5th Joint SIGHUM Workshop on Computational Linguistics for Cultural Heritage, Social Sciences, Humanities and Literature (LaTeCH-CLfL-2021)

Held online

Punta Cana, Dominican Republic
11 November 2021

ISBN: 978-1-7138-9175-8

Printed from e-media with permission by:

Curran Associates, Inc.
57 Morehouse Lane
Red Hook, NY 12571

Some format issues inherent in the e-media version may also appear in this print version.

Printed with permission by Curran Associates, Inc. (2024)

For permission requests, please contact the Association for Computational Linguistics at the address below.

Association for Computational Linguistics
209 N. Eighth Street
Stroudsburg, Pennsylvania 18360

Phone: 1-570-476-8006
Fax: 1-570-476-0860

acl@aclweb.org

Additional copies of this publication are available from:

Curran Associates, Inc.
57 Morehouse Lane
Red Hook, NY 12571 USA
Phone: 845-758-0400
Fax: 845-758-2633
Email: curran@proceedings.com
Web: www.proceedings.com

EMNLP 2021

The 5th Joint SIGHUM Workshop on Computational Linguistics for Cultural Heritage, Social Sciences, Humanities and Literature

Co-located with the 2021 Conference on Empirical Methods in Natural Language Processing EMNLP 2021

Proceedings

November 11, 2021
Punta Cana, Dominican Republic (Online)

Preface

Another virtual workshop... Oh well: maybe next year we will go back to the (new) normal.

Looking at submission numbers, this year's edition of the workshop was a huge success. We have received *really* unusually many submissions (thanks, everyone!). Out of those, we have accepted 22 papers for a 38 % acceptance rate. A round of applause for our wonderful program committee!

The workshop programme consists of brief eight-minute Q&A sessions for ten oral presentations (which you will have watched by then!), and a twelve-poster session during which you will be able to chat with any author you like. Thematically, the papers cover the entire range of "Cultural Heritage, Social Sciences, Humanities and Literature". The programme shows that this area of applied language technology is mature and active.

Last but not least, Sara Tonelli will give a live invited talk. We are grateful, and we look forward to it.

Keep well.

Stefania, Anna, Nils, Stan

`https://sighum.wordpress.com/events/latech-clfl-2021/`

Invited Talk

Dissecting offensive language detection: does it work, and what can we do with it?

Social media messages are often written to attack specific groups of users based on their religion, ethnicity or social status, and they can be particularly threatening to vulnerable users such as teenagers. It is therefore very important to develop reliable, unbiased and robust detection systems to support stakeholders in fighting online hatred. Although state-of-the-art systems yield very good classification results, the problem is far from being solved. In my talk, I will discuss which issues still affect the development of abusive language detection systems, for example the problem of dealing with annotators' disagreement in the creation of training data, and the issues related to contextual information in threads. On the other hand, I will show how the output of offensive language detection systems can be integrated with network-based information to study the behavioral patterns of different types of users, also in relation to misinformation.

About the speaker

Sara Tonelli
Digital Humanties
Fondazione Bruno Kessler
Trento, Italy

Sara Tonelli holds a PhD in Language Sciences from Università Ca' Foscari, Venice. Since 2013 she has been the head of the Digital Humanities research group at Fondazione Bruno Kessler in Trento, Italy. Among many projects in digital humanities, she is currently involved in the H2020 ODEUROPA project (focusing on olfactory information extraction), and in the H2020 PERCEPTIONS project (online perception and migration narratives related to EU). Since January 2021 she is also the scientific coordinator of the KID ACTIONS European project (addressing cyberbullying among children and adolescents). Sara's main research interests are related to temporal and event-based processing of texts, especially in the historical domain, and social media processing, including the detection of abusive language.

Organizers:

Stefania Degaetano-Ortlieb, Department of Language Science and Technology, Universität des Saarlandes
Anna Kazantseva, National Research Council of Canada
Nils Reiter, Institute for Natural Language Processing (IMS), Stuttgart University / Institute for Digital Humanities (IDH), Cologne University
Stan Szpakowicz, School of Electrical Engineering and Computer Science, University of Ottawa

Program Committee:

Beatrice Alex, University of Edinburgh, United Kingdom
Melanie Andresen, Hamburg University, Germany
JinYeong Bak, Sungkyunkwan University, Suwon, South Korea
Andre Blessing, University of Stuttgart, Germany
Anne-Sophie Bories, Universität Basel, Switzerland
Paul Buitelaar, National University of Ireland, Galway, Ireland
Miriam Butt, University of Konstanz, Germany
Gerard de Melo, Tsinghua University, China
Thierry Declerck, Deutsche Forschungszentrum für Künstliche Intelligenz GmbH, Germany
Stefanie Dipper, Ruhr-University, Bochum, Germany
Jacob Eisenstein, Georgia Institute of Technology, United States
Peter Fankhauser, IDS Mannheim, Germany
Anna Feldman, Montclair State University, United States
Mark Finlayson, Florida International University, United States
Antske Fokkens, Vrije Universiteit Amsterdam, The Netherlands
Heather Froehlich, Pennsylvania State University, United States
Francesca Frontini, National Research Council, Italy
Michael Hahn, Stanford University, United States
Udo Hahn, Friedrich-Schiller-Universität Jena, Germany
Mika Hämäläinen, University of Helsinki, Finland
Serge Heiden, École normale supérieure de Lyon, France
Graeme Hirst, University of Toronto, Canada
Labiba Jahan, Florida International University, United States
Fotis Jannidis, Würzburg University, Germany
Gard Jenset, Springer Nature, London, United Kingdom
Mike Kestemont, University of Antwerp, Belgium
Dimitrios Kokkinakis, University of Gothenburg, Sweden
Stasinos Konstantopoulos, National Centre of Scientific Research "Demokritos", Greece
Markus Krug, Würzburg University, Germany
John Lee, City University of Hong Kong, Hong Kong
Chaya Liebeskind, Jerusalem College of Technology, Israel
Tom Lippincott, Johns Hopkins University, United States
Barbara McGillivray, The Alan Turing Institute, United Kingdom
David Mimno, Cornell University, United States

Syrielle Montariol, INRIA Paris, France
Vivi Nastase, University of Stuttgart, Germany
Borja Navarro Colorado, University of Alicante, Spain
John Nerbonne, University of Freiburg, Germany
Pierre Nugues, Lund University, Sweden
Petya Osenova, Sofia University and IICT-BAS, Bulgaria
Janis Pagel, University of Stuttgart, Germany
Andrew Piper, McGill University, Canada
Petr Plecháč, Institute of Czech Literature of the CAS, Czechia
Thierry Poibeau, CNRS Paris and Lattice, France
Jelena Prokic, Leiden University Centre for Digital Humanities, The Netherlands
Georg Rehm, DFKI, Germany
Martin Reynaert, Tilburg University, Radboud University Nijmegen, The Netherlands
Pablo Ruiz Fabo, Université de Strasbourg, France
Marijn Schraagen, Utrecht University, The Netherlands
Matthew Sims, University of California, Berkeley, United States
Pia Sommerauer, Vrije Universiteit Amsterdam, The Netherlands
Elke Teich, Saarland University, Germany
Laure Thompson, University of Massachusetts Amherst, United States
Ulrich Tiedau, University College London, United Kingdom
Ted Underwood, University of Illinois, Urbana-Champaign, United States
Rob Voigt, Northwestern University, United States
Menno van Zaanen, South African Centre for Digital Language Resources, Potchefstroom, South Africa
Albin Zehe, University of Würzburg, Germany
Heike Zinsmeister, University of Hamburg, Germany

Invited Speaker:

Sara Tonelli, Fondazione Bruno Kessler, Italy

Table of Contents

Workshop Program

Talks, part I

The Early Modern Dutch Mediascape. Detecting Media Mentions in Chronicles Using Word Embeddings and CRF
Alie Lassche and Roser Morante

Batavia asked for advice. Pretrained language models for Named Entity Recognition in historical texts.
Sophie I. Arnoult, Lodewijk Petram and Piek Vossen

Quantifying Contextual Aspects of Inter-annotator Agreement in Intertextuality Research
Enrique Manjavacas Arevalo, Laurence Mellerin and Mike Kestemont

WMDecompose: A Framework for Leveraging the Interpretable Properties of Word Mover's Distance in Sociocultural Analysis
Mikael Brunila and Jack LaViolette

A Mixed-Methods Analysis of Western and Hong Kong–based Reporting on the 2019–2020 Protests
Arya D. McCarthy, James Scharf and Giovanna Maria Dora Dore

Talks, part II

FrameNet-like Annotation of Olfactory Information in Texts
Sara Tonelli and Stefano Menini

End-to-end style-conditioned poetry generation: What does it take to learn from examples alone?
Jörg Wöckener, Thomas Haider, Tristan Miller, The-Khang Nguyen, Thanh Tung Linh Nguyen, Minh Vu Pham, Jonas Belouadi and Steffen Eger

Automating the Detection of Poetic Features: The Limerick as Model Organism
Almas Abdibayev, Yohei Igarashi, Allen Riddell and Daniel Rockmore

Translationese in Russian Literary Texts
Maria Kunilovskaya, Ekaterina Lapshinova-Koltunski and Ruslan Mitkov

Stylometric Literariness Classification: the Case of Stephen King
Andreas van Cranenburgh and Erik Ketzan

Posters

The Early Modern Dutch Mediascape. Detecting Media Mentions in Chronicles Using Word Embeddings and CRF

Alie Lassche
Leiden University
a.w.lassche@hum.leidenuniv.nl

Roser Morante
VU University Amsterdam
r.morantevallejo@vu.nl

Abstract

While the production of information in the European early modern period is a well-researched topic, the question how people were engaging with the information explosion that occurred in early modern Europe, is still underexposed. This paper presents the annotations and experiments aimed at exploring whether we can automatically extract media related information (source, perception, and receiver) from a corpus of early modern Dutch chronicles in order to get insight in the mediascape of early modern middle class people from a historic perspective. In a number of classification experiments with Conditional Random Fields, three categories of features are tested: *(i)* raw and binary word embedding features, *(ii)* lexicon features, and *(iii)* character features. Overall, the classifier that uses raw embeddings performs slightly better. However, given that the best F-scores are around 0.60, we conclude that the machine learning approach needs to be combined with a close reading approach for the results to be useful to answer history research questions.

1 Introduction

It is well known from previous studies that early modern Europe witnessed an eruption of news, which was due to developments such as the burgeoning business of print, the professionalization of postal networks, and the invention of the newspaper (Pettegree, 2014; Rosenberg, 2003). While the production of information by various media is a well-researched topic, the question how people were engaging with this information explosion is still underexposed aside from a few studies (van Groesen, 2016; Blaak, 2009). Historians find it difficult to answer questions such as 'who owned book shelves?', 'who read which books?', and 'who bought newspapers?', since they have not yet found a suitable source and method to research these issues concerning the spread of information from the perspective of the consumer.

A source of information that might contain the key to answer these questions are early modern chronicles. A chronicle is a text from someone who keeps a record of events happening in their surroundings, who believes that these events are worth recording, and that the best way to structure this information is to do so chronologically (Pollmann, 2016). To fill their chronicle with useful information, early modern chroniclers used a wide variety of information sources, such as pamphlets, newspapers, official announcements, gossips, conversations, songs and other sounds, letters from friends or relatives, or the chronicler themselves functioned as eyewitness. All the sources that a modern chronicler had available constitute the early modern 'mediascape', a term coined by Appadurai (1990). Furthermore, the genre of the chronicle has remained rather stable over the centuries, and since many texts have been preserved in both public and private archives, a rather homogeneous collection of manuscripts still exists.

This is why chronicles are a suitable source for historians to get more insight in the reception of news and information. Two aspects are interesting to analyse from a history perspective: (i) the media that are mentioned by the author of the chronicle (such as 'my uncle', 'the newspaper', 'a rumour'), and *(ii)* the information that the chronicler is reporting on, which they have obtained from the media. These data are contained in the chronicles and traditionally close reading methods would be applied. However, in order to generalise across chroniclers, it is necessary to analyze as many chronicles as possible. Since close reading is a time consuming process, computational methods should be applied to automatically find the data.

This is the goal of this study. We focus on the first aspect (media) and present a computational approach to automatically extract media related information from Dutch early modern chronicles. This has been possible thanks to the availability of

Proceedings of LaTeCH-CLfL 2021, pages 1–10
Punta Cana, Dominican Republic (Online), November 11, 2021.

a corpus of 350 Dutch chronicles from the period 1500-1850 fully digitized. Our research question is: to which extent is it possible to automatically extract media mentions from a corpus of early modern Dutch chronicles? Addressing this issue is relevant because having this information available would allow historians to find out which books chroniclers owned, which newspapers they read, and in what other ways they received new information. It also provides insights in how the media use of chroniclers differs among each other. It would be possible to investigate, for example, how the mediascape of a chronicler from a large city such as Ghent, relates to that of a chronicler from a small provincial town such as Hoorn. Furthermore, it tells us something about how the preferences for certain media develop over time. The broader context of this study is to explore whether the use of computational methods can help historians to analyse the data concerning the mediascape of early modern chroniclers.[1]

Section 2 presents related work, Section 3 describes the data, Section 4 the methods, Section 5 the experiments, and Section 6 the results. Finally, in Section 7 we put forward some conclusions.

2 Related work

Historical text mining is an incipient field (Piotrowski, 2012). Regarding the Dutch language, historical text mining studies are limited. Stylometric methods have been applied in authorship verification tasks on medieval and early modern texts (Kestemont et al., 2017; Kestemont, 2018). Furthermore, Dutch early modern songs have been quantitatively researched (Lassche et al., 2019; Lassche, 2019). Corpora of historical Dutch newspapers have been subject to research in several studies, including Wevers and Verhoef (2018), Wevers et al. (2020), and Ros (2019). This work is the first to investigate chronicles on a large scale and with the use of text mining methods. Early modern Dutch chronicles have only been qualitatively researched up until now (Blaak, 2009; Pollmann, 2016, 2017). The same goes for chronicles in other languages, such as German, where only case studies on a handful chronicles have been published (Rau, 2002; Mauer, 2001).

Word embedding models (or word vector models) have recently become a popular way to describe a corpus of texts. Well known implementations are `word2vec` and `fasttext` (Bojanowski et al., 2017). Regarding the Dutch language, they have been used for relation evaluation and dialect identification (Tulkens et al., 2016), and to detect semantic change in Dutch newspapers (Wevers and Koolen, 2020; Wevers, 2019) and parliamentary debates (Lange, van and Futselaar, 2019). Word embeddings have been used as features in classification tasks (see for example Beelen et al. (2021)), but to the best of our knowledge, this has never been done for the historic Dutch language. Studies with corpora in other languages show that there are multiple ways to implement the word embeddings as features of a classifier. In Huang et al. (2015), every one hot encoding word representation is simply replaced with its corresponding 50-dimensional embedding vector. The authors of (Wu et al., 2015) compared three strategies for deriving distributed word representations in a corpus of English clinical texts. They base their method on earlier work (Guo et al., 2014), in which three different approaches for utilizing the embedding features are compared. In Wu et al. (2015) it is shown that the binarized word embedding features caused the largest improvement of the performance of the CRF system, while Guo et al. (2014) concluded that a distributional prototype approach performed the best. Bansal et al. (2014) perform agglomerative hierarchical clustering of the embedding vectors to take into account all dimensions of a vector simultaneously. Dařena and Süss (2020) use a neural network that is allowed to update the word vectors during training, since their Czech corpus from which a word embedding model was build, was rather small.

As far as we know, the current study is the first in which historic Dutch word embeddings are used as features of a classifier. We also do not know of any studies in other historical languages, in which a similar classification task is performed.

3 Data

In the context of the research project 'Chronicling Novelty. New knowledge in the Netherlands, 1500-1850', led by Judith Pollmann (Leiden University) and Erika Kuijpers (VU), a corpus of about 350 early modern Dutch chronicles has been built over

[1]The underlying code and materials of this paper are accessible via Github, see `https://github.com/awlassche/media-mentions-latech`.

the last three years.[2] The texts included in the corpus have the following characteristics: they are written between 1500 and 1850, they are organised chronologically, they cover events that happened in the lifetime of the author, and they focus on local events more than national, individual or familial.

About 100 of these chronicles had been published before as a contribution to a journal, on the initiative of an archive, or in the private domain, and were digitised by the DBNL (Digital Library for Dutch Literature). The other 250 chronicles were kept in libraries and archives throughout the Netherlands and Belgium. Every manuscript page was scanned, and afterwards transcribed with both the Handwritten Text Recognition tool Transkribus (Kahle et al., 2017), and the help of volunteers on the online crowd sourcing platform Vele Handen. Currently, the corpus contains about 70,000 pages.

In order to improve the searchability of the corpus of chronicles, a second group of volunteers is labeling useful information in the completely transcribed chronicles. They annotate both content and lay out in the chronicle pages, using labels including `date`, `location`, and `person name`, as well as `page number`, `lists and tables`, and `copied text`. Besides, a select group of volunteers has labeled media mentions in the chronicles. These are the annotations that are used in this study, which will be discussed in more detail in the next subsection.

3.1 Annotated media corpus

A group of four volunteers, all having an above average knowledge of the early modern Dutch language and culture, has been annotating media mentions in the chronicles. They were provided with extensive guidelines in which media mentions were explained.[3] To extract media related information, three types of annotations are relevant:

- a `receiver`, who is the person receiving information;
- a `source`, which is the instance bringing information to the receiver;
- a `perception`, which is the way in which the source is bringing information to the receiver.

[2] On `http://www.chroniclingnovelty.com/kronieken/`, an overview of the corpus can be found.

[3] The annotation guidelines are accessible via the Github repository.

The label `perception` has four possible attributes: `oral/heard`, `written/read`, `seen`, or `else`. See the following examples translated from Dutch into English:

1. 'This morning <source> mayor Vorsterman </source> came <perception: oral/heard> telling </perception> <receiver> us </receiver> that because of the disease, no one was allowed to be buried in the church.'
2. 'On 18 February <receiver> we </receiver> have <perception: written/read> seen </perception> in the <source> Amsterdammer Courant </source> of that day that Her Royal highness had given birth to a healthy and well-made Prince on the 16th at 11 in the evening in The Hague!'
3. '<receiver> I </receiver> have been to Broek and have <perception: seen> seen </perception> the Prince having dinner and walking through the village.'
4. '<receiver> They </receiver> <perception: oral/heard> heard </perception> how a farmer hanged himself.'
5. '<source> They </source> <perception: oral/heard> said </perception> that he had two letters in his pocket.
6. 'After this oddity had been <perception: seen> shown </perception> in Bruges for 8 days...'

The examples show that a `source` can be a person (1) or a printed text (2). In (5), the `source` is 'they', but this word also often functions as `receiver`, as can be seen in (4). The different perceptions are in most cases obvious ('telling' is `oral/heard` in (1), 'seen' is `seen` in (3)), but sometimes they are not. In (2), the word 'seen' suggests a `perception: seen`, but the context makes clear that this word should get the `perception: written/read`. Finally, the examples show that the mention of a medium does not necessary consist of the 3 labels: in (3) and (4) there is no `source`, in (5) there is no `receiver`, and in (6), there is only a `perception`.

Inter annotator agreement (IAA) was calculated at two moments during the process of improving the guidelines, using the balanced F-measure (Hripcsak, 2005) (see Table 1). After the first calculation of the IAA, the F-scores were analysed. They showed that the guidelines caused the most confusion among the annotators regarding the label `source`. Annotators found it hard to distinguish between the description of an event ('Our Aldermen Court were heard') and the mention of a medium ('We heard a strange rumour'). Guidelines were also not clear about self references of a chronicler ('as I wrote on p. 23'). Some annotators interpreted this wrongly as a medium mention.

Table 1: IAA in the media annotation task.

	F-score phase 1		F-score phase 2	
	A1 - A2	*A2 - A1*	*A1 - A2*	*A2 - A1*
all	0.589	0.589	0.755	0.729
source	0.208	0.208	0.768	0.760
receiver	0.777	0.777	0.667	0.571
perception	0.707	0.707	0.754	0.699

The labels `receiver` and `perception` are less ambiguous: the receiver is often the chronicler referring to him- or herself, and a perception is usually a verb such as 'read', 'hear', 'tell', or 'see'. Annotators more often agreed on those. However, they also sometimes mixed up the `source` and the `receiver`, because the same word could have a different meaning in different contexts: in 'they heard', they is a `receiver`, but in a construction with 'they said', they is a `source`. In the updated guidelines, this definition of a `source` was more clearly explained, as well as the difference between a `source` and a `receiver`. Several examples were added, both in which media mentions appeared, as well as sentences which we considered not to contain media mentions. The F-scores obtained in the second inter annotator agreement after improvement of the guidelines made it clear that a lot of the confusion was cleared up: especially the F-score of the label `source` was much higher than before, as shown in Table 1.

In general, the F-scores show that we are dealing with a difficult annotation task. While annotating dates, person names and locations is something annotators hardly disagree on, labeling media mentions requires prior knowledge about the early modern Dutch society and language. The fact that the phrase 'de vliegende poste' (the flying post) is actually a reference to a carrier pigeon, and therefore should be labeled as a `source`, is something that is easily overlooked. Still, the final F-scores were considered good enough to let the volunteers make the annotations. About 25% of the total corpus of 350 Dutch chronicles is currently annotated with medium mentions, a percentage that is increasing everyday.

For the experiments reported in this study, we use four eighteenth century chronicles that are fully annotated with media mentions. Detailed corpus characteristics are presented in Table 2.

All experiments were performed on two different training and test sets. Set 1 contained the 12 volume chronicle from the late eighteenth century, written by Jozef Van Walleghem about his city Bruges (Van Walleghem, 2016). In set 2, three other eighteenth century chronicles were added (Abbing and S., 1794; Anoniem, 1795; Callion, 1789). For all experiments, of every chronicle, 70% was used for training, and 30% was used for testing.

Statistics about the datasets are displayed in Table 3. They show that set 2 is about 2.5 times bigger than set 1 regarding the number of tokens. This does not apply to the number of labels of `source-B`, `receiver-B`, `perception-B` and `perception-I`. This means that set 1 contains more labels per x tokens than set 2, in other words: the chronicle of Van Walleghem contains an above average number of media mentions. However, the labeled sources are longer in set 2: the number of `source-I` labels in set 2 is more than 4 times larger than in set 1.

4 Methods

The manually labeled data was used to train a CRF-classifier that is able to recognize media mentions in unseen chronicles. We use the Python library `sklearn-crfsuite` and the default parameters of CRF (Pedregosa et al., 2011). The classification task consists in labelling tokens with one of the following labels: `O` (no medium mention), `source-B`, `source-I`, `receiver-B`, `receiver-I`, `perception-B`, or `perception-I`.

Conditional Random Fields is a frequently used method in Named Entity Recognition (NER) labeling tasks, because CRF is able to deal with sequential data implicitly, without adding this information as features. Since the media mentions are tagged on token level using the IOB-tagging scheme, this task is also one in which labels of consecutive points can influence each other. There are, however, a few aspects in which this labeling task differs from a NER-task performed on modern texts, and complicates it.

Preprocessing of the data was limited: upper cases and punctuation were not removed, since these can be an indication of a media mention (consider the 'Gentsche Gazette'). Since chronicles were handwritten by authors from different areas, different time periods, and with different levels of literacy and dialects, there is a large variation in the vocabulary used. As a result of that, features such as POS-tags – which are often used in classi-

Table 2: Corpus characteristics.

set	chronicle	# pages	% labeled	# sources	# receivers	# perceptions
1 & 2	Brugge, Van Walleghem (1779-1800)	1165	17%	519	272	510
2	Gent, Callion (1780-1789)	248	100%	93	18	22
2	Hoorn, Abbing (1630-1794)	665	51%	241	94	53
2	Maastricht, Anonymous (1698-1742)	216	56%	63	74	36

Table 3: Statistics of tokens and labels per dataset.

set	1		2	
train/test	*train*	*test*	*train*	*test*
n tokens	107,351	46,006	284,160	121,781
source-B	373	122	772	251
source-I	486	152	2130	444
receiver-B	179	83	251	136
receiver-I	50	9	122	55
perception-B	335	134	470	235
perception-I	41	12	79	54

fication tasks that are performed on modern texts – can not be used in this task. Previous studies have shown, though, how the use of word embeddings as features of a classifier can improve its quality (Collobert et al., 2011; Wu et al., 2015; Bansal et al., 2014; Seok et al., 2016). Vectors of historical spelling variants are often each other's nearest neighbors. The hypothesis is therefore that using them as features will positively affect the quality of a model.

4.1 Features

We distinguish three categories of features: *(i)* word embedding features, *(ii)* character features, and *(iii)* lexicon features.

4.1.1 Word embedding features

We have used `fastText` to train a word embedding model (Bojanowski et al., 2017). In contrast to `word2vec`, `fastText` treats each word as composed of character n-grams, which enables the application to create a vector for a word that is not in the training data. The `skipgram` method was used, which was in previous studies shown to be better suited for this task than `cbow` (Ljubešić, 2018). The trained embeddings contained 100 dimensions. Three different word embedding models were used, in which the time span of the documents varied: model *a* was trained only on Van Walleghem's chronicle, model *b* was trained on chronicles that were finished between 1750 and 1800, and model *c* was trained on chronicles that were written between 1700 and 1850.

Regarding the obtained embeddings, two different ways of implementing them as features were tested: *(i)* RawEmb, and *(ii)* BinEmb. Both methods are also used by Wu et al. (2015). With RawEmb, the real values from the embedding matrix are directly used as feature weights for the classifier, without any post processing. The BinEmb refer to binarized embedding features, which are used to discretize the real-valued matrix and omit the insignificant dimensions. Given a word embedding matrix with the raw embeddings, the binarized embedding features are derived by converting the real-valued embedding matrix to another discrete-valued matrix with the discrete symbolic values in $[+, -, 0]$.

4.1.2 Character features

The character features that were calculated during training included the following features of a $token_n$, the previous $(token_{n-1})$, and the next $(token_{n+1})$:

- First 5 characters;
- Last 5 characters;
- Boolean value whether the token is a digit;
- Boolean value whether the token consists of only lower cases;
- Boolean value whether the token is a title.

4.1.3 Lexicon features

We also defined a boolean feature indicating whether the token occurred in a lexicon of media words. This lexicon consists of tokens that were extracted from the train corpus manually annotated data. Different lexicons were used in the two sets of experiments, consisting of `source` labeled words that appeared in the texts that were included in the specific set of training data.[4]

5 Experiments

We perform several experiments:

Experiment 1: Baseline. We performed three baseline experiments. In the first, only the lexicon

[4]The lexicons are available upon request.

Table 4: F-scores of all experiments.

Train/test	Model Embeddings	1. Baseline *lex.*	*ch.*	*lex.+ch.*	2. RawEmb *emb.+ch.*	*emb.+ch.+lex.*	3. BinEmb *emb.+ch.*	*emb.+ch.+lex.*
set 1	Walleghem	0.573	0.569	0.575	**0.606**	0.600	0.581	0.571
	1750-1800				0.611	**0.612**	0.551	0.596
	1700-1850				0.594	**0.597**	0.586	0.593
set 2	1750-1800	0.346	0.359	0.359	0.391	**0.395**	0.367	0.367
	1700-1850				0.387	0.387	**0.402**	0.387

feature was used, in the second, only the character features were used, and in the third, both the lexicon feature and the character features were used.

Experiment 2: RawEmb. We performed two experiments with raw embeddings. In the first, only the character features and the word embedding features were used. In the second, the lexicon feature was added as well.

Experiment 3: BinEmb. We performed two experiments with the binarized embeddings. In the first, only the character features and the word embedding features were used. In the second, the lexicon feature was added as well.

6 Results

6.1 Performance of the classifiers

In Table 4, we present the F-scores of the classifiers for all experiments.[5] The F-scores were calculated with the function `metrics.flat_f1_score`. The label `O` was excluded from this score. The baseline experiments with solely the lexicon features show that using the lexicon with media mentions provides relatively high results.

Regarding the **baseline experiments** on train and test set 1, the best performance was achieved with a combination of the lexicon features and the character features. Adding the word embeddings as RawEmb features results in an increase of the F-score with around 4%. The differences between the scores of the experiments with and without the lexicon features are very small and negligible. Using the BinEmb version of the word embedding features, together with the lexicon features, results also in an increase of the F-score with around 4%.

The highest scores with train and test **set 1** were achieved with the RawEmb features obtained from the corpus of chronicles written between 1750 and 1800. Presumably, the word embedding model made from the chronicle of Van Walleghem solely contained not enough tokens to create a coherent model. The fact that the quality of the word embedding model of chronicles between 1700 and 1850 did not outperform the 1750-1800 model suggests that taking a too wide time span of texts enlarges the spelling variation, and does not improve the quality of a word embedding model. Over all, because of the relatively low number of tokens, decreasing the number of dimensions of the word embedding models to 75 or 50 might improve its performance.

Concerning train and test **set 2**, all experiments show that the system had a lower performance than the ones trained on set 1. However, adding word embedding features to the model causes a higher increase of the F-score than in set 1. This time, the highest scores with train and test set 2 were achieved with the BinEmb features obtained from the corpus of chronicles written between 1700 and 1850. The experiment with the lexicon features and the RawEmb features obtained from the corpus of chronicles written between 1750 and 1800 comes in second place.

Tables 5 and 6 contain the F-scores per label from the baseline experiments on set 2, with the lexicon features and the character features respectively. These numbers were obtained with the function `metrics.flat_classification_report`. They show that the classifiers obtain a better precision than recall.

Table 5: Precision and recall of experiment 1 (set 2, baseline, lexicon features)

	precision	recall	F-score	support
source-B	0.518	0.287	0.369	251
source-I	0.639	0.212	0.318	444
perception-B	0.707	0.298	0.419	235
perception-I	0.333	0.019	0.035	54
receiver-B	0.823	0.375	0.515	136
receiver-I	0.250	0.018	0.034	55

The two best performing experiments on set 2 are in bold in Table 4, and their detailed F-scores are displayed in Table 7 and 8. The precision and recall scores of the distinct labels show that the system obtains the highest precision in labeling

[5] We use an abbreviation for the used features. 'lex.' refers to the lexicon feature, 'ch.' to the character features, and 'emb.' to the embedding features.

Table 6: Precision and recall of experiment 1 (set 2, baseline, character features)

	precision	recall	F-score	support
source-B	0.493	0.263	0.343	251
source-I	0.616	0.245	0.351	444
perception-B	0.645	0.340	0.446	235
perception-I	0.167	0.019	0.033	54
receiver-B	0.803	0.390	0.525	136
receiver-I	0.200	0.018	0.033	55

perception-B and receiver-B. However, the low recall implies that the system is still missing a lot. It would therefore be useful to explore in future experiments the effect of different cut-offs for label probabilities, rather than using the default argmax for the various labels. Furthermore it would be worth to experiment in future research with other classifiers. A bidirectional long short-term memory system (BiLSTM) might for example be more suitable for this task. This model relies on neural networks and has shown in other studies to outperform the CRF-system when the level of non-standardness of the text increases.

In the current experiments, the very low scores for perception-I and receiver-I are probably caused by the scarcity of these labels. The scores for source-B and source-I show that both models gain a similar performance regarding this label, although different features were used. An evaluation at sequence level could provide more insight in possible tendencies.

Table 7: Precision and recall of experiment 2 (set 2, 1750-1800, RawEmb, lexicon)

	precision	recall	F-score	support
source-B	0.558	0.347	0.428	251
source-I	0.580	0.302	0.397	444
perception-B	0.643	0.345	0.449	235
perception-I	0.125	0.019	0.032	54
receiver-B	0.794	0.397	0.529	136
receiver-I	0.111	0.018	0.031	55

Table 8: Precision and recall of experiment 2 (set 2, 1700-1850, BinEmb)

	precision	recall	F-score	support
source-B	0.555	0.323	0.408	251
source-I	0.570	0.338	0.424	444
perception-B	0.647	0.366	0.467	235
perception-I	0.143	0.019	0.033	54
receiver-B	0.750	0.375	0.500	136
receiver-I	0.125	0.018	0.032	55

6.2 Error analysis

Manually comparing the gold labels with the predicted labels of the best performing systems shows that five types of issues occur frequently.

Errors in labeling sources with long spans. This became already clear from the numbers in Table 3, as we discussed earlier. The mention of a medium is rarely limited to one or two labeled words ('Gentsche Gazette', 'letters', or 'amendment'), but is often part of a phrase such as 'the amendment of our most honorable Lord Bishop' or 'letters from their Royal Highnesses the Governors General of the Netherlands'. The classifier is in most cases able to label words such as 'Gazette', 'letters' and 'amendment' as source, but does not label the surrounding words as source, while the annotators often do. When precision and recall is calculated on token level, this results in a low recall.

Labels source-B and source-I and the way in which annotators define the start of a medium mention. Some annotators have included articles or demonstrative pronouns in a medium mention, while others have not. This means that a word such as 'declaration' is in some cases labeled as source-B, and in other situations as source-I, while the pronoun 'this' is labeled as source-B. This again results in a mismatch, when calculating precision and recall on token level.

The third type of error concerns the so-called **lonely tokens**. When there is a sequence of labeled tokens, the model is better in predicting labels than when there is no labeled context. When a source such as 'decree' is mentioned without companion of a perception or receiver label, the model often does not label it as such. Using the lexicon feature does partially overcome this problem, but still there are infrequent tokens in the test set, which are not in the lexicon, and therefore not labeled as a source. The same issue occurs for a perception such as 'said', or a receiver such as 'they': when there are no labeled tokens in the close context, the tokens are often not labeled.

A fourth issue that also concerns the use of a lexicon, are the **ambiguous sources**. The term 'placard', or 'rumours', for example, is sometimes labeled as a source, but in other contexts, it is not interpreted as a source by the annotator. This inconsistency might confuse the classifier, thus improving the chance of a wrongly predicted label.

The final issue involves the fact that the **classifier labels in a more consistent way** than human annotators do. The word 'they', for example, refers in most cases to the `receiver` of a news item. However, the chronicler sometimes also uses it in other contexts, in which no media mention appears. Annotators did not label this word, but the model sometimes wrongly did. On the positive, from this uniformity of the model sometimes also follows that media mentions that were overlooked by the human annotator, are anyway labeled by the model. There are also a few cases in which the annotator confused a `receiver` with a `source`, but the computer assigned the correct labels.

6.3 Sequence level evaluation of the task

In Subsection 6.1 we presented the evaluation results at token level for each of the labels predicted. However, the full task involves finding the sequences of words that express sources, perceptions and receivers. Here we present results of evaluating at sequence level in terms of full match and partial match. In full match all the tokens in the sequence need to be correctly labeled, in partial match at least one token in the sequence needs to be correctly labelled. We evaluate the output of the two best performing classifiers on set 2 (based on the F-scores in Table 4).

Table 9: F-measures at sequence level of the two best systems for source (S), perception (P) and receiver (R), in terms of full match (fm) and partial match (pm). Column REL contains results on set2 1750-1800 RawEmb, emb+ch+lex; column BE contains results for set2 1700-1850 BinEmb (emb+ch).

	Precision		Recall		F-score	
	REL	BE	REL	BE	REL	BE
S fm	0.127	0.112	0.060	0.052	0.081	0.071
S pm	0.571	0.566	0.351	0.351	0.435	0.433
P fm	0.319	0.317	0.157	0.157	0.211	0.211
P pm	0.483	0.486	0.298	0.306	0.368	0.376
R fm	0.806	0.777	0.368	0.371	0.505	0.503
R pm	0.806	0.777	0.368	0.371	0.505	0.503

For `source` and `perception` the full match scores are much lower than the partial match scores, whereas this is not the case for `receiver`. This is due to the fact that `receiver` labels span over one token. The `receiver` obtains the highest scores, with a high precision, caused by the fact that there is less lexical variation in the expression of `receivers`. The `perception` obtains the lowest partial match scores, whereas the `source` gets the lowest full match scores. This is due to the fact that `source` labels tend to be longer sequences.

In the view of these results, with partial match F-scores not higher than 0.51 for `receiver`, 0.38 for `perception` and 0.44 for `source`, we can answer our research question: we can automatically extract from the chronicles some of the media related information, but the results are not high enough so as to perform the analysis of the chronicles fully automatically because too many media mentions are missed by the system. This is not surprising, given the amount of spelling and lexical variation present in the chronicles. The train corpus is not big enough for this type of machine learning experiments. Additional improvements need to be done to the system in order to improve its performance before historians can rely on it to obtain data to answer their research questions. We consider that the output of the current system can be used to perform exploratory studies. One of the possible improvements should focus on obtaining a higher recall, which now is much lower than precision. A higher recall would be desirable if the system would be used to select examples for the annotation of more data.

7 Conclusions

In this paper we have presented experiments aimed at extracting media related information from Early Modern Dutch chronicles with the purpose of investigating to which extent it is possible to perform this task automatically and to which extent are the results of automatic systems useful to facilitate history research. We have described the manual annotation task, which consisted in labeling sequences of tokens with the labels `source`, `perception` and `receiver`, considered by historians to be of relevance for their research. The IAA scores, with F-scores of around 0.73, show that the annotation task is well defined but that it is not easy. The label that produced more confusion was `source`, due to different interpretations of when to assign this label.

Four fully annotated chronicles were used to perform experiments with a CRF algorithm and different types of features that included several models of raw and binary word embeddings. We performed evaluations on token and sequence level. Both reveal that the systems obtain a much better precision than recall. In any case, the results of baseline experiments without word embeddings are only 0.04 F-score lower than the experiments with word embeddings, indicating that the word embedding models are not rich enough, probably due to the size of the corpus used to generate them. Experiments with set 2, which contains more variety in authors, and therefore also in vocabulary, benefit more from word embedding features than experiments with set 1, where only one chronicle was used. The classifier with raw embeddings performs slightly better than the one with binary embeddings. As expected, the scores of the sequence level evaluation are lower than the scores of the token level evaluation.

In this paper we aimed at determining whether it was possible to automatically extract media related information from chronicles and whether the extracted information can be used by historians to answer their research questions. Since the sequence level partial match F-scores are not higher than 0.51 for receiver, 0.38 for perception and 0.44 for source, we conclude that the methods that we applied are not precise enough to extract the information and that it is not possible for historians to solely use such a system to obtain data to answer their research questions because too much information is missed. Both the data used to train the classifiers and the methods need to be improved. For future work we aim at experimenting with more algorithms and with larger corpora that include more chronicles, both for creating the embedding models and to train the systems.

Acknowledgements

Research for this paper was conducted at Leiden University and the Vrije Universiteit Amsterdam, and funded through the NWO VC project 'Chronicling Novelty. New knowledge in the Netherlands, 1500-1850'. We are thankful to the anonymous reviewers for their insightful comments, and to the annotators.

References

D.C.A. Abbing and H. S. 1794. Vervolg op de kroniek van Hoorn van D. Velius, eerste deel tot 1794.

Anoniem. 1795. Manuscripta wegens de stad Maestricht de anno 998 usque anno 1742.

Arjun Appadurai. 1990. Disjuncture and Difference in the Global Cultural Economy. *Theory, Culture & Society*, 7(2-3):295–310.

Mohit Bansal, Kevin Gimpel, and Karen Livescu. 2014. Tailoring Continuous Word Representations for Dependency Parsing. In *Proceedings of the 52nd Annual Meeting of the Association for Computational Linguistics (Volume 2: Short Papers)*, pages 809–815, Baltimore, Maryland. Association for Computational Linguistics.

Kaspar Beelen, Federico Nanni, Mariona Coll Ardanuy, Kasra Hosseini, Giorgia Tolfo, and Barbara McGillivray. 2021. When time makes sense: A historically-aware approach to targeted sense disambiguation. In *Findings of the Association for Computational Linguistics: ACL-IJCNLP 2021*, pages 2751–2761, Online. Association for Computational Linguistics.

Jeroen Blaak. 2009. *Literacy in Everyday Life. Reading and Writing in Early Modern Dutch Diaries.* Egodocuments and History Series ; v. 2. Brill, Leiden ; Boston.

Piotr Bojanowski, Edouard Grave, Armand Joulin, and Tomas Mikolov. 2017. Enriching Word Vectors with Subword Information. *arXiv:1607.04606 [cs].*

Edouard Callion. 1789. Gentsche kronijke : 1525-1835 / door Edou. Callion. 1780-1789.

Ronan Collobert, Jason Weston, Leon Bottou, Michael Karlen, Koray Kavukcuoglu, and Pavel Kuksa. 2011. Natural Language Processing (almost) from Scratch. *arXiv:1103.0398 [cs].*

František Dařena and Martin Süss. 2020. Quality of Word Vectors and its Impact on Named Entity Recognition in Czech. *European Journal of Business Science and Technology*, 6(2):154–169.

Jiang Guo, Wanxiang Che, Haifeng Wang, and Ting Liu. 2014. Revisiting embedding features for simple semi-supervised learning. In *Proceedings of the 2014 Conference on Empirical Methods in Natural Language Processing (EMNLP)*, pages 110–120, Doha, Qatar. Association for Computational Linguistics.

G. Hripcsak. 2005. Agreement, the F-Measure, and Reliability in Information Retrieval. *Journal of the American Medical Informatics Association*, 12(3):296–298.

Zhiheng Huang, Wei Xu, and Kai Yu. 2015. Bidirectional LSTM-CRF Models for Sequence Tagging. *arXiv:1508.01991 [cs].*

P. Kahle, S. Colutto, H. Hackl, and H. Mühlberger. 2017. Transkribus - A Service Platform for Transcription, Recognition and Retrieval of Historical Documents. In *2017 14th IAPR International Conference on Document Analysis and Recognition (ICDAR)*, volume 04, pages 19–24.

Mike Kestemont. 2018. Stylometric Authorship Attribution for the Middle Dutch Mystical Tradition from Groenendaal. *Dutch Crossing*, 42(3):203–237.

Mike Kestemont, Els Stronks, Martine de Bruin, and Tim de Winkel. 2017. *Van Wie Is Het Wilhelmus? De Auteur van Het Nederlandse Volkslied Met de Computer Onderzocht*. Amsterdam University Press, Amsterdam.

Milan Lange, van and Ralf Futselaar. 2019. Debating evil: Using word embeddings to analyse parliamentary debates on war criminals in the netherlands. *Prispevki za novejšo zgodovino / Inštitut za zgodovino delavskega gibanja*, 59(1):140–156.

Alie Lassche. 2019. *Cultural Evolution in Dutch Early Modern Songs. Topical Fluctuations in the Dutch Song Database (1550-1750)*. Master's thesis, Utrecht University, Utrecht.

Alie Lassche, F.B. Karsdorp, and Els Stronks. 2019. *Repetition and Popularity in Early Modern Songs*.

Nikola Ljubešić. 2018. Comparing CRF and LSTM performance on the task of morphosyntactic tagging of non-standard varieties of South Slavic languages. In *Proceedings of the Fifth Workshop on NLP for Similar Languages, Varieties and Dialects (VarDial 2018)*, pages 156–163, Santa Fe, New Mexico. Association for Computational Linguistics.

Benedikt Mauer. 2001. *"Gemain Geschrey" und "teglich Reden": Georg Kölderer - ein Augsburger Chronist des konfessionellen Zeitalters*. Number 29 in Veröffentlichungen der Schwäbischen Forschungsgemeinschaft Reihe 1, Studien zur Geschichte des bayerischen Schwaben. Wißner, Augsburg.

F. Pedregosa, G. Varoquaux, A. Gramfort, V. Michel, B. Thirion, O. Grisel, M. Blondel, P. Prettenhofer, R. Weiss, V. Dubourg, J. Vanderplas, A. Passos, D. Cournapeau, M. Brucher, M. Perrot, and E. Duchesnay. 2011. Scikit-learn: Machine learning in Python. *Journal of Machine Learning Research*, 12:2825–2830.

Andrew Pettegree. 2014. *The Invention of News: How the World Came to Know about Itself*. Yale University Press, New Haven ; London, England.

Michael Piotrowski. 2012. *Natural Language Processing for Historical Texts*, volume 5 of *Synthesis Digital Library of Engineering and Computer Science*. Morgan & Claypool, San Rafael, Calif.

Judith Pollmann. 2016. Archiving the Present and Chronicling for the Future in Early Modern Europe. *Past & Present*, 230(suppl 11):231–252.

Judith Pollmann. 2017. *Memory in Early Modern Europe, 1500-1800*, first edition edition. Oxford University Press, Oxford ; New York, NY.

Susanne Rau. 2002. *Geschichte Und Konfession: Städtische Geschichtsschreibung Und Erinnerungskultur Im Zeitalter von Reformation Und Konfessionalisierung in Bremen, Breslau, Hamburg Und Köln*. Number Bd. 9 in Hamburger Veröffentlichungen Zur Geschichte Mittel- Und Osteuropas. Dölling und Galitz, Hamburg.

R.S Ros. 2019. The birth of the foreign : A digital conceptual history of buitenland in dutch newspapers 1815-1914.

Daniel Rosenberg. 2003. Early Modern Information Overload. *Journal of the History of Ideas*, 64(1):1–9.

Miran Seok, Hye-Jeong Song, Chan-Young Park, Jong-Dae Kim, and Yu-seop Kim. 2016. Named Entity Recognition using Word Embedding as a Feature. *International Journal of Software Engineering and Its Applications*, 10(2):93–104.

Stéphan Tulkens, Chris Emmery, and Walter Daelemans. 2016. Evaluating Unsupervised Dutch Word Embeddings as a Linguistic Resource. *arXiv:1607.00225 [cs]*.

Michiel van Groesen. 2016. Reading Newspapers in the Dutch Golden Age. *Media History*, 22(3-4):334–352.

Jozef Van Walleghem. 2016. *Merckenweerdigste voorvallen en Daegelijcksche gevallen Brugge 1779-1800*. Gemeentebestuur, Brugge.

Melvin Wevers. 2019. Using Word Embeddings to Examine Gender Bias in Dutch Newspapers, 1950-1990. *arXiv:1907.08922 [cs, stat]*.

Melvin Wevers, Jianbo Gao, and Kristoffer Nielbo. 2020. Tracking the Consumption Junction: Temporal Dependencies between Articles and Advertisements in Dutch Newspapers. *Digital Humanities Quarterly*, 14(1).

Melvin Wevers and Marijn Koolen. 2020. Digital begriffsgeschichte: Tracing semantic change using word embeddings. *Historical Methods: A Journal of Quantitative and Interdisciplinary History*, pages 1–18.

Melvin Wevers and Jesper Verhoef. 2018. Coca-cola: An icon of the american way of life. an iterative text mining workflow for analyzing advertisements in dutch twentieth-century newspapers. *Digital humanities quarterly*, 11(4).

Yonghui Wu, Jun Xu, Min Jiang, Yaoyun Zhang, and Hua Xu. 2015. A Study of Neural Word Embeddings for Named Entity Recognition in Clinical Text. *AMIA ... Annual Symposium proceedings. AMIA Symposium*, 2015:1326–1333.

FrameNet-like Annotation of Olfactory Information in Texts

Sara Tonelli, Stefano Menini
Fondazione Bruno Kessler
Via Sommarive 18, Trento (Italy)
[satonelli|menini]@fbk.eu

Abstract

Although olfactory references play a crucial role in our cultural memory, only few works in NLP have tried to capture them from a computational perspective. Currently, the main challenge is not much the development of technological components for olfactory information extraction, given recent advances in semantic processing and natural language understanding, but rather the lack of a theoretical framework to capture this information from a linguistic point of view, as a preliminary step towards the development of automated systems. Therefore, in this work we present the annotation guidelines, developed with the help of history scholars and domain experts, aimed at capturing all the relevant elements involved in olfactory situations or events described in texts. These guidelines have been inspired by FrameNet annotation, but underwent some adaptations, which are detailed in this paper. Furthermore, we present a case study concerning the annotation of olfactory situations in English historical travel writings describing trips to Italy. An analysis of the most frequent role fillers show that olfactory descriptions pertain to some typical domains such as religion, food, nature, ancient past, poor sanitation, all supporting the creation of a stereotypical imagery related to Italy. On the other hand, positive feelings triggered by smells are prevalent, and contribute to framing travels to Italy as an exciting experience involving all senses.

1 Introduction

In the humanities and social sciences, the senses, which have traditionally received little attention from researchers, are now very high on the academic agenda (Smith, 2007). In fact, in the last two decades, scholarly attention has shifted away from the visual and textual to the embodied and multi-sensory, following a so-called 'sensorial revolution' (Howes, 2006; Classen, 1999). In the field of history, for example, recent works have focused on describing the meaning of odours in particular places and times (Dugan, 2011), or on the role played by smells in signalling identity, community and otherness in the past – especially race (Smith, 2006; Tullett, 2016). This turn, however, has received little attention from the NLP community, probably due to a number of inherent challenges related to the intangible nature of scents and odours. The few existing works in the field have mainly focused on building resources aimed at capturing and modelling sensory vocabularies (Tekiroğlu et al., 2014b) and analysing how the different senses interfere from a lexical point of view (Winter, 2019). This lack of attention may be partly explained by the fact that Western languages, which are prevalent in NLP studies, do not contain rich vocabularies for describing odorants as opposed to other senses (Majid and Burenhult, 2014). The only exception in this direction is the work in (Brate et al., 2020), where the authors present two semi-supervised approaches to identify smell experiences in English literature after annotating a gold standard of 700 sentences with smell-related information.

In this work, we present a more comprehensive scheme for the annotation of olfactory information, which has been developed within the ODEUROPA H2020 Project[1]. The goal of this effort is to capture smell events and situations in texts and manually label the main participants in the scene. Our guidelines are inspired by frame semantics (Fillmore and Baker, 2001) and the FrameNet annotation project (Ruppenhofer et al., 2006), although we carry out some modifications both to the olfactory-related frames and to the annotation practice. This work will guide a subsequent annotation task, which will lead to the creation of a multi-domain multilingual benchmark of historical texts annotated with olfactory information. The guidelines and the benchmark represent also the backbone upon which an

[1] https://odeuropa.eu/

Proceedings of LaTeCH-CLfL 2021, pages 11–20
Punta Cana, Dominican Republic (Online), November 11, 2021.

automated system for olfactory information extraction will be built. As a preliminary study, we apply the annotation scheme to a set of English travel narratives describing trips to Italy, and present the results obtained by analysing the most frequent role fillers and grouping them by domains.

2 Related work

Only very little research within the NLP community has dealt with sensory information extraction. Most works have focused on the creation of structured resources to capture the sensory domain, automatically deriving them from WordNet (Tekiroğlu et al., 2014b,a). Other works have dealt with the automated analysis of texts related to specific domains like wine reviews, where olfaction plays a central role (Lefever et al., 2018). Other studies have focused on synaesthetic aspects of language, starting from a controlled lexicon of perception (Lievers and Huang, 2016). To our knowledge, only the work by (Brate et al., 2020) proposes both a simple annotation scheme to capture smelly experiences and two semi-supervised approaches to automatically replicate this annotation. Another line of research has addressed so-called urban smellscapes, i.e. how modern cities can be described from an olfactory point of view. More specifically, (Quercia et al., 2015, 2016) obtain descriptions of different urban areas by asking annotators to walk around cities and take note of the smell characterising different places. Such descriptions are then combined with social media posts about the same places, allowing the authors to build an olfactory representation of different cities and categorise urban smells into odour wheels.

3 FrameNet and Olfactory Information

Our annotation of olfactory information is inspired by frame semantics (Fillmore and Baker, 2001), a theory which has been implemented through the FrameNet annotation project (Ruppenhofer et al., 2006)[2], whose goal is to capture situations and events present in texts. In FrameNet, events and situations are so-called *frames*, which from a cognitive point of view, are defined as components of the internal model of the world that a language-user has created by interpreting his/her environment (Fillmore, 1976). Frames are used as synonyms for schemata, semantic memory or scenarios, and represent the perceptual base of our knowledge that is necessary to understand the meaning of words. For example, the predicate 'marry' refers to a scenario where two partners get involved in some kind of social relationship.

According to frame semantics, a frame includes two main components: *lexical units* (LUs) and *frame elements* (FEs). The former are words, multiwords or idiomatic expressions that evoke a specific frame, while the latter are frame-specific semantic roles that, in case of verbal LUs, are usually realized by the syntactic dependents of the verb. For example, the *Commerce pay* frame includes as lexical units 'pay', 'payment', 'disburse', 'disbursement', 'shell out', and has the following frame elements: Buyer, Goods, Money, Rate, Seller.

FrameNet aims at being a general-purpose resource, capturing all possible situations and events that may happen in real life. Therefore, in the last FrameNet version, more than 1,200 frames are listed. Since in our study we are only interested in olfactory situations, we narrow the scope of the annotation and we simplify the frame repository, while adopting the same structure as the original FrameNet based on lexical units and related frame elements.

For example, in FrameNet the 'smell' lexical unit is present as a noun or verb in five frames: *Sensation*, *Perception active*, *Give impression*, *Perception experience* and *Chemical sense description*. Their distinctions are rather fine-grained, for example *Perception active* and *Perception experience* both capture perception events but in the former the perceptual experience is intentional, while in the second it can be unintentional. On the other hand, *Chemical sense description* captures mainly descriptions of tastes and smells, while *Give impression* includes characterisations and appraisals of smells and *Sensation* includes nouns that refer to sensations in different modalities. All these distinctions are not needed in our framework, whose final goal is to build a methodology and techniques for olfactory information extraction. Therefore, we only define a single frame, the *Olfactory event*, where all relevant roles of the above frames are captured. We also create domain-specific semantic roles that are the outcome of discussions with experts in olfactory heritage and history. For example, we introduced the roles of *Smell source*, *Evoked odorant* and *Odour carrier*, while we borrowed from FrameNet some generic roles such as *Perceiver*, *Time*, *Location* and *Circumstances*. For

[2] https://framenet.icsi.berkeley.edu

details, see Section 4.2. Also the list of lexical units (LUs) is defined with the help of domain experts, choosing smell-related lexical units that evoke olfactory situations and events. Our goal is to develop an annotation scheme that may be applied to different languages, therefore the LU lists are being created in seven languages, namely English, Dutch, Italian, French, German, Slovenian, Latin. They include both translations and synonyms of words such as 'to smell', 'odour' 'odorous', 'smelly', 'perfume' and language-specific terms. For example, German includes a list of compound nouns created with the roots '-gestank', '-geruch', '-duft' (e.g. Regengeruch, Viehgestank, Lavendelduft). We report in Table 1 the lexical units defined so far for English and Italian, while for the other languages the definition is still in progress.

With this annotation, we pursue several objectives: we want our guidelines to be generic enough to accomodate all possible smell-related events which may be mentioned in a text, and also to cover all languages, without the need to provide language-specific adaptations from a semantic point of view. We also want our framework to be flexible enough to deal with meaning change of terms over time, enabling annotators to add new smell-related terms to our initial list during the annotation process. Finally, we define semantic roles using labels that are self-explanatory and not ambiguous (e.g. *Evoked odorant*, *Smell source*), so to facilitate the role selection ensuring a good agreement among annotators.

4 Annotation of Olfactory Events

4.1 Lexical unit annotation

Following FrameNet guidelines, the annotation of olfactory situations and events should be carried out in two steps: given a sentence, first frame-evoking words or expressions should be marked as lexical units, and then their related semantic roles should be identified, labeled and connected to the LU.

The *Olfactory event* frame is typically evoked by 'smell' words, i.e. terms (different for each language) that unambiguously evoke or describe an odor-related situation or event. Using the same terminology of FrameNet, smell words are the lexical units. These include nouns, verbs, adverbs and adjectives. To create an initial set of smell words, we asked domain experts to prepare a list of possible lexical units for each language, which is reported in Table 1 and can be further expanded during annotation. The **Other** category covers (ambiguous) smell words, that should be annotated only if they refer to a smell experience or an olfactory situation. We report few example sentences below, underlying the smell-related lexical units:

(1) The guardsmen drenched their beards in scent.

(2) Hungry dogs scent a meal in the refuse heaps of the gutters.

(3) Beside the road the tall asphodel is smelling of cats.

Each olfactory situation can be evoked only by one smell word. If more smell-related terms are present, they have to be annotated as different frame instances. If a smell word can correspond also to a frame element, it has to be labeled with both tags, following the same convention as in FrameNet. Consider for example the following sentence:

(4) The air in the room was mephitic.

The term 'mephitic' would be a quality, but since no other smell-word is present in the sentence, it is clearly this term that evokes the smell event, and it should therefore be marked as lexical unit (this is also part of the seed words listed in Table 1).

If a text clearly describes an olfactory situation but smell words from the pre-defined list cannot be found, other terms can be considered as lexical units if they are used as near-synonyms of 'smell', even if out of context they may have another meaning. See for example 'composition', 'essence', 'perceive', etc.

4.2 Annotation of Frame Elements (FEs)

Each odor-related event or situation is evoked by a smell-word but can involve one or more participants in the event, each having a specific role. These olfactory frame elements (i.e. semantic roles) have to be identified and annotated as well. The list of participants or semantic roles pertaining to an odour-related situation is reported below.

Smell source: the person, object or place that has a specific smell. It can also refer to (non)human / object that produces an odour (e.g. plant, animal, perfume, human). This FE is the entity or phenomenon that the perceiver experiences through his or her senses.

Odour carrier: this FE corresponds to the carrier of an odor, which can be either an object (e.g.

English
Nouns: stink, scent, scents, smell, smells, odour, odor, odours, odors, stench, reek, aroma, aromas, aromatic, whiff, foetor, fetor, fragrance, musk, rankness, redolence, pong, pungency, niff, deodorant, olfaction **Verbs**: smelling, smelled , reeked, sniff, sniffed, sniffing, whiffed, fragrance, deodorized, deodorizing, snuffing, snuffed **Adjectives**: stinking, stank, stunk, scented, odourless, odoriferous , odorous, malodorous , reeking, aromatic , whiffy, fetid, foetid, fragrant, fragranced, redolent, frowzy, frowsy, pungent, funky, musty, niffy, unscented, scentless, deodorized, noisome , smelly, mephitic, olfactory **Adverbs**: musky, pungently **Other**: atmosphere, essence, putrid
Italian
Nouns: lezzo, morbo, putidore, fiatore, puzzo, puzza, fetore, miasma, putrefazione, effluvio, esalazione, estratto, odore, aroma, olezzo, fragranza, profumo, aulimento, odoramento, afrore, tanfo, tanfata, zaffata **Verbs**: odorare, puzzare, profumare, deodorare, odorizzare, aromatizzare, fiutare, annusare, nasare, olezzare, ammorbare, appestare, impestare, impuzzare, impuzzire, impuzzolentire, impuzzolire, intanfare **Adjectives**: puzzolente, fetente, fetido, deodorizzato, putrefatto, odorato, odoroso, odorifero, aromatizzato, profumante, profumato, suave, soave, olfattivo, olfattorio, maleodorante, aromatico, pestilenziale, puzzoso, fragrante **Adverbs**: profumatamente, odorosamente **Other**: essenza, atmosfera, sentire

Table 1: Initial list of possible lexical units for English and Italian

pomander, bottle of perfume, handkerchief) or atmospheric elements like wind and air. Note that the *Odor carrier* has a different role from the *Source*, since the *Source* produces an odour, while the *Carrier* carries a smell that is produced by something else (possibly unknown). A *Carrier* should be annotated only when there is a clear distinction w.r.t. the *Source*. When this distinction cannot be understood or inferred from the text, a *Source* label should be selected. This means that when an odour is described as coming generically from an object or entity and it is not specified or clear from the context whether the object or entity actually produced the odour it should be annotated as *Source*.

Quality: This is a quality associated with a smell and used to describe it. For example 'rancid', 'fresh', etc. This is typically expressed by qualitative adjectives. It is often preceded by an intensifier such as 'very, really'. The intensifier has to be annotated with the related adjective in the same span. Qualities include intensity ('not perceptible', 'weak', 'distinct', 'strong'), volume / reach ('far reaching'), duration ('lasting', 'permanent'), state ('old', 'deteriorated'), character ('humid', 'dry', 'garlicky', 'fruity', 'woody'), hedonic characteristics ('malodorous', 'aromatic', 'healthy').

Perceiver: The being that perceives an odour, who has a perceptual experience, not necessarily on purpose. The perceiver is mostly a person or an animate entity. The perceiver can also be expressed by mentioning the perceptive organ (e.g. nose, nostrils, nerves) used in the olfactory experience

Evoked Odorant: This frame element describes the object, place or similar that is evoked by the odour, even if it is not visible in the scene. In English, this is often part of a comparison or similarity using the verb 'to smell' and introduced by 'like'. *Evoked Odorants* also include situations, recollections or abstract concepts that are evoked in the *Perceiver*'s mind by smelling an odour.

In some cases, there is no linguistic evidence that a frame element is an *Evoked Odorant* and not a *Smell source*. The former is usually evoked in the mind of the perceiver, often as a recollection of past experiences, while the latter is the actual entity emitting an odour. In these cases, annotators need to interpret the whole sentence and infer if the smell source is real or only evoked, as in the following example where 'nothing but painted paper and tinsel' would be *Smell source*:

(4) The horrid stench [of the leek]$_{Evoked\_odorant}$ was composed of [nothing but painted paper

Frame Element	Example Sentence
Smell Source	The waiter smelled [something] foul in the kitchen. He carefully smelt [the soup] for any trace of poison.
Odour Carrier	[An Egyptian gale] came rushing upon me, impregnated with pestilential vapours. [The pomander] emitted a smell of musk.
Quality	The coffee had a [pungent] smell. The waiter smelled something [foul] in the kitchen.
Perceiver	The olfactory [nerves of women of quality] are amazingly tender. They have the old smell which [to me] would bring back Knole.
Evoked Odorant	He smells [like flowers]. I have no desire to reek [like the floor of a florist's stall].
Location	[In Venice] the canals have an offensive smell. The peaceful odour of Mrs. Dillon was prevalent [in the hall of the house].
Time	[In Summer] the city was inundated with a pungent fish smell. [By day] they have little or no smell except in rainy weather, but [in the evening] they are delightfully fragrant.
Circumstances	[The alteration] it made in him would sometimes fill the room with a musty scent. [At high heat] the smell of mud was pungent.
Effect	The odour was so strong [that I fainted].

Table 2: Frame Elements (FEs) related to Olfactory situations and events with corresponding examples. Lexical units are underlined and the FE of interest is put between squared brackets.

and tinsel]$_{Smell\_source}$.

Location: This frame element describes the location where the smell event takes place. *Locations* can include both named places (for example names of cities) and common nouns describing locations such as garden, street, kitchen, cliffs, promenade, neighborhoods, etc. Similar to the annotation of *Odour Carrier*, *Locations* are to be marked only when they are different from the *Smell source*. Otherwise, if it is not possible to distinguish whether a place produces a smell or is just impregnated by it, the more generic *Smell source* label is preferred.

Example of annotation of a place as *Smell source*:

(5) They kneel on the wet flags of this foetid [cave]$_{Smell\_source}$.

Time: an expression describing when the smelling event occurred. It includes expressions of duration, frequency and point(s) or period(s) of time.

Circumstances: This frame element describes the state of the world under which the smell event takes place. Note that this does not include places and temporal expressions, which should be annotated as *Location* and *Time* respectively. The role can describe causal implications that lead to or influence the smell event. *Circumstances* may also describe bigger events that include the smell event, for example historical (named) events. Annotators should first try to assign to the FE a *Time* or *Location* role and, only if it does not apply to the specific case, resort to *Circumstances*.

Effect: This frame element describes an effect or reaction caused by the smell. This can include entire sentences or clauses describing another event, that is not necessarily a smell event. This can include also the description of emotions triggered in the *Perceiver* by the smell event.

Creator: This frame element describes the person that creates an (usually pleasant) smell. This role is frequent in documents in the perfumery domain, while it is almost never found in other types of texts.

Each semantic role may be present or not, or be expressed through multiple instances, if they appear separately in the text. For example, in the following sentence both 'the excrements of animals' and 'their sweat' are to be labeled as *Smell source*.

(6) Usually, [the excrements of animals]$_{Smell\_source}$, and in particular [their sweat]$_{Smell\_source}$, are faetid.

For an olfactory event to be present, however, at least a smell word should be annotated.

4.3 Annotation Conventions

Following FrameNet annotation practice, we annotate whole constituents that realize frame elements relative to smell words, rather than just tagging the head words of these constituents. That is, we work with a phrase structure grammar, rather than a dependency grammar. A consequence of this is that many frame element labels cover words that have no direct relation of their own to the target, but only to the head of their constituent. For instance, when a frame element is expressed by a noun which takes adjectival, prepositional or clausal complements or which is modified by such elements, these complements and modifiers are included in the frame element tag. This means also that, when a frame element is expressed by a noun phrase, also articles at the beginning of the phrase are labeled. The same holds with prepositions at the beginning of a prepositional phrase (Example 7).

(7) The peaceful <u>odour</u> of Mrs. Dillon was prevalent [in the hall of the house]$_{Location}$.

In some cases, the same FE label appears multiple times relative to a given target. This can apply to two cases: *i)* multiple separate instances of the same frame element, for example when several Smell sources are mentioned for the same smell event; *ii)* a single instance of a frame element, which is realized in two discontinuous pieces rather than as a single constituent. The cases of discontinuous FEs are particularly frequent in languages that foresee separable terms, for example German split verbs. Both segments have to be annotated and tagged with the same label, and a relation has to be specified going from the peripheral elements to the head of the constituent (see Section 4.4).

Concerning negated events or texts describing the lack of smell events, we annotate them as if they were standard smell events. This is because we are interested in understanding how smells (or a lack thereof) were described at scale and in extracting odor-related terminology, not so much in distinguishing whether a specific event description refers to the presence or absence of a smell. Therefore, the following example would be annotated ignoring the presence of negation:

(8) The <u>aroma</u> cannot be described [as a floral emanation]$_{Evoked\_odorant}$.

Since we are also interested in metaphorical use of smell-related expressions, we include them in our annotation. This decision is in line with past annotation efforts related to emotions in Dutch texts from 1600 to 1800: no distinction was made between the references to body parts or bodily processes in a literal and a metaphorical sense because such a distinction is often quite difficult to make in early modern texts, where expressions which we now consider to be metaphorical often had a quite material basis in humoral theories of the passions (Leemans et al., 2017).

4.4 Deviations from FrameNet annotation

In FrameNet only one relation type is foreseen, that is the relation connecting a lexical unit and the different frame elements. We consider this relation type to hold also for our annotation as the standard relation, which should go from each annotated frame element to the related smell word. However, we introduce two additional relation types. One is used to mark discontinuous frame elements, roles that are expressed by two or more non contiguous strings. While in FrameNet discontinuous FEs are annotated, no specific relation is set to connect them. On the contrary, we introduce this relation to explicitly link strings of text belonging to the same FE. We create a **Discontinuous** relation oriented towards the head or governor of the FE. For example, in the case of a separable verb, the relation will be directed from the prefix to the verb root.

The second relation type is **Anaphoric**, which is not present in FrameNet annotation because it is outside the scope of the project, as stated in the official guidelines (Ruppenhofer et al., 2006). Indeed, FrameNet was originally designed for sentence-level annotation, so no ways to capture relations across sentence boundaries are foreseen. In ODEUROPA, instead, we plan to perform annotation at document level, therefore we introduce anaphoric relations for cases where a frame element is a pronoun and its antecedent is mentioned in discourse (usually preceding the pronoun). In this case, we would annotate the pronoun as bearing a FE label (for example, *Smell source* or *Perceiver*) but we would also manually mark the string explicitly stating whom the pronoun refers to.

This kind of annotation is reported below with *Perceiver1* as the antecedent and *Perceiver2* as the pronoun. In the annotation tool, an arrow has to be set connecting the first to the second element, and the label *Anaphoric* should be selected.

(9) There was no persuading [the lady in question]$_{Perceiver1}$ that [she]$_{Perceiver2}$ had the [most powerful]$_{Quality}$ scent.

(10) He detected [persons of impure life]$_{Smell\_source1}$ by [their]$_{Smell\_source2}$ smell.

Concerning the annotation tool, we selected INCEpTION (Klie et al., 2018), a highly flexible web-based system that supports multiple languages and is extremely user-friendly. The platform foresees three different levels of control i.e. administrator, curator and annotator, so that multiple annotators can perform the task in parallel, the curator can check the annotation quality and compute the agreement, and finally the administrator can close the task, export the data and make further assignments. A screenshot of the annotation window is displayed in Figure 1.

Two expert linguists were trained to annotate English texts containing olfactory situations using the tool. They first annotated the same three historical documents (from 1630, 1833 and 1921) in two training sessions, after which cases of disagreement were discussed and adjudicated. Then, a fourth document was annotated in parallel and used to compute IAA, which was 0.68 Krippendorf's Alpha on FEs extension and labels.

5 Case Study: Olfactory Annotation in Travel Writings

In order to validate the proposed annotation guidelines, we test them on a set of smell-related sentences extracted from 51 books on travel narratives presented in (Sprugnoli et al., 2017) and (Sprugnoli et al., 2018). The books include non-fictional narratives (reports, diaries, letters) and guidebooks about Italy written by English native authors and published between 1860 and 1930[3]. This period was chosen because it followed Italy unification and was characterised by the new phenomenon of leisure-oriented tourists' travels. Indeed, after unification, new routes to Southern Italy and the islands were opened, so that travelers could reach less visited sites, beyond the classic destinations such as Venice, Florence and Rome.

We first extract from the corpus all sentences containing an English smell word, taken from the LU list for English. We try to exclude highly ambiguous words such as "essence" or "atmosphere". Overall, we obtain 650 sentences, corresponding to olfactory events or situations. Then, the sentences are annotated following the guidelines described in the previous sections.

5.1 Annotation statistics

We report an overview of FE occurrences in our dataset in Table 3. The most frequent FE is Smell Source, which appears in 84% of the cases. If it is not present, Evoked Odorant is usually mentioned. Since we deal with travel writings, Locations are also frequently mentioned, while Time, Effect and Circumstances do not seem to be equally relevant. Usually Time is specified in text or can be inferred by the reader without being part of the Olfactory event. For example, in reports and diaries it often appears at the beginning of the document. Such long-range relations, however, are not captured by our guidelines.

Frame Element	Frequency
Smell Source	546
Quality	272
Evoked Odorant	70
Time	42
Location	159
Odour Carrier	84
Perceiver	79
Effect	26
Circumstances	7
Creator	0

Table 3: Number of annotated FEs over 650 olfactory events found in text

We further extract the list of FE fillers and rank them by frequency. An overview of the output is presented in Fig. 2. We do not include the FEs that have less than 50 occurrences and *Perceiver*, since it is often expressed through the 1st person pronoun 'I' or through generic nouns such as 'the traveler', "the observer" or 'the nostrils'.

The list of FE fillers reveals the most striking aspects of Italy to the travelers' eyes (and nose): the vegetation, typical of the Mediterranean landscape, including 'violets' but also 'rosemary', 'oranges and lemons', 'primroses', 'tall asphodels', 'white roses', 'lentisk' and 'cistus'. These are frequently associated with positive qualities such as 'delicious', 'sweet' and 'delicate', but also 'strange'

[3]https://sites.google.com/view/travelwritingsonitaly/

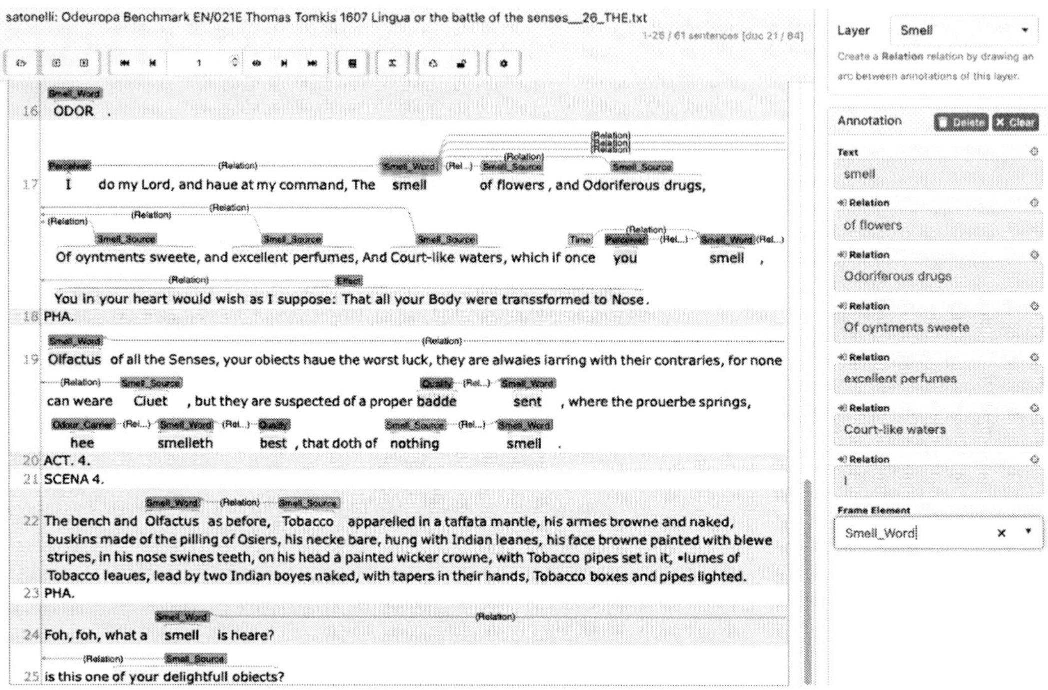

Figure 1: Annotation interface in INCEpTION

and 'peculiar'. Food is also mentioned in relation with odours, mainly typical ingredients of Italian cuisine such as garlic, spaghettis, frying oil, fish and cheese. Another aspect that is often mentioned in the context of olfactory scenes is religion, not only because travelers mention often the 'smell of sanctity', i.e. the belief in the Catholic church that saints were characterised by a sweet smell. They were also struck by the pungent odour of churches, smelling of incense after religious rites, or by the stale odour of catacombs. Finally, travelers are negatively struck by the lack of sanitation of Italian cities, mentioning the 'intolerable', 'pestilential' and 'villanous' odours emanating from 'filth , mud and garbage', 'the vile streets' and 'the litter of horses and cattle'. These aspects were noted by travelers coming from Northern Europe where, already in the 18th Century, processes of urban modernisation and sanitation had been initiated (Wrigley, 2012), while Italy, including Rome, was lagging behind the rest of Europe on this issue.

Overall, travelers describe their experiences as full of excitement for being on classic soil and involving all senses. Indeed, smell is often mentioned together with other senses, for example sweet odours are often associated with music, while bad smells characterise noisy places.

6 Conclusions

In this paper, we first present annotation guidelines to capture olfactory information in texts, and then describe a first use case aimed at analysing travel writings through the lens of smell descriptions. Although this analysis is carried out on English texts, our guidelines have been designed to be language-independent, and the preparation of LU lists covering different European languages is ongoing. As a next step, we plan to extend the annotation with emotion information, so to capture the effect or reactions triggered by smells. Once a multilingual benchmark with manually annotated olfactory information is available, we will also investigate different approaches to perform the task automatically, exploring cross-language frame information transfer (Tonelli and Pianta, 2008) as well as semi-supervised and few-shot classification.

More broadly, analysing how olfactory experiences are described in texts can offer fresh perspectives for humanities research in this field. Through the connection of different, multilingual sources, especially historical ones, we can promote scholarship in the field of sensory history, and engage audiences with more (nuanced) stories about their olfactory past. Once information extraction sys-

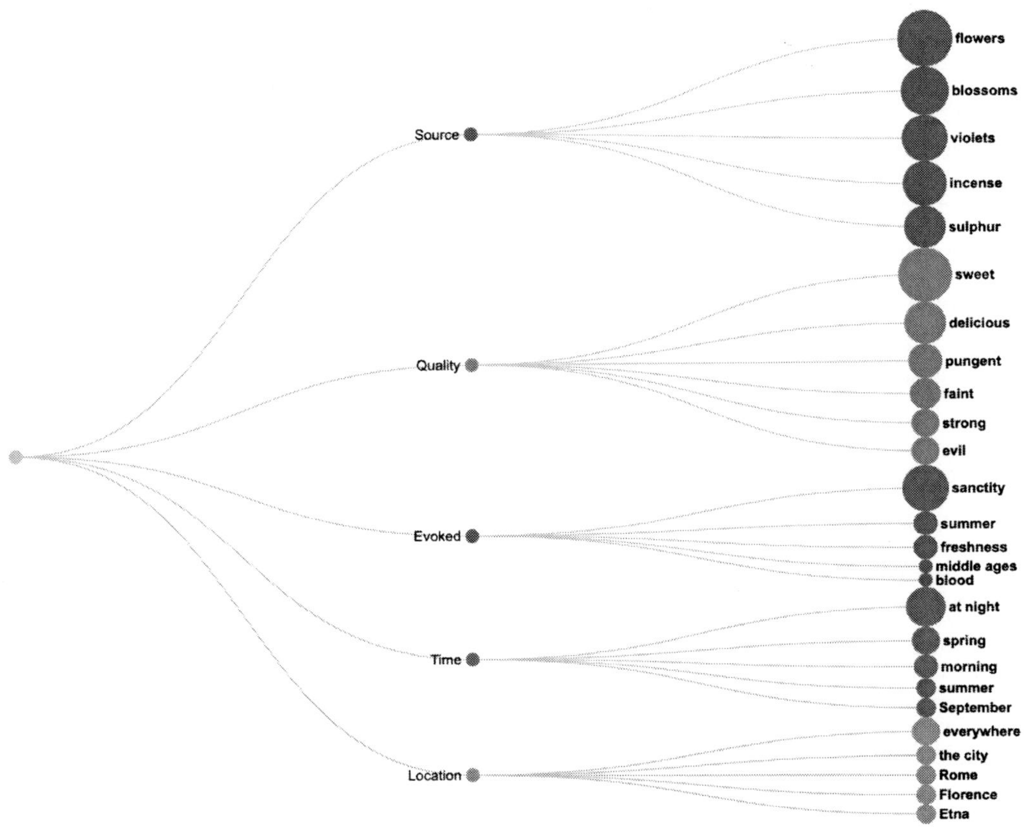

Figure 2: Most frequent FE fillers

tems trained on our annotated data are developed, we will be able to analyse extensive digital archives and trace how scent and smelling were instrumental in shaping communities in the past and how these bound and separated groups and nations.

Acknowledgements

This research has been supported by the European Union's Horizon 2020 program project ODEUROPA under grant agreement number 101004469. We thank in particular Inger Leemans, William Tullet, Caro Verbeek and Cecilia Bembibre for their suggestions on how to define and model olfactory events.

References

Ryan Brate, Paul Groth, and Marieke van Erp. 2020. Towards olfactory information extraction from text: A case study on detecting smell experiences in novels. In *Proceedings of the The 4th Joint SIGHUM Workshop on Computational Linguistics for Cultural Heritage, Social Sciences, Humanities and Literature*, pages 147–155, Online. International Committee on Computational Linguistics.

Constance Classen. 1999. Other Ways to Wisdom: Learning Through the Senses Across Cultures. *International Review of Education*, 45(3-4):269–280.

Holly Dugan. 2011. *The Ephemeral History of Perfume: Scent and Sense in Early Modern England*. Baltimore: Johns Hopkins University Press.

C. Fillmore. 1976. Frame semantics and the nature of language *. *Annals of the New York Academy of Sciences*, 280.

Charles J. Fillmore and Collin F. Baker. 2001. Frame semantics for text understanding. In *In Proceedings of WordNet and Other Lexical Resources Workshop*.

David Howes. 2006. Charting the sensorial revolution. *The Senses and Society*, 1(1):113–128.

Jan-Christoph Klie, Michael Bugert, Beto Boullosa, Richard Eckart de Castilho, and Iryna Gurevych. 2018. The inception platform: Machine-assisted and knowledge-oriented interactive annotation. In *Proceedings of the 27th International Conference on Computational Linguistics: System Demonstrations*, pages 5–9. Association for Computational Linguistics.

I. Leemans, J. V. D. Zwaan, I. Maks, E. Kuijpers, and K. Steenbergh. 2017. Mining embodied emotions: A comparative analysis of sentiment and emotion in dutch texts, 1600-1800. *Digital Humanities Quarterly*, 11.

Els Lefever, Iris Hendrickx, Ilja Croijmans, Antal van den Bosch, and Asifa Majid. 2018. Discovering the language of wine reviews: A text mining account. In *Proceedings of the Eleventh International Conference on Language Resources and Evaluation (LREC 2018)*, Miyazaki, Japan. European Language Resources Association (ELRA).

Francesca Strik Lievers and Chu-Ren Huang. 2016. A lexicon of perception for the identification of synaesthetic metaphors in corpora. In *Proceedings of the Tenth International Conference on Language Resources and Evaluation (LREC'16)*, pages 2270–2277, Portorož, Slovenia. European Language Resources Association (ELRA).

Asifa Majid and Niclas Burenhult. 2014. Odors are expressible in language, as long as you speak the right language. *Cognition*, 130(2):266–270.

D. Quercia, R. Schifanella, L. Aiello, and K. McLean. 2015. Smelly maps: The digital life of urban smellscapes. In *Proceedings of ICWSM*.

Daniele Quercia, Luca Maria Aiello, and Rossano Schifanella. 2016. The emotional and chromatic layers of urban smells. *Proceedings of the International AAAI Conference on Web and Social Media*, 10(1).

Josef Ruppenhofer, Michael Ellsworth, Miriam R. L. Petruck, C. R. Johnson, and J. Scheffczyk. 2006. Framenet ii: Extended theory and practice.

M. M. Smith. 2006. *How race is made: Slavery, segregation, and the senses*. Chapel Hill : The University of North Carolina Press.

Mark Smith. 2007. *Sensing the past: seeing, hearing, smelling, tasting, and touching in history*. Berkeley: University of California Press.

Rachele Sprugnoli, Sara Tonelli, Giovanni Moretti, and Stefano Menini. 2017. A little bit of bella pianura: Detecting code-mixing in historical english travel writing. In *Proceedings of the Fourth Italian Conference on Computational Linguistics (CLiC-it 2017)*, pages 304–309.

Rachele Sprugnoli, Sara Tonelli, Giovanni Moretti, and Stefano Menini. 2018. Two days we have passed with the ancients...: a digital resource of historical travel writings on italy. In *In the Book of Abstracts of AIUCD 2018*.

Serra Sinem Tekiroğlu, Gözde Özbal, and Carlo Strapparava. 2014a. A computational approach to generate a sensorial lexicon. In *Proceedings of the 4th Workshop on Cognitive Aspects of the Lexicon (CogALex)*, pages 114–125, Dublin, Ireland. Association for Computational Linguistics and Dublin City University.

Serra Sinem Tekiroğlu, Gözde Özbal, and Carlo Strapparava. 2014b. Sensicon: An automatically constructed sensorial lexicon. In *Proceedings of the 2014 Conference on Empirical Methods in Natural Language Processing (EMNLP)*, pages 1511–1521, Doha, Qatar. Association for Computational Linguistics.

Sara Tonelli and Emanuele Pianta. 2008. Frame information transfer from English to Italian. In *Proceedings of the Sixth International Conference on Language Resources and Evaluation (LREC'08)*, Marrakech, Morocco. European Language Resources Association (ELRA).

William Tullett. 2016. Grease and sweat: Race and smell in Eighteenth-Century English culture. *Cultural and Social History*.

Bodo Winter. 2019. *Sensory linguistics: Language, perception and metaphor*, volume 20. John Benjamins Publishing Company.

Richard Wrigley. 2012. Making sense of rome. *Journal of Eighteenth-Century Studies*, 35(4).

Batavia asked for advice. Pretrained language models for Named Entity Recognition in historical texts.

Sophie Arnoult
Vrije Universiteit Amsterdam
s.i.arnoult@vu.nl

Lodewijk Petram
Huygens ING
lodewijk.petram@huygens.knaw.nl

Piek Vossen
Vrije Universiteit Amsterdam
p.t.j.m.vossen@vu.nl

Abstract

Pretrained language models like BERT have advanced the state of the art for many NLP tasks. For resource-rich languages, one has the choice between a number of language-specific models, while multilingual models are also worth considering. These models are well known for their crosslingual performance, but have also shown competitive in-language performance on some tasks. We consider monolingual and multilingual models from the perspective of historical texts, and in particular for texts enriched with editorial notes: how do language models deal with the historical and editorial content in these texts? We present a new Named Entity Recognition dataset for Dutch based on 17th and 18th century United East India Company (VOC) reports extended with modern editorial notes. Our experiments with multilingual and Dutch pretrained language models confirm the crosslingual abilities of multilingual models while showing that all language models can leverage mixed-variant data. In particular, language models successfully incorporate notes for the prediction of entities in historical texts. We also find that multilingual models outperform monolingual models on our data, but that this superiority is linked to the task at hand: multilingual models lose their advantage when confronted with more semantical tasks.

1 Introduction

Pretrained language models (Peters et al., 2018; Radford et al., 2018; Devlin et al., 2019) have recently advanced the state-of-the-art in many NLP tasks, providing deep contextual language representations and ease of deployment. BERT (Devlin et al., 2019) has proven particularly successful, combining the attention-based contextual representations of Transformers (Vaswani et al., 2017) with a simple fine-tuning procedure, allowing to deploy quickly to any sequence or document classification task.

BERT has given birth to a myriad of variants, differing by their training procedure, model size or language. Resource-rich languages in particular are spoilt for choice. Dutch for instance has two main monolingual models: the BERT-based BERTje (de Vries et al., 2019) and RobBERT (Delobelle et al., 2020), itself based on RoBERTa (Liu et al., 2019), a revision of BERT's training procedure. But multilingual models like mBERT (Devlin, 2018) and XLM-R (Conneau et al., 2020) are also applicable. These models, which are trained on 104, respectively 100 languages at once, perform well on crosslingual transfer (Pires et al., 2019; Wu and Dredze, 2019; Conneau et al., 2020). Pires et al. (2019) notably show that mBERT learns generic representations over different input languages and scripts. This makes multilingual models particularly interesting for historical texts, not only because these contain noncontemporary language, but also because they exhibit language variation due to language change over long periods of time or unstandardized spelling. But what when historical texts are accompanied by modern notes? How do monolingual and multilingual models compare on the historical and editorial parts of such texts, and on their combination?

If we only consider modern notes, it is not given that monolingual models outperform multilingual models on their training language. Notwithstanding possible differences in genre, the nature of the linguistic task at hand is an important factor in determining whether a monolingual or multilingual model is more appropriate. de Vries et al. (2019) and Delobelle et al. (2020) show for Dutch that mBERT is competitive with monolingual models on POS tagging (on Universal Dependencies POS), while Dutch models perform better at semantic tasks like Semantic Role Labelling or language-specific tasks like agreement resolution. For Named Entity Recognition (NER), results appear mixed, as both BERTje and RobBERT

Proceedings of LaTeCH-CLfL 2021, pages 21–30
Punta Cana, Dominican Republic (Online), November 11, 2021.

perform in-between mBERT and a version optimized by Wu and Dredze (2019). How semantic or language-specific does a task need to be for monolingual models to perform better than multilingual models in historical texts with editorial notes?

In this article, we consider these questions in the context of NER in 17th and 18th century Dutch texts. We introduce a new NER dataset based on the *General Letters of the United East India Company* (VOC)[1]. These official letters were written to the board of the VOC between 1610 and 1795. They report on the activities of the VOC (trade, conflicts, intelligence) in and around Indonesia and up to Japan and South Africa. Between 1960 and 2017, a selection of this corpus, spanning the time period 1610-1767, was transcribed and edited by the Huygens Institute for the History of the Netherlands (Huygens ING) and its predecessors. Annotating entities in these letters is part of a larger effort to facilitate historical research on these texts.

Our dataset[2] consists of 24.5k entities, with a repartition of 40%/60% between historical text and editorial notes, where the historical text covers the period 1621 to 1760. We introduce a semantic component in this dataset by distinguishing metonymical uses of locations (which represent almost half of all entities). This allows us to compare two NER variants: a standard one, where locations form a single entity type; and a more semantic one, where models additionally must distinguish locations in agent-like roles, as in for instance, *Batavia asked for advice*.

We compare the performance of monolingual and multilingual models on both NER variants through BERTje (de Vries et al., 2019), RobBERT (Delobelle et al., 2020), mBERT (Devlin, 2018) and XLM-R (Conneau et al., 2020). On standard NER, we find that multilingual models outperform monolingual models on both historical text and modern notes. In crosstext finetuning and evaluation, we confirm the strong crosslingual transfer ability of multilingual models in the context of historical language variation. We also show that notes and historical text are complementary for NER, as all pretrained models, multilingual *and* monolingual, benefit from their combination. On the more semantic-oriented NER task, we find that monolingual and multilingual models perform competitively, with RobBERT and mBERT performing best. This confirms the importance of the semantic nature of a task as a factor in choosing between monolingual and multilingual models.

[1] http://resources.huygens.knaw.nl/vocgeneralemissiven/index_html_en

[2] Dataset and code are available at https://github.com/cltl/voc-missives

2 Annotations

The labelset consists of five base labels—LOC, ORG, PER, REL and SHP—for the entity types *locations*, *organisations*, *persons*, *religions* and *ships*. Following (Benikova et al., 2014), this labelset is extended with secondary labels of the form X_{deriv} or X_{part} for expressions derived from entity names by grammatical derivation (as with for instance, the location *Banda* and the derived *Bandanezen*[3]) or composition (as with *Java* and *Javakoffie*[4]). The labelset is extended with a GPE label (*geopolitical entities*) to distinguish metonymical use of location names.

2.1 Data selection

The data selected for annotations consist of letters spread out through the *General Letters* corpus[5]. In editing these letters, Huygens ING transcribed parts of the letters, and summarized other parts, which appear as in-text paragraph notes in the digital version of the corpus[6]. Editorial comments appear as footnotes.

We use the post-OCR version of the corpus[7] made available in Text-Fabric (Roorda, 2016, 2019). This is a clean text overall, with some errors in character recognition (e.g., *Ib* instead of *lb*, *S* Malo* instead of *St Malo*), page-to-text formatting (*Chris -toffel* for *Christoffel*) or tokenization (*Schippers ,* instead of *Schippers,*).

We selected 25 letters for annotation, keeping the historical text and editorial notes of these letters apart to facilitate their separate use. Our final dataset consists of 43 documents: 22 historical *text* documents and 21 editorial *notes* documents[8].

[3] Bandanese

[4] Java coffee

[5] The original corpus contains fourteen volumes, the first thirteen of which were available for annotations.

[6] http://resources.huygens.knaw.nl/retroboeken/generalemissiven/#page=0&accessor=toc&view=homePane

[7] https://github.com/annotation/app-missieven, version 0.8.1

[8] A number of documents were unfortunately lost because of server errors. From the 25 letters, 18 are annoted for both *text* and *notes*, 4 for *text* only, and 3 for *notes* only.

	text	notes	total
tokens	233k	201k	434k
entities	9.57k	14.9k	24.5k
density (%)	4.1	7.4	5.6
entity types			
LOC	3927	6525	10.5k
LOC_{deriv}	2227	1414	3641
LOC_{part}	14	21	35
GPE	43	854	897
ORG	994	995	1989
ORG_{part}	8	41	49
PER	1665	3337	5002
REL	10	4	14
REL_{deriv}	159	73	232
REL_{part}	7	10	17
SHP	520	1652	2172

Table 1: Annotation counts

2.2 Annotation counts

Summary statistics are provided in Table 1. Compared to the historical text, the editorial notes show a higher density of entities per token, and they refer less to peoples (through derived forms of *locations* and *religions*), and more to *locations*, *persons* and *ships*. This agrees with notes commenting on *primary* named entities. In contrast, the skewed distribution of *geopolitical entities* between text and notes appears to be a stylistic artefact: metonymical use of locations is in fact concentrated in three notes documents (from volumes 11 and 12), which contain 88.0% of all *geopolitical entities* (for 14.8% of all entities and 11.3% of all tokens). While we consider here the editorial notes as being linguistically homogeneous, their writing spanned more than fifty years and they are at least stylistically varied.

2.3 Guidelines

Our annotations focus on named entities and their derived forms, aiming at annotations that are both consistent for NER and adaptable for extensions. We present here the main considerations in annotating different types of entities.

Locations Only the named entity is marked as an entity in compositional location names (*rif van* $[Luang]_{LOC}$), except when the full expression is treated as a given name. This is in particular the case with coastal areas, which were often the only known part of an island for the VOC:

(1) $[\text{Java's Oostkust}]_{LOC}$, $[\text{Sumatra's Westkust}]_{LOC}$, $[\text{Malabar}]_{LOC}$ en $[\text{Ceylon}]_{LOC}$ [9]

The *Coast* then refers to a specific coastal area, like in this note:

(2) de $[\text{Custe}]_{LOC}$ is hier en elders de $[\text{Kust van Coromandel}]_{LOC}$ [10]

Practically, we annotate compositional location names as entities when their constituents are capitalized:

(3) expeditie ter $[\text{Oostkust van Java}]_{LOC}$ [11]

(4) nabij de noordkust van $[\text{Java}]_{LOC}$ [12]

Derived (adjectival) forms of locations are annotated with LOC_{deriv} and composed names with LOC_{part}:

(5) de $[\text{Bandanezen}]_{LOC_{deriv}}$

(6) Sijn $[\text{Portugeesche}]_{LOC_{deriv}}$ Majesteyt

(7) $[\text{Javakoffie}]_{LOC_{part}}$

Location names with a semantic role of *agent*, *theme*, *experiencer*, *benefactive*, or of *trading* or *political actor* are marked with a distinct GPE label (we use this label for our semantic-oriented NER experiments; GPE entities are relabelled as LOC for standard NER experiments).

(8) $[\text{Batavia}]_{GPE}$ heeft advies gevraagd[13]

(9) er is aan $[\text{Coromandel}]_{GPE}$ opgedragen[14]

(10) de inkomsten van $[\text{Malakka}]_{GPE}$ [15]

(11) de vrede met $[\text{Frankrijk}]_{GPE}$ [16]

[9] *Java's Eastcoast, Sumatra's Westcoast, [...]*

[10] *The Coast refers here and elsewhere to the Coast of Coromandel*

[11] *expedition to the Eastcoast of Java*

[12] *near the north coast of Java*

[13] *Batavia has asked for advice*

[14] *Coromandel has been ordered to*

[15] *the revenues of Malakka*

[16] *peace with France*

Organisations Compositional organisation names are annotated as a whole in principle (*Rade van India, College van Schepenen*). An exception is made for *Kamer* and *Compagnie* which are used productively in the context of the VOC:

(12) de $[\text{kamers}]_{ORG}$ $[\text{Delft}]_{LOC}$, $[\text{Rotterdam}]_{LOC}$ en $[\text{Hoorn}]_{LOC}$

(13) de respective $[\text{Comp.en}]_{ORG}$ van $[\text{Engelant}]_{LOC}$ ende $[\text{Nederlant}]_{LOC}$

(14) wegen d'$[\text{Engelse}]_{LOCderiv}$ en de $[\text{Nederlantse}]_{LOCderiv}$ $[\text{Comp.en}]_{ORG}$

(15) de $[\text{France}]_{LOCderiv}$ $[\text{Comp.ie}]_{ORG}$ van $[\text{S* Malo}]_{LOC}$

Common nouns denoting organisations are not annotated[17]:

(16) het $[\text{Siamse}]_{LOCderiv}$ hoff[18]

Persons Person names are annotated without qualifiers or titles[19]:

(17) ingenieur $[\text{Albert Legrand}]_{PER}$

(18) Radja $[\text{Simorang}]_{PER}$

Religions Religion names and derived forms are a small but relevant group of entities in the context of the VOC:

(19) concurrentie van $[\text{Engelsen}]_{LOCderiv}$ en $[\text{Moren}]_{RELderiv}$[20]

We systematize the annotation of religious groups by including non-capitalized names:

(20) De $[\text{heidense}]_{RELderiv}$ bewoners [...] de $[\text{Moslimse}]_{RELderiv}$ kustbewoners[21]

Ships Ships form a considerable part of the annotations. They are annotated without determiners or qualifiers:

(21) de $[\text{Loenderveen}]_{SHP}$

[17]These are historically relevant while falling out of a linguistic definition of named entities. We might extend *organisations* to terms like *hof, gouvernement* or *comptoir* in a future version of the dataset.

[18]*the Siamese court*

[19]Following (Benikova et al., 2014). The time and space covered by the *General Letters* corpus entails however a great variety of personal titles, that can be hard to tell from person names. We might extend our labelset with titles in the future.

[20]*competition from Englishmen and Moors*

[21]*the pagan inhabitants [...] the Moslim coastal inhabitants*

2.4 Annotation process

Annotations were performed with Inception (Klie et al., 2018) by two annotators, following guidelines inspired from (Benikova et al., 2014). To disambiguate difficult cases, the annotators could rely on the indices of persons, locations and ships accompanying each volume of the corpus, as well as on a glossarium[22]. Annotations were performed for the most part on raw text[23] with the help of a gazetteer compiled from the indices; a few documents were preannotated with either string matching from the gazetteer or with a preliminary NER system.

Agreement was measured halfway through the annotation process, on three documents (two with historical text and one with editorial notes). We measure inter-annotator agreement with F score: like Brandsen et al. (2020) and Deleger et al. (2012), we question the use of Cohen's kappa for NER, as it is unclear how chance agreement should be defined for NER.

Table 2 provides F scores for the text and notes and details cases of agreement and disagreement between both annotators. To this end, we first pair up annotations with a same span to isolate cases of agreement and cases of *label* disagreement. We then attempt to pair remaining annotations, and count annotations that overlap with annotations of the other annotator; those that do are cases of *span* disagreement, while the remaining cases are mentions that only one of the annotators identifies as *entities*.

The analysis of disagreements presented next revealed some inherent difficulties with annotating historical texts, errors in the annotations, but also unclarities in the guidelines. We used this analysis to streamline guidelines and correct annotations[24].

Disagreement analysis Most cases of label disagreement result from the confusion between person names and location or ship names, or between location names and derived forms thereof. Person names cannot always be distinguished from location or ship names by the linguistic context alone, especially with earlier language variants. In this example for instance:

[22]`http://resources.huygens.knaw.nl/vocglossarium/VocGlossarium/zoekvoc`

[23]Extracted from TEI post-OCR files. Annotations on this text were later ported to the Text-Fabric release of the corpus.

[24]Corrections were performed by one of the authors, after annotations were gathered.

	text	notes	total
F1	88.5	92.1	90.8
entities	492/484	910/877	1402/1361
agreeing	432	823	1255
disagreeing			
- label	10	24	34
- span	39/39	24/25	63/64
- entity	11/3	39/5	50/8

Table 2: Inter-annotator agreement. Pairs of counts correspond to the respective annotation counts of each annotator.

(22) vroeg de sengadji van Lamakera Mauwadasje[25]

the indices tell us that *Lamakera* refers to a location and *Mauwadasje* to a person (and the glossarium that *sengadji* denotes the head of a village or district). Linguistic context alone is not enough to distinguish person from location, and the form of the apposition of *Mauwadasje* is also unusual for contemporary Dutch.

Most cases of span disagreement[26] concern infix abbreviations like *Comp.e* for *Compagnie* and qualifiers like *Edele* (*noble*) for *Compagnie*, person titles like *Khan* or *Radja* and location qualifiers as in *engte van Pambenaar*[27] or *Noord-Celebes*.

Most cases of entity disagreement are due to omissions. Other cases concern whether or not to annotate: political actors in general like *gouvernement*; derived forms of location names not denoting peoples, as in *het Engels schip*; compositional location names like *Oostkust*; metonymical uses of locations[28].

3 Experimental Setup

3.1 Models

BERTje (de Vries et al., 2019) is a Dutch model trained on 12GB of data from mixed, mainly contemporary sources. The model is structurally equivalent to BERT_{base}, with 12 Transformer layers of size $H = 768$ and 12 attention heads. The tokenizer is based on Sentence-Piece (Kudo and Richardson, 2018), and has a vocabulary size of 30k. Unlike BERT, BERTje is trained on a Sentence-Order Prediction objective next to Masked Language Modelling (MLM).

RobBERT (Delobelle et al., 2020) is a Dutch model trained on 39GB of data from the OSCAR corpus (Ortiz Suárez et al., 2019). The model is structurally equivalent to BERT_{base} while following the training procedure of RoBERTa (Liu et al., 2019), with a dynamic MLM objective, and a tokenizer based on byte-level BPE following (Radford et al., 2019), with a vocabulary size of 40k (we consider RobBERT v2).

mBERT (Devlin, 2018) is a multilingual model trained on Wikipedia dumps of the 104 languages best represented on Wikipedia (we consider the *cased* version); the model is trained without knowledge of which languages are input, while data are sampled to compensate for less represented languages. The vocabulary is shared across languages and built with Word-Piece (Wu et al., 2016) and has a size of 110k. The model is structurally equivalent to BERT_{base}, and is trained with an MLM and Next Sentence Prediction objective.

XLM-R (Conneau et al., 2020) is a multilingual model trained on a CommonCrawl corpus of 2.5TB, with a vocabulary of 250k tokens built with the Sentence-Piece tokenizer. Like RoBERTa (and RobBERT), XLM-R is trained with an MLM objective, taking sequences of tokens of fixed length as input instead of sentences. We use XLM-R_{base}, which is structurally equivalent to BERT_{base}.

3.2 Data

The data are split in train/dev/test sets so as to obtain comparable splits for the notes and historical text while keeping the notes and text of a same letter together. Besides, we selected the test set for the historical text from the earliest part of the corpus, so as to make it more challenging for a model trained and validated on later text; as the earlier letters contain little notes, the test set for the notes is complemented with a letter for which only the notes were annotated. Data selection for

[25] *asked the sengadji of Lamakera Mauwadasje*

[26] Annotation counts differ for the notes because one entity (*Castor en Pollux*) was marked as two entities by the second annotator.

[27] *Pambenaar's strait*

[28] These were first marked by double LOC/ORG labels. In these cases, the annotators would disagree on adding an ORG label.

training	1658-1730, 1743-44, 1759-60
validation	1731-40, 1741^t, 1750^n
test	1621-43, 1647^n, 1752^n

Table 3: Year ranges of selected letters for each data subset. t: text only; n: notes only

	text	notes	all
training			
tokens	170k	160k	330k
entities	7192	11.5k	18.7k
avg. length	56.6	89.4	68.9
validation			
tokens	30.3k	24.4k	54.7k
entities	981	1991	2972
avg. length	106.8	71.9	87.8
test			
tokens	32.3k	16.7k	49.0k
entities	1401	1436	2837
avg. length	142.9	32.5	66.3

Table 4: Data split. Average sequence lengths are in tokens, before subword tokenization.

the notes also accommodates for GPE labels being concentrated in three letters (from 1744, 1750 and 1752). Data selection is summarized in Table 3.

The data are tokenized with the IXA-pipe tokenizer (Agerri et al., 2014). We do not segment sentences with the tokenizer, but take paragraphs and separate notes as text units, splitting sequences longer than 256 subword units for each language model. This is motivated practically by the tokenizer being to greedy (the letters abound with abbreviations), but we also believe that working at the paragraph level may be beneficial as it provides more context for NER. Summary statistics are provided in Table 4.

For both standard and semantic-oriented experiments, rare labels are mapped to lexically-related labels: REL and REL_{part} to REL_{deriv}, LOC_{part} to LOC_{deriv}, ORG_{part} to ORG. Additionally, GPE labels are remapped to LOC for standard NER.

3.3 Hyperparameter settings

All models are fine-tuned with the HuggingFace Transformers library (Wolf et al., 2020). Adam parameters are: $\beta_1 = 0.9$; $\beta_2 = 0.999$, $\epsilon = 10^{-8}$. We used training batch sizes of 16, a learning rate of $5 \cdot 10^{-5}$ and no weight decay. We did not perform hyperparameter search, but we fine-tuned all models with three different seeds (1, 10 and 100), and we report average values with standard deviation across the three runs. For each run, we selected the best model within 4 epochs, taking loss on the validation set as a criterion and keeping checkpoint models every 100 steps when fine-tuning on the text or notes only, and every 200 steps when fine-tuning on all the data[29]. All experiments were run on a single Tesla P100 GPU. Fine-tuning on all the data takes around 15 minutes per run for all models.

4 Results

We first present results on standard NER, comparing the in-text (text or notes) and crosstext performance of monolingual and multilingual models, and assessing the reciprocal contribution of text and notes. We end with results on semantic-oriented NER.

4.1 In-text performance

Table 5 presents results with fine-tuning and evaluation on the same part of the dataset (text, notes or both). Multilingual models perform better than monolingual models on average, albeit with a smaller margin for the notes and the entire dataset. Results are higher for all models on the notes than on the text; this may have to do with a more homogeneous language in the notes, but also with differences in sequence lengths, which are long on average in the text's testset and short in the notes[30]. The length of text sequences coupled with our working at the paragraph level may also explain the higher unstability of results of BERTje and mBERT, as these were trained on the sentence level.

4.2 Crosstext performance

Crosstext results are presented in Table 6. These confirm the superiority of multilingual models in crosslingual transfer: while all models fine-tuned on text loose a few points when predicting on notes,

[29]Fine-tuning takes about 550 steps for the notes, 850 for the text and 1400 for all the data.

[30]This resulted by chance from our data split. While it might be interesting to try another split resulting in more even sequence lengths, the other constraints we followed, combined with the limited number of letters, limit possibilities in that direction.

	text	notes	all
BERTje	84.4 (2.5)	91.8 (0.4)	90.4 (0.5)
RobBERT	86.1 (0.8)	92.7 (0.5)	91.1 (0.9)
mBERT	**88.7** (3.2)	**93.4** (0.7)	92.2 (0.6)
XLM-R$_{base}$	88.2 (0.6)	**93.4** (0.4)	**92.3** (0.3)

Table 5: In-text fine-tuning and evaluation (F1 scores and standard deviation)

		text	notes
BERTje	text	84.4 (2.5)	82.8 (2.9)
	notes	68.7 (3.3)	91.8 (0.4)
RobBERT	text	86.1 (0.8)	84.1 (1.5)
	notes	71.9 (1.8)	92.7 (0.5)
mBERT	text	88.7 (3.2)	**86.8** (3.6)
	notes	**79.5** (1.2)	93.4 (0.7)
XLM-R$_{base}$	text	88.2 (0.6)	84.7 (0.6)
	notes	77.9 (2.9)	93.4 (0.4)

Table 6: Crosstext fine-tuning and evaluation. Models fine-tuned on the text or notes (rows) and evaluated on text and notes (columns).

		in-text	all
BERTje	text	84.4 (2.5)	87.8 (0.8)
	notes	91.8 (0.4)	92.9 (0.6)
RobBERT	text	86.1 (0.8)	89.3 (1.1)
	notes	92.7 (0.5)	92.9 (0.7)
mBERT	text	88.7 (3.2)	90.8 (0.7)
	notes	93.4 (0.7)	93.6 (0.6)
XLM-R$_{base}$	text	88.2 (0.6)	91.0 (0.5)
	notes	93.4 (0.4)	93.6 (0.1)

Table 7: Reciprocal contribution of notes and text: fine-tuning on in-text data (text or notes) or on all data, and predicting on text or notes (rows).

	text		notes	
	in-text	all	in-text	all
LOC	93.0 (0.6)	94.4 (0.4)	96.7 (0.3)	96.7 (0.1)
LOCd	92.0 (0.3)	93.1 (0.1)	89.6 (0.4)	92.5 (1.0)
ORG	87.5 (1.9)	90.2 (1.6)	89.8 (1.3)	90.9 (2.2)
PER	74.1 (4.2)	79.3 (2.2)	89.4 (1.2)	88.4 (1.1)
RELd	92.3 (1.9)	92.1 (2.3)	39.1 (36.7)	90.0 (5.8)
SHP	60.0 (5.0)	76.2 (1.0)	86.8 (0.4)	86.4 (1.5)
all	88.2 (0.6)	91.0 (0.5)	93.4 (0.4)	93.6 (0.1)

Table 8: Detailed contribution of notes and text fine-tuning data to text and notes predictions, for XLM-R$_{base}$.

multilingual models fine-tuned on notes are more robust when predicting on text, their performance dropping then by about 15 points compared to 20 points or more for monolingual models.

4.3 Reciprocal contribution of notes and text

Table 7 shows the effect of adding out-of-text data for fine-tuning. We see that notes are informative for NER in historical text, as performance on the text increases by 2 to 3 points when fine-tuning on all data. The reverse does not hold: performance on the notes also increases when fine-tuning on all data, but only minimally (by 0.2 point for all models except BERTje, for which scores improve by 1.1 point). These trends hold for all models, monolingual or multilingual, pointing to the general contextual value of notes for named entities combined with a general ability of pretrained language models to exploit context—while monolingual models are trained on a single language, they retain the ability to adapt to a variety of language variants in fine-tuning.

Table 8 details the contribution of notes and text per label for XLM-R. Notes are informative for all entities except *religions* and derived forms, which are poorly represented in the notes (results for the REL$_{deriv}$ label are also very unstable in the notes, as witnessed by the high standard deviation). The highest gains are obtained for *persons* and *ships*, which are also much better represented in the notes than the text. But notes are also informative for entities that are well represented in the text (*locations*, derived forms thereof and *organisations*). Reciprocally, the text is informative for entities that are comparatively better represented: derived forms of *locations*, *organisations* and *religions*.

4.4 Locations as political actors

We end with a semantic oriented NER experiment, where models additionally must distinguish between metonymical (GPE) and standard uses (LOC) of locations. Results are presented in Table 9. Adding this semantic orientation makes it

	-GPE	+GPE
BERTje	90.4 (0.5)	88.4 (0.5)
RobBERT	91.1 (0.9)	**89.0** (0.5)
mBERT	**92.2** (0.6)	**89.1** (1.2)
XLM-R_{base}	**92.3** (0.3)	88.4 (2.2)

Table 9: Distinguishing metonymical uses of locations. -GPE: no distinction; +GPE: distinction between LOC and GPE labels. Models fine-tuned and evaluated on all the data. Boldface marks the two best performing models per case.

	mBERT		RobBERT	
	-GPE	+GPE	-GPE	+GPE
GPE	-	82.0 (0.3)	-	84.0 (1.5)
LOC	95.7 (0.6)	93.0 (0.8)	94.8 (0.5)	92.2 (0.7)
LOCd	92.7 (0.4)	91.0 (1.3)	92.2 (0.4)	91.1 (1.1)
ORG	90.6 (3.4)	90.5 (1.5)	88.6 (1.7)	88.7 (1.8)
PER	84.7 (0.6)	84.0 (1.6)	83.8 (0.4)	82.7 (1.4)
RELd	93.4 (3.9)	78.1 (23.8)	91.3 (4.1)	92.8 (1.9)
SHP	82.1 (1.9)	77.0 (1.6)	79.6 (4.4)	80.6 (0.3)
all	92.2 (0.6)	89.1 (1.2)	91.1 (0.9)	89.0 (0.5)

Table 10: Distinguishing metonymical uses of locations: detailed label scores.

a harder task for all models. Monolingual models however perform relatively better, with RobBERT almost equalling mBERT as best performing model. Multilingual models suffer a larger drop in performance than monolingual models, coupled with more instable results.

We compare detailed label scores for RobBERT and mBERT in Table 10. GPE-label distinction negatively affects prediction of all entity types for mBERT. In contrast, RobBERT performs better than mBERT on GPE prediction, and benefits from the GPE/LOC distinction for the prediction of a few entity types (derived forms of *religions* and *ships*). We observe similar trends with XLM-R_{base} and BERTje, respectively (for BERTje, scores improve for REL_{deriv} and LOC_{deriv} by 1 point).

5 Conclusion

We have introduced a new Dutch dataset for Named Entity Recognition, consisting of Early Modern Dutch VOC letters and modern editorial notes. Comparing monolingual and multilingual pretrained language models, we confirm the stronger crosslingual abilities of multilingual models, while showing that both monolingual and multilingual models can leverage on mixed language variants at fine-tuning. For Named Entity Recognition, pretrained language models are notably able to leverage on notes to improve text predictions. We have further shown that multilingual pretrained language models not only perform better on the historical part of this dataset, but also on modern Dutch notes. However, the superiority of multilingual models on modern Dutch is very much linked to the task at hand, as orienting the data to more semantic distinctions can turn the tables for monolingual models.

Acknowledgements

This work is part of a *Clariah Work Package 6: Text* project, and supported by NWO project number CP-WP6-19-005. We thank the members of the *VOC use case* group for interesting discussions and the anonymous reviewers for their pertinent comments.

References

Rodrigo Agerri, Josu Bermudez, and German Rigau. 2014. IXA pipeline: Efficient and Ready to Use Multilingual NLP tools. In *Proceedings of the Ninth International Conference on Language Resources and Evaluation (LREC'14)*, Reykjavik, Iceland. European Language Resources Association (ELRA).

Darina Benikova, Chris Biemann, and Marc Reznicek. 2014. NoSta-D Named Entity Annotation for German: Guidelines and Dataset. In *Proceedings of the Ninth International Conference on Language Resources and Evaluation (LREC'14)*, pages 2524–2531, Reykjavik, Iceland. European Language Resources Association (ELRA).

Alex Brandsen, Suzan Verberne, Milco Wansleeben, and Karsten Lambers. 2020. Creating a Dataset for Named Entity Recognition in the Archaeology Domain. In *Proceedings of the 12th Language Resources and Evaluation Conference*, pages 4573–4577, Marseille, France. European Language Resources Association.

Alexis Conneau, Kartikay Khandelwal, Naman Goyal, Vishrav Chaudhary, Guillaume Wenzek, Francisco Guzmán, Edouard Grave, Myle Ott, Luke Zettlemoyer, and Veselin Stoyanov. 2020. Unsupervised Cross-lingual Representation Learning at Scale. In *Proceedings of the 58th Annual Meeting of the Association for Computational Linguistics*, pages 8440–8451, Online. Association for Computational Linguistics.

Wietse de Vries, Andreas van Cranenburgh, Arianna Bisazza, Tommaso Caselli, Gertjan van Noord, and Malvina Nissim. 2019. BERTje: A Dutch BERT Model. ArXiv: 1912.09582.

Louise Deleger, Qi Li, Todd Lingren, Megan Kaiser, Katalin Molnar, Laura Stoutenborough, Michal Kouril, Keith Marsolo, and Imre Solti. 2012. Building Gold Standard Corpora for Medical Natural Language Processing Tasks. *AMIA Annual Symposium Proceedings*, 2012:144–153.

Pieter Delobelle, Thomas Winters, and Bettina Berendt. 2020. RobBERT: a Dutch RoBERTa-based Language Model. In *Findings of the Association for Computational Linguistics: EMNLP 2020*, pages 3255–3265, Online. Association for Computational Linguistics.

Jacob Devlin. 2018. Multilingual BERT release. Original-date: 2018-10-25T22:57:34Z.

Jacob Devlin, Ming-Wei Chang, Kenton Lee, and Kristina Toutanova. 2019. BERT: Pre-training of Deep Bidirectional Transformers for Language Understanding. In *Proceedings of the 2019 Conference of the North American Chapter of the Association for Computational Linguistics: Human Language Technologies, Volume 1 (Long and Short Papers)*, pages 4171–4186, Minneapolis, Minnesota. Association for Computational Linguistics.

Jan-Christoph Klie, Michael Bugert, Beto Boullosa, Richard Eckart de Castilho, and Iryna Gurevych. 2018. The INCEpTION Platform: Machine-Assisted and Knowledge-Oriented Interactive Annotation. In *Proceedings of the 27th International Conference on Computational Linguistics: System Demonstrations*, pages 5–9. Association for Computational Linguistics.

Taku Kudo and John Richardson. 2018. SentencePiece: A simple and language independent subword tokenizer and detokenizer for Neural Text Processing. In *Proceedings of the 2018 Conference on Empirical Methods in Natural Language Processing: System Demonstrations*, pages 66–71, Brussels, Belgium. Association for Computational Linguistics.

Yinhan Liu, Myle Ott, Naman Goyal, Jingfei Du, Mandar Joshi, Danqi Chen, Omer Levy, Mike Lewis, Luke Zettlemoyer, and Veselin Stoyanov. 2019. RoBERTa: A Robustly Optimized BERT Pretraining Approach. ArXiv: 1907.11692.

Pedro Javier Ortiz Suárez, Benoît Sagot, and Laurent Romary. 2019. Asynchronous Pipeline for Processing Huge Corpora on Medium to Low Resource Infrastructures. In *7th Workshop on the Challenges in the Management of Large Corpora (CMLC-7)*, Cardiff, United Kingdom. Leibniz-Institut für Deutsche Sprache.

Matthew E. Peters, Mark Neumann, Mohit Iyyer, Matt Gardner, Christopher Clark, Kenton Lee, and Luke Zettlemoyer. 2018. Deep Contextualized Word Representations. In *Proceedings of the 2018 Conference of the North American Chapter of the Association for Computational Linguistics: Human Language Technologies, Volume 1 (Long Papers)*, pages 2227–2237, New Orleans, Louisiana. Association for Computational Linguistics.

Telmo Pires, Eva Schlinger, and Dan Garrette. 2019. How Multilingual is Multilingual BERT? In *Proceedings of the 57th Annual Meeting of the Association for Computational Linguistics*, pages 4996–5001, Florence, Italy. Association for Computational Linguistics.

Alec Radford, Karthik Narasimhan, Tim Salimans, and Ilya Sutskever. 2018. Improving Language Understanding by Generative Pre-Training. Technical report, OpenAI.

Alec Radford, Jeffrey Wu, Rewon Child, David Luan, Dario Amodei, and Ilya Sutskever. 2019. Language Models are Unsupervised Multitask Learners. Technical report, OpenAI.

Dirk Roorda. 2016. Text-Fabric. Software. Version 8.3.4.

Dirk Roorda. 2019. Text-fabric: handling Biblical data with IKEA logistics. *HIPHIL Novum*, 5(2):126–135.

Ashish Vaswani, Noam Shazeer, Niki Parmar, Jakob Uszkoreit, Llion Jones, Aidan N. Gomez, Lukasz Kaiser, and Illia Polosukhin. 2017. Attention Is All You Need. ArXiv: 1706.03762.

Thomas Wolf, Lysandre Debut, Victor Sanh, Julien Chaumond, Clement Delangue, Anthony Moi, Pierric Cistac, Tim Rault, Remi Louf, Morgan Funtowicz, Joe Davison, Sam Shleifer, Patrick von Platen, Clara Ma, Yacine Jernite, Julien Plu, Canwen Xu, Teven Le Scao, Sylvain Gugger, Mariama Drame, Quentin Lhoest, and Alexander Rush. 2020. Transformers: State-of-the-Art Natural Language Processing. In *Proceedings of the 2020 Conference on Empirical Methods in Natural Language Processing: System Demonstrations*, pages 38–45, Online. Association for Computational Linguistics.

Shijie Wu and Mark Dredze. 2019. Beto, Bentz, Becas: The Surprising Cross-Lingual Effectiveness of BERT. In *Proceedings of the 2019 Conference on Empirical Methods in Natural Language Processing and the 9th International Joint Conference on Natural Language Processing (EMNLP-IJCNLP)*, pages 833–844, Hong Kong, China. Association for Computational Linguistics.

Yonghui Wu, Mike Schuster, Zhifeng Chen, Quoc V. Le, Mohammad Norouzi, Wolfgang Macherey, Maxim Krikun, Yuan Cao, Qin Gao, Klaus Macherey, Jeff Klingner, Apurva Shah, Melvin Johnson, Xiaobing Liu, Łukasz Kaiser, Stephan Gouws, Yoshikiyo Kato, Taku Kudo, Hideto Kazawa, Keith

Stevens, George Kurian, Nishant Patil, Wei Wang, Cliff Young, Jason Smith, Jason Riesa, Alex Rudnick, Oriol Vinyals, Greg Corrado, Macduff Hughes, and Jeffrey Dean. 2016. Google's Neural Machine Translation System: Bridging the Gap between Human and Machine Translation. ArXiv: 1609.08144.

Quantifying Contextual Aspects of Inter-annotator Agreement in Intertextuality Research

Enrique Manjavacas
Leiden University
Leiden, The Netherlands
enrique.manjavacas@gmail.com

Laurence Mellerin
Source Chrétiennes Institute
Lyon, France
laurence.mellerin@mom.fr

Mike Kestemont
University of Antwerp
Antwerp, Belgium
mike.kestemont@uantwerpen.be

Abstract

We report on an inter-annotator agreement experiment involving instances of text reuse focusing on the well-known case of biblical intertextuality in medieval literature. We target the application use case of literary scholars whose aim is to document instances of biblical references in the 'apparatus fontium' of a prospective digital edition. We develop a Bayesian implementation of Cohen's κ for multiple annotators that allows us to assess the influence of various contextual effects on the inter-annotator agreement, producing both more robust estimates of the agreement indices as well as insights into the annotation process that leads to the estimated indices. As a result, we are able to produce a novel and nuanced estimation of inter-annotator agreement in the context of intertextuality, exploring the challenges that arise from manually annotating a dataset of biblical references in the writings of Bernard of Clairvaux. Among others, our method is able to unveil the fact that the obtained agreement depends heavily on the biblical source book of the proposed reference, as well as the underlying algorithm used to retrieve the candidate match. Finally, a discussion of the hurdles encountered by annotators supplements the results of the statistical analysis, contributing a qualitative insight into the difficulties involved in the identification of literary text reuse.

1 Introduction

The automatic detection of cases of text reuse in literary collections has the ultimate goal of enabling literary scholars to explore networks of intertextual references between literary works. This goal materializes in more concrete use cases for computationally-aided scholarly work, which include, for instance, visualizing high-level patterns in the referential connections between collections of texts (Jänicke et al., 2015; Yousef and Janicke, 2021), or studying the influence[1] that a given writer has had on subsequent generations (Bloom, 1973). More generally, curators of (nowadays more commonly digital) editions of literary works are concerned with making even the more subtle intertextual connections accessible to the contemporary public.

In this quest, automated retrieval algorithms play a crucial role, since they can accelerate the task of identification at different retrieval phases. At the beginning, a focus on precision can help editors dealing with the bulk of more obvious cases. Towards the end of the process, the majority of the references have been spotted, and high-recall algorithms can help suggesting potential candidates. In this context, the curation of benchmark datasets on which retrieval algorithms can be put to the test is an important milestone of applied research, since benchmark datasets are necessary not only for assessing the relative advantage of particular approaches but also in order to reliably measure the level of precision and recall that editors can expect from automated systems.

However, the curation of benchmark datasets depends on reliable annotation processes. Two aspects of text reuse studies in literary contexts turn the process of benchmark corpus compilation into a problematic enterprise. The first one is that the assessment of intertextual references is a highly interpretative matter. The second one is that the interpretation of these links demands a specific set of skills and expertise that is scarce. In this context, an important question—which has been however rarely approached in previous research—addresses the level of agreement that expert anno-

[1] A recent example is the HyperHamlet project, which aimed at documenting influential passages of Shakespeare on later literature in an exhaustive manner (Hohl Trillini, 2018).

Proceedings of LaTeCH-CLfL 2021, pages 31–42
Punta Cana, Dominican Republic (Online), November 11, 2021.

tators may reach. Still, as it has been noted before (Manjavacas et al., 2019b), inter-annotator agreement studies of intertextuality are rare.[2]

The present paper starts by addressing such research question, but moves beyond it and further aims towards an examination and understanding of the contextual factors that may affect inter-annotator agreement in intertextuality research. Thus, we not only seek to establish an estimate of the achieved inter-rater agreement, but crucially to investigate contextual aspects in the experimental design that influence the process of agreement and can therefore serve as explanatory variables for the obtained agreement scores. We approach this research by means of a re-formulation of Cohen's κ for multiple raters (Artstein, 2017) that bases the computation of the observed agreement on a hierarchical statistical model. Thanks to the incorporation of the statistical model, we are able to infer the dependency of agreement on a number of factors of variation present in the experimental design. Finally, using modern Bayesian modeling techniques to fit the statistical model we obtain estimates of agreement that naturally incorporate uncertainty arising from the inferential process.

We target the text reuse retrieval context of ongoing efforts towards a digital edition of the sermons written by the influential medieval author Bernard of Clairvaux (1090–1153). Bernard's sermons are known for their pervasive biblical intertextuality and are, therefore, rich in potential cases of reuse. The digital edition is currently in a late-stage retrieval phase in which the goal is to exhaustively find relevant but missed cases of reuse.

In this context, we examine the effect of the following contextual factors. First, we investigate the influence of the underlying retrieval method—examining two competitor algorithms from the literature that, a priori, obtain similar performance results but target different aspects of intertextuality. Depending on the biases towards particular types of reuse, algorithms may retrieve candidate pairs that are consistently more or less prone to disagreement. Secondly, we inspect the effect of the biblical book from which the suggested source verse stems. Annotators may be more or less familiar with particular books, and may have diverging expectations on what biblical book the author is likely to borrow from. From this point of view, the source book could constitute an important factor of influence for the obtained agreement. Third, we look into the effect of the amount of lexical overlap between the suggested documents. The level of literality in the suggested matches may constitute a source for disagreement when, for example, annotators expectations on the author's style of reuse diverge. Finally, we tackle the issue of intra-biblical intertextuality, the fact that biblical verses may refer to each other and, as a result, annotators must decide which of the possible verses a Bernardine passage actually refers to.

Contributions Our contributions are as follows. We present a novel study of the inter-annotator agreement on the task of identifying cases of biblical intertextuality in a real-world scenario. We implement a Bayesian variant of a popular inter-annotator agreement index that allows us to compute robust estimates of agreement in the presence of small sample sizes as well as control for and examine relevant factors of variation.

We find that under certain circumstances a semantically motivated text reuse algorithm produces slightly higher inter-annotator agreement scores than an alternative retrieval method based on the text alignment paradigm—which has a bias towards more literal reuse styles. Secondly, we statistically inspect additional factors of variation—related to both objective (style of reuse retrieved by the system) and subjective variables (knowledge of the collection from which the passages are borrowed)—that may help explain the obtained agreement scores. Specifically, we find that the biblical book from which the source of the reference stems is a significant factor of variation and overshadows the effects of other variables. Furthermore, we find that agreement is lowest with average values of lexical overlap in the candidate pair, and that the overall shape of the effect of lexical overlap on agreement diverges depending on whether the Bernardine passage was already known to contain a reference or not.

Finally, we contribute a quantitative assessment of the main hurdles to agreement that our annotators encountered during the experiment, highlighting that not only expert knowledge on the target collections can have important consequences on the assessment of intertextual links, but also that choices in the experimental design may contribute

[2] Bär et al. (2012) include an ad-hoc study of inter-annotator agreement of the annotation guidelines for their evaluation corpus—the Wikipedia Rewrite Corpus (Clough and Stevenson, 2011). This corpus, however, contains examples that are hardly related to literary cases of reuse.

Method	Matches	Sermons	Matches/ Sermon
`S-C`	296 (72)	24	12.33 ($\pm$ 10.66)
`S-W`	292 (56)	22	13.27 ($\pm$ 18.5)

Table 1: Summary statistics of the annotation dataset, displaying the number of matches per method (including the number of matches that had no previous annotation), the number of sermons involved, and the mean (+ standard deviation) of matches per sermon.

to inflated levels of disagreement.

2 Experimental Design

In the present section, we explain the underlying resources and methods used in this study.

2.1 Dataset

Underlying Collections The target collection consists in the 85 *Sermons on the Song of Songs* by Bernard of Clairvaux—made available at the Sources Chrétiennes Institute as part of the BiblIndex project (Mellerin, 2013, 2014)—which we segmented into "documents" using a sliding window of 20 tokens with an overlap of 10 tokens. The processed collection comprises 19,987 such documents. The source collection is the Vulgate Bible, available in digital form from the Perseus repository (Crane, 1996). For the Vulgate, we follow the traditional segmentation into verses, which amounts to 36,663 documents. Both collections were lemmatized using the neural Latin lemmatizer provided by the software library `pie` (Manjavacas et al., 2019a).

Focus Dataset The focus dataset underlying the inter-annotator agreement experiment contains candidate matches between target documents from Bernard and source documents from the Bible. The matches represent optimized guesses about potential misses by the editors in a late-stage retrieval phase during the curation of the digital edition of Bernard's sermons. The current version of this digital edition contains already a total of 6,689 manually identified biblical references. On the basis of the available annotations, we fine-tuned two text reuse retrieval algorithms: one using the local alignment algorithm `Smith-Waterman` (Smith and Waterman, 1981), with a bias towards verbatim cases, and another one based on the `Soft-Cosine` similarity measure (Sidorov et al., 2014), which takes into account lexical similarity using word embeddings and has been used in a previous study on Bernard (Manjavacas et al., 2019b).[3] These algorithms were then applied to the remaining dataset in order to find references potentially overlooked by the editors. From the candidate set of each algorithm we took 300 candidate matches for a total of 600 items. An example candidate match, retrieved with the `Smith-Waterman` algorithm is shown in Figure 1.

Some of the suggested matches involve target documents that are already annotated with a reference to the Bible, whereby the labeled source diverges from the suggested one. In principle, referencing passages in Bernard need not be restricted to a single biblical source. For this reason, we did not exclude such cases from the final target dataset. Table 1 displays dataset statistics about the focus dataset.

2.2 Inter-annotator Agreement

Our experiment involved a total of three expert editors of Bernard,[4] who were shown candidate matches retrieved by the algorithms. The guideline provided to the participants was limited to indicate whether the candidate match would be considered for inclusion in the 'apparatus fontium' of the prospective edition.

In order to quantify agreement, we chose a chance-corrected inter-annotator agreement index for multiple raters based on Cohen's κ. As shown in (Artstein and Poesio, 2008), a series of chance-corrected indices can be formulated as follows:

$$S, \pi, \kappa = \frac{A_o - A_e}{1 - A_e} \quad (1)$$

Here, A_e expresses the expected agreement due to chance as the probability of agreement based on a theoretical annotator casting judgments on a random fashion. In contrast, A_o expresses the observed agreement as the probability—commonly computed as the proportion of instances of agreement in the dataset—that agreement actually

[3] A careful comparison on the basis of Average Precision showed that these algorithms are likely to perform equally with a probability of 0.91 within a margin (region of practical equivalence) of 0.02 points. See Benavoli et al. (2017) for a detailed description of the Bayesian modeling approach to retrieval performance comparison taken in the present study. See Manjavacas (2021) for a thorough discussion of these retrieval methods.

[4] The annotators were Jacqueline Picard, Yasmine Ech Chael and Laurence Mellerin, from the BiblIndex project. The biblical analysis was prepared by Jean Figuet, Marie-Imelda Huille and Laurence Mellerin.

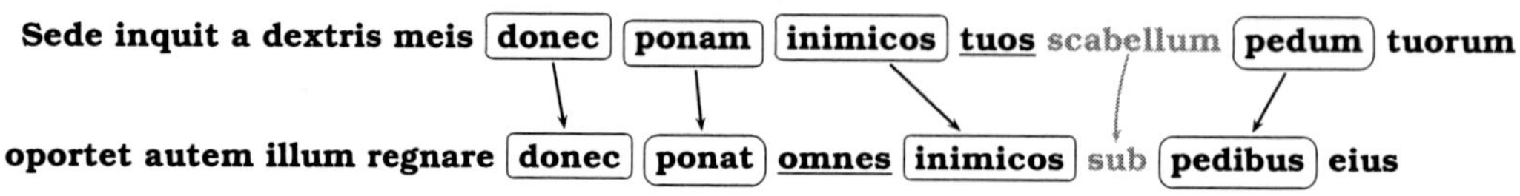

Figure 1: Example of a candidate pair retrieved by the `Smith-Waterman` algorithm, matching a passage from Bernard's 6th Sermon-—document on top—and the biblical verse *1 Corinthians, 15:25*—document on the bottom. Boxes mark tokens that matched based on their lemmata. Underlined tokens represent gaps and tokens highlighted in red represent mismatches.

occurs—i.e. based on the evidence provided by the collected judgments. The difference between S (Bennett et al., 1954), π (Scott, 1955) and κ (Cohen, 1960) resides on the posited model of random annotator behaviour used to compute A_e, where Cohen's κ—the preferred approach—is the only one taking annotator bias towards particular labels into account.

In order to compute agreement indices for more than two raters, we follow the common approach of decomposing the total agreement into the agreement between pairs of annotators, normalizing by the total number of possible annotator pairs.

2.3 A Probabilistic Model for Cohen's κ

As already mentioned, the common approach to obtaining A_o consists in computing the proportion of pairs of judgements that are in agreement over the total number of pairs of judgments implied by the dataset. For each candidate match i, the corresponding agreement agr(i) is given by:

$$\text{agr}(i) = \frac{1}{\binom{c}{2}} \sum_{j=1}^{k} \binom{n_{ij}}{2} \tag{2}$$

where c and k refer respectively to the number of raters and labels, and n_{ij} refers to the number of times label j was assigned to candidate match i. The dataset-level A_o is given by the average $agr(i)$ on the entire dataset: $A_o = \frac{1}{N}\sum_i agr(i)$, where N indicates the total number of candidate matches.

Our approach differs in that we base the computation of A_o on a statistical model of the possible outcomes of a pairwise judgement comparison, as we will show below. Relying on a statistical model allows us to both control for contextual factors as well as look for explanatory variables through the incorporation of statistical co-variates. Moreover, through the deployment of a statistical model we can naturally incorporate uncertainty and provide more robust estimates of the agreement indices.

We resort to a hierarchical multinomial regression model to capture the probabilities of the outcomes of the pairwise judgement comparison. For k labels, this approach uses $m-1$ log-linear models, where $m = k^2$ indicates the number of possible outcomes from pairwise comparisons of casted judgements, using the remaining outcome as a "pivot". For the present case, let θ_{01} refer to the probability of the outcome in which one annotator assigns label 0 and the second assigns label 1.[5] Then, the proposed model is given by Equations 3, 4 and 5.

$$\begin{aligned} \log\left(\frac{\theta_{01}}{\theta_{00}}\right) &= \alpha_{01} + \beta_{01p} \cdot X_p + \nu_{01q} \\ \log\left(\frac{\theta_{10}}{\theta_{00}}\right) &= \alpha_{10} + \beta_{10p} \cdot X_p + \nu_{10q} \\ \log\left(\frac{\theta_{11}}{\theta_{00}}\right) &= \alpha_{11} + \beta_{11p} \cdot X_p + \nu_{11q} \end{aligned} \tag{3}$$

$$\theta_{00} + \theta_{01} + \theta_{10} + \theta_{11} = 1 \tag{4}$$

More specifically, Equation 3 shows the log-odds of the responses θ_{01}, θ_{10} and θ_{11} with respect to the pivot: θ_{00}. Each log-odds are computed by a multi-level linear model where $\alpha_{..}$ refers to the fixed intercepts, $\beta_{..p}$ to the fixed coefficient corresponding to the pth independent variable X_p and $\nu_{..q}$ to the qth-level random intercept, which captures within-group variation for the corresponding grouping factor.

$$\begin{bmatrix} \nu_{01q} \\ \vdots \\ \nu_{11q} \end{bmatrix} \sim \text{MVN}(0, \Sigma_q); \Sigma_q = \begin{bmatrix} \sigma^2_{01q} & & \\ \vdots & \ddots & \\ \sigma_{01-11q} & \cdots & \sigma^2_{11q} \end{bmatrix} \tag{5}$$

As shown in Equation 5, these group-level random intercepts are modeled jointly, coming from

[5] For illustration purposes, the formulation considers only the binary case. The extension to any number of labels is, however, straight-forward.

a multi-variate normal (MVN) centered around a zero-mean with a variance-covariance matrix Σ_q.[6] Letting i refer to the ith outcome, we can turn the log-odds into actual probabilities employing the softmax function, shown in Equation 6.

$$\begin{aligned}
\theta_{00} &= 1 - \sum_{i=1}^{m} \theta_{00} \cdot e^{\alpha_i + \beta_{ip} \cdot X_p + \nu_{iq}} \\
\implies \theta_{00} &= \frac{1}{1 + \sum_{i=1}^{m-1} e^{\alpha_i + \beta_{ip} \cdot X_p + \nu_{iq}}} \\
\implies \theta_i &= \frac{e^{\alpha_i + \beta_{ip} \cdot X_p + \nu_{iq}}}{1 + \sum_{i'=1}^{m-1} e^{\alpha_{i'} + \beta_{i'p} \cdot X_p + \nu_{i'q}}}
\end{aligned} \tag{6}$$

As we can see, the probability of the pivot (θ_{00}, in this case) can be computed as the remaining probability after subtracting the probabilities of the other $m-1$ models.

The probabilities computed by Equation 6 represent baseline probabilities of the outcomes without regard to the annotators that produced the judgements. In order to take into account the observed annotator behaviour, we fit random intercepts that capture the annotator pair underlying the observed outcome. For c annotators, this approach introduces $\binom{c}{2}$ random intercepts per outcome, one for each of the pairwise combinations of the annotators in set C. Letting θ_{00}^{xy} be the probability of the 00 outcome for annotators x and y, A_o can be computed by Equation 7.

$$A_o = \sum_{i=1}^{k} \frac{1}{\binom{c}{2}} \sum_{x,y \in C} \theta_{ii}^{xy} \tag{7}$$

Finally, we compute κ from Equation 1 using A_o from Equation 7 and the dataset-level computation of A_e given by Equation 8.

$$A_e = \sum_{i=1}^{k} \frac{1}{\binom{c}{2}} \sum_{x,y \in C} P(i|x)P(i|y) \tag{8}$$

where $P(i|x)$ corresponds to the probability that annotator x assigns label i, which we obtain as the relative proportion of i-judgements casted by annotator x.[7]

Bayesian Modeling Moreover, in this study we turn to Bayesian inference methods in order to fit the multi-level model. Bayesian inference has a number of advantages in this context, as it has superior modeling capacity in multi-level modeling scenarios with reduced number of cases (Gelman and Hill, 2006), and it produces a posterior distribution over model parameters, upon which further computation can be run in order to propagate parameter uncertainty to the agreement coefficients.

3 Results

3.1 Model Validation

In order to address the effect of contextual aspects on agreement, we identify a number of relevant factors and incorporate them into the computation of the agreement index as fixed effects and random intercepts. Besides modeling the underlying annotator pair as random intercepts, we model (i) the *familiarity* (Known) of the target document (i.e. whether the Bernardine fragment was known already to contain a reference to a different biblical verse) as a binary fixed effect—this allows us to estimate agreement in cases where annotators are asked to re-assess the actual reference of a given passage. Secondly, we incorporate (ii) the *lexical overlap* between source and target documents[8] as a continuous fixed effect. Moreover, we model (iii) the underlying retrieval *method* using random intercepts, seeking to capture whether the underlying retrieval methods have a tendency to suggest more or less controversial matches. Finally, we model (iv) the biblical *source book* (Book) as random intercepts with 50 levels—one for each of the biblical books attested in the dataset—in order to test whether references to particular biblical books tend to be more or less controversial.

First, we test the explanatory power of these

[6]The variance-covariance matrix is, in practice, decomposed into a diagonal variance matrix and a correlation matrix. The inferred models, thus, contain posterior distributions of the group-level correlations between random intercepts across linear models—this resembles the setup introduced by Koster and McElreath (2017).

[7]The utilized index corresponds to a generalization of Cohen's κ to multiple annotators. This is in contrast to the multi-rater agreement index, commonly known as Fleiss κ, which was introduced by Fleiss in (Fleiss, 1971) but that, as (Artstein and Poesio, 2007) argue, actually corresponds to a generalization of Scott's π. Following (Artstein and Poesio, 2007), we will refer to our index as multi-κ, in order to avoid confusion.

[8]We compute lexical overlap using the weighted Jaccard similarity shown in the following Equation:

$$J(D_i, D_j) = \sum_{w \in D_i \cup D_j} \frac{min[c(w, D_i), c(w, D_j)]}{max[c(w, D_i), c(w, D_j)]}$$

where D_i refers to the ith document, and $c(w, D_i)$ refers to the count of word w in document D_i. As it is customary, we rescale the predictor variable to be centered around a zero-mean and unit standard deviation.

Model	ELPD (SE)	P	ELPDΔ(SE)
m.klMB	-1570.05 (35.62)	99.08	0.00
m.kMB	-1733.29 (33.45)	96.15	-163.24 (16.78)
m.MB	-1793.92 (31.55)	92.70	-223.87 (19.10)
m.M	-2136.21 (21.63)	12.12	-566.15 (28.64)
m	-2150.97 (20.84)	8.98	-580.92 (29.13)

Table 2: Evaluation of the statistical models in terms of ELPD. First column shows the absolute ELPD (higher ELPD indicates a better model fit). The second columns shows an estimate of the effective number of parameters. The third column displays the absolute difference in ELPD with respect to the best model.

	-Book			+Book		
Known	-95%	κ	+95%	-95%	κ	+95%
Soft-Cosine						
False	0.66	0.76	0.84	0.22	0.72	0.97
True	0.66	0.74	0.82	0.29	0.73	0.97
Smith-Waterman						
False	0.45	0.58	0.29	0.08	0.54	0.93
True	0.52	0.62	0.71	0.16	0.62	0.95

Table 3: Median, lower and upper 95% quantiles for posterior agreement scores obtained with the full model (m.mlBK), while keeping similarity at the zero-centered mean value. (-/+ Book refers to whether variation stemming from the source book is taken into account or not.)

effects using a statistical model comparison approach based on the expected log pointwise predictive density (ELPD) as measure. This quantity provides an estimate of the predictive accuracy of a model on out-of-sample datasets. These estimates can be efficiently obtained—i.e. without having to refit the model on the different splits—using an approximatation to leave-one-out (LOO).[9]

We consider a total of 5 models of increasing complexity, and seek to establish the relevance of the information taken into account by the different models through model comparison.[10] Specifically, m is a baseline model that has a single intercept and adds neither predictors nor grouping factors. The second model—m.M—adds the underlying retrieval method as binary predictor. The third model—m.MB—adds varying intercepts corresponding to the biblical source book of the candidate reference. The fourth model—m.kMB—includes an additional binary predictor for the "familiarity" with the Bernardine passage. Finally, model m.klMB adds a continuous predictor accounting for lexical overlap.

Table 2 shows the results of the model comparison. As we can see the full model m.klMB can be identified as the model with superior predictive performance. We take this as a justification for the inclusion of all considered predictors and base any further inference on this model.

[9]In particular, we use the Pareto-smoothed Importance Sampling (PSIS-LOO) method—see (Vehtari et al., 2017) for a description of the method and (Vehtari et al., 2018) for an implementation in the **R** programming language.

[10]Details about the model fitting process as well as the software used for inference are shown in Appendix A.

3.2 Effects of Contextual Factors

We now inspect the effects of the different contextual factors on the output inter-annotator agreement index. Table 3 shows the resulting inter-annotator agreement scores by a number of contextual factors. As we can see, the average agreement is fairly high across conditions ranging from 0.54 to an eventual 0.76. In order to gain a better picture of the underlying phenomena, we first zoom in on the effect of the retrieval method.

Effects of the retrieval method Figure 2 shows the posterior distributions obtained for the κ scores, computed using Equation 1. The plot on the left-hand side of Figure 2 shows the resulting scores obtained for references to an "average" biblical book. These estimates, thus, ignore the variability arising from the fact that references to particular books may result in more or less inter-annotator agreement. The plot on the right-hand, however, includes this variability through marginalization. Technically, the marginalization procedure is accomplished by sampling $\nu_{..q}$ from the inferred multi-variate normal distribution from which the random intercepts are modeled to arise—see Equation 5. For each MCMC draw of parameters, we add the sampled $\nu_{..q}$ value, before computing the output softmax. For the case of books, this marginalization results in a posterior that corresponds to the agreement that we could expect for a reference to any (possibly unobserved) given book.

As we can see, the agreement is decisively higher for candidates suggested by the Soft-Cosine retrieval algorithm. However,

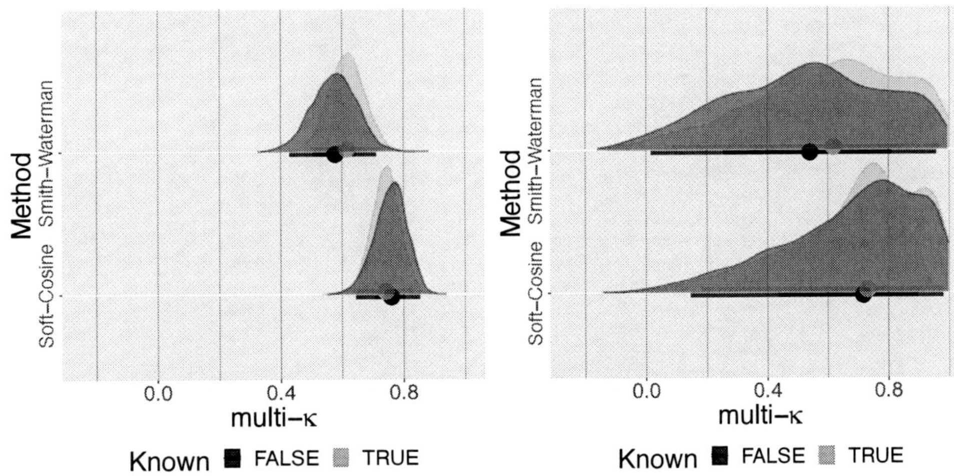

Figure 2: Posterior multi-κ scores inferred from the full model (m.m1BK), displayed according to retrieval method, on the y-axis, and whether the candidate borrowing passage is known to contain a reference to a different biblical verse, on the x-axis. Word overlap is kept to the zero-centered mean value. Left plots and right plots differ on whether the variation coming from the books is excluded or not. The mean estimate is shown by a point with a 0.89 probability interval (shown by the surrounding horizontal bar).

when the variability stemming from books is taken into account through marginalization, we obtain very wide posterior distributions, as shown by the right plot. This is a strong indication of the importance of the target reference book for annotator behavior and supplements the evidence from the ELPD comparisons in Section 3.1, where including book-level varying intercepts resulted in a large ELPD increase of 342.29 points—model m.MB vs. model m.M—, corresponding to a 58.92% ELPD increase with respect to the total increase between worst and best models—i.e. model m vs model m.k1MB.

Effects of lexical overlap Figure 3 shows the effect of lexical overlap on agreement under different combinations of underlying retrieval method and familiarity of the target passage, using counter-factual plots. These plots visualize the statistical dependency relying on the posterior predictions for the entire range of the lexical overlap variable—i.e. including values for which no observation is attested in the original dataset (McElreath, 2018). The plots on the left hand-side do not take into account variability arising from the source book, while those in the right hand-side do. As we can see, the effect of overlap on agreement is primarily decreasing and, at least for unknown passages, monotonic—i.e. an increase in overlap is associated with a decrease in agreement. Judging by the small credible intervals, this seems to suggest that annotators find it easy to agree on candidates with very low overlap—probably because the match can be discarded. At average and above-average overlap values the effect of overlap is neutralized and, in the case of target passages with known reference, the effect is even inverted—i.e. starting at an above-average overlap value agreement increases with an increase in overlap.

Similarly to the other considered predictors—i.e. the effect of underlying retrieval method—we find that the shape and magnitude of the effect overlap on agreement is much more uncertain when the biblical source book is taken into account.

3.3 Post-experimental Report

In order to gain insight on the sources of disagreement, we extracted a set of document pairs in which one of the annotators systematically disagreed with the other two, and asked her to elucidate the reasons for the disagreement. The annotator in charge of the discussion was the one with the highest level of familiarity with Bernard, based on self-report capacity and experience. Four illustrative examples along explanations are shown in Appendix B.

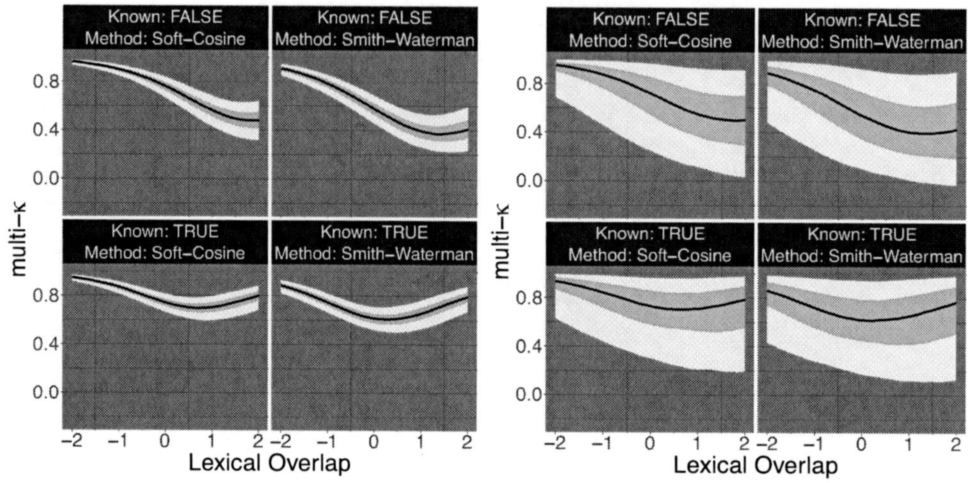

Figure 3: Posterior multi-κ scores over lexical overlap. Note that the lexical overlap scale is centered such that a unit on the x-axis indicates a standard deviation away from the zero-mean. Left plot and right plot differ respectively on whether the variation coming from the books is excluded (left) or not (right). Black lines indicate median κ scores with credible intervals at 0.5 and 0.89 probabilities shown in shaded grey areas.

Segmentation Related Problems The first issue relates to ambiguity problems arising from the approach employed in order to segment Bernard's sermons into documents. Bernard's Sermons were segmented using a sliding window of 20 words with an overlap of 10 words. This strategy resulted in a number of difficult cases in which the annotators have to decide subjectively whether to validate a candidate pair in the presence of fuzzy segmentation. For example, eventually segmentation left crucial words out of the target document, which lead to an artificial increase in the pool of candidate verses that can be interpreted as source. These problems have a significant incidence on the annotator disagreements and generate a lack of consistency, even by the same annotator.

Knowledge of the Bible When dealing with biblical texts, it is important to take intra-biblical intertextuality into account, a known phenomenon that consists in internal borrowing within the Bible. As an example, verses from the Old Testament are frequently referenced in the New Testament, and the so-called synoptical Gospels are known to contain parallel accounts of the same events. As a result, disagreements can appear when annotators diverge with respect to which of the parallel variants they consider to be the actual source of the biblical reference.

Knowledge of Bernard Finally, annotators must combine their knowledge of the Bible with other abilities regarding the borrowing author. In the case of the current case study, dedicated scholarship can show authors to hold a general preference towards specific biblical passages. For example, a biblical passage has a higher probability of being quoted by an author if he uses it in daily prayers. Moreover, an author of exegetical commentaries of a biblical book may quote this book more often than others. Depending on the level of familiarity with the author's preferences, annotators choices will be in disagreement.

4 Conclusion & Future Work

Our study has shown how to apply Bayesian statistical methods to the computation of inter-annotator agreement indices. On the basis of a multi-level model, we were able to isolate the influence of co-variates on agreement and show how the inter-annotator agreement scores vary depending on the value of the independent variables.

While the overall average inter-annotator agreement reached is fairly high, the amount of uncertainty arising from the source book resulted in very wide posterior distributions which drastically nuance the reported coefficients.

Our approach fits random intercepts in order to capture individual annotator behaviour and should, therefore, scale reasonably well to higher number of annotators. However, the multinomial approach presented in the current research requires fitting a number of linear models that is quadratic on the number of labels, and, thus, more complex tasks may become unfeasible to model in the same manner. Future work should address this shortcoming. Moreover, our approach is limited to annotation tasks defined in terms of categorical outcomes, and, thus, ordinal or continuous outcomes would require further research in order to be accommodated.

As the post-experimental report highlighted, some of the experimental design choices introduced artificial hurdles to agreement, and future research should take this into account in order to produce a more robust experimental settings.

Finally, while our study constitutes one of the first dedicated to the problem of inter-annotator agreement in intertextual studies, the specific experimental setting and design should be complemented in the future by other case studies in order to offer a more general picture of the matter.

References

Ron Artstein. 2017. Inter-annotator agreement. In *Handbook of linguistic annotation*, pages 297–313. Springer.

Ron Artstein and Massimo Poesio. 2007. Inter-Coder Agreement for Computational Linguistics. This reference corresponds to an extended version of the survey article appearing in the Computational Linguistics journal under the same name.

Ron Artstein and Massimo Poesio. 2008. Inter-Coder Agreement for Computational Linguistics. *Computational Linguistics*, 34(4):555–596.

Daniel Bär, Torsten Zesch, and Iryna Gurevych. 2012. Text reuse detection using a composition of text similarity measures. In *24th International Conference on Computational Linguistics - Proceedings of COLING 2012: Technical Papers*.

Alessio Benavoli, Giorgio Corani, Janez Dem˘sar, and Marco Zaffalon. 2017. Time for a Change: A Tutorial for Comparing Multiple Classifiers Through Bayesian Analysis. *The Journal of Machine Learning Research*, page 36.

E. M. Bennett, R. Alpert, and A. C. Goldstein. 1954. Communications Through Limited Response Questioning. *Public Opinion Quarterly*, 18(3):303.

Harold Bloom. 1973. *The Anxiety of Influence: A Theory of Poetry*. Oxford University Press.

Paul Christian Bürkner. 2018. Advanced Bayesian multilevel modeling with the R package brms. *R Journal*.

Paul Clough and Mark Stevenson. 2011. Developing a corpus of plagiarised short answers. *Language Resources and Evaluation*, 45(1):5–24.

Jacob Cohen. 1960. A Coefficient of Agreement for Nominal Scales. *Educational and Psychological Measurement*, 20(1):37–46.

Gregory Crane. 1996. Building a digital library: The Perseus Project as a case study in the humanities. In *Proceedings of the First ACM International Conference on Digital Libraries*, pages 3–10.

Joseph L. Fleiss. 1971. Measuring nominal scale agreement among many raters. *Psychological Bulletin*, 76(5):378–382.

Andrew Gelman and Jennifer Hill. 2006. *Data Analysis Using Regression and Multilevel/Hierarchical Models*. Cambridge University Press, Cambridge.

Regula Hohl Trillini. 2018. *Casual Shakespeare : Three Centuries of Verbal Echoes*. Routledge.

Ross Ihaka and Robert Gentleman. 1996. R: A Language for Data Analysis and Graphics. *Journal of Computational and Graphical Statistics*, 5(3):299–314.

Stefan Jänicke, Thomas Efer, Marco Büchler, and Gerik Scheuermann. 2015. Designing Close and Distant Reading Visualizations for Text Re-use. In *Computer Vision, Imaging and Computer Graphics - Theory and Applications*, Communications in Computer and Information Science, pages 153–171, Cham. Springer International Publishing.

Jeremy Koster and Richard McElreath. 2017. Multinomial analysis of behavior: statistical methods. *Behavioral Ecology and Sociobiology*, 71(9):138.

Enrique Manjavacas. 2021. *Computational approaches to intertextuality. from retrieval engines to statistical analysis : thesis*. Proefschriften UA-LW : letterkunde: 2021: 2.

Enrique Manjavacas, Ákos Kádár, and Mike Kestemont. 2019a. Improving Lemmatization of Non-Standard Languages with Joint Learning. In *Proceedings of the 2019 Conference of the North American Chapter of the Association for Computational Linguistics: Human Language Technologies, Volume 1 (Long and Short Papers)*, pages 1493–1503, Minneapolis, Minnesota. Association for Computational Linguistics.

Enrique Manjavacas, Brian Long, and Mike Kestemont. 2019b. On the Feasibility of Automated Detection of Allusive Text Reuse. In *Proceedings of the 3rd Joint {SIGHUM} Workshop on Computational Linguistics for Cultural Heritage, Social Sciences, Humanities and Literature*, pages 104–114, Minneapolis, USA. Association for Computational Linguistics.

Richard McElreath. 2018. *Statistical Rethinking*. Chapman and Hall/CRC.

Laurence Mellerin. 2013. Methodological issues in biblindex, an online index of biblical quotations in early christian literature. In Laurence Mellerin, Markus Vinzent, and Hugh Houghton, editors, *Biblical Quotations in Patristic Texts (Papers Presented at the Sixteenth International Conference on Patristic Studies Held in Oxford 2011)*, volume 2 of *Studia Patristica*, pages 11–32. Peeters.

Laurence Mellerin. 2014. New ways of searching with biblindex, the online index of biblical quotations in early christian literature. In Claire Clivaz, Gregory Andrew, and Hamidovic David, editors, *Digital Humanities in Biblical, Early Jewish and Early Christian Studies*, volume 2 of *Digital Humanities in Biblical, Early Jewish and Early Christian Studies*, pages 175–192. Brill.

William A. Scott. 1955. Reliability of Content Analysis: The Case of Nominal Scale Coding. *Public Opinion Quarterly*, 19(3):321.

Grigori Sidorov, Alexander Gelbukh, Helena Gómez-Adorno, and David Pinto. 2014. Soft similarity and soft cosine measure: Similarity of features in vector space model. *Computación y Sistemas*, 18(3):491–504.

T.F. Smith and M.S. Waterman. 1981. Identification of common molecular subsequences. *Journal of Molecular Biology*, 147(1):195–197.

Aki Vehtari, Jonah Gabry, Yuling Yao, and Andrew Gelman. 2018. loo: Efficient leave-one-out cross-validation and waic for bayesian models. *R package version*, 2(0):1003.

Aki Vehtari, Andrew Gelman, and Jonah Gabry. 2017. Practical Bayesian model evaluation using leave-one-out cross-validation and WAIC. *Statistics and Computing*, 27(5):1413–1432.

Tariq Yousef and Stefan Janicke. 2021. A Survey of Text Alignment Visualization. *IEEE Transactions on Visualization and Computer Graphics*, 27(2):1149–1159.

A Model Fitting

In the present study, we deploy Bayesian linear models as implemented by the `brms` library (Bürkner, 2018), an **R** (3.6.3) package (Ihaka and Gentleman, 1996) providing a user-friendly interface to `Rstan`, which utilizes a powerful Hamiltonian Monte Carlo sampler. In order to ensure the validity of the resulting posterior distributions, we make sure that the following diagnostics check: first, effective sample sizes are large enough; secondly, the samples are homogeneous across chains (i.e. $\hat{R}$ values should be close to 1), and, finally, divergent transitions are kept to a minimum. This was accomplished using 4 chains for 2000 iterations with the first 1000 used as warmup iterations. Some models required fine-tuning the "adapt delta" and the "maximum tree depth" parameters.

Moreover, we choose weakly informative priors to avoid exploring highly unlikely regions of the parameter space.

B Post-experimental Report Examples

Table 4 shows a number of candidate pairs that illustrate common sources of disagreement. The subset consists of instances retrieved with the `Smith-Waterman` algorithm and has, thus, a slight bias towards literal quotations.

The first instance in Table 4 corresponds to an example of a segmentation problem. The words "quia mirabilia facit" have been left out by the applied segmentation. Without these words, two annotators were inclined to accept *Psalms, 95:1*, a verse with which the overlap is high. The dissident annotator, however, rejected it under the assumption that the fitting reference was instead *Psalms, 97:1*, for which the missing words provide stronger evidence. As we can see, these segmentation-related issues already point towards a second difficulty, which consists in the biblical knowledge required for the interpretation of these intertextual references.

The second example in Table 4 refers to a general idea that first appears in *Genesis, 2:24*, which is the unity of man and woman becoming one flesh through marriage. Two annotators, however, validated the suggested reference to *Mark, 10:8*, even though in the typical Bernardine style, the reference is most likely to allude to the original passage, rather than a direct quote to the Gospel. This example already suggests a further source of disagreement, which corresponds to the familiarity with the referential practices of the borrowing author.

In the third example in Table 4, Bernard's chunk lies in a context at the end of a paragraph in which the main points of a previous argumentation are being summarized. In that argumentation, *Mark, 12:30* has been referenced explicitely and in the current location it is being referred to implicetely. *Luke, 10:27*, however, is a more closely related match in terms of lexical overlap, which may lead annotators with more superficial knowledge of Bernard's oeuvre to select it.

In the last example in Table 4, Bernard refers to

a passage that appears both in a Psalm and in the Letter to the Hebrews, in which the Psalm is, in turn, referenced. An expert annotator of Bernard can identify that the introduction formula contains a decisive clue: Bernard puts these words in the Father's mouth adressing to Son ("Pater ad Filium"). Moreover, in the context surrounding this passage, Psalms are being repeatedly referenced, as evidenced by the usage of the word "psalmist" (not shown in the example).

Bernardian Chunk	Proposed Verse	Alternative Verse
vestra, et in exitu vestro de lacu miseriae et de luto faecis, **cantastis et ipsi Domino canticum novum** *quia mirabilia facit* *S. 1, 9 (SC 414, p. 72)*	quando domus aedificabatur post captivitatem canticum huic David **cantate Domino canticum novum** cantate Domino omnis terra *Psalms, 95:1*	psalmus David **cantate Domino canticum novum quoniam mirabilia fecit** salvavit sibi dextera eius et brachium sanctum eius *Psalms, 97:1*
carnale matrimonium constituit **duos in carne una**, cur non magis spiritualis copula duos coniunget in uno spiritu? Denique *S. 8, 9 (SC 414, p. 192)*	et erunt **duo in carne una** itaque iam non sunt duo sed una caro *Mark, 10:8*	quam ob rem relinquet homo patrem suum et matrem et adherebit uxori suae et erunt **duo in carne una** *Genesis, 2:24*
blanditiis, seduci fallaciis, nec iniuriis frangi, **toto corde, tota anima, tota virtute diligere** est. *S. 20, 5 (SC 431, p. 136)*	ille respondens dixit diliges Dominum Deum tuum ex **toto corde tuo et ex tota anima** tua et ex omnibus viribus tuis et ex omni mente tua et proximum tuum sicut te ipsum *Luke, 10:27*	et diliges Dominum Deum tuum ex **toto corde** tuo et ex **tota anima** tua et ex tota mente tua et ex **tota virtute** tua hoc est primum mandatum *Mark, 12:30*
cognoscentur. Hinc rursus Pater ad Filium: **Sede**, inquit, **a dextris meis, donec ponam inimicos tuos** ***scabellum pedum tuorum*** *S. 6, 5 (SC 414, p. 144)*	ad quem autem angelorum dixit aliquando **sede a dextris meis quoadusque ponam inimicos tuos scabillum pedum tuorum** *Hebrews, 1:13*	david canticum dixit Dominus Domino meo **sede a dextris meis donec ponam inimicos tuos scabillum pedum tuorum** *Psalms, 109:1*

Table 4: Examples from the dataset, showcasing different types of agreement problems. The first one highlights **segmentation** issues, and the second one and the last two relate respectively to *diverging degrees of familiarity* with the **Bible** and **Bernard**. The Bernardine chunk on the left is accompanied by the retrieved candidate in the center and a better verse proposed by the annotator during the post-experimental report in the right. Words in bold correspond to lexical overlap with the biblical references, while words in italics indicate a relevant fragment left out by the applied segmentation. Biblical references contain hyper-links re-directing to the BiblIndex online version that includes English translations.

The Multilingual Corpus of Survey Questionnaires Query Interface

Danielly Sorato
Universitat Pompeu Fabra
Barcelona, Spain
danielly.sorato@upf.edu

Diana Zavala-Rojas
European Social Survey ERIC
Universitat Pompeu Fabra
Barcelona, Spain
diana.zavala@upf.edu

Abstract

The dawn of the digital age led to increasing demands for digital research resources, which shall be quickly processed and handled by computers. Due to the amount of data created by this digitization process, the design of tools that enable the analysis and management of data and metadata has become a relevant topic. In this context, the Multilingual Corpus of Survey Questionnaires (MCSQ) contributes to the creation and distribution of data for the Social Sciences and Humanities (SSH) following FAIR (Findable, Accessible, Interoperable and Reusable) principles, and provides functionalities for end-users that are not acquainted with programming through an easy-to-use interface. By simply applying the desired filters in the graphic interface, users can build linguistic resources for the survey research and translation areas, such as translation memories, thus facilitating data access and usage.

1 Introduction

In the last decade, research in the Social Sciences and Humanities (SSH) field has consolidated a paradigmatic transformation from theoretically-oriented approaches to data-driven methodologies (Kitchin, 2014; Manovich, 2011). Digitizing SSH data otherwise distributed as non-machine readable formats to convenient electronic ones is a decisive and necessary step in the SSH research life-cycle (Gómez et al., 2016). However, the digitization process of artifacts, documentation, and other research objects produces enormous amounts of data, which must be systematically stored and managed. This presents both a necessity and an opportunity to design and implement tools to manage and use such data in a FAIR (Findable, Accessible, Interoperable, and Reusable) way, allowing not only the preservation of SSH data but facilitating scientifically sound and transparent research processes.

Focusing on strengthening this paradigmatic transformation in the SSH field, the Multilingual Corpus of Survey Questionnaires (MCSQ) provides easy access to textual survey data in a machine-readable format and related services streamlined to the needs of the SSH community. In this context, we present the MCSQ interface: a tool that offers easy-to-use functionalities for end-users unacquainted with programming or data manipulation libraries. Other than common search functionalities offered by off-the-shelf corpus management tools such as IMS Open Corpus Workbench (Evert and Hardie, 2011) and Sketch Engine (Kilgarriff et al., 2014), the MCSQ interface provides features that are convenient for translators and survey practitioners, such as allowing users to build their own translation memories and facilitating the retrieval and comparison of multilingual data.

This paper is organized as follows. In Section 2, we briefly describe the MCSQ, and discuss how it follows the FAIR principles. Subsequently, in Section 3, we describe the interface infrastructure and its functionalities. Finally, in Section 4, we present our conclusions and future work.

2 The Multilingual Corpus of Survey Questionnaires

The Multilingual Corpus of Survey Questionnaires (MCSQ) is the first publicly available corpus of survey questionnaires. The MCSQ is an open-source and open-access resource that was designed and implemented following the FAIR principles. The current version 3 of the corpus (entitled Rosalind Franklin) contains approximately 4 million tokens and includes 306 distinct questionnaires designed in the source (British) English language and their translations into Catalan, Czech, French, German, Norwegian, Portuguese, Spanish, and Russian, adding to 30 country-language combinations (e.g., French from Switzerland). Questionnaires in the MCSQ comprise more than 40 years of

Proceedings of LaTeCH-CLfL 2021, pages 43–48
Punta Cana, Dominican Republic (Online), November 11, 2021.

survey research from large-scale comparative survey projects that provide cross-national and cross-cultural data to the SSH, namely, the European Social Survey (ESS), the European Values Study (EVS), the Survey of Health Ageing and Retirement in Europe (SHARE), and the WageIndicator Survey (WIS).

Within a questionnaire, a *survey item* (Saris and Gallhofer, 2014) is a unit for data collection. It includes the question, the response options, and other textual elements presented to the participants in the study. The questionnaires in the MCSQ were designed for in-person interviews. Except in the case of the WIS, the translation process was implemented according to the TRAPD (Translation, Review, Adjudication, Pretesting and, Documentation) method (Harkness et al., 2003), a team approach for the translation of survey questionnaires.

In the TRAPD method, two translators ('*T*' in the TRAPD acronym) should produce independent translations into the respective target language. Optionally, they could split a source questionnaire and work independently on one of its parts. In a team meeting with the translators, a reviewer ('*R*') assesses the two translations, and an adjudicator '*A*' takes the final decisions on the different translation options. Teams can opt for one of the translation options or create a new one by combining the strengths of each translation. The translated questionnaire is pretested before fieldwork ('*P*'), and the whole process is documented ('*D*'). Ideally, the team is composed of survey experts and language experts (e.g. professional translators) capable of assessing not only translatability aspects, but also necessary adaptations for the culture where it will be administered and to achieve the measurement objectives.

Questionnaires included in the MCSQ were obtained from the survey projects' archives in distinct formats such as spreadsheets, Extensible Markup Language (XML), and Portable Document Format (PDF) files. The PDF files had to undergo an additional step of conversion to plain texts before going through the preprocessing pipeline. Then, the texts were extracted from the input files and preprocessed, sentence aligned with respect to the English source and annotated with Part-of-speech (POS) and Named Entity Recognition (NER) tags.

During the preprocessing steps, in addition to text cleaning and normalization, we attributed metadata to the text segments to identify and navigate among the items in the MCSQ:

- The study or survey project, among ESS, EVS, SHARE or WIS;
- The round or wave, that is, a sequential number survey projects use to identify the edition of the study;
- The year in which the survey data and questionnaire were published;
- Language and country of the questionnaire. As the survey questionnaires texts are country-localized, this attribute helps to account for the language varieties included in the corpus;
- The name of each survey item, referred to as item name in the corpus;
- The item type, which indicates the role each sentence has in the questionnaire, among introduction, instruction (both for the participants and for the interviewers), request (or question) and response (or answer) (Saris and Gallhofer, 2014)
- The survey item ID, which is a combination of the study (S), round (R), year (Y), language (L), and country (C), with the following digits $SSS\_RRR\_YYYY\_LLL\_CC\_i$[1], where i is a sequential number that uniquely identifies and indicates the text segment order.

To align the survey items, we developed our own sentence alignment algorithm, which leverages metadata available in MCSQ to minimize the search space for candidates of a given alignment. Namely we use the module, item name, and item type metadata to this end. Additionally, we take into account the sentence length and information from domain specific bilingual dictionaries built with *Word2Word*(Choe et al., 2020) as alignment heuristics.

For the POS tagging task, we used *Flair* (Akbik et al., 2019) pre-trained models for the Czech, English, German, French, Norwegian, and Spanish languages, whereas for Catalan, Portuguese and Russian languages we trained our own models, also using the *Flair* framework. The Named Entity Recognition (NER) annotation was executed using pre-trained models from different sources. Namely,

[1]Language codes follow the ISO 639-2/B standard (three-digit standard) and country codes follow the ISO 3166 Alpha-2 standard (two digits).

Flair for English, German, French, and Spanish, *SpaCy*(Honnibal et al., 2020) for Catalan, Norwegian and Portuguese, and *Slavic BERT* (Arkhipov et al., 2019) for Czech and Russian. Due to the domain specificity and nature of the texts, some of the models (e.g., Catalan) performed worse than others, especially in instruction segments.

We developed the MCSQ aiming to be as FAIR (Findable, Accessible, Interoperable, and Reusable) as possible. To be *Findable*, we attributed the rich metadata described above. The code and data used to compile the corpus are publicly available and it has attached a persistent identifier [2]. Furthermore, the MCSQ will be submitted for permanent preservation to a CLARIN ERIC[3] repository in 2021, where the data will receive a persistent identifier.

In order to be *Accessible*, we made the MCSQ data available in open format (CSV with tab separators) and safeguarded accessibly, i.e. through user registration, via the interface hereby described[4] .

The *Interoperability* aspect of the MCSQ is a work in progress. Currently, our metadata is a simplified subset of the DDI codebook[5], adapted for CSV files instead of XML ones, and including linguistic metadata such as part-of-speech tags. We use the Universal POS tags[6] for part-of-speech metadata tags. Furthermore, the data model that describes and structures the MCSQ metadata will be submitted to FAIRsharing[7].

To ensure *re-usability* aspects, we are currently acquiring a license for the MCSQ that will allow users to remix, adapt, and build upon the work done in MCSQ. Moreover, we upload publicly available documentation and materials about the corpus with persistent identifiers[8][9][10] in the Zenodo repository[11].

Making data FAIR is a process. Although we consider that findability, accessibility, and reusability facets are well underway, interoperability is yet a work in progress and needs enhancement, such as producing mappings of the MCSQ metadata to the DDI standard.

[2]`doi.org/10.5281/zenodo.5153300`

[3]`https://www.clarin.eu/`

[4]Permanent preservation in a CLARIN repository aims at improving accessibility as well

[5]`https://ddialliance.org/Specification/DDI-Codebook/`

[6]`https://universaldependencies.org/u/pos/`

[7]`https://fairsharing.org`

[8]`doi.org/10.5281/zenodo.4785196`

[9]`doi.org/10.5281/zenodo.4555099`

[10]`doi.org/10.5281/zenodo.4696181`

[11]`https://zenodo.org/`

3 The interface of the Multilingual Corpus of Survey Questionnaires

Aiming at combining searches in the MCSQ contents and functionalities that facilitate the usage of the MCSQ data for end-users, we developed the MCSQ interface[12]. To have complete control over the technology stack and freedom to include innovative functionalities, instead of using off-the-shelf corpus management tools, we developed our infrastructure from scratch. Users must register to access all functionalities in the interface[13]. The corpus and all its metadata are available for visualization and download through the interface.

3.1 Infrastructure

The MCSQ is hosted in a virtual machine provided by Universitat Pompeu Fabra, which runs a Debian Linux Operating System. The data is stored in an Entity-Relationship (ER) database, implemented in PostgreSQL[14]. The user interface of the MCSQ is a Flask application[15], that runs on top of the ER database. We use the SQLalchemy library (Bayer, 2012) to facilitate the manipulation of data and SQL objects in a high-level programming language. The interface is currently in the Alpha stage since new functionalities are still being added as we receive users' feedback. Nonetheless, it is fully functional.

3.2 Functionalities

In order to define which functionalities should be implemented, we consulted with corpus linguists, survey practitioners, translators with experience in questionnaire translation, and computational linguists. Our objective was to develop functionalities that would allow for data usage in real research contexts, such as questionnaire design, multilingual resources for domain-specific machine translation, translation verification, among others. The functionalities of the MCSQ interface can be divided into three main blocks, which are presented in the following subsections.

[12]`http://easy.mcsq.upf.edu`

[13]The MCSQ interface is European Union GDPR compliant (General Data Protection Regulation), registration requires an email used exclusively for managing access to the MCSQ. Users about the purpose of the processing and the data controller. They can request to delete their account at any given time.

[14]`https://www.postgresql.org`

[15]`https://flask.palletsprojects.com`

3.2.1 Linguistic

The linguistic functionalities in the MCSQ interface are those commonly found in other corpus query engines. This block of functionalities consists of (i) word searches; (ii) retrieving and comparing word collocations; (iii) word frequencies and; (iv) POS-tag sequence search. *Word searches* can be conducted both in aligned and non-aligned data, comprising partial[16], single and multiple word search. By applying the metadata filters, one can search for words or word sequences restricting results by item type (e.g., introductions, response options), language variation, year, study, etc.

The *word collocation* functions allow searching for bigram or trigram collocations of a word, ranked by raw frequency. It is possible to compare the collocations of two words, being that the words can be selected from any sub-portion of the corpus. The interface allows users to retrieve and compare up to 30 collocations. The *word frequencies* can be computed for single or multiple words. Word frequency results can be filtered by item type, language variation, year, and study. Finally, *POS-tag sequence search* is available as well, since the corpus is POS annotated, which can be useful for analyzing syntactic patterns.

The application encapsulates all queries to the database, hiding them completely from the users. Hence, users build their queries by simply selecting the desired filters in the graphic interface, which facilitates the access and use of the data. An example of the aforementioned filters is shown in the search for word usage in the sentence aligned data, in Figure 1. This functionality allows users to search for source andor target words in the aligned sentences of the MCSQ to see how the source segments were translated to the target languages, filter results by metadata, see POS-tagging and NER annotations, and optionally, download the results.

Most of the results, except for the the ones that are exclusively downloadable, are presented as depicted in Figure 2. In addition to the text and POS tag annotation, which is shown when the display annotation option is selected, the survey item IDs of the segments are also exhibited. The IDs simplify the identification of the texts by providing immediate reference to the study, edition and year of publication of every segment. In the case of functionalities that calculate statistics or information about the texts, such as frequencies and collocations, the results are shown in a table similar to the one depicted in Figure 3. The aforementioned functionalities allow researchers to analyze linguistic aspects of the questionnaires, for instance, to investigate linguistic patterns, or assess translation equivalence.

3.2.2 Data resources

The *data resource* functionalities allow for the selection of any given subset of the corpus data to visualize and/or download fully customized datasets, which is useful for expanding the analysis of the data, or use the texts as input to design new questionnaires. Mainly, data resources are downloaded as CSV files with tab separators, with the exception of downloadable files to build a translation memory. We specifically chose the CSV format because it is easy to use across different domains of research, other file formats such as XML require knowledge about parsing to be used. In the case of customized translation memories, a TMX file is built in the back-end and outputted for the user. Translators can customize their translation memories and upload them into a CAT tool. It is possible to create subsets of the data to build a translation memory by filtering the corpus according to (i) the language; (ii) the language variation (language/country); (iii) the study and; (iv) the year.

3.2.3 Comparison

This feature allows comparing questionnaires in multiple languages, without filters, by item type, or by word. Features to compare texts are useful for survey practitioners and questionnaire designers who can examine entire questionnaires in multiple languages, without having to search for and compare various files separately.

4 Conclusion

The MCSQ is a valuable contribution to open-source, open-access, and high-quality SSH data that follows FAIR principles, whilst its interface provides useful functionalities for researchers across different disciplines, such as linguists, survey practitioners, computational linguists, and translators. Aside from traditional corpus search functionalities, we developed features to support end-users that are not acquainted with programming, thus facilitating the accessibility of the data and related resources to all audiences. Through this work, we hope to stimulate the creation of FAIR

[16]A partial word search for the word "run" would retrieve "runs", "running", etc, for instance

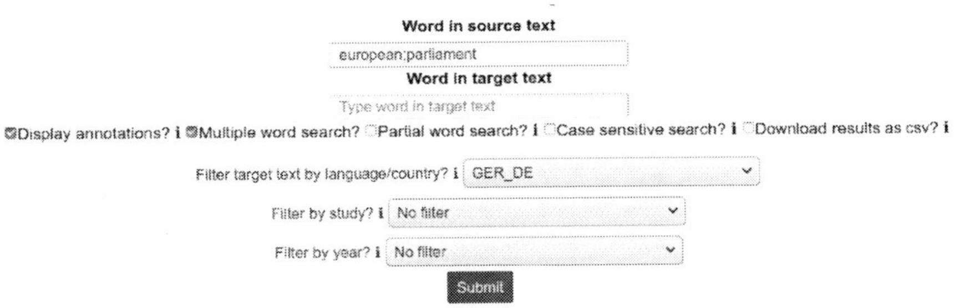

Figure 1: Searching for translations of the words "European Parliament" in German from Germany MCSQ alignments.

source_survey_itemid	target_survey_itemid	Source Text	Target Text	POS Tagged Source Text	POS Tagged Target Text	NER Tagged Source Text	NER Tagged Target Text
ESS_R01_2002_ENG_SOURCE_198	ESS_R01_2002_GER_DE_181	... the European Parliament?	...dem Europäischen Parlament?	... <PUNCT> the <DET> European <PROPN> Parliament <PROPN> ? <PUNCT>	... <PUNCT> dem <DET> Europäischen <PROPN> Parlament <PROPN> ? <PUNCT>	... the European <B-ORG> Parliament <E-ORG> ?	... dem Europäischen <B-ORG> Parlament <E-ORG> ?
ESS_R08_2016_ENG_SOURCE_118	ESS_R08_2016_GER_DE_107	... the European Parliament?	...dem Europäischen Parlament?	... <PUNCT> the <DET> European <PROPN> Parliament <PROPN> ? <PUNCT>	... <PUNCT> dem <DET> Europäischen <PROPN> Parlament <PROPN> ? <PUNCT>	... the European <B-ORG> Parliament <E-ORG> ?	... dem Europäischen <B-ORG> Parlament <E-ORG> ?

Figure 2: Sample of results for the search in Figure 1. Response segments in the source language appear next to their German alignments. It is possible to examine the study, round, year, and language variation of the segments by examining the *source_survey_itemid* and *target_survey_itemid* columns.

word 1 (first word)	word 2 (first word)	word 3 (first word)	word 1 (second word)	word 2 (second word)	word 3 (second word)
examiner	la	carte	use	this	card
veuillez	examiner	la	using	this	card
de	cette	carte	please	use	this
sur	cette	carte	on	this	card
utiliser	cette	carte	please	look	at
l'aide	de	cette	this	card	please
veuillez	utiliser	cette	look	at	card
dans	quelle	mesure	please	tell	me
cette	carte	pour	card	please	tell
à	l'aide	de	which	of	the

Figure 3: Comparing trigram collocations for the words "card" in the English source and "carte" in French from France sub portions of the MCSQ.

and user-friendly infrastructures for secondary research.

As future work, we aim to explore the following three aspects: i) the possibility of allowing users to add new data to the corpus through the interface; ii) functionalities for the construction of domain-specific bilingual dictionaries and, iii) the comparison of similar questions across rounds and studies. Additionally, we aim at producing hands-on tutorials with a comprehensive overview of the interface functionalities and guidance on how to use them.

Acknowledgements

The MCSQ is part of the SSHOC project, an EU Horizon 2020 Research and Innovation Programme (2014-2020) under Grant Agreement No. 823782. It was developed as part of the European Social Survey ERIC work in the SSHOC, and it had the support of the European Values Survey team.

References

Alan Akbik, Tanja Bergmann, Duncan Blythe, Kashif Rasul, Stefan Schweter, and Roland Vollgraf. 2019. Flair: An easy-to-use framework for state-of-the-art nlp. In *NAACL 2019, 2019 Annual Conference of the North American Chapter of the Association for Computational Linguistics (Demonstrations)*, pages 54–59.

Mikhail Arkhipov, Maria Trofimova, Yuri Kuratov, and Alexey Sorokin. 2019. Tuning multilingual transformers for language-specific named entity recognition. In *Proceedings of the 7th Workshop on Balto-Slavic Natural Language Processing*, pages 89–93,

Florence, Italy. Association for Computational Linguistics.

Michael Bayer. 2012. Sqlalchemy. In Amy Brown and Greg Wilson, editors, *The Architecture of Open Source Applications Volume II: Structure, Scale, and a Few More Fearless Hacks*. aosabook.org.

Yo Joong Choe, Kyubyong Park, and Dongwoo Kim. 2020. word2word: A collection of bilingual lexicons for 3,564 language pairs. In *Proceedings of the 12th International Conference on Language Resources and Evaluation (LREC 2020)*.

Stefan Evert and Andrew Hardie. 2011. Twenty-first century corpus workbench: Updating a query architecture for the new millennium.

Nancy-Diana Gómez, Eva Méndez, and Tony Hernández-Pérez. 2016. Social sciences and humanities research data and metadata: A perspective from thematic data repositories. *El profesional de la información*, 25(4):545–555.

Janet A Harkness, Fons JR van de Vijver, Peter Ph Mohler, and John Wiley. 2003. *Cross-cultural survey methods*, volume 325. Wiley-Interscience Hoboken, NJ.

Matthew Honnibal, Ines Montani, Sofie Van Landeghem, and Adriane Boyd. 2020. spaCy: Industrial-strength Natural Language Processing in Python.

Adam Kilgarriff, Vít Baisa, Jan Bušta, Miloš Jakubíček, Vojtěch Kovář, Jan Michelfeit, Pavel Rychlý, and Vít Suchomel. 2014. The sketch engine: ten years on. *Lexicography*, pages 7–36.

Rob Kitchin. 2014. Big data, new epistemologies and paradigm shifts. *Big data & society*, 1(1):2053951714528481.

Lev Manovich. 2011. Trending: The promises and the challenges of big social data. *Debates in the digital humanities*, 2(1):460–475.

Willem E Saris and Irmtraud N Gallhofer. 2014. *Design, evaluation, and analysis of questionnaires for survey research*. John Wiley & Sons.

The FairyNet Corpus - Character Networks for German Fairy Tales

David Schmidt, Albin Zehe, Janne Lorenzen, Lisa Sergel, Sebastian Düker, Markus Krug, Frank Puppe
Universität Würzburg, Germany
firstname.lastname@informatik.uni-wuerzburg.de

Abstract

This paper presents a data set of German fairy tales, manually annotated with character networks which were obtained with high interrater agreement. The release of this corpus provides an opportunity of training and comparing different algorithms for the extraction of character networks, which so far was barely possible due to heterogeneous interests of previous researchers. We demonstrate the usefulness of our data set by providing baseline experiments for the automatic extraction of character networks, applying a rule-based pipeline as well as a neural approach, and find the neural approach outperforming the rule-approach in most evaluation settings.

1 Introduction

The creation and publication of data sets that can be shared without restrictions is a driving factor in the progress of digital humanities. In this paper we describe a new resource, comprising 40 German fairy tales by the Brothers Grimm. Our corpus contains the annotation of all fictional entities and their references as well as a manually created character network for each of the texts. The main contribution of this work is a publicly available resource[1] that serves the purpose of supporting the creation of automatic algorithms for character network extraction. The paper is structured as follows: First, we give a small overview of the most prominent works that deal with automatic extraction of character networks as well as the very heterogeneous ways the authors evaluate the networks. We then describe the data and its origin, our guidelines and the interrater agreement we achieved on the different layers of annotation in more detail in section 3. In section 4 we present preliminary experiments that can be referred to as baselines in future projects using the corpus, before concluding the paper.

[1]https://gitlab2.informatik.uni-wuerzburg.de/kallimachos/fairynet-latech-clfl

2 Related Work

Since to the best of our knowledge no freely available data set comprising character networks for prose texts that originate a standardized set of guidelines exist, we cover the different approaches that dealt with the automatic extraction of character networks and depict how they went around this issue of a missing data set. For a wide overview of this field we refer to Labatut and Bost (2019). For textual media, the methods to create character networks share many similarities, especially in regard to the lexical preprocessing involved. The similiarities end, when we compare how character networks are evaluated. The field is still very heterogeneous, rendering direct comparisons of different approaches almost infeasible. By publication of this data set we hope to address this point and help to support convergence in terms of character network evaluation.

Most previous work only evaluates their extracted networks by proxies. The system of Park et al. (2013) evaluate by assuming the character and co-occurence frequencies (between characters) are distributed by a power law, which they were able to recover. The work of Dekker et al. (2019) uses modern and classical literature and compare their character networks using Social Network Analysis (SNA), but found that there is no significant difference between these two sets. The work of Coll Ardanuy and Sporleder (2014) extracted networks and subsequently clustered them to examine whether the networks can be used as proxies for unsupervised genre and authorship attribution, but could only slightly exceed their baselines. The work of Elson et al. (2010) can be seen as one of the first papers that dealt with the automatic extraction of character networks. They validated their networks by the verification of different literary theories (e.g. they suspected that the more characters are involved in a story, the less dialogue is con-

Proceedings of LaTeCH-CLfL 2021, pages 49–56
Punta Cana, Dominican Republic (Online), November 11, 2021.

tained). Agarwal et al. (2012) and Jayannavar et al. (2015) extracted interactions between characters using relations of the categories *interact* and *observe* which they learn using a kernel Support Vector Machine. They evaluated their system based on SNA metrics, such as the Node-In-Degree-Centrality or Out-Centrality. The method of Jing et al. (2007) evaluated the networks by measuring the overlap between nodes and edges. Their results suggest that coreference resolution is the limiting factor of their approach, only reaching F1-scores of 0.3. The work of Krug (2020), extracted gold character networks from labeled expert summaries of novels, and compared the gold networks with system networks extracted from the full text novels using ranking metrics.

3 Data and Annotation

The texts that we plan to annotate are the fairy tales of the seventh edition of the *Children's and Household Tales* by the Brothers Grimm for the German language[2]. Currently, we finished annotating 40 fairy tales alongside their character networks. Each fairy tale now consists of two files: The first file is the text (modernized with a tool from Deutsches Textarchiv[3] (Jurish, 2012)) with markup representing the references of the characters (including coreference annotations) and the second file contains a manually annotated character network in the form of a ".xlsx" file (for automatic usability we will release .json as well), containing several layers of annotations, described in the following section.

3.1 Annotation Guidelines

This section describes the guidelines that were used to annotate the different layers of the annotations.

3.1.1 Texts

The characters and coreferences were annotated simply by their heads in a fashion similar to that of DROC (Krug et al., 2018), instead of marking complete noun phrases like in Ontonotes (Weischedel et al., 2011)[4]. On top of the three **syntactic categories** of a mention (name, noun phrase, pronoun), we also attributed each mention with a **semantic category** ("human", "legendary creature", "transcendent creature" and "generic"). The semantic category "human" is attached to all human character references, while the category "legendary creature" is attached to all references of entities which show some inhuman traits (e.g. a speaking animal, a sorcerer, dead people showing unexpected behaviour, giants or dwarves.). A transcendent character is reserved for religious entities that do not actually appear in the story but are referenced in sayings (e.g. "god" or "devil"). The last category is a "generic" reference. It is used for mentions which do not refer to a concrete entity (e.g. "[nobody] could have saved him"). This label overrides potential labels "human" or "legendary creature" if the character is considered to be abstract.

We also annotate **grammatical number** and **biological sex** (i.e., a reference to a girl with the German neuter pronoun "es" (it), as in "das Mädchen" would be marked as a singular female).

3.1.2 Networks

Each character that plays an important role in the plot is deemed relevant enough to be in the final network of the story (linked via their coreference ID into the text file) and is assigned one of the **character types** of Vladimir Propp (1972) (e.g. hero, villain, etc..).[5] Examples for characters that are not relevant enough for the networks are the cook and the kitchen boy in *Dornröschen* (*Sleeping Beauty*) because their existence and actions have no influence on the plot whatsoever. In cases where only the actions of a group of characters but not those of the individual characters are important for the plot, the networks contain only a node for the group (e.g. the dwarves in *Schneewittchen* (*Snow White*) or the parents of the princess in *Dornröschen* (*Sleeping Beauty*).

For the **age** of the entities, we use a set of five distinct labels: (1) Baby: should be assigned to newborns only (2) Growing-up: An entity that is either a child or adolescent. (3) Grown-up: Entities that take on responsibility on their own (having children is one such responsibility). (4) Aged: Requires a clear mention in the text ("alte Hexe"/"old witch", "Großvater"/"grandfather" - here we assume third generation people to take the value by default) (5) Unknown: This category is used if there are no clear indicators, for instance for legendary creatures.

The **entity sentiment** of a character corresponds

[2]https://de.wikisource.org/wiki/Kinder-_und_Hausmärchen

[3]https://www.deutschestextarchiv.de/demo/cab/

[4]Example: In the noun phrase "eine kleine süße Dirne" (a little sweet girl) we only mark "Dirne" (girl).

[5]We restricted the networks to the important characters to prevent them from being cluttered and to keep the amount of work manageable.

to the sentiment of the entity as it is depicted by the *author*. We only make use of three possible values for the sentiment of a character: (1) positive: This value is assigned if the entity is described to be social and acts in an ethical manner (e.g. the entity cares for the well-being of someone else) and/or is attributed positive character traits, e.g. "Das Mädchen [...] blieb fromm und gut." (The girl [...] stayed pious and good.) (2) negative: This value is assigned if the character only cares about themselves and/or acts unsocial and unethical and/or is attributed negative character traits, e.g. "eine böse Hexe". (3) neutral: By default, a character receives this sentiment value. The sentiment can change over the course of the plot (though it only happened once in the 40 documents we have annotated).

The edges in the network correspond to the sentiment between characters and the social relations: By analyzing all thoughts an entity has towards another entity as well as all actions taken between them, we are trying to subsume the **sentiment between characters** in a label with the values: (1) positive: Entity has either positive feelings, thoughts or had actions that she would repeat. (2) negative: Entity has negative feelings (such as fear), negative thoughts or fear of reliving certain actions with the other entity (e.g. being eaten by the other entity). (3) neutral (4) none/empty cell: There is no mention of thoughts or interaction between the characters. The set of **social relations** is currently spanning 29 labels, with more to be expected to come if we continue to label more texts. These contain family relations (16 labels), a label that expresses a love relation between the characters and currently 12 other social relations (see Appendix A for the complete list).

We suspect there would be no problems using these guidelines for fairy tales from different author or in different languages (one would probably need to expand the set of relation types as we expect to do when we annotate the remaining Grimm fairy tales). Outside of the domain of fairy tales, the character types of Propp will most likely not make much sense, so they would have to be discarded or replaced.

3.2 Annotation Procedure

For annotation, two annotators were asked to label all these layers on their own and afterwards had the task to discuss the differences and unify their individual solutions to form a final document. We measured inter-rater agreement of the individual layers using Cohen's Kappa: The values for age (61.2%), where the main source of disagreement was between the labels "unknown" and "aged", characters in the network (81.5%), entity sentiment (69.9%), character types (69.7%), sentiment between characters (71.5%) and social relations between characters (67.3% overall; 83.6% when only regarding family relations and 60.3% for all other relations) correspond to substantial agreement according to Landis and Koch (1977).

3.3 Dataset Statistics

The 40 annotated texts have an average length of 1823 tokens and contain a total of 11873 mentions in 1218 clusters (about 9.75 mentions per cluster). 589 of the clusters are singletons.

The networks contain 244 characters (6.1 plot-relevant characters per network). For detailed information about the distribution of the labels in the text files and in the networks, see Appendix A.

4 Baseline Experiments

In order to demonstrate the usefulness of our data set, both for the automatic extraction and evaluation of character networks, we conduct baseline experiments using a rule-based pipeline and an approach based on neural networks. Both approaches detect and cluster character references. The rule-based version uses the Named Entity Recognition of Jannidis et al. (2017) and the coreference module of Krug et al. (2015), while the neural network **c2f** (Lee et al., 2018) conducts both steps in an end-to-end fashion. c2f was pre-trained on DROC and fine-tuned on the fairy tales using 5 folds, so that the entirety of our corpus could be labeled by the system.[6] The resulting entities form the nodes in the networks. As a proxy for interactions (which represent the edges in the networks) we used co-occurence counts for a given discours (in our work we differentiate between a sentence or a paragraph as discours). The corresponding edge weights are the number of times the two entities appear in the same discours. Currently, we do not infer relation types, which is left for future work.

[6]We actually used an additional six fairy tales, for which we did not have character networks yet, for fine-tuning.

4.1 Social Network Analysis

The resulting networks are evaluated by two means. The first evaluation setting is directed at the network structure itself. We compare networks based on the gold coreference annotations and the system annotations using a set of metrics from Social Network Analysis:

- Average Weighted Degree: average number of neighbours of an entity weighted by the corresponding edge weight. A high degree means than an entity has interacted with a lot of other entities.
- Average Path Length: average length of all shortest paths in the graph.
- Network Diameter: longest of all shortest paths in the network.
- Graph Density: ratio of edges in the graph compared to the number of possible edges. The higher this number is, the more other entities each entity interacts with.
- Average Betweenness Centrality: average number of shortest paths that go through the node but do not start or end there. This is high if an entity connects many other entities to each other.

Table 1 shows the results of this experiment. No approach is currently capable of recovering the network structure (at least according to these statistics). For the discourse of sentences, the entities in the neural approach seem to be connected more strongly than required (as can be seen by the much higher density and the higher average degree) and the rule-based pipeline proposes entities that are linked too sparsely. Interestingly, this phenomenon is almost shifted when the discourse is changed to paragraphs, where the rule-based system appears to overestimate the inter-connectedness of the characters and the neural system underestimates it. Since these metrics do not compare a system and gold network directly and are difficult to interpret we performed a second experiment where the system networks were scored against the gold networks.

4.2 Precision at k

The second evaluation rates the quality of the most important entities that appear in the networks. For this setting, we extract a ranking of the k most important entities (using frequency of appearance in the text, which was shown by Krug et al. (2016) to correlate with the actual importance). The resulting rankings were matched in several ways against the gold entities:

	Deg	PL	Dia	Den	B Cen
Gold Sent	15.69	2.80	6.05	0.33	18.92
Rules Sent	10.81	2.55	5.53	0.21	29.86
c2f Sent	19.56	2.82	5.70	0.53	8.86
Gold Para	13.22	1.93	3.38	0.48	7.33
Rules Para	15.75	1.58	2.77	0.40	11.47
c2f Para	11.77	1.70	3.00	0.64	3.66

Table 1: Average Weighted **Deg**ree, **P**ath **L**ength, **Dia**meter, **Den**sity and **B**etweenness **Cen**trality of entity graphs from the rule-based pipeline and c2f.

- **Soft:** In this setting a suggested entity by the system is correct if it does appear at all in the network (no matter the rank)
- **Soft-Ranked:** In this setting the rank of the system and gold solution need to agree in order to obtain a correct match
- **Spearman-Ranked:** In this setting the entire ranking was compared to the ranking obtained from the gold networks using Spearman correlation Spearman (1904)

In order to find a corresponding system entity for each gold entity (which are both represented by clusters of mentions in the text), we use the Kuhn-Munkres algorithm used in the CEAF metric (Luo, 2005). The similarity of two entities is measured by the relative number of common mentions, like in the entity-based variant of CEAF. That means even if multiple system entities would be determined as compatible, only the "best" match will be chosen.

We introduced a cutoff parameter k in order to artificially limit the rankings at position k and therefore obtain insight into the quality at different levels of the ranking (e.g. is the ranking of the top 2 entities more reliable than that of the top 6).
Figure 1 shows Precision-at-k for soft (Soft) and soft-ranked gold entities as well as Spearman correlation for the results of the rule-based pipeline and the neural algorithm.

Interpreting the results first shows that the neural system outperformed the rule-based pipeline in every setting. In the **Soft** evaluation setting, the proposed most important entity is always part of

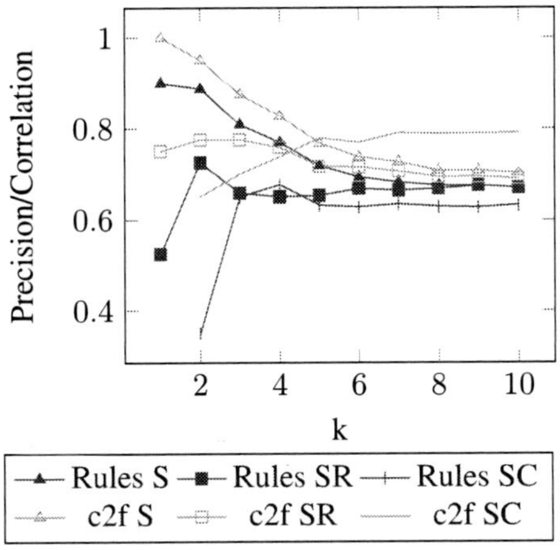

Figure 1: Precision and Spearman Correlation (SC) of the top k entities found via rule-based pipeline and neural algorithm (c2f). SR is short for the *Soft-ranked* setting and S is an abbreviation for the *Soft* setting

the network, but only about 75% of the time also the most important entity in the gold data. Both scores severly decline up to about 70% Precision with k at ten. That means, if we were to form a network comprising ten characters, three characters would be spurious and unwanted. In the most severe setting Spearman-Ranked, the correlation starts at about 0.75 (for k=2, since rankings of size 1 cannot be evaluated) and dropping to about 0.6 in the process. This correlation shows, that at least the relative importances of the entities seems to be maintained when an automatic attempt is made.

5 Conclusion

We present a corpus of 40 German fairy tales by the Brothers Grimm with hand-annotated coreference information and character networks. This data set can be used to train and compare different approaches for the automatic extraction of character networks and helps to homogenize the evaluation of research on this topic. We demonstrated its usefulness by comparing two different systems available for the automatic extraction of character networks. We found that even state-of-the-art approaches can not reliably extract character networks, even for a seemingly easy domain such as fairy tales, evaluated on the overlap of characters in the network and the general shape of the resulting graph. For future work, we plan to conduct experiments for the automatic prediction of all further annotated layers, especially sentiment, attributes and relations of/between the characters.

References

Apoorv Agarwal, Augusto Corvalan, Jacob Jensen, and Owen Rambow. 2012. Social network analysis of alice in wonderland. In *Proceedings of the NAACL-HLT 2012 Workshop on Computational Linguistics for Literature*, pages 88–96, Montréal, Canada. Association for Computational Linguistics.

Mariona Coll Ardanuy and Caroline Sporleder. 2014. Structure-based clustering of novels. In *Proceedings of the 3rd Workshop on Computational Linguistics for Literature (CLFL)*, pages 31–39, Gothenburg, Sweden. Association for Computational Linguistics.

Niels Dekker, Tobias Kuhn, and Marieke van Erp. 2019. Evaluating named entity recognition tools for extracting social networks from novels. *PeerJ Computer Science*, 5:e189.

David Elson, Nicholas Dames, and Kathleen McKeown. 2010. Extracting social networks from literary fiction. In *Proceedings of the 48th Annual Meeting of the Association for Computational Linguistics*, pages 138–147, Uppsala, Sweden. Association for Computational Linguistics.

Fotis Jannidis, Isabella Reger, Lukas Weimer, Markus Krug, Martin Toepfer, and Frank Puppe. 2017. Automatische Erkennung von Figuren in deutschsprachigen Romanen. *Proceedings of DhD*.

Prashant Jayannavar, Apoorv Agarwal, Melody Ju, and Owen Rambow. 2015. Validating literary theories using automatic social network extraction. In *Proceedings of the Fourth Workshop on Computational Linguistics for Literature*, pages 32–41, Denver, Colorado, USA. Association for Computational Linguistics.

Hongyan Jing, Nanda Kambhatla, and Salim Roukos. 2007. Extracting social networks and biographical facts from conversational speech transcripts. In *Proceedings of the 45th Annual Meeting of the Association of Computational Linguistics*, pages 1040–1047, Prague, Czech Republic. Association for Computational Linguistics.

Bryan Jurish. 2012. *Finite-State Canonicalization Techniques for Historical German*. Ph.D. thesis, Universität Potsdam. (completed 2011, published 2012).

Markus Krug. 2020. *Techniques for the Automatic Extraction of Character Networks in German Historic Novels*. doctoralthesis, Universität Würzburg.

Markus Krug, Frank Puppe, Fotis Jannidis, Luisa Macharowsky, Isabella Reger, and Lukas Weimar. 2015. Rule-based coreference resolution in German historic novels. In *Proceedings of the Fourth Workshop on Computational Linguistics for Literature*, pages 98–104, Denver, Colorado, USA. Association for Computational Linguistics.

Markus Krug, Frank Puppe, Fotis Jannidis, Isabella Reger, Lukas Weimer, and Luisa Macharowsky. 2016. Comparison of methods for the identification of main characters in german novels. In *Digital Humanities 2016: Conference Abstracts*, pages 578–582.

Markus Krug, Frank Puppe, Isabella Reger, Lukas Weimer, Luisa Macharowsky, Stephan Feldhaus, and Fotis Jannidis. 2018. Description of a corpus of character references in german novels - DROC [Deutsches ROman Corpus]. In *DARIAH-DE Working Papers*. DARIAH-DE.

Vincent Labatut and Xavier Bost. 2019. Extraction and analysis of fictional character networks: A survey. *ACM Computing Surveys (CSUR)*, 52(5):1–40.

J Richard Landis and Gary G Koch. 1977. The measurement of observer agreement for categorical data. *biometrics*, pages 159–174.

Kenton Lee, Luheng He, and Luke Zettlemoyer. 2018. Higher-order coreference resolution with coarse-to-fine inference. In *Proceedings of the 2018 Conference of the North American Chapter of the Association for Computational Linguistics: Human Language Technologies, Volume 2 (Short Papers)*, pages 687–692, New Orleans, Louisiana. Association for Computational Linguistics.

Xiaoqiang Luo. 2005. On coreference resolution performance metrics. In *Proceedings of Human Language Technology Conference and Conference on Empirical Methods in Natural Language Processing*, pages 25–32, Vancouver, British Columbia, Canada. Association for Computational Linguistics.

Gyeong-Mi Park, Sung-Hwan Kim, Hye-Ryeon Hwang, and Hwan-Gue Cho. 2013. Complex system analysis of social networks extracted from literary fictions. *International Journal of Machine Learning and Computing*, 3(1):107.

Vladimir Propp. 1972. Morphologie des märchens [1928]. *Hrsg. Karl Eimermacher. Übs. Christel Wendt. München: Carl Hanser Verlag*.

Charles Spearman. 1904. The proof and measurement of association between two things. *The American Journal of Psychology*, 15(1):72–101.

Ralph Weischedel, Sameer Pradhan, Lance Ramshaw, Martha Palmer, Nianwen Xue, Mitchell Marcus, Ann Taylor, Craig Greenberg, Eduard Hovy, Robert Belvin, et al. 2011. Ontonotes release 4.0. *LDC2011T03, Philadelphia, Penn.: Linguistic Data Consortium*.

A Inter Annotator Agreement and Corpus Statistics

Label	Precision	Recall	F1
unlabeled	96.9%	98.7%	97.7%
human	91.1%	95.7%	92.8%
legendary	83.1%	83.1%	79.0%
generic	85.8%	68.0%	73.1%
transcendent	95.1%	98.2%	96.2%
mixed	93.3%	91.7%	91.5%

Table 2: Agreement on annotated mention spans.

Metric	Precision	Recall	F1
MUC	96.5%	96.8%	96.7%
B^3	92.4%	91.0%	91.6%
$CEAF_E$	88.1%	84.3%	85.8%
$CEAF_M$	94.2%	92.5%	93.3%
LEA	90.0%	89.2%	89.9%

Table 3: Agreement on annotated mentions (including coreference id).

Label Type	Cohen's Kappa
Character Age	61.2
Character Type	69.7
Character Sentiment	69.9
Relation Type	67.3
Relation Sentiment	71.5

Table 4: Agreement on labels in the networks.

(a) Sex

Label	Ratio
female	29.0%
male	58.1%
unknown	12.9%

(b) Number

Label	Ratio
Singular	83.5%
Plural	13.0%
unknown	3.5%

(c) Syntactic Category

Label	Ratio
name	4.4%
noun phrase	30.8%
pronoun	64.8%

(d) Semantic Category

Label	Ratio
human	69.7%
legendary	24.0%
generic	5.8%
transcendent	0.4%
mixed	0.1%

Table 5: Distribution of Sex, Number, Syntactic Category and Semantic Category labels in the annotated texts.

(a) Sex

Label	Ratio
female	28.3%
male	56.6%
unknown	15.2%

(b) Sentiment

Label	Ratio
positive	31.1%
negative	19.7%
neutral	49.6%

(c) Character Type

Label	Ratio
dispatcher	10.2%
donor	3.3%
false hero	2.0%
helper	15.6%
hero	20.1%
plot relevant	32.8%
prize	4.9%
villain	13.1%

(d) Age

Label	Ratio
baby	0.8%
growing-up	16.0%
grown-up	32.8%
aged	7.0%
unknown	43.4%

Table 6: Distribution of Sex, Character Sentiment, Character Type and Age labels in the annotated character networks. Note that the percentages do not always add up to 100% since some entities can have several labels.

(a) Relation Type

Label	Ratio
none	57.0%
victim	4.2%
friend	9.9%
enemy	5.8%
desires	1.2%
loves	0.7%
parent	3.8%
child	3.5%
sibling	2.4%
spouse	3.6%
grandparent	0.3%
grandchild	0.3%
uncle	0.1%
nephew	0.1%
parent-in-law	1.1%
child-in-law	1.3%
stepparent	0.3%
stepchild	0.3%
stepsibling	0.1%
fosterparent	0.2%
fosterchild	0.2%
fostersibling	0.1%
ruler	1.8%
subject	1.4%
employee	1.3%
employer	1.3%
owner	0.6%
property	0.6%
tradepartner	0.6%
workmate	0.1%

(b) Relation Sentiment

Label	Ratio
none	51.7%
positive	16.0%
negative	11.5%
neutral	21.2%

Table 7: Distribution of Relation Type and Relation Sentiment labels in the annotated character networks. Note that the percentages do not always add up to 100% since some relations can have several labels.

End-to-end style-conditioned poetry generation: What does it take to learn from examples alone?

Jörg Wöckener[1] and **Thomas Haider**[2] and **Tristan Miller**[3]
Thanh Tung Linh Nguyen[1] and **The-Khang Nguyen**[1] and **Minh Vu Pham**[1]
Jonas Belouadi[1] and **Steffen Eger**[1]

[1] Technische Universität Darmstadt [2] Universität Göttingen
[3] Austrian Research Institute for Artificial Intelligence

Abstract

In this work, we design an end-to-end model for poetry generation based on conditioned recurrent neural network (RNN) language models whose goal is to learn stylistic features (poem length, sentiment, alliteration, and rhyming) from examples alone. We show this model successfully learns the 'meaning' of length and sentiment, as we can control it to generate longer or shorter as well as more positive or more negative poems. However, the model does not grasp sound phenomena like alliteration and rhyming, but instead exploits low-level statistical cues. Possible reasons include the size of the training data, the relatively low frequency and difficulty of these sublexical phenomena as well as model biases. We show that more recent GPT-2 models also have problems learning sublexical phenomena such as rhyming from examples alone.

1 Introduction

Poetry is a very old form of human language use which is deeply embedded in the heritage of many cultures (Beissinger, 2012; Fabb and Halle, 2010). It is characterized by refined, creative, and sublime expressions and linguistic structure. Thus, it comes as little surprise that automatic poetry generation has long captivated artificial intelligence (AI) researchers (Gervás, 2001; Gonçalo Oliveira et al., 2017), for any general solution to this task will have assuredly brought us a step closer to understanding human creativity.[1]

```
-   +  | -     + | -     +    | -   +  |
I  felt  a    funeral    in     my brain ,

-   +  | -        + | -    +    |
And mourners ,    to and   fro   ,

-   +  | -       + | -     +    | -   +   |
Kept treading ,  treading , till   it seemed

-   +  | -     + | -     +     |
That sense was breaking through .
```

Figure 1: Example of alliteration (red), a (near) rhyme (blue), and metre (black/grey). This is the first stanza of 'I felt a Funeral, in my Brain' by Emily Dickinson. The rhyme scheme is 'abcb', the overall lexical sentiment of the stanza is negative (many words are associated with negative sentiment), and the time period is the 19th century.

A crucial factor when producing poetry (either by humans or automatically) is *style*. While definitions of style have varied considerably over time, space, and fields of study (Herrmann et al., 2015), there is widespread agreement that the study of literary *form*, not (just) *content*, is what allows us to determine the criteria for aesthetic appreciation and impact. That is, it is formal or stylistic features that often distinguish sophisticated, effectual, or simply 'good' poetry from poetry that is pedestrian, mundane, or just plain 'bad' (Jakobson, 1960; Shlovsky, 1965; Ganjigunte Ashok et al., 2013; Kao and Jurafsky, 2015; Menninghaus et al., 2017).

In this work, we consider the problem of *style-conditioned poetry generation*, where the user may specify stylistic factors that the generated text has to fulfil. Our stylistic factors include rhyme, alliteration, sentiment, text length, and time period. Examples of some of our stylistic features (particularly rhyme and alliteration) can be found in Figure 1. (We include metre in the example, but do not consider it in the experiments.)

In generating poetry conditioned upon stylistic factors, we explore a theme in the automatic gen-

[1]Poetry generation systems may have manifold applications. For example, an AI tool that could assist songwriters in composing lyrics to a given tune, or even generate them entirely automatically, would have commercial potential. Besides such entertainment-oriented applications, producing tools for poetry generation will necessarily involve the development of poetry analysis tools – since generation and analysis are complementary aspects of poetry (Jhamtani et al., 2019) – which may prove useful in their own right. And the production and application of these analysis tools could result in insights into the structural and aesthetic features that distinguish human-penned poetry from its artificially produced counterpart.

Proceedings of LaTeCH-CLfL 2021, pages 57–66
Punta Cana, Dominican Republic (Online), November 11, 2021.

eration of poetry that we believe will dominate the field in the upcoming years: *end-to-end generation* of formal poetry *from examples alone*, without the need for human involvement in designing the model or filtering its output (e.g., via hard-coded stylistic constraints on rhyme, alliteration, etc.). We believe advances in this task serve as an indicator of the maturity of natural language processing (NLP) systems as they progress towards true AI. Indeed, the recent success of GPT-3 (Brown et al., 2020) with its focus on few-shot learning (i.e., learning from a few illustrative examples, even without model updating) is inspiration for our work to design poetry generation models that learn relevant stylistic features without any other form of human intervention.

We find that, while our models can capture sentiment, time epoch, and text length, they have trouble learning intricate phonetic stylistic features from examples alone, instead learning low-level statistical cues that are weakly correlated with these target features. This holds both for a classical RNN language model and more recent transformer models (GPT-2). We take this as a negative result and as a challenge for future poetry generation systems, viz., to be able to produce typical relevant stylistic factors of poetry without hard-coding them into the model architecture.

2 Related work

Poetry analysis. Computational analysis of poetry has been concerned largely with formal features such as metre (Greene et al., 2010; Agirrezabal et al., 2016; Estes and Hench, 2016), rhyme (Reddy and Knight, 2011; Haider and Kuhn, 2018), and enjambment (Ruiz et al., 2017; Baumann et al., 2018). More recently, higher-level phenomena, including semantic coherence (Herbelot, 2015), metaphor (Reinig and Rehbein, 2019; Kesarwani et al., 2017), and diachronic analysis of tropes (Haider and Eger, 2019) have come into focus. Haider et al. (2020) annotate poetry for fine-grained aesthetic emotion categories elicited in readers.

Poetry generation. In the era of statistical NLP, text generation has evolved along the path of n-gram language models (Kneser and Ney, 1995), whose inherent modelling limitations allow them to consider only a finite amount of history when generating next output symbols, to recurrent neural network (RNN) language models (Sutskever et al., 2011), which can take an infinite history into account but suffer from vanishing and exploding gradients, to transformer models (Vaswani et al., 2017), which have constant path lengths between inputs and outputs. Transformers are feed-forward networks that use self-attention between consecutive layers. Their shorter paths between inputs and outputs make it easier to learn long-range dependencies. They can also be parallelized easier. As a consequence, they can be pre-trained on massive amounts of data, where they acquire general text generation abilities (Radford et al., 2019).

Approaches to poetry generation can be categorized into pre- and post-deep learning era approaches. Pre-deep learning approaches were highly hand-engineered and 'top-down', using specific grammar formalisms and linguistic resources to generate poetry; they typically built stylistic aspects such as rhyme and rhythm into their model architectures (Manurung et al., 2000; Gervás, 2001; Gonçalo Oliveira, 2013; Colton et al., 2012).

Neural approaches to poetry generation learn from collections of real poetry data. Most of them use RNN language models (Zhang and Lapata, 2014; Lau et al., 2018). This framework has also been extended to related tasks such as generating poetry from images (Liu et al., 2018), translating poetry (Ghazvininejad et al., 2018), and generating song lyrics given an input melody (Watanabe et al., 2018). A drawback shared by most poetry generation systems, including even very recent ones (Van de Cruys, 2020; Agarwal and Kann, 2020), is that they require hard- and hand-coded rules to generate poetry with specific properties, such as rhyming and alliteration, or to filter output not having these properties. For example, to ensure rhyming, Lau et al. (2018) exploit the fact that their data (sonnets) has a particular structure from which they can infer that certain word pairs must rhyme, which they incorporate in the modelling. Hämäläinen and Alnajjar (2019) define rules for style features. Agarwal and Kann (2020) tell the model when a rhyming word is required and then modify the prediction process. This means that the models themselves lack the ability to discover elementary properties of poetry themselves, but instead rely on the modeller's intention and ingenuity to do so.

Recently, Jhamtani et al. (2019) introduced an intriguing approach to poetry generation that learns rhyming constraints using an adversarial model: an RNN language model (the *generator*) generates poetry and a discriminator (the *adversary*) decides whether the line endings of the generated text are plausible for poetry. The generator and the discriminator compete against each other: the generator tries to generate poetry that the discriminator misclassifies and the discriminator aims at distinguishing generated poetry from human-authored poetry. The authors show that this competition leads to models learning rhyming with higher probability. While this model comes close to our envisioned ideal of a poetry generation system learning from examples alone, it still has the drawback that the modellers need to make the model aware of what to pay attention to (i.e., character information of ending words). This is unsatisfactory given the large space of possible features to consider in generated poetry.

Formally similar approaches to ours are those of Ficler and Goldberg (2017) and Manjavacas et al. (2019) (without emphasizing the 'examples-only' aspect, however). Ficler and Goldberg (2017) conditioned RNN language models on stylistic features such as length and whether the text appears to be professionally written, and on sentiment and theme. They showed this approach to be successful for the given conditions in the movie reviews domain, though they did not deal with the much more challenging case of poetry. Manjavacas et al. (2019) generate hip-hop lyrics conditional upon rhythm and rhyme. To enforce rhyming, they feed phonetic rhyme representations to the model, and thus also encode relevant knowledge top-down into the model.

2.1 Poetry evaluation

Evaluation of generated poetry is usually done either automatically or manually. Zhang and Lapata (2014) compare generated lines to manually produced 'gold-standard' lines using BLEU (Papineni et al., 2002), a metric borrowed from machine translation, for the task of continuing an initial line of poetry. They also report perplexity, a widely used metric for language model evaluation. For manual evaluation, they ask human annotators to rate the generated poems for fluency, coherence, meaning, and poeticness. Hopkins and Kiela (2017) and Lau et al. (2018) use a sort of Turing test where they ask human participants to distinguish between human- and computer-generated poems. Lau et al. (2018) additionally have an expert rate generated poetry with respect to metre, rhyme, readability, and emotion. Ghazvininejad et al. (2017) ask crowd-workers to give star ratings for the general quality of the generated poems, and then investigate whether users give higher scores to style-adjusted poems compared to the default poems.

In our work, we choose a simple evaluation scheme that measures whether the generated poetry satisfies user constraints. We do not measure other qualities of the generated poetry as we are mostly interested in whether end-to-end systems can successfully generate poetry from examples alone, without human intervention.

3 Models

Our goal is to design an end-to-end poetry generation model that learns to associate a desired style feature vector with poetic content and form purely inductively, using examples rather than hand-coded knowledge about what rhyming, alliteration, metre, and sentiment are. To do so, we implement a *conditioned language model* that samples the next word w_{t+1} to be generated conditioned on the history of past words $w_0, \ldots, w_t$ and a style constraint c. That is, it samples w_{t+1} from the conditional distribution $P(w_{t+1} \mid w_0, w_1, \ldots, w_t, c)$. We implement the model in this formula by a unidirectional RNN language model. At every time step, the RNN predicts the next word to be generated by sampling from a softmax distribution over the whole vocabulary, taking the current word vector $\mathbf{w}_t$ as well as the current history vector $\mathbf{h}_t$, which summarizes all past inputs, into account. The model starts generation from a special input token, 'SOS', and generates until it encounters an end-of-sentence token 'EOS'. To take the context c into account, we encode it as a feature vector $\mathbf{c}$ and concatenate it to every input representation. While there are other possible ways of including $\mathbf{c}$, our way constantly 'reminds' the model of the style context, which we hope better enforces that style in the output. The model is illustrated in Figure 2. Our RNN language model also uses character-level information to build input representations, which may help it to generalize to rare words or sublexical phenomena, such as rhyming. Our implementation is taken from that of Reimers and Gurevych (2017).[2]

For the conditions c, we consider the following:

Rhyming: How much rhyming is present in a base unit (e.g., a stanza or full poem) of poetry? We measure the degree of rhyming by using a

[2]https://github.com/UKPLab/emnlp2017-bilstm-cnn-crf

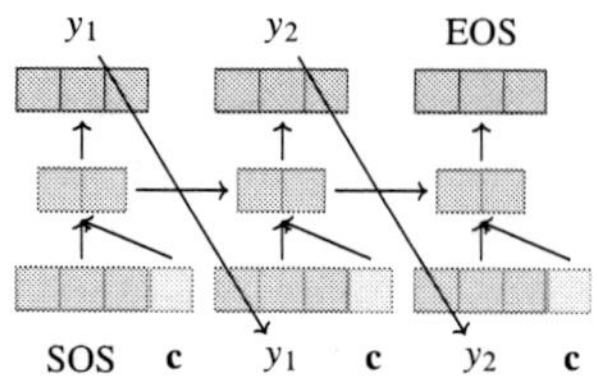

Figure 2: A conditioned RNN language model.

supervised rhyme model based on character-level Siamese bidirectional long short-term memory (BiLSTM) networks (Haider and Kuhn, 2018), available for English and German. We count both internal and end rhymes as contributing to the rhyme level of a base unit of poetry.

Alliteration: Alliteration is a device, often associated with humour (Mihalcea and Strapparava, 2006), where consecutive words begin with the same sound or sounds. As a character does not uniquely specify a sound in most writing systems (cf. *cat* and *chase*), it is not sufficient to compare the first characters of the words. Instead, we use the CMU Sphinx Sequence-to-Sequence grapheme-to-phoneme toolkit[3] for converting words into a phonemic representation and then check whether subsequent words start with the same phoneme. We measure the degree of alliteration by counting how many alliterating word sequences occur within a base unit of poetry.

Sentiment: To determine the sentiment of a base unit of poetry, we use a lexicon lookup approach. For English, we use the opinion lexicon developed by Hu and Liu (2004) and for German, we use the German polarity clues word lists by Waltinger (2010). The English lexicon consists of 2,007 positive and 4,782 negative words and the German lexicon consists of 17,627 positive and 19,962 negative words. In each base unit of poetry, we count the number of words that appear in the positive and negative lists of the lexicon, respectively, and then calculate the difference between these two numbers. The final result is normalized by dividing by the number of total matches for this unit, resulting in the formula $c_\sigma = \frac{p-n}{p+n}$, where p is the number of positive words found and n is the number of negative words found. For instance, if four words of the unit were found in the positive list and six words in the negative list, the final rating is $-2/10 = -0.2$.

[3]https://github.com/cmusphinx/g2p-seq2seq

3.1 Training and testing mode

In **training mode**, we extract sentiment, rhyme, and alliteration levels of poems (or stanzas) and pair them with the poems themselves. The model then predicts the text of poems (next words) based on the previous text and the context vector **c**. The model is end to end and has no built-in understanding of rhyme, sentiment, nor alliteration, except for what it gleans from its input examples. In **testing mode**, the user may select a context specification in terms of rhyme, alliteration, and sentiment, which is fed into the RNN language model. The model starts generating from the SOS token and terminates when it has produced the EOS token.

4 Experiments

4.1 Experimental setup

For training data, we use two small corpora, one English and one German. The English corpus, the Chicago Rhyming Poetry Corpus,[4] has 15,672 training and 1,979 development quatrains, and the German corpus is a small curated subset of Textgrid[5] with 67,054 training and 6,697 development quatrains. We generate quatrain stanzas instead of full poems for speed reasons. As our network architecture, we use a single hidden layer RNN with 64 hidden units, a dropout of 0.2 and input word embeddings of 300 (trained on poetry data using word2vec (Mikolov et al., 2013)) with an additional character-level word representation of dimensionality 25. As optimizer, we use Adam (Kingma and Ba, 2014) with a learning rate of 0.001; we set the batch size to 25.

In general, we obtained very similar results across our two English and German datasets. We report results only for one language per experimental condition.

4.2 Results

Text length. As a sanity check, we test whether we can generate stanzas of a desired length. We select lines that have between 4 and 14 tokens from the English Chicago corpus. We then calculate a normalized condition c_λ which divides the number of tokens in a line by the maximum number available in the subcorpus, which is 14. The values for c_λ thus range from 4/14 to 1 in the training data. For evaluation, we let the condition c_λ range from 0 to 1 in steps of 1/10; we also include the value 2. Note

[4]https://github.com/sravanareddy/rhymedata
[5]https://textgrid.de

that all values below $4/14 \approx 0.2857$ as well as 2 were not seen during training. Figure 3 (top) shows average line length per condition c_λ, averaged over 100 generated lines for any value of c_λ. We see that the value of c_λ and the length of the generated output lines correlate strongly. The average line length for $c_\lambda = 0.3$ is 4, which matches the length of training lines with that value. The model can even extrapolate to unseen values, at least to a certain degree – with a value of 2, the line length exceeds the limit of 100 tokens, indicating overgeneralization, while values smaller than $4/14$ are smoothly extrapolated.

Sentiment. We infer sentiment from the corpus with the help of word lists: each quatrain receives a rating c_σ as previously defined which we then divide by the maximum sentiment rating of the corpus, normalizing the values to a range of -1 (for very negative sentiment) to 1 (for very positive sentiment). After training, we generate 100 quatrains for each c_σ ranging from -1 to $+1$ in steps of $1/10$. Additionally, we add the extreme values of -2 and $+2$, which were never seen during training. Figure 3 (right) shows the average sentiment rating value in the generated test data as a function of the c_σ condition. The average rating of the sentiment in the test data increases linearly with c_σ. The model can even extrapolate to the unseen extreme values. Table 1 shows examples of quatrains generated with positive and negative c_σ. With a positive c_σ, the model tends to sample stanzas containing positively connotated words like '*himmels*' (heaven), '*liebe*' (love), and '*kuesst*' (kisses), while a negative c_σ increases the selection of negatively connotated words like '*schwache*' (weak), '*angst*' (fear), and '*heuchler*' (hypocrite). Apparently, the model has understood the semantics of positive and negative sentiment on the sole basis of examples.

Alliteration. In order to control the alliteration level in the generated quatrains, we count how many alliterating sequences there are in a quatrain, as described in Section 3. To normalize these values, we divide them by the maximum number of alliterating sequences in the quatrains of the corpus and add the normalized values as conditional information c_α. We then generate 100 quatrains for each c_α ranging from 0 to 1 in steps of $1/10$. Figure 4 (left) shows that the alliteration level in the test data indeed increases as c_α increases. However, Figure 4 (right) shows that increasing c_α for the test poems has

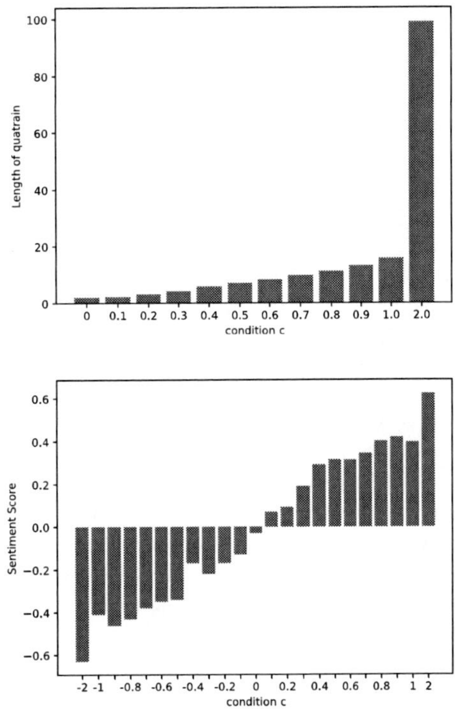

Figure 3: Conditioning on length (c_λ, top) and polar sentiment (c_σ, bottom). The input condition (a real number) is shown on the x axis and the average value measured in the generated output is on the y axis.

the effect that the model generates longer stanzas; when we further normalize the degree of alliteration measured in the output by the number of tokens in the output, then the correlation between the input condition and the measured normalized alliteration degree in the output disappears. Thus, the model apparently does not understand the phenomenon of alliteration, but instead increases the number of words generated: the longer a poem, the more likely it is to (coincidentally) contain instances of alliteration. We also experimented with the input condition $c_{\alpha_{\text{norm}}}$, which measures the degree of alliteration *per token* in a poem, to see if the models would understand the phenomenon of alliteration when they cannot rely on length. Figure 5 (left) shows that this is not the case. There is no clearly visible effect of the input condition on the measured normalized alliteration degree in the generated test data.

Rhyme. We similarly experiment with internal rhymes within a verse and end rhymes within a quatrain. We consider all possible pairs of distinct

ein zeuge o der schoenen du fuer die schuldlos buch bluehend dein schoenstes und noch sieht ein licht jedwedes blatt zum joche ein tor	schwerer streit und weinend flehn vom letzten wort mit farb ergeben hirn und bluete in die der natur ist freude ist des ihm thut
in liebe die streng umgekehret eins sei mein ewig zugethan erfuelle des himmels wieder dass das mit kuesst den lauf	komm doch er sey der heuchler sei nicht dann im spott du solltest eh mir geschrieben die schwache angst

Table 1: Examples of automatically generated sentiment-conditioned quatrains using the sentiment conditions $c_\sigma = +1$ (left) and $c_\sigma = -1$ (right).

words in a verse and feed them into the rhyme classifier described in Section 3, which returns a cosine distance for each pair. If the distance is smaller than a threshold of 0.2, the pair is classified as rhyming. The number of rhyming word pairs in a quatrain is normalized by division by the maximum number of rhyming word pairs found in the quatrains of the corpus. The results are values between 0 (for no rhyming word pair) and 1 (for quatrains with the most rhyming word pairs). Since also the degree of rhyming is positively correlated with the number of tokens in a stanza, we further divide these values by the number of tokens of the respective quatrain, then scale them again to a range between 0 and 1. We denote this rhyme level as $c_{\rho_{\text{norm}}}$. As before, we let $c_{\rho_{\text{norm}}}$ range from 0 to 1 in steps of 1/10 and generate 100 quatrains for each value. Figure 5 (right) shows the fraction of rhyming words among all generated words in the output as a function of $c_{\rho_{\text{norm}}}$. Similar to the results of conditioning on alliterations, there is no positive correlation of the measured output rhyme level and the input rhyme degree condition when stanza length is accounted for.

4.3 Discussion

In our experiments, we found that end-to-end learning of word-level properties such as sentiment and poem length works – the models successfully learn to generate longer or shorter, and more positive or negative poems, when we condition them on these variables. This means that they have understood the semantics of these conditions on the sole basis of examples – i.e., without the need to explicitly encode the conditions into the model architecture. In contrast, conditioning on sublexical phenomena such as rhyming and alliteration was not successful. Instead, we found that the models learned dataset artifacts and biases – in particular, they learned to generate longer stanzas, which coincidentally have higher degrees of rhyming and alliteration. When controlling for this factor, we could not find evidence that the models learn rhyming or alliteration from examples alone. There are several possible explanations for this finding:

Dataset size. All our datasets were relatively small in size. It is unclear how model results depend on dataset size in terms of the conditioning variables considered here. In terms of the fluency, coherence, etc. of the generated texts, there is clear evidence that size improves model output – see our discussion of GPT-2 in Section 4.4.

Frequency of phenomena. On a per-token level, very few words rhyme or alliterate: for example, less than 3% of tokens in our datasets are part of an alliteration. This makes it harder to detect the meaning of these phenomena from examples alone. Also, very few stanzas have alliteration or rhyming levels that exceed 0.5, meaning that the model is in 'extrapolation mode' for most of them. A possible remedy for this would be to artificially augment the training data with stanzas having large degrees of alliteration or rhyming.

Word-level vs. sublexical phenomena. We note that sentiment is mostly expressed on the word level and rhyme and alliteration are expressed sublexically (i.e., on the sub-word-level). As RNNs (and other text generation models) produce lexical tokens (one after the other), they may be more naturally suited for the former types of phenomena.

Size of character-level representation. For computational reasons, we kept our RNN language models small, with few hidden units (64) and a small dimensionality of character-level representations for words (25). It is possible that the model simply did not have enough capacity to store the

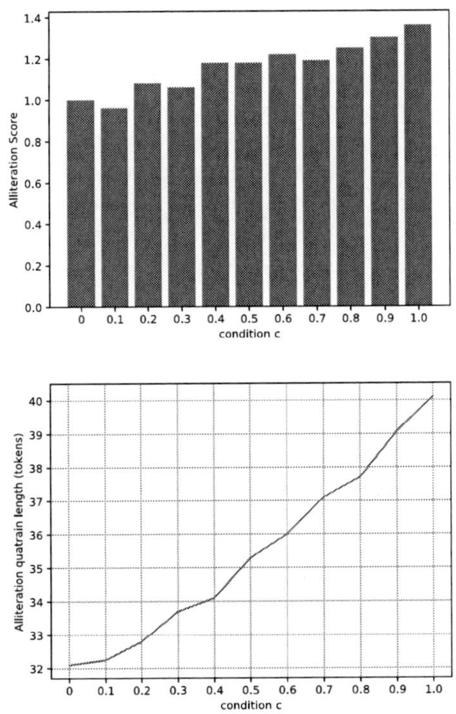

Figure 4: Top: Conditioning on degree of alliteration (c_α) on the English Chicago corpus data. The input condition (a real number) is shown on the x axis and the average value measured in the generated output is reported on the y axis. Bottom: Increasing c_α generally leads to an increase in the length of the generated poems.

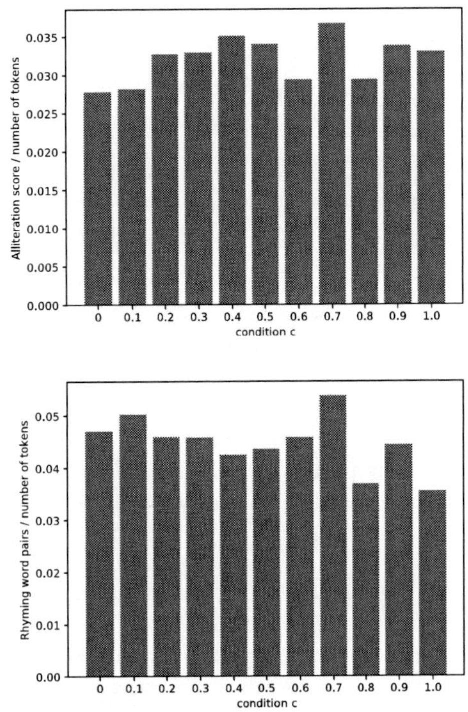

Figure 5: Conditioning on normalized alliteration degree ($c_{\alpha_{\text{norm}}}$, top) and normalized rhyme degree ($c_{\rho_{\text{norm}}}$, bottom) on the English Chicago corpus data. The input condition (a real number) is shown on the x axis and the average value measured in the generated output is reported on the y axis.

relevant information about the sublexical phenomena of interest. However, it must also be said that increasing model capacity runs the risk of severe overfitting when the training data size is small, as is the case for our datasets.

Heterogeneity of poetry data. It is possible that the heterogeneity of the poetry data (with some stanzas having high and others very low degrees of rhyming and alliteration) confuses the models (Hopkins and Kiela, 2017), particularly when some of these phenomena are very infrequent.

While the explanations above are specific to our task of style-conditioned poetry generation, the more general problem of deep models learning dataset artifacts or shortcuts that exploit low-level statistical regularities has often been remarked upon in recent years: Such observations have been made for natural language inference (Poliak et al., 2018) and argumentation mining (Niven and Kao, 2019), among many other tasks.

In the following subsection, we re-evaluate our findings using a different model architecture trained on more data.

4.4 Using GPT-2 instead of an RNN

In order to explore the capabilities of a transformer model over a generic RNN, we also tuned style-conditioned GPT-2 models on poetry. The main advantage of GPT-2 (based on transformer networks) over standardly trained RNNs is their transfer learning ability: While a standardly trained RNN needs to learn language modelling capabilities only from small amounts of poetry data, GPT-2 is already equipped with general language modelling abilities, obtained from having seen billions of tokens of written English. This makes the output of GPT-2 much more semantically coherent, fluent, and grammatically correct. Nevertheless, we believe that even GPT-2 may have the same problems learning poetry-specific characteristics such as rhyme, metre, and alliteration that our RNN

And much, in fact, this lesser world can show
Of grief and crime that in the greater grow
"You saw," said George, "in that still-hated school
How the meek suffer, how the haughty rule

Table 2: Example pseudo-quatrain in our data for GPT-2, with (predicted) rhyme scheme 'aabb', negative sentiment, and 18th-century time period.

had, presumably because these characteristics have low statistical support in the pre-trained data (e.g., Wikipedia) and for the other reasons named above. We therefore conducted two sets of experiments concerning the generation of style-conditioned poetry where the conditions include rhyme, sentiment, and the time epoch of the poetry to be produced, in English poetry.

Rhyme, sentiment, time epoch. We used a GPT-2 model[6] trained on a larger English poetry corpus[7] that additionally contains information about the time period in which the poems were written; we used pseudo-quatrains (any consecutive sequence of four lines), amounting to over 770K unique examples.[8] A sample pseudo-quatrain from the data is shown in Table 2.

Since GPT-2 can more naturally be run with discrete input text, we trained the model on the 24 different rhyming patterns ('abab', 'abcd', etc.) that we found in the corpus, three sentiment values (positive, negative, neutral), and five different time periods (16th to 20th centuries). We determine the sentiment of a newly generated poem as above but using thresholding (e.g., a poem has a positive sentiment if it has more positive than negative terms), rhyming is predicted as for the RNN, and the time period is learned on the annotated data using a multi-layer perceptron. We tested various hyperparameter configurations and in all cases observed the same result: the model has great difficulty learning rhyming, but can capture the other two stylistic features. The last two phenomena are informed largely by lexical choice while rhyming is informed by sublexical information. To illustrate, with the default configuration, we see accuracy of 7.5% for rhyming (with a random baseline performance of 4.2%), 63% for sentiment (random baseline of 33%) and 63% for time period (random performance of 20%) when generating about 5,000 poems with the desired styles. Even though the model is not entirely at the random guessing baseline for rhyming, it does not perform much above it and is considerably below the majority baseline of 22% (always producing a poem with 'aabb' rhyme style). Also, the rhyme scheme predicted best by far is 'abcd' involving no rhyming. This requires the model not to rhyme, which the model then also satisfies. Here, the model satisfies 53% of all such user constraints, while it satisfies only 0.4% of more complex constraints such as 'aabb'.

[6]https://huggingface.co/gpt2

[7]https://github.com/tnhaider/english-gutenberg-poetry

[8]Our model is available at https://github.com/thekhangnguyen/poetry-gen.

5 Concluding remarks

Traditional, 'formal' poetry is characterized by intricate form that often expresses itself on the sound level: among the key features are rhyme, metre, and alliteration. Computational treatments typically handle these phenomena by hard-coding them as in purely symbolic AI, by exploiting dataset-specific properties (Lau et al., 2018), or by having models pay special attention to the phenomena in question (e.g., making the models concentrate on the character-level structure of line-ending words) (Jhamtani et al., 2019). However, as we show, current models still seem unable to learn sound-level stylistic aspects from examples alone, without priming them, and *even when we specifically condition on such features*. This raises the question of where this discrepancy between human and machine text processing (Eger et al., 2019) comes from and how it can be addressed *in the general case*. We envision several solutions for future work: It is possible that end-to-end modelling of phonetic stylistic features is an *emergent* phenomenon that appears once dataset sizes are large enough; it is also possible that datasets need to be sufficiently clean (e.g., containing only very few different rhyming schemes); or that new model architectures, which do not operate on words or sublexical units, are required (Xue et al., 2021).

Acknowledgments

This work has been supported by the Austrian Science Fund (FWF) under project M 2625-N31 and by the German Research Foundation as part of the Research Training Group Adaptive Preparation of Information from Heterogeneous Sources (AIPHES) at the Technische Universität Darmstadt under grant GRK 1994/1.

References

Rajat Agarwal and Katharina Kann. 2020. Acrostic poem generation. In *Proc. EMNLP*, pages 1230–1240.

Manex Agirrezabal, Iñaki Alegria, and Mans Hulden. 2016. Machine learning for metrical analysis of English poetry. In *Proc. COLING*, pages 772–781.

Timo Baumann, Hussein Hussein, and Burkhard Meyer-Sickendiek. 2018. Style detection for free verse poetry from text and speech. In *Proc. COLING*, pages 1929–1940.

M. H. Beissinger. 2012. Oral poetry. In R. Greene *et al.*, editor, *The Princeton Encyclopedia of Poetry and Poetics*, 4th edition, pages 978–81. Princeton University Press.

Tom Brown, Benjamin Mann, Nick Ryder, Melanie Subbiah, Jared D Kaplan, Prafulla Dhariwal, Arvind Neelakantan, Pranav Shyam, Girish Sastry, Amanda Askell, Sandhini Agarwal, Ariel Herbert-Voss, Gretchen Krueger, Tom Henighan, Rewon Child, Aditya Ramesh, Daniel Ziegler, Jeffrey Wu, Clemens Winter, Chris Hesse, Mark Chen, Eric Sigler, Mateusz Litwin, Scott Gray, Benjamin Chess, Jack Clark, Christopher Berner, Sam McCandlish, Alec Radford, Ilya Sutskever, and Dario Amodei. 2020. Language models are few-shot learners. In *Advances in Neural Information Processing Systems*, volume 33, pages 1877–1901. Curran Associates, Inc.

Simon Colton, Jacob Goodwin, and Tony Veale. 2012. Full-FACE poetry generation. In *Proc. 3rd International Conference on Computational Creativity*, pages 95–102.

Steffen Eger, Gözde Gül Şahin, Andreas Rücklé, Ji-Ung Lee, Claudia Schulz, Mohsen Mesgar, Krishnkant Swarnkar, Edwin Simpson, and Iryna Gurevych. 2019. Text processing like humans do: Visually attacking and shielding NLP systems. In *Proc. NAACL*, volume 1, pages 1634–1647.

Alex Estes and Christopher Hench. 2016. Supervised machine learning for hybrid meter. In *Proc. 5th Workshop on Comp. Ling. for Literature*, pages 1–8.

Nigel Fabb and Morris Halle. 2010. *Meter in Poetry: A New Theory*. Cambridge University Press.

Jessica Ficler and Yoav Goldberg. 2017. Controlling linguistic style aspects in neural language generation. In *Proc. Workshop on Stylistic Variation*, pages 94–104.

Vikas Ganjigunte Ashok, Song Feng, and Yejin Choi. 2013. Success with style: Using writing style to predict the success of novels. In *Proc. EMNLP*, pages 1753–1764.

Pablo Gervás. 2001. An expert system for the composition of formal Spanish poetry. *Knowledge-based Syst.*, 14(3–4):181–188.

Marjan Ghazvininejad, Yejin Choi, and Kevin Knight. 2018. Neural poetry translation. In *Proc. NAACL*, volume 2, pages 67–71.

Marjan Ghazvininejad, Xing Shi, Jay Priyadarshi, and Kevin Knight. 2017. Hafez: An interactive poetry generation system. In *Proc. ACL (System Demonstrations)*, pages 43–48.

Hugo Gonçalo Oliveira. 2013. PoeTryMe: A versatile platform for poetry generation. In *Proc. Workshop on Computational Creativity, Concept Invention, and General Intelligence*, volume 1-2012, pages 21–26.

Hugo Gonçalo Oliveira, Raquel Hervás, Alberto Díaz, and Pablo Gervás. 2017. Multilingual extension and evaluation of a poetry generator. *Nat. Lang. Eng.*, 23(6):929–967.

Erica Greene, Tugba Bodrumlu, and Kevin Knight. 2010. Automatic analysis of rhythmic poetry with applications to generation and translation. In *Proc. EMNLP*, pages 524–533.

Thomas Haider and Steffen Eger. 2019. Semantic change and emerging tropes in a large corpus of New High German poetry. In *Proc. 1st International Workshop on Computational Approaches to Historical Language Change*, pages 216–222.

Thomas Haider, Steffen Eger, Kim Evgeny, Roman Klinger, and Winfried Menninghaus. 2020. PO-EMO: Conceptualization, annotation, and modeling of aesthetic emotions in German and English poetry. In *Proc. LREC*, pages 1652–1663.

Thomas Haider and Jonas Kuhn. 2018. Supervised rhyme detection with Siamese recurrent networks. In *Proc. LaTeCH-CLfL*, pages 81–86.

Mika Hämäläinen and Khalid Alnajjar. 2019. Let's FACE it. Finnish poetry generation with aesthetics and framing. In *Proc. 12th International Conference on Natural Language Generation*, pages 290–300.

Aurélie Herbelot. 2015. The semantics of poetry: A distributional reading. *Digit. Scholarsh. Humanit.*, 30(4):516–531.

J. Berenike Herrmann, Karina van Dalen-Oskam, and Christof Schöch. 2015. Revisiting style, a key concept in literary studies. *J. Lit. Theory*, 9(1):25–52.

Jack Hopkins and Douwe Kiela. 2017. Automatically generating rhythmic verse with neural networks. In *Proc. ACL*, volume 1, pages 168–178.

Minqing Hu and Bing Liu. 2004. Mining and summarizing customer reviews. In *Proc. ACM SIGKDD*, pages 168–177.

Roman Jakobson. 1960. Linguistics and poetics. In *Style in Language*, pages 350–377. MIT Press.

Harsh Jhamtani, Sanket Vaibhav Mehta, Jaime Carbonell, and Taylor Berg-Kirkpatrick. 2019. Learning rhyming constraints using structured adversaries. In *Proc. EMNLP/IJCNLP*, pages 6025–6031.

Justine T. Kao and Dan Jurafsky. 2015. A computational analysis of poetic style: Imagism and its influence on modern professional and amateur poetry. *Linguist. Issues Lang. Technol.*, 12(3):1–31.

Vaibhav Kesarwani, Diana Inkpen, Stan Szpakowicz, and Chris Tanasescu. 2017. Metaphor detection in a poetry corpus. In *Proc. LaTeCH-CLfL*, pages 1–9.

Diederik P. Kingma and Jimmy Ba. 2014. Adam: A method for stochastic optimization. *arXiv e-prints*, 1412.6980.

Reinhard Kneser and Hermann Ney. 1995. Improved backing-off for m-gram language modeling. In *Proc. 1995 International Conference on Acoustics, Speech, and Signal Processing*, volume 1, pages 181–184.

Jey Han Lau, Trevor Cohn, Timothy Baldwin, Julian Brooke, and Adam Hammond. 2018. Deep-speare: A joint neural model of poetic language, meter and rhyme. In *Proc. ACL*, volume 1, pages 1948–1958.

Bei Liu, Jianlong Fu, Makoto P. Kato, and Masatoshi Yoshikawa. 2018. Beyond narrative description: Generating poetry from images by multi-adversarial training. In *Proc. 26th ACM International Conference on Multimedia*, pages 783–791.

Enrique Manjavacas, Mike Kestemont, and Folgert Karsdorp. 2019. Generation of hip-hop lyrics with hierarchical modeling and conditional templates. In *Proc. 12th International Conference on Natural Language Generation*, pages 301–310.

Hisar Maruli Manurung, Graeme Ritchie, and Henry Thompson. 2000. Towards a computational model of poetry generation. In *Proc. AISB Symposium on Creative and Cultural Aspects and Applications of AI and Cognitive Science*, pages 79–86.

Winfried Menninghaus, Valentin Wagner, Eugen Wassiliwizky, Thomas Jacobsen, and Christine A Knoop. 2017. The emotional and aesthetic powers of parallelistic diction. *Poetics*, 63:47–59.

Rada Mihalcea and Carlo Strapparava. 2006. Learning to laugh (automatically): Computational models for humor recognition. *Comp. Intel.*, 22(2):126–142.

Tomas Mikolov, Kai Chen, Greg Corrado, and Jeffrey Dean. 2013. Efficient estimation of word representations in vector space. *arXiv e-prints*, 1301.3781.

Timothy Niven and Hung-Yu Kao. 2019. Probing neural network comprehension of natural language arguments. In *Proc. ACL*, pages 4658–4664.

Kishore Papineni, Salim Roukos, Todd Ward, and Wei-Jing Zhu. 2002. BLEU: A method for automatic evaluation of machine translation. In *Proc. ACL*, pages 311–318.

Adam Poliak, Jason Naradowsky, Aparajita Haldar, Rachel Rudinger, and Benjamin Van Durme. 2018. Hypothesis only baselines in natural language inference. In *Proc. 7th Joint Conference on Lexical and Computational Semantics*, pages 180–191.

Alec Radford, Jeff Wu, Rewon Child, David Luan, Dario Amodei, and Ilya Sutskever. 2019. Language models are unsupervised multitask learners. Article on openai.com.

Sravana Reddy and Kevin Knight. 2011. Unsupervised discovery of rhyme schemes. In *Proc. ACL*, pages 77–82.

Nils Reimers and Iryna Gurevych. 2017. Reporting score distributions makes a difference: Performance study of LSTM-networks for sequence tagging. In *Proc. EMNLP*, pages 338–348.

Ines Reinig and Ines Rehbein. 2019. Metaphor detection for German poetry. In *Proc. KONVENS*, pages 149–160.

Pablo Ruiz, Clara Martínez Cantón, Thierry Poibeau, and Elena González-Blanco. 2017. Enjambment detection in a large diachronic corpus of spanish sonnets. In *Proc. LaTeCH-CLfL*, pages 27–32.

Victor Shlovsky. 1965. Art as technique. In Lee T. Lemon and Marion J. Reis, editors, *Russian Formalist Criticism: Four Essays*, pages 3–24. University of Nebraska Press.

Ilya Sutskever, James Martens, and Geoffrey Hinton. 2011. Generating text with recurrent neural networks. In *Proc. 28th International Conference on Machine Learning*, pages 1017–1024.

Tim Van de Cruys. 2020. Automatic poetry generation from prosaic text. In *Proc. ACL*, pages 2471–2480.

Ashish Vaswani, Noam Shazeer, Niki Parmar, Jakob Uszkoreit, Llion Jones, Aidan N. Gomez, Łukasz Kaiser, and Illia Polosukhin. 2017. Attention is all you need. In *Advances in Neural Information Processing Systems 30*, pages 5998–6008. Curran Associates.

Ulli Waltinger. 2010. GermanPolarityClues: A lexical resource for German sentiment analysis. In *Proc. LREC*, pages 1638–1642.

Kento Watanabe, Yuichiroh Matsubayashi, Satoru Fukayama, Masataka Goto, Kentaro Inui, and Tomoyasu Nakano. 2018. A melody-conditioned lyrics language model. In *Proc. NAACL*, volume 1, pages 163–172.

Linting Xue, Aditya Barua, Noah Constant, Rami Al-Rfou, Sharan Narang, Mihir Kale, Adam Roberts, and Colin Raffel. 2021. Byt5: Towards a token-free future with pre-trained byte-to-byte models.

Xingxing Zhang and Mirella Lapata. 2014. Chinese poetry generation with recurrent neural networks. In *Proc. EMNLP*, pages 670–680.

Emotion Classification in German Plays with Transformer-based Language Models Pretrained on Historical and Contemporary Language

Thomas Schmidt
Media Informatics Group
University of Regensburg, Germany
thomas.schmidt@ur.de

Katrin Dennerlein
German Literary Studies
University of Würzburg, Germany
katrin.dennerlein@uni-wuerzburg.de

Christian Wolff
Media Informatics Group
University of Regensburg, Germany
christian.wolff@ur.de

Abstract

We present results of a project on emotion classification on historical German plays of *Enlightenment*, *Storm and Stress*, and *German Classicism*. We have developed a hierarchical annotation scheme consisting of 13 sub-emotions like *suffering*, *love* and *joy* that sum up to 6 main and 2 polarity classes (positive/negative). We have conducted textual annotations on 11 German plays and have acquired over 13,000 emotion annotations by two annotators per play. We have evaluated multiple traditional machine learning approaches as well as transformer-based models pretrained on historical and contemporary language for a single-label text sequence emotion classification for the different emotion categories. The evaluation is carried out on three different instances of the corpus: (1) taking all annotations, (2) filtering overlapping annotations by annotators, (3) applying a heuristic for speech-based analysis. Best results are achieved on the filtered corpus with the best models being large transformer-based models pretrained on contemporary German language. For the polarity classification accuracies of up to 90% are achieved. The accuracies become lower for settings with a higher number of classes, achieving 66% for 13 sub-emotions. Further pretraining of a historical model with a corpus of dramatic texts led to no improvements.

1 Introduction

Transformer-based language models like BERT (Devlin et al., 2019) and ELECTRA (Clark et al., 2019) have recently gained a lot of attention and achieve state-of-the-art results for various tasks in natural language processing (NLP) (Qiu et al., 2020). These language models are usually trained via deep learning on large amounts of texts acquired from the internet. Unlike previous methods in NLP, these models use context-sensitive word representations and they can better deal with out-of-vocabulary words. These attributes are, of course, advantageous for various text sorts in digital humanities (DH) and computational literary studies (CLS). Furthermore, transformer-based language models can be adapted to specific domain texts by either training a model from scratch on large amounts of these texts or taking an existing model and further pretraining it with domain-specific texts (Beltagy et al., 2019; Gururangan et al., 2020; Rietzler et al., 2020). Transformer-based models as well as these approaches have been successfully applied in DH contexts with historical or poetic German texts for named entity recognition (NER) (Schweter and Baiter, 2019; Labusch et al., 2019) and speech type recognition (Brunner et al., 2020). We present a study for the task of textual emotion classification in the same line of research for the use case of German historical plays.

Emotion classification deals with the prediction of (multiple) emotion categories in text. Its neighbouring field sentiment analysis primarily focuses on the prediction of the overall polarity (or valence) of a text, meaning if it is rather positive or negative (Mäntylä et al., 2018). Both methods have been explored in DH and CLS to analyze emotion/sentiment distributions and progressions in social media (Schmidt et al., 2020b) or literary texts like plays (Nalisnick and Baird, 2013; Schmidt and Burghardt, 2018; Schmidt et al., 2019b; Schmidt, 2019), novels (Zehe et al., 2016; Reagan et al., 2016) and fairy tales (Alm and Sproat, 2005; Mo-

Proceedings of LaTeCH-CLfL 2021, pages 67–79
Punta Cana, Dominican Republic (Online), November 11, 2021.

hammad, 2011) (see Kim and Klinger (2019) for an in-depth review of this research area). However, as the review of Kim and Klinger (2019) and recent tool developments in DH show (Schmidt et al., 2021a), the application of rather basic lexicon-based methods is frequent although these methods are usually outperformed by more modern approaches in sentiment and emotion classification (Cao et al., 2020; Dang et al., 2020; Cortiz, 2021; González-Carvajal and Garrido-Merchán, 2021) and are especially problematic for literary texts (Fehle et al., 2021). Furthermore, performance evaluation of computational approaches compared to human annotations ("gold standard") are rare. Thus, we present an evaluation study for the use case of German historical plays (from *Enlightenment, Storm and Stress* and *German Classicism*) for emotion classification. Our goal is to develop emotion classification algorithms with a satisfactory performance for the described use case to investigate in later stages of our research, for example, emotion progressions throughout time or genre-based differences concerning emotion distributions on a larger set of plays. We primarily focus on current state-of-the-art transformer-based language models.

The main contributions of this paper are as follows: (1) the development of an emotion annotation scheme directed towards the interest of literary scholars for the time frame of our corpus, (2) the annotation results for the annotation of 11 plays by 2 annotators for each play, (3) a systematic evaluation of traditional textual machine learning (ML)-approaches, transformer-based models pretrained on contemporary and historical language and further pretrained on dramatic texts on different instances of the annotated corpus. The goal of this contribution is to work towards the development of emotion classification algorithms with a satisfactory performance for the described use case.

2 Training and Evaluation Corpus

In the following section, we describe the conceptual framework and process for the acquisition of the annotated corpus that serves as training and evaluation corpus for the emotion classification ("Gold Standard").

2.1 Emotion Scheme

The main goal of the scheme development was to create an annotation scheme that includes the interests of literary scholars and the interpretative and historical dimensions of these literary texts. Common emotion annotation schemes in NLP are mostly inspired by psychology, oftentimes consisting of 6-8 established emotion classes (cf. Wood et al., 2018a,b). However, we regard these concept sets as unfit for our specific case, since important emotion and affect concepts from the perspective of literary criticism for the time of our plays are missing, while other concepts are not specifically important for our text genre. Thus, we developed a novel annotation scheme based on literary theory and redesigned the scheme in an iterative process of small pilot annotations and discussions. Our final scheme deviates heavily from more common schemes in emotion annotation in NLP. Some concepts well-known in NLP and psychology are included like *joy*, *fear* or *anger* while other standard emotion concepts like *disgust* and *surprise* showed in pilot annotations to be not of great importance. Concepts, important for literary critique for that time that are not usually regarded as emotions, that we include are *desire*, *suffering* or *compassion*. Please refer to Schmidt et al., (2021b) for more information about the scheme creation and the annotation process.

The final scheme consists of 13 *sub-emotions* that are hierarchically clustered including one special concept (*emotional movement*). The *sub-emotions* are summarized in six *main classes* which can then be clustered in a final binary setting of two classes (similar to sentiment): (per default) positive and negative emotions (marked in the upcoming list as + and - respectively; we refer to this concept as *polarity*). In the following list we name the *sub-emotions* and *main classes* with the original German term in brackets (since we perform annotations in German) and an English translation.

- emotions of affection (*Emotionen der Zuneigung*)
  - desire (*Lust*) (+)
  - love (*Liebe*) (+)
  - friendship (*Freundschaft*) (+)
  - admiration (*Verehrung*) (+)
- emotions of joy (*Emotionen der Freude*)
  - joy (*Freude*) (+)

- Schadenfreude (The joy about the misfortune of others) (+)

- emotions of fear *(Emotionen der Angst)*
  - fear *(Angst)* (-)
  - despair *(Verzweiflung)* (-)
- emotions of rejection *(Emotionen der Ablehnung)*
  - anger *(Ärger)* (-)
  - hate, disgust *(Hass, Abscheu)* (-)
- emotions of suffering *(Emotionen des Leids)*
  - suffering *(Leid)* (-)
  - compassion *(Mitleid)* (-)
- emotional movement

Emotional movement has no polarity and is used to describe astonishment, emotional turmoil, excitation and oscillation between several emotions. We will refer to the combination of the *positive*- and the *negative*-class as well as *emotional movement* as *triple polarity*. The various hierarchical structures are later used for classification approaches with different class numbers.

2.2 Annotation Process

Annotators are instructed to assign sub-emotions, as defined in our scheme, to text. We regard the character's state of mind as expressed in the text as the emotion to be annotated. Annotations are performed context-sensitive, meaning annotators should take into account the plot and content of the entire play and annotate what the character really means as determined by the literary interpretation. Thus, plays are read and annotated from beginning to end concerning *stage directions* and *speeches* (single utterances of characters separated by the utterances of other characters). Depending on the emotional expression in the text, annotators can mark text sequences of varied lengths (ranging from one word to an entire speech) and are not limited to a concrete annotation size. Furthermore, annotators can annotate multiple annotations per text sequence fully or partially (see figure 1) and adjust the default polarity of sub-emotions for certain cases. The annotation procedure just presented is closer to the interpretation process of literary scholars than context-free approaches with fixed text sizes for annotation attribution that are more common in NLP (Mäntylä et al., 2018). It has been deemed as more fitting throughout multiple pilot annotations with literary scholars.

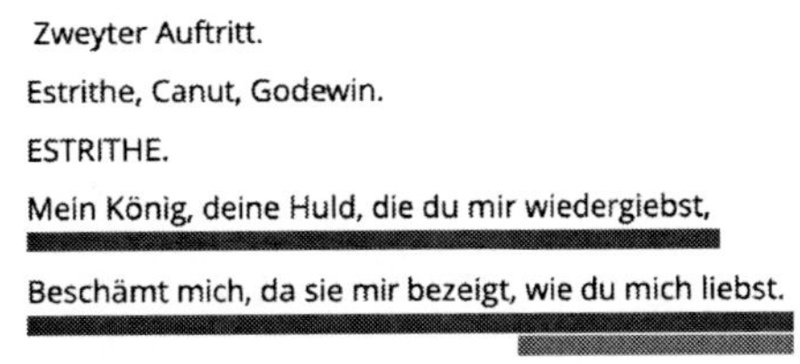

Figure 1: Example annotation in CATMA. The annotator marked two lines as *suffering* (purple), and the last part additionally as *love* (blue). (Excerpt from *Canut*)

The annotation process itself is performed with the tool CATMA[1] (Gius et al., 2020). Two annotators annotate each play independently from each other in a time span of 1-2 weeks depending on the length of the play. All annotators are students of German literary studies and are compensated monetarily for the annotation. They have access to an annotation instruction manual with descriptions of the scheme and examples. They also participated in test annotations under the guidance of an expert literary scholar. Indeed, the entire annotation process is iterative (cf. Reiter, 2020) meaning scheme and instructions changed based on feedback throughout the project cycle and might be due to change (the study presented here has been performed consistently in the way described, however).

2.3 Annotated Plays

As part of our larger project, we intend to analyze emotion classification on historical German plays between 1650-1815. Our current corpus of plays consists of around 300 digitized plays. For this evaluation study, we annotated a representative sub-corpus of 11 plays of varying epochs and genres. However, we focus on more recent plays for this first evaluation study since older ones are more likely to pose more challenges to the applied language models:

- *Das Testament* by Gottsched (1745/comedy)
- *Canut* by Schlegel (1746/tragedy)
- *Die zärtlichen Schwestern* by Gellert (1747/comedy)
- *Lucie Woodvil* by Pfeil (1757/tragedy)

[1] https://catma.de/

- *Der Freigeist* by Brawe (1758/tragedy)
- *Minna von Barnhelm* by Lessing (1767/comedy)
- *Der Postzug* by Ayrenhoff (1769/comedy)
- *Kabale und Liebe* by Schiller (1784/tragedy)
- *Kasperl' der Mandolettikrämer* by Eberl (1789/tragedy)
- *Menschenhass und Reue* by Kotzebue (1790/comedy)
- *Faust* by Goethe (1807/tragedy)

Most of the plays were acquired as part of the *GerDracor*-Corpus (Fischer et al., 2019) except for *Kasperl' der Mandolettikrämer* which was acquired via an open web repository.[2]

2.4 Annotation Statistics

Depending on the length of a play, the annotation duration for each play was 8-15 hours in absolute numbers. We collected 13,264 annotations of varying lengths. Table 1 illustrates the distributions for the *sub-emotions* as well as the resulting sums for the *main classes*.

Emotion category	absolute	%
MC: emotions of affection	2,928	22
desire	52	0
love	1,755	13
friendship	345	3
admiration	776	6
MC: emotions of joy	1,943	15
joy	1,619	12
Schadenfreude	324	2
MC: emotions of fear	1,257	9
fear	721	5
despair	536	4
MC: emotions of rejection	3,028	23
anger	1,625	12
hate, disgust	1,403	11
MC: emotions of suffering	2,700	20
suffering	2,069	16
compassion	631	5
emotional movement	1,408	11
Overall	13,264	100

Table 1: Distribution of emotion categories. First, the summed results of the *main classes* (MC; marked in bold) are listed followed by the *sub-emotions*. Percentages are rounded.

The most frequent *sub-emotion* are *suffering* (16%) and *love* (13%) and the *emotions of rejection* and (23%) *affection* (22%) for the *main classes* respectively. The overall distribution is rather imbalanced with certain sub-emotions being rarely annotated (e.g. *desire*). Considering the overall *triple polarity*, the majority of annotations are *negative* (53%), followed by *positive* (37%) and *emotional movement* (11%). We also examined token statistics about annotation lengths: On average an annotation consists of 25 tokens, however with a large variance ranging from 1-token annotations to multiple sentences consisting of over 500 tokens. This shows that annotators make significant use of the possibility of varied annotation lengths.

Due to the varied annotation lengths, calculating inter-annotator agreement is not possible with common metrics. However, to get an overall understanding of the agreement we calculate agreement according to the following speech-based heuristic: For each speech, the emotion that is annotated the most per speech (measured in number of tokens) is assigned the specific emotion (or a neutral class if no emotion is annotated) for each annotator. This results in a *Cohen's* κ value of 0.5 for *polarity* (percentage wise agreement: 68%) and 0.4 for *main classes* (62%) and *sub-emotions* (58%) respectively. This is regarded as moderate agreement (Landis and Koch, 1977), which is low compared with sentiment analysis research with other text sorts (cf. Mäntylä et al., 2018) but in line with similar annotation projects with literary and historical texts (Alm and Sproat, 2005; Sprugnoli et al., 2015; Schmidt et al., 2018, 2019a,c; Öhman, 2020; Schmidt et al., 2020a).

2.5 Corpus Manifestations

Due to the varied annotation text sequence lengths and the moderate agreement statistics, we evaluated and trained the chosen emotion classification approaches on different "manifestations" of our corpus. We refer to the first one as *full corpus*. This manifestation includes all text annotations of the two annotators for every play. Thus, it does include annotations for which the annotators disagree upon fully or partially. This is the largest corpus manifestation consisting of 13,264 annotations (for more statistics see table 1). For the classification of

[2] http://lithes.uni-graz.at/maezene/eberl_mandolettikraemer.html

polarity, we reduce corpora by filtering out annotations with *emotional movement*, which results in 11,883 annotations for the *full corpus*. The second manifestation is referred to as *filtered corpus*. For this corpus instance, we filter out all annotations for which annotators either fully or partially disagree, meaning annotations of different categories that overlap at least for one token. We do not filter out annotated text sequences by one annotator that are not annotated by the other one. We do however filter all overlapping contrary annotations by a single annotator. While our annotation scheme enables these kind of annotations, we want to evaluate how the filtering of all contrary overlaps influences emotion classification. Depending of the emotion hierarchy, this results in different annotation numbers for the final filtered corpus: 9,962 (*polarity*), 10,247 (*triple polarity*), 8,552 (*main class*), 7,503 (*sub-emotions*). Thus, the filtering reduces the corpus size between 15-44% depending of the categorical system.

The last manifestation, the *speech corpus*, is focused on the central units of plays: speeches and stage directions. It is designed as follows: Each speech (we include stage directions in the following when speaking about speeches) of the plays is assigned with the emotion category that is annotated the most by both annotators (as measured by number of tokens). If tied among multiple classes, the class is assigned that is overall chosen the least (to counteract class imbalances). The entire corpus consists of 11,617 speeches; we filter out speeches with no annotation by either annotator to avoid adding an extra neutral-like class to our already multi-class setting (adding neutrality is something we intend to explore in future work). This reduces the amount of speeches to 6,741 and affects especially stage directions which are rarely annotated. We apply the above heuristic to acquire emotion assignments. Please note that emotion distributions change compared to the other manifestations since underrepresented classes become even more rare due to the applied heuristic; thus the class imbalances intensify. Distribution statistics for the *filtered* and *speech corpus* can be found in the appendix (table 6, 7, 8).

We separate the corpus in these three manifestations in order to explore performance on different classification levels and text sizes, which will influence our decision for later large-scale emotion prediction tasks on larger corpora of plays which we plan for future stages of our project.

3 Emotion Classification Methods

We regard the emotion classification as single-label classification on text sequences of varied lengths. The amount of classes differs depending on the hierarchical system: *polarity* (2 classes), *triple valence* (3 classes), *main classes* (6), *sub-emotions* (13). We have implemented reference baselines based on traditional ML-approaches but otherwise focus on transformer-based language models for German pretrained on contemporary and historical texts since transformer-based models have been shown to achieve state-of-the-art results for emotion classification (Shmueli and Ku, 2019; Yang et al., 2019; Cao et al., 2020) and performed best in a pre-study (Schmidt et al., 2021c). We also explore further fine-tuning/pretraining of a pretrained model with our domain texts since research suggests performance improvements for this method (Beltagy et al., 2019; Gururangan et al., 2020; Rietzler et al., 2020).

3.1 Baseline Methods

The following "classical" ML-methods for text are implemented (methods like this are usually outperformed by transformer-based approaches in other settings (González-Carvajal and Garrido-Merchán, 2021) and thus serve as lower baselines in the following evaluation): (1) Representation of text units with term frequencies in a bag-of-words model and subsequently *Multinomial Naive Bayes* as training algorithm. (2) Same representation format as above but *Support Vector Machines* as training algorithm.

We implemented the approaches with the *scikit-learn machine learning library*[3] (Pedregosa et al., 2011) and trained and evaluated the algorithms in a stratified 5x5 cross evaluation setting. We refer to the first approach as *bow-nb* and the second one as *bow-svm*. We will also report the random and majority baseline for each classification task. Please note that depending on the corpus type, these values migh vary.

3.2 Transformer-based Models

We selected the (to our knowledge) most well-known and established transformer-based language models in German that are freely available. Table 2 summarizes the selected models (the identifiers

[3]https://scikit-learn.org/stable/

are used in the following to reference the models). All models are acquired via the *Hugging Face platform*[4] and are also implemented with the corresponding library (Wolf et al., 2020).

One main point of interest are performance differences between models pretrained on contemporary texts (e.g. like the *Wikipedia*, subtitles etc.) for general purpose tasks and models pretrained on historical texts (e.g. historical newspapers, historical fictional texts). In Table 2 we attribute the label "historical" to a model if a significant part of the texts dates from before the 20th century. We want to evaluate if these models perform better since the language is closer to the ones of our plays, which are of the 18th and 19th century.

For the contemporary models, we evaluate, among others, the models *gbert-large* and *gelectra-large* by *Deepset*[5] which achieve state-of-the-art results in standardized NLP-tasks (Chan et al., 2020) and are, to our knowledge, the largest German BERT- and ELECTRA-based models. On the historical side, we evaluate two models provided by the European Digital Library *Europeana* pretrained on historical newspaper (Schweter and Baiter, 2019; Schweter, 2020) and a model focused on fictional texts (Brunner et al., 2020). To perform the training and evaluation, each model is fine-tuned to the downstream task of emotion classification for the specific hierarchy and corpus. We apply the recommended settings for the training of downstream tasks, depending on the architecture: BERT (Devlin et al., 2019) or ELECTRA (Clark et al., 2019) as well as by the *Hugging Face*-library. Each model is fine-tuned for 4 epochs, a batch size of 32, learning rate of 4e-5 and *Adam* optimizer for stochastic gradient descent. The models are trained and evaluated in a 5x5 cross evaluation setting, thus averages over 5 runs are reported. As GPU a *Tesla P100* was used.

All of the above models are trained from scratch on large amounts of texts. However, recent research also suggests further pretraining of already existing models with texts that are close to the texts of the downstream task may improve results (domain-specific fine-tuning) (Gururangan et al., 2020; Rietzler et al., 2020). We explore this approach and further pretrain the model *bert-base-german-europeana-cased* solely with German dramatic texts that we acquired of our corpus sources (including the annotated texts). The texts consist of all German plays of *GerDracor* (Fischer et al., 2019), the platform *TextGrid*[6] and around 60 plays we acquired via various other sources. Altogether the texts sum up to 300 MB consisting of 1,224 plays that range from the 16th to the 20th century. We use the *simpletransformer*-library[7] and further pretrain the model *bert-base-german-europeana-cased* for 10 epochs. The setting and parameters for the emotion classification training are the same as for the general models. We refer to this model as *bert-europeana-further-pretrained.*

4 Results

We report accuracies and F1-scores for all models and category systems as well as corpus manifestations in tables 3, 4 and 5. Considering F1-scores, we report weighted F1 due to the imbalanced class distributions.

In general, transformer-based models outperform traditional ML-approaches. For every corpus manifestation the performance of the different transformer-based models is rather similar regardless whether contemporary or historical language is the basis for the pretraining. The best models are the large contemporary models *gbert-large* and *gelectra-large* achieving up to 90% for *polarity* (2 classes), 85% for *triple polarity* (3 classes), 75% for *main classes* (6 classes) and 66% *for sub-emotions* (13 classes) on the *filtered corpus*. The historical models perform rather similar but consistently slightly below the large contemporary ones, but also slightly above the smaller contemporary model *bert-base-german-europeana-cased*. Considering the different corpus manifestations, all models perform best on the *filtered corpus* and worst for the speech-based prediction. The difference becomes larger with increasing number of classes. For example, *gbert-large* achieves an accuracy of 75% for main class prediction on the *filtered corpus* which reduces to 51% on the *speech corpus*. As the analysis of recall and F1-macro statistics show, this is mostly due to the bad prediction accuracies for low-frequency classes.[8]

Further pretraining the model *bert-base-german-europeana-cased* with dramatic texts did not result

[4] https://huggingface.co/

[5] https://deepset.ai/german-bert

[6] https://textgrid.de/digitale-bibliothek

[7] https://simpletransformers.ai/

[8] Additional data about the results can be found via the following repository: https://github.com/lauchblatt/Emotions_in_Drama

Identifier	Hugging Face-identifier	Pretrained language	Pretrained texts and size if reported	Related paper (if available) and provider
bert-base	bert-base-german-cased	contemporary	Wikipedia, legal texts, news (~12 GB)	Deepset
gbert-large	gbert-large	contemporary	Crawled web data, Wikipedia, subtitles, book, legal texts (~161 GB)	Deepset (Chan et al., 2020)
gelectra-large	gelectra-large	contemporary	Crawled web data, Wikipedia, subtitles, book, legal texts (~161 GB)	Deepset (Chan et al., 2020)
bert-europeana	bert-base-german-europeana-cased	historical	*Europeana* newspaper (51 GB)	MDZ Digital Library (Schweter, 2020)
electra-europeana	electra-base-german-europeana-cased-discriminator	historical	*Europeana* newspaper (51 GB)	MDZ Digital Library (Schweter, 2020)
bert-historical-rw	bert-base-historical-german-rw-cased	historical	Fairy tales, historical newspapers, magazine articles, narrative texts, texts of Projekt Gutenberg	(Brunner et al., 2020)
bert-europeana-further-pretrained	-	contemporary, further pretrained on historical texts	Based on *bert-base-german-europeana-cased*. Further pretrained with dramatic texts of *GerDracor*, *TextGrid* and other (300 MB)	-

Table 2: Transformer-based models for the evaluation. *Hugging Face*-identifier can be used to retrieve the models from the *Hugging Face*-platform, bert-europeana-further-pretrained was created by the authors of this paper via further pretraining.

in improvements. Indeed, the accuracies become slightly worse and significantly lower looking at settings with multiple classes (e.g. 29% for *sub-emotions* on the *filtered corpus*).

5 Discussion and Future Work

As the results show, we can confirm general findings of NLP-research for classification tasks for various text genres, in the sense that transformer-based models perform better than traditional textual ML-approaches in our setting with German historical plays. However, we cannot confirm our assumption that models pretrained on historical language achieve better results because they are closer to the language of our annotated material. Indeed, the best performing models are *gbert-large* and *gelectra-large* by *deepset* (Chan et al., 2020). These are, to our knowledge, the largest German models trained on contemporary texts, primarly internet texts. The difference between historical and these contemporary models is however small. Since the differences in the amount of text for the pretraining are significant (around 20 GB) it opens up the question if the performance of historical models improves with similarly large amounts of texts.

Considering the different corpus instances, we showed that filtering out overlapping annotations annotators disagree upon results into the strongest performance boost, although the training and test size become smaller. Thus, it is crucial for our project to find ways to deal with disagreements among annotators. Due to the varied and overlapping annotation lengths, we cannot rely on standard solutions like majority voting. Furthermore, the inherent subjectivity of literary texts and the resulting low agreement among annotators is a specific feature of these kind of texts. We do however think that we can reduce disagreement with further training of the annotators and also by implementing a subsequent step after the first annotations of two annotators, in which a literary scholar expert creates a *consensus annotation* resolving disagreement. Additionally, we intend to switch from single-label classification to multi-label emotion classification since this is more in line with the annotation process. This will open up further possibilities to deal with overlapping annotations and integrates this phenomenon into the classification task. Applying a heuristic to map single emotion classes to entire speeches led to the models performing rather poorly compared to the other corpus manifestations. For *sub-emotion* prediction with 13 classes, accuracies became 25% worse for certain

Method	acc (pol)	F1 (pol)	acc (t-p)	F1 (t-p)	acc (m-c)	F1 (m-c)	acc (s-e)	F1 (s-e)
random baseline	0.50	-	0.33	-	0.17	-	0.08	-
majority baseline	0.59	-	0.53	-	0.23	-	0.16	-
bow-svm	0.74	0.72	0.66	0.62	0.47	0.45	0.35	0.32
bow-bayes	0.78	0.78	0.70	0.68	0.52	0.50	0.39	0.35
bert-base	0.83	0.83	0.76	0.76	0.60	0.60	0.49	0.48
bert-europeana	0.84	0.84	0.76	0.76	0.61	0.61	0.50	0.49
electra-europeana	0.84	0.84	0.77	0.76	0.61	0.61	0.50	0.48
bert-historical-rw	0.84	0.84	0.76	0.76	0.61	0.61	0.51	0.50
gbert-large	**0.85**	0.85	**0.78**	0.77	0.63	0.63	0.52	0.52
gelectra-large	**0.85**	0.85	**0.78**	0.78	**0.64**	0.64	**0.53**	0.52
bert-europeana-further-pretrained	0.81	0.81	0.74	0.71	0.53	0.50	0.38	0.32

Table 3: Evaluation results for the *full corpus*. F1-scores are weighted F1. pol=*polarity*, t-p=*triple polarity*, m-c=*main class*, s-e=*sub-emotion*. Best result per classification is marked in bold for accuracies.

Method	acc (pol)	F1 (pol)	acc (t-p)	F1 (t-p)	acc (m-c)	F1 (m-c)	acc (s-e)	F1 (s-e)
random baseline	0.50	-	0.33	-	0.17	-	0.08	-
majority baseline	0.60	-	0.55	-	0.25	-	0.15	-
bow-svm	0.77	0.75	0.70	0.66	0.53	0.51	0.41	0.38
bow-bayes	0.83	0.83	0.76	0.74	0.59	0.56	0.46	0.41
bert-base	0.88	0.88	0.83	0.83	0.70	0.70	0.61	0.60
bert-europeana	0.88	0.88	0.83	0.83	0.71	0.70	0.60	0.59
electra-europeana´	0.89	0.89	0.83	0.83	0.70	0.69	0.56	0.53
bert-historical-rw	0.88	0.88	0.83	0.83	0.72	0.72	0.63	0.63
gbert-large	0.89	0.89	0.84	0.84	**0.75**	0.75	**0.66**	0.66
gelectra-large	**0.90**	0.90	**0.85**	0.85	0.74	0.74	0.64	0.63
bert-europeana-further-pretrained	0.83	0.83	0.76	0.74	0.45	0.38	0.29	0.23

Table 4: Evaluation results for the *filtered corpus*. F1-scores are weighted F1. pol=*polarity*, t-p=*triple polarity*, m-c=*main class*, s-e=*sub-emotion*. Best result per classification is marked in bold for accuracies.

models. While one reason is that this corpus is the smallest of all manifestations, we argue that the main problem is, as annotations showed, that most speeches consist of multiple, oftentimes differing emotion categories. Mapping them heuristically to one results in text units including various emotional expressions that are falsely mapped to one emotion. This problem intensifies due to the fact that many speeches are rather long and that the class imbalances for *main classes* and *sub-emotions* are significant. Thus, we plan to focus on smaller text unit sizes like sentences or n-grams in the future emotion prediction task over the entire corpus.

Considering the results for *filtered* and *full corpus*, the transformer-based models achieve state-of-the-art accuracies for polarity classification (88-90%) compared to results with sentiment analysis with similar amounts of classes on contemporary German (Chan et al., 2020). The results achieved by the transformer-based models for *polarity* are also around 20% above results on German dramatic texts predicted by lexicon-based sentiment analysis, which yields results around 70% (Schmidt and Burghardt, 2018). For the *main class* and *sub-emotion* classification, results are, however, for the best models (75% for main classes, 66% for sub-emotions), below state-of-the-art results on emotion classification tasks with 4 or more classes for contemporary English texts for which accuracies of up to 86% are reported (Shmueli and Ku,

Method	acc (pol)	F1 (pol)	acc (t-p)	F1 (t-p)	acc (m-c)	F1 (m-c)	acc (s-e)	F1 (s-e)
random baseline	0.50	-	0.33	-	0.17	-	0.08	-
majority baseline	0.60	-	0.51	-	0.23	-	0.16	-
bow-svm	0.62	0.53	0.53	0.42	0.28	0.23	0.22	0.16
bow-bayes	0.70	0.69	0.59	0.55	0.39	0.36	0.29	0.25
bert-base	0.73	0.73	0.63	0.62	0.46	0.45	0.36	0.34
bert-europeana	0.72	0.69	0.66	0.65	0.48	0.47	0.37	0.35
electra-europeana	0.74	0.74	0.66	0.65	0.46	0.45	0.36	0.32
bert-historical-rw	0.74	0.74	0.64	0.64	0.47	0.47	0.39	0.37
gbert-large	**0.77**	0.77	0.67	0.67	**0.51**	0.51	**0.40**	0.39
gelectra-large	**0.77**	0.77	**0.68**	0.67	**0.51**	0.51	0.39	0.36
bert-europeana-further-pretrained	0.65	0.57	0.54	0.43	0.29	0.23	0.19	0.12

Table 5: Evaluation results for the *speech corpus*. F1-scores are weighted F1. pol=*polarity*, t-p=*triple polarity*, m-c=*main class*, s-e=*sub-emotion*. Best result per classification is marked in bold for accuracies.

2019; Yang et al., 2019; Cao et al., 2020), however, for the most part, with larger training corpora and fewer classes as in our setting. We intend to improve the performance to satisfactory levels by hyperparameter-tuning and especially by exploring recommended ML-methods like over- and undersampling to deal with the class imbalances (Buda et al., 2018), which is one of the main problems of the *main class* and *sub-emotion* classification.

Among all transformer-based models, the *bert-europeana*-model further pretrained on dramatic texts yields the lowest accuracies. The performance becomes especially low for *main classes* and *sub-emotions* (see table 4). A reason might be that, while research argues that further pretraining with even low amount of texts can show improvements, the amount of text used in our setting (300 MB) is below the amounts reported in similar research (Kameswara Sarma et al., 2018; Gururangan et al., 2020; Rietzler et al., 2020). The usage of solely dramatic texts instead of varied forms of texts for training might also lead to problems in generalizing the specific language of the annotated material. Furthermore, a significant proportion of the selected dramatic texts is actually of the middle to the end of the 19th century and also of the beginning of the 20th century. Thus, the language might again deviate strongly from the time span of our plays (1745-1807). This might also be a reason why the historical transformer-based models in our evaluation show no relevant improvements. Investigating the training corpora for these models (Schweter, 2020; Brunner et al., 2020) shows that large proportions of the texts are actually of the 19th and 20th century. For our future studies, we plan to continue our exploration of domain-specific fine-tuning by acquiring larger amounts of general text material (and not only dramatic texts) focused on the time span of our interest, 1650-1815, to train models from scratch and evaluate if we can identify performance improvements. We intend to achieve satisfactory levels of accuracies to perform large-scale analysis of emotion distributions and progressions for our entire corpus of around 300 plays.

Acknowledgements

We want to thank the following student annotators for their contributions to this project: Carlina Eizenberger, Viola Hipler, Emma Ruß, Leon Sautter and Lisa Schattmann.

Funding

This research is part of the project "Emotions in Drama" (Emotionen im Drama), funded by the German Research Foundation (DFG) and part of the priority programme SPP 2207 Computational Literary Studies (CLS).

References

Cecilia Ovesdotter Alm and Richard Sproat. 2005. Emotional Sequencing and Development in Fairy Tales. In *Affective Computing and Intelligent Interaction*, Lecture Notes in Computer Science, pages 668–674, Berlin, Heidelberg. Springer.

Iz Beltagy, Kyle Lo, and Arman Cohan. 2019. SciBERT: A Pretrained Language Model for Scientific Text. *arXiv:1903.10676 [cs]*. ArXiv: 1903.10676.

Annelen Brunner, Ngoc Duyen Tanja Tu, Lukas Weimer, and Fotis Jannidis. 2020. To bert or not to bert-comparing contextual embeddings in a deep learning architecture for the automatic recognition of four types of speech, thought and writing representation. In *SwissText/KONVENS*.

Mateusz Buda, Atsuto Maki, and Maciej A. Mazurowski. 2018. A systematic study of the class imbalance problem in convolutional neural networks. *Neural Networks*, 106:249–259. ArXiv: 1710.05381.

Lihong Cao, Sancheng Peng, Pengfei Yin, Yongmei Zhou, Aimin Yang, and Xinguang Li. 2020. A Survey of Emotion Analysis in Text Based on Deep Learning. In *2020 IEEE 8th International Conference on Smart City and Informatization (iSCI)*, pages 81–88, Guangzhou, China. IEEE.

Branden Chan, Stefan Schweter, and Timo Möller. 2020. German's Next Language Model. *arXiv:2010.10906 [cs]*. ArXiv: 2010.10906.

Kevin Clark, Minh-Thang Luong, Quoc V. Le, and Christopher D. Manning. 2019. ELECTRA: Pre-training Text Encoders as Discriminators Rather Than Generators.

Diogo Cortiz. 2021. Exploring Transformers in Emotion Recognition: a comparison of BERT, DistillBERT, RoBERTa, XLNet and ELECTRA. *arXiv:2104.02041 [cs]*. ArXiv: 2104.02041.

Nhan Cach Dang, María N. Moreno-García, and Fernando De la Prieta. 2020. Sentiment Analysis Based on Deep Learning: A Comparative Study. *Electronics*, 9(3):483. ArXiv: 2006.03541.

Jacob Devlin, Ming-Wei Chang, Kenton Lee, and Kristina Toutanova. 2019. BERT: Pre-training of deep bidirectional transformers for language understanding. In *Proceedings of the 2019 Conference of the North American Chapter of the Association for Computational Linguistics: Human Language Technologies, Volume 1 (Long and Short Papers)*, pages 4171–4186, Minneapolis, Minnesota. Association for Computational Linguistics.

Jakob Fehle, Thomas Schmidt, and Christian Wolff. 2021. Lexicon-based sentiment analysis in german: Systematic evaluation of resources and preprocessing techniques. In *Proceedings of the 17th Conference on Natural Language Processing (KONVENS 2021)*, Düsseldorf, Germany.

Frank Fischer, Ingo Börner, Mathias Göbel, Angelika Hechtl, Christopher Kittel, Carsten Milling, and Peer Trilcke. 2019. Programmable Corpora: Introducing DraCor, an Infrastructure for the Research on European Drama. Conference Name: Digital Humanities 2019: "Complexities" (DH2019) Publisher: Zenodo.

Evelyn Gius, Jan Christoph Meister, Marco Petris, Malte Meister, Christian Bruck, Janina Jacke, Mareike Schuhmacher, Marie Flüh, and Jan Horstmann. 2020. CATMA.

Santiago González-Carvajal and Eduardo C. Garrido-Merchán. 2021. Comparing BERT against traditional machine learning text classification. *arXiv:2005.13012 [cs, stat]*. ArXiv: 2005.13012.

Suchin Gururangan, Ana Marasović, Swabha Swayamdipta, Kyle Lo, Iz Beltagy, Doug Downey, and Noah A. Smith. 2020. Don't Stop Pretraining: Adapt Language Models to Domains and Tasks. *arXiv:2004.10964 [cs]*. ArXiv: 2004.10964.

Prathusha Kameswara Sarma, Yingyu Liang, and Bill Sethares. 2018. Domain Adapted Word Embeddings for Improved Sentiment Classification. In *Proceedings of the Workshop on Deep Learning Approaches for Low-Resource NLP*, pages 51–59, Melbourne. Association for Computational Linguistics.

Evgeny Kim and Roman Klinger. 2019. A Survey on Sentiment and Emotion Analysis for Computational Literary Studies. *Zeitschrift für digitale Geisteswissenschaften*. ArXiv: 1808.03137.

Kai Labusch, Clemens Neudecker, and David Zellhofer. 2019. BERT for Named Entity Recognition in Contemporary and Historical German. page 9.

J. Richard Landis and Gary G. Koch. 1977. The Measurement of Observer Agreement for Categorical Data. *Biometrics*, 33(1):159–174. Publisher: [Wiley, International Biometric Society].

Saif Mohammad. 2011. From Once Upon a Time to Happily Ever After: Tracking Emotions in Novels and Fairy Tales. In *Proceedings of the 5th ACL-HLT Workshop on Language Technology for Cultural Heritage, Social Sciences, and Humanities*, pages 105–114, Portland, OR, USA. Association for Computational Linguistics.

Mika V. Mäntylä, Daniel Graziotin, and Miikka Kuutila. 2018. The evolution of sentiment analysis—A review of research topics, venues, and top cited papers. *Computer Science Review*, 27:16–32.

Eric T. Nalisnick and Henry S. Baird. 2013. Character-to-Character Sentiment Analysis in Shakespeare's Plays. In *Proceedings of the 51st Annual Meeting of the Association for Computational Linguistics (Volume 2: Short Papers)*, pages 479–483, Sofia, Bulgaria. Association for Computational Linguistics.

Fabian Pedregosa, Gaël Varoquaux, Alexandre Gramfort, Vincent Michel, Bertrand Thirion, Olivier Grisel, Mathieu Blondel, Peter Prettenhofer, Ron Weiss, Vincent Dubourg, and others. 2011. Scikit-learn: Machine learning in Python. *Journal of machine learning research*, 12(Oct):2825–2830.

Xipeng Qiu, Tianxiang Sun, Yige Xu, Yunfan Shao, Ning Dai, and Xuanjing Huang. 2020. Pre-trained Models for Natural Language Processing: A Survey. *arXiv:2003.08271 [cs]*. ArXiv: 2003.08271.

Andrew J. Reagan, Lewis Mitchell, Dilan Kiley, Christopher M. Danforth, and Peter Sheridan Dodds. 2016. The emotional arcs of stories are dominated by six basic shapes. *EPJ Data Science*, 5(1):31. ArXiv: 1606.07772.

Nils Reiter. 2020. *Anleitung zur Erstellung von Annotationsrichtlinien*, pages 193–202. De Gruyter.

Alexander Rietzler, Sebastian Stabinger, Paul Opitz, and Stefan Engl. 2020. Adapt or Get Left Behind: Domain Adaptation through BERT Language Model Finetuning for Aspect-Target Sentiment Classification. In *Proceedings of the 12th Language Resources and Evaluation Conference*, pages 4933–4941, Marseille, France. European Language Resources Association.

Thomas Schmidt. 2019. Distant reading sentiments and emotions in historic german plays. In *Abstract Booklet, DH_Budapest_2019*, pages 57–60. Budapest, Hungary.

Thomas Schmidt and Manuel Burghardt. 2018. An Evaluation of Lexicon-based Sentiment Analysis Techniques for the Plays of Gotthold Ephraim Lessing. In *Proceedings of the Second Joint SIGHUM Workshop on Computational Linguistics for Cultural Heritage, Social Sciences, Humanities and Literature*, pages 139–149, Santa Fe, New Mexico. Association for Computational Linguistics.

Thomas Schmidt, Manuel Burghardt, and Katrin Dennerlein. 2018. Sentiment Annotation of Historic German Plays: An Empirical Study on Annotation Behavior. In Sandra Kübler and Heike Zinsmeister, editors, *Proceedings of the Workshop on Annotation in Digital Humanities 2018 (annDH 2018)*, pages 47–52. RWTH Aachen, Sofia, Bulgaria.

Thomas Schmidt, Manuel Burghardt, Katrin Dennerlein, and Christian Wolff. 2019a. Sentiment Annotation for Lessing's Plays: Towards a Language Resource for Sentiment Analysis on German Literary Texts. In Thierry Declerck and John P. McCrae, editors, *2nd Conference on Language, Data and Knowledge (LDK 2019)*, pages 45–50. Leipzig, Germany.

Thomas Schmidt, Manuel Burghardt, and Christian Wolff. 2019b. Toward Multimodal Sentiment Analysis of Historic Plays: A Case Study with Text and Audio for Lessing's Emilia Galotti. In *Proceedings of the Digital Humanities in the Nordic Countries 4th Conference*, volume 2364 of *CEUR Workshop Proceedings*, pages 405–414, Copenhagen, Denmark. CEUR-WS.org.

Thomas Schmidt, Johanna Dangel, and Christian Wolff. 2021a. Senttext: A tool for lexicon-based sentiment analysis in digital humanities. In Thomas Schmidt and Christian Wolff, editors, *Information Science and its Neighbors from Data Science to Digital Humanities. Proceedings of the 16th International Symposium of Information Science (ISI 2021)*, volume 74, pages 156–172. Werner Hülsbusch, Glückstadt.

Thomas Schmidt, Katrin Dennerlein, and Christian Wolff. 2021b. Towards a Corpus of Historical German Plays with Emotion Annotations. In *3rd Conference on Language, Data and Knowledge (LDK 2021)*, volume 93 of *Open Access Series in Informatics (OASIcs)*, pages 9:1–9:11, Dagstuhl, Germany. Schloss Dagstuhl – Leibniz-Zentrum für Informatik.

Thomas Schmidt, Katrin Dennerlein, and Christian Wolff. 2021c. Using Deep Learning for Emotion Analysis of 18th and 19th Century German Plays. In Manuel Burghardt, Lisa Dieckmann, Timo Steyer, Peer Trilcke, Niels-Oliver Walkowski, Joëlle Weis, and Ulrike Wuttke, editors, *Fabrikation von Erkenntnis. Experimente in den Digital Humanities*.

Thomas Schmidt, Isabella Engl, David Halbhuber, and Christian Wolff. 2020a. Comparing live sentiment annotation of movies via arduino and a slider with textual annotation of subtitles. In *Post-Proceedings of the 5th Conference Digital Humanities in the Nordic Countries (DHN 2020)*, pages 212–223.

Thomas Schmidt, Florian Kaindl, and Christian Wolff. 2020b. Distant reading of religious online communities: A case study for three religious forums on reddit. In *Proceedings of the Digital Humanities in the Nordic Countries 5th Conference (DHN 2020)*, pages 157–172, Riga, Latvia.

Thomas Schmidt, Brigitte Winterl, Milena Maul, Alina Schark, Andrea Vlad, and Christian Wolff. 2019c. Inter-rater agreement and usability: A comparative evaluation of annotation tools for sentiment annotation. In *INFORMATIK 2019: 50 Jahre Gesellschaft für Informatik – Informatik für Gesellschaft (Workshop-Beiträge)*, pages 121–133, Bonn. Gesellschaft für Informatik e.V.

Stefan Schweter. 2020. Europeana BERT and ELECTRA models.

Stefan Schweter and Johannes Baiter. 2019. Towards Robust Named Entity Recognition for Historic German. In *Proceedings of the 4th Workshop on Representation Learning for NLP (RepL4NLP-2019)*, pages 96–103, Florence, Italy. Association for Computational Linguistics.

Boaz Shmueli and Lun-Wei Ku. 2019. SocialNLP EmotionX 2019 Challenge Overview: Predicting Emotions in Spoken Dialogues and Chats. *arXiv:1909.07734 [cs]*. ArXiv: 1909.07734.

Rachele Sprugnoli, Sara Tonelli, Alessandro Marchetti, and Giovanni Moretti. 2015. Towards sentiment analysis for historical texts. *Digital Scholarship in the Humanities*, 31:762–772. Publisher: Oxford : Oxford University Press.

Thomas Wolf, Lysandre Debut, Victor Sanh, Julien Chaumond, Clement Delangue, Anthony Moi, Pierric Cistac, Tim Rault, Rémi Louf, Morgan Funtowicz, Joe Davison, Sam Shleifer, Patrick von Platen, Clara Ma, Yacine Jernite, Julien Plu, Canwen Xu, Teven Le Scao, Sylvain Gugger, Mariama Drame, Quentin Lhoest, and Alexander M. Rush. 2020. HuggingFace's Transformers: State-of-the-art Natural Language Processing. *arXiv:1910.03771 [cs]*. ArXiv: 1910.03771.

Ian Wood, John McCrae, Vladimir Andryushechkin, and Paul Buitelaar. 2018a. A Comparison of Emotion Annotation Approaches for Text. *Information*, 9(5):117.

Ian Wood, John P. McCrae, Vladimir Andryushechkin, and Paul Buitelaar. 2018b. A Comparison Of Emotion Annotation Schemes And A New Annotated Data Set. In *Proceedings of the Eleventh International Conference on Language Resources and Evaluation (LREC 2018)*, Miyazaki, Japan. European Language Resources Association (ELRA).

Kisu Yang, Dongyub Lee, Taesun Whang, Seolhwa Lee, and Heuiseok Lim. 2019. EmotionX-KU: BERT-Max based Contextual Emotion Classifier. *arXiv:1906.11565 [cs]*. ArXiv: 1906.11565.

Albin Zehe, Martin Becker, Lena Hettinger, Andreas Hotho, Isabella Reger, and Fotis Jannidis. 2016. Prediction of Happy Endings in German Novels. In *DMNLP@PKDD/ECML*.

Emily Öhman. 2020. Challenges in Annotation: Annotator Experiences from a Crowdsourced Emotion Annotation Task. In *Proceedings of the Digital Humanities in the Nordic Countries 5th Conference*, pages 293–301. CEUR Workshop Proceedings.

A Appendix: Class Distributions for Corpus Manifestations

Emotion category	absolute	%
MC: emotions of affection	1,965	23
MC: emotions of joy	1,348	16
MC: emotions of fear	614	7
MC: emotions of rejection	2,153	25
MC: emotions of suffering	1,566	18
emotional movement	906	9
Overall	8,552	100

Table 6: Distributions of *main classes* for the *filtered corpus*. Percentages are rounded.

Emotion category	absolute	%
desire	28	0
love	1,032	14
friendship	185	2
admiration	468	6
joy	1,103	15
Schadenfreude	181	2
fear	390	5
despair	160	2
anger	1,002	13
hate, disgust	690	9
suffering	1,045	14
compassion	313	4
emotional movement	906	9
Overall	7,503	100

Table 7: Distributions of *sub-emotions* for the *filtered corpus*. *Polarity* distribution is 6,018 *negative* (60%) and 3,944 *positive* (40%). Percentages are rounded.

Emotion category	absolute	%
MC: emotions of affection	1,198	18
desire	27	0
love	602	9
friendship	126	2
admiration	441	7
MC: emotions of joy	1,088	16
joy	881	13
Schadenfreude	201	3
MC: emotions of fear	725	11
fear	391	6
despair	339	5
MC: emotions of rejection	1,538	23
anger	919	14
hate, disgust	660	10
MC: emotions of suffering	1,175	17
suffering	833	12
compassion	297	4
emotional movement	1,022	15
Overall	6,741	100

Table 8: Distributions of emotions for the *speech corpus*. *Polarity* distribution is 3,414 *negative* (60%) and 2,305 *positive* (40%). Percentages are rounded.

Automating the Detection of Poetic Features: The Limerick as Model Organism

Almas Abdibayev
Department of Computer Science
Sudikoff Lab
Dartmouth College
Hanover, NH 03755
almas.abdibayev.gr@dartmouth.edu

Yohei Igarashi
Department of English
University of Connecticut
Storrs, CT 06269-4025
yohei.igarashi@uconn.edu

Allen Riddell
Department of Information & Library Science
Indiana University Bloomington
Bloomington, IN 47408
riddella@indiana.edu

Daniel Rockmore
Department of Computer Science
Dartmouth College
Hanover, NH 03755
daniel.n.rockmore@dartmouth.edu

Abstract

In this paper we take up the problem of "limerick detection" and describe a system to identify five-line poems as limericks or not. This turns out to be a surprisingly difficult challenge with many subtleties. More precisely, we produce an algorithm which focuses on the structural aspects of the limerick – rhyme scheme and rhythm (i.e., stress patterns) – and when tested on a a culled data set of 98,454 publicly available limericks, our "limerick filter" accepts 67% as limericks. The primary failure of our filter is on the detection of "non-standard" rhymes, which we highlight as an outstanding challenge in computational poetics. Our accent detection algorithm proves to be very robust. Our main contributions are (1) a novel rhyme detection algorithm that works on English words including rare proper nouns and made-up words (and thus, words not in the widely used CMUDict database); (2) a novel rhythm-identifying heuristic that is robust to language noise at moderate levels and comparable in accuracy to state-of-the-art scansion algorithms. As a third significant contribution (3) we make publicly available a large corpus of limericks that includes tags of "limerick" or "not-limerick" as determined by our identification software, thereby providing a benchmark for the community. The poetic tasks that we have identified as challenges for machines suggest that the limerick is a useful "model organism" for the study of machine capabilities in poetry and more broadly literature and language. We include a list of open challenges as well. Generally, we anticipate that this work will provide useful material and benchmarks for future explorations in the field.

1 Introduction

The application of natural language processing methods to the field of poetry and poetics has led to much promising work. In particular, advances in machine learning-based language models have spurred investigations into various kinds of automated poetic analysis and synthesis. There has been recent work pursuing automated scansion ("scansion" denoting the marking of feet, accents, and caesuras or pauses in lines of poetry) (Agirrezabal et al., 2017a; Anttila and Heuser, 2016; de la Rosa et al., 2020; Marco et al., 2021; Greene et al., 2010; Hammond, 2013; McCurdy et al., 2015; Lau et al., 2018) and probing the ability of language models to encode rhyme (Abdibayev et al., 2021). Other work is devoted to the automatic classification of poetic kinds, like the haiku in English (Long and So, 2016) and free verse (Baumann et al., 2018). On the generative or machine writing side of the problem, models have been trained to output synthetic poems that are increasingly difficult to tell apart from human-made poetic compositions; such work includes the generation of sonnets (Ghazvininejad et al., 2017) and, especially relevant to the present paper, limericks (Wang et al., 2021). These computational approaches to poet-

Proceedings of LaTeCH-CLfL 2021, pages 80–90
Punta Cana, Dominican Republic (Online), November 11, 2021.

ics share many of the same objects of inquiry as recent scholarship in literary criticism, especially those associated with the "New Formalism" and "Historical Poetics" (Adams et al., 2016; Levinson, 2007; Culler and Glaser, 2019). Such scholarship and computational poetics together prompt us to attend once again to the particularities of poetic form – meter and rhythm, poetic sound generally, aspects of lyric poetry, and related concerns. This kind of joined work promises to advance our understanding of the formal elements of poetry while also making progress in our understanding of the capabilities of language models to gain what might be called poetic knowledge.

In this paper we hope to contribute to computational poetics and formalist literary criticism alike by offering an account of our work in the automatic detection of poetic features, using the limerick form. The limerick is a comedic, light, and primarily oral poetic kind. While there is but a scattering of scholarship on the genre (see e.g., (Baring-Gould, 1988; Belknap, 1981; Bibby, 1978; Legman, 1969, 1980)) there are nevertheless important reasons to take up the limerick. State-of-the-art language models still tend to perform better with short texts (Liu et al., 2019), and the limerick is a short verse form. Even better, limericks have a high density of conspicuous poetic-formal features compared to other short verse forms (Wang et al., 2021). Haiku, for example, do not have rhymes or consistent accentual patterning, and epigrammatic couplets are less interesting than limericks in terms of rhyme scheme and rhythmic variation between lines. For these reasons, the limerick is a particularly promising case study for computational poetics. In biological terms, it is a useful model organism, an object of study tactically chosen for its relative simplicity and potential to provide insights into broader phenomena (Hedges, 2002; Poovey, 2001) – in our case, poetry more broadly.

Specifically, with this paper we offer the following. First, a large, clean limerick data set as a resource to other researchers: Wang et. al, noting the unavailability of large limerick data sets, have offered a novel corpus of their own, made up of 2,000 limericks (Wang et al., 2021) We offer a data set of 98,454 highly regular limericks drawn from the *The Omnificent English Dictionary in Limerick Form* ("OEDILF") website. Second, we outline our methods for detecting two of the three main features of limericks: their rhyme scheme and accentual pattern. (We discuss the third feature of the limerick, its triplet meter, which is closely related to its accentual pattern, in our "Future Directions" section.)

The "limerick decision" problem, of deciding whether or not a poem is a limerick through the automatic discernment of formal features, may appear to be of only narrow interest. But, as per the model organism conceit we see it as not only enabling the construction of a well-defined poetic, even literary laboratory, but also as a direct pathway to a range of broader potential applications for computational poetics and formal feature detection. These include the automated discernment of latent poetic features of songs, advertising and marketing copy, political speeches, and more. We take this up in the concluding "Future Directions" section. The case or model organism of the limerick has implications that reach well beyond the form itself.

2 Recognizing The Limerick

According to the *New Princeton Encyclopedia of Poetry and Poetics* the limerick is "the most popular form of comic, light verse in English." The origins of the form and its very name "limerick" are obscure, but the form was popularized by Edward Lear's *A Book of Nonsense* (1846) and became widespread by the early 20th century (Preminger et al., 1993).

The limerick form has three main formal features:

Rhyme scheme. The limerick's rhyme scheme is *AABBA*. In written form, limericks are almost always arranged as five-line poems, but it is also possible to view the limerick as a four-line poem by combining the third and fourth lines as a pair of *hemistichs* (half-lines of verse) that are separated by a *caesura* (a pause). It is even possible to understand the limerick as comprised of two long verse lines, the first (merging lines 1 and 2) having six accents and the second (merging lines 3-5) having seven accents. (Preminger et al., 1993; Attridge, 1982). Whatever its written form, all recited limericks conform aurally to the *AABBA* rhyme scheme.

Accents or Stresses. The number of stresses in each line is organized as follows: line 1 (3 stresses), line 2 (3 stresses), line 3 (2 stresses), line 4 (2 stresses), and line 5 (3 stresses). The 3-stress lines– lines 1, 2, and 5–typically have seven to ten syllables, while the two shorter lines–lines 3 and 4– typically have five to seven syllables. But, being an instance of accentual verse like the traditional ballad, the limerick allows for much variation in the total number of syllables per line in realizing the necessary 3-3-2-2-3 stress pattern.

Meter. The main metrical foot of limericks is debatable. Depending on how one hears or recites limericks, the limerick's metrical foot is either anapestic, amphibrachic (Preminger et al., 1993), or (if one treats the initial unstressed syllable as something like a musical pick-up note or *anacrusis*) dactyllic. What is unequivocal is that there are trisyllabic feet (or, triplets, musically speaking) driving the rhythm. Another interesting aspect of limerick rhythm is known to all reciters and auditors of limericks: the pauses at the end lines, which themselves can be sorted into the typically lengthier pauses at the end of lines 1, 2, and 5 and the shorter pauses at the end of lines 3 and 4. These lines can be classified as "catalectic" (an incomplete line of verse). But isochronic approaches to meter, though out of fashion today, have historically incorporated musical notation, and they are therefore best at revealing these important rests which are not registered by scansion (Attridge, 1982; Lanier, 1979).

The content of limericks is usually bawdy, which can raise problems in data curation. Nevertheless, it is a poetic form whose relative brevity, rhyme scheme, distinct accentual pattern, and meter make it not only an ideal form for introducing poetry to elementary school students, but a valuable testbed for computational poetics. We can see these primary formal elements at work in one of Lear's most well-known limericks, "There was an Old Man with a Beard" (Foundation, 2021):

> There was an Old Man with a beard,
> Who said, "It is just as I feared! –
> Two Owls and a Hen,
> four Larks and a Wren,
> Have all built their nests in my beard!"

Note the adherence to the *AABBA* rhyme scheme – "beard," "feared," "Hen," "Wren," "beard" – and how the final line's end rhyme circles back to the A rhyme, giving a sense of circularity and closure. We can also hear the 3-3-2-2-3 accentual pattern: in line 1, "there **was** an Old **Man** with a **beard**," and in line 3, "Two **Owls** and a **Hen**." The dominance of trisyllabic feet (dactyllic, anapestic, or amphibrachic) is audible too: if predominantly dactyllic, the initial syllable of each line is unstressed, then followed by a series of dactyls ("**all** built their **nests** in my . . . ").

Herein we focus on the detection of limerick rhyme scheme and accentual pattern. While these appeared to be the most tractable formal elements (compared to the ambiguities of the metrical system), even rhyme and accent detection turn out to be nontrivial problems.

3 Data

We scraped from the website *The Omnificent English Dictionary in Limerick Form* ("OEDILF"). The OEDILF, established in 2004, is an amateur, crowd-sourced project whose goal is to have at least one limerick for every meaning of every word found in the *Oxford English Dictionary*. User-submitted limericks are subject to approval by moderators, and, if approved, are published on the website.[1] We turned to OEDILF in order to get a large number of limericks which we could then sort according to different categories of metadata.[2] At the time of writing this paper, OEDILF contained 112,609 submitted limericks, of which 110,610 were approved and posted to the site.

On the website, the limericks are organized according to different categories:

Authors. Our scrape of OEDILF contains limericks by 1624 unique authors. The distribution of limericks by author is not uniform (Figure 1), with the top ten authors responsible for ca. 40% of all limericks.

Topics. The topics are generated by the contributors to the website as well as by the moderators.

Words. OEDILF is interested in words as found in the dictionary, as described above. The website allows users to search limericks by keywords: for instance, there are 52 limericks featuring the word, "bridge," spanning its denotations as card game, infrastructure, a platform found on vessels, segment of a pop song, and so on. Currently, OEDILF is focusing on words beginning with the letters "Aa-" through "Ha-," and indicates the projected date of completion (presumably having a limerick for every meaning of every word found in the OED) as November 3, 2063.[3]

For our detection experiments below, we first filtered limericks based on simple criteria: limericks must have 5 lines and must use words (as opposed to symbols, such as emojis or formulae). This excludes a range of unorthodox limericks such as

[1] http://http://www.oedilf.com/db/Lim.php?View=About
[2] http://www.oedilf.com/db/Lim.php
[3] http://http://www.oedilf.com/db/Lim.php?View=About

ASCII art limericks. The result was a corpus of 98,454 limericks, dated 1998 to the present.

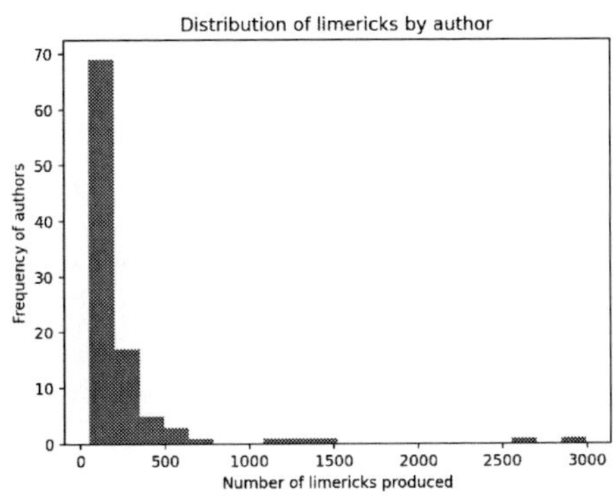

Figure 1: Histogram plotting distribution of top 100 authors within the entire scraped dataset. The y-axis shows the number of authors within a bin, while the x-axis shows the number of limericks those authors produced.

4 Method

4.1 Rhyme Detection

Detecting the correct rhyme scheme (*AABBA*) was the first step we took in order to sort out limericks that did not adhere to the rhyme scheme. We employed two models trained on CMUDict[4]: one to predict phoneme structure and another to predict stress patterns across these phones. Using this method, we determine that two words rhyme if after breaking them down into phonemes with stressed vowels, the last stressed vowels in the syllables match and any following phonemes also match. For example, words *fire* and *rewire* are broken down into `F AY1 ER0` and `R IY0 W AY1 ER0`. The spaces separate phones and numbers indicate stress pattern, `0` for no stress, `2` for secondary stress, and `1` for primary stress. In this case the algorithm would walk through the phonemes until encountering `AY1` in both phoneme sequences and then compare `AY1 ER0` with `AY1 ER0`, concluding that the words are in fact rhyming. In some cases words may have several pronunciations which results in two different phone sequences. Here, we assume that if one of the phoneme sequences matches with the phoneme sequence of another end-of-the-line word in the limerick, then that is the intended pronunciation.

We choose a two-model approach since joint models of phoneme and stress tend show lower accuracy for the stress prediction task. The first model, the phoneme predictor, is an open source Transformer (Vaswani et al., 2017) model (out of the box implementation available in the Tensor2Tensor toolkit (Vaswani et al., 2018)) that was trained on CMUDict[5]. Transformer is a neural network that consists of several layers of attention (Bahdanau et al., 2014) interspersed with fully connected layers. The variation of the model trained to predict phonemes was released by researchers at Carnegie Mellon University, under the umbrella name CMU Sphinx. It features 3 layers with an embedding size of 256. The second model is a custom phoneme LSTM (Hochreiter and Schmidhuber, 1997) that we also trained on CMUDict to predict the stress pattern for a sequence of phonemes produced by the previous grapheme to phoneme model. In particular, our model is a simple bidirectional LSTM (biLSTM) with 3 layers and hidden size of 30 units, followed by a linear projection layer that outputs probabilities for all three possible stress patterns. We do not use dropout or other regularization techniques (such as variational dropout) as we found they lower performance on the test set. We trained this network for 10 epochs using learning rate of 10^{-4} using AdamW on a test set of 107,498 examples, validation set of 13,437 examples, and test set of 13,438 examples, until validation loss plateaued. We obtain 84% accuracy on our test set. This model has a total of 60,393 parameters. We have experimented with other more complex architectures (such as a vanilla GPT model of varying number of layers and embedding sizes) and hyperparameter setups, but found that biLSTM performs the best (our best Transformer model achieved 70% accuracy on the task), perhaps due to the size of the data set, while also featuring 2 orders of magnitude fewer parameters.

As a result of rhyme scheme filtering using predicted stressed phonemes, we were left with 65,971 limericks out of 98,454 of the original data set (a 70% yield). The associated labeled data set ("limerick" or "non-limerick") can be found at `http://dx.doi.org/10.5281/zenodo.5520078`.

A random sample of limericks that did not pass

[4]http://www.speech.cs.cmu.edu/cgi-bin/cmudict. For a different method based on eSpeak, see Alnajjar and Hämäläinen 2018

[5]https://github.com/cmusphinx/g2p-seq2seq

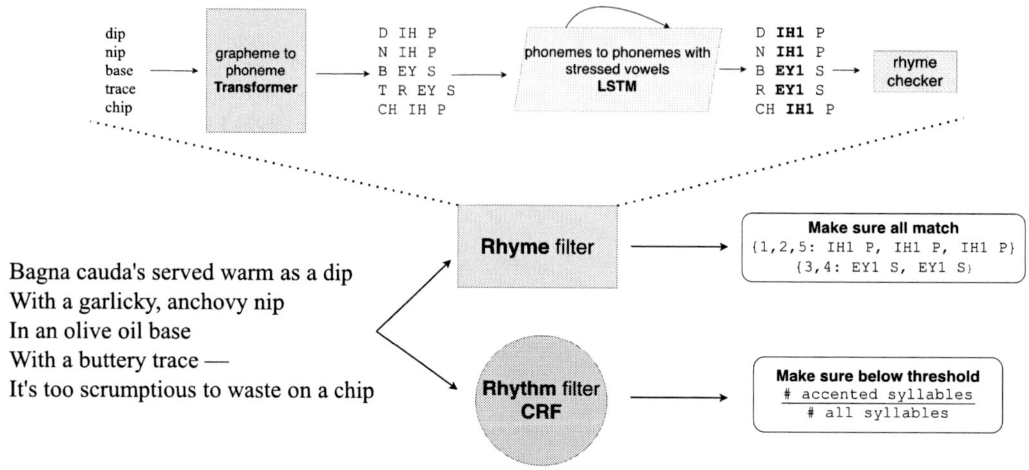

Figure 2: Overview of our filter.

the rhyming test (30% of all limericks) yielded fifteen examples where the non-rhyme could be attributed to non-standard or difficult word spellings (and thus an associated difficulty in producing the phones). There were four examples of "near" or "imperfect" rhymes (e.g., "groaned" and "crooned") and one example of an "eye" or "sight" rhyme (e.g., "prove" and "love") (Abrams, 1999). In Table 1, there are examples of these, while in the Appendix we include five other examples of "failures." The detection of near and eye rhymes is an outstanding challenge for computational poetics.

4.2 Rhythm (Accentual Pattern) Detection

To characterize the rhythm of a poem, we "scan" a poem (that is, perform a scansion). Numerous studies have documented that it is possible to use familiar models from computational linguistics to scan poetry (Haider, 2021; Agirrezabal et al., 2017b; Estes and Hench, 2016). These models are trained on poems that have been scanned by human annotators. We use a conditional random field (CRF) model (Lafferty et al., 2001; Okazaki, 2007), trained on the *For Better for Verse* corpus (Bet, Accessed July 1, 2021). We extract a range of simple features from each word (e.g., character trigrams, syllable count) and predict each word's "label"—the word-specific scansion. For example, in a particular poem the word *evening* might be scanned as +−, where "+" indicates a stressed syllable and "-" an unstressed one. The CRF, sometimes called a discriminative random field, jointly models the input features and the labels. The CRF model has the virtue of being more than a decade old and being widely used in computational linguistics for named entity recognition, among other applications (Murphy, 2012, Sec. 19.6).

A simple approach to identifying five-line poems that feature the limerick rhythm would be to use a model which infers, for each line, a probability distribution over the number of accented syllables. If the number of accents conspicuously departs from the (3, 3, 2, 2, 3) pattern, the poem would be rejected as a non-limerick. Unfortunately, such an approach is not available at present because the best models that perform scansion frequently make mistakes when considering whole lines (Haider, 2021). No method exists which has line-level accuracy above 90% for English poetry. Moreover, the limerick form poses special difficulties because its pattern of stresses and unstresses oftentimes depends on a departure from word or lexical stress: for example, ordinarily, in the line, "There was an Old Man with a beard," "Old Man" would be two consecutive stresses (a spondee), but the three beats of this line dictate that "Old" is demoted a to non-stressed syllable in recitation, while "was" becomes stressed. Limericks and their comedic effects depend on such "wrenched accents" (Abrams, 1999), which mark the difference between lexical stress and the recited poetic rhythm, but this makes word-based scansion impractical.

We therefore choose a simpler approach and instead attempt to identify poems which have, in

Near Rhyme	Eye Rhyme
This sign, where the road intersects	In my audio-lingual exam,
With the train track, is shaped like an X.	I recited from Omar Khayyam.
It's a crossbuck, which works	I am fortunate, still,
As a warning to jerks	For this Arabic drill:
Who might otherwise end up in wrecks.	Jug of wine, loaf of bread, lots of jam.

Table 1: Two limericks whose rhyming defeated our filter. The rhyming of "X" with "intersects" and " wrecks" is a near rhyme and the rhyming of "Khayyam" rhyming with "exam" and "jam" is an eye rhyme. Both limericks by Chris Doyle, available at OEDILF as limericks #60115 and #9508 (accessed July 1, 2021).

aggregate, more accented syllables than would be expected given the (3, 3, 2, 2, 3) pattern found in conventional limericks. We use the ratio of accented syllables to total syllables as our measure of the prevalence of stressed syllables. Because this approach considers the entire poem, it averages over the line-level inaccuracy of the scansion model.

To determine a cutoff beyond which we say a poem contains too many accented syllables, we look at the ratios associated with a small number of published conventional limericks. The mean and standard deviation of these ratios are 0.47 and 0.038 respectively. Assuming that the ratio follows a normal distribution in conventional limericks, we set our cutoff to be 2.33 standard deviations higher than the mean ($\Phi^{-1}(0.99) \approx 2.33$). So any poem associated with a ratio higher than this value, 0.562, will be rejected as featuring too many accented syllables to be a limerick.[6]

Of the 98,454 poems in the OEDILF corpus, 4,773 (5%) were flagged as having more accented syllables than would be expected in a limerick. To estimate the performance of this method, we randomly sampled 20 flagged limericks as well as 20 limericks which were not flagged. We then manually assessed whether or not our approach succeeded in identifying poems which did not feature the conventional limerick rhythm. We estimate that this method has an accuracy of about 95% and an F1 score of about 0.096. Because the vast majority of limericks in the OEDLIF corpus use the expected rhythm, estimating the true negative rate of this classifier is a challenge. (A corpus of almost-correct limericks would be helpful here.) The only poem correctly flagged as flawed was the following:[7]

Upset tum from a dubious chef?
Coughing? Lame? Itchy? Sore? Sleepy? Deaf?
Deaf? My old British National
Formulary ration 'll
List the pills for your ills — BNF.

We view this poem as flawed in terms of rhythm because it is extremely difficult to recite the third line of the poem using only two accented syllables.

Clearly there is considerable opportunity for improvement here. A corpus of obviously flawed limericks (in terms of rhythm) would be particularly valuable for future research as such a corpus would allow researchers to accurately estimate the performance of a classifier designed to detect flawed rhythm.

5 Results

After applying all of our rhyming and meter filters we identify a final clean set of 65,971 limericks, which constitutes 67% of our original set of limericks that we scraped (Table 2).

One implication of our results is that in the limerick form, at least as understood by the poetizing users and editors of OEDILF, accentual pattern predominates as a necessary formal trait. 95% of the limericks in the data set satisfied our accent measure, and 70% cleared our rhyme filter. Ideally, a poem is an "organic whole" (Poovey, 2001) with its different formal features and the work's meaning working harmoniously together. Yet our findings suggest that, practically speaking, there is a hierarchy of formal features. All formal features are not emphasized equally by writers and readers of poems: some features matter more than others in the quiddity of the form – in the limerick-ness of

[6]Note that these values are all calculated using our particular CRF model. The particular values (mean, standard deviation, cutoff) should be re-calculated if a different model is used.

[7]By Chris Young, Limerick #83205 in the OEDILF.

the limerick. Another way to put this is that we (humans) have laxer expectations about some formal elements of poems (like syllables), a higher toleration for variation among these elements while still identifying the work as an instance of the poetic kind. (For example, a sonnet with 13 lines may seem less like sonnet than a sonnet whose rhyme scheme is slightly aberrant: in other words, in practice, the number of lines is a more essential feature of the sonnet than strict adherence to the rhyme scheme.)

6 Difficult Examples

The previous subsections take the limerick and break out fundamental structural components that need to be identified for limerick detection. That said, the human – poet or not – can readily create new difficult limericks that might defeat these state-of-the-art poetic classification engines.

We tested our rhyme detection and accent detection algorithms on the following poems[8] with made-up words for end rhymes. These are words that are definitely not included in CMUDict. Our rhyme and accent detectors both correctly evaluated these examples, accepting all three limericks as featuring legitimate limerick rhyme schemes and stress patterns.

My favorite food is red schnook,
It is best when eaten with glook,
Or with sauce from meef,
Or with sides of dreef,
It always makes me feel so trook.

I like to walk in the dark fraze,
At my side a furry brown braze,
It lopes on its broops,
And shakes his sharp croops,
That stir up the hidden small snays.

It's so tough to fagrewzin a kloom,
Its frantabulous frinks are a croom,
To brillig the shneezles,
Or traming the dreaszels,
The sturmping coughs up shnayble and stoom.

7 Future Directions

As mentioned, in this paper we have only addressed the problem of the structural identification of the limerick. But, of course there is much more to the limerick than just patterns of rhyme and rhythm.

The limerick is typically a narrative. These brief, comic stories fall into different narrative types and structures. For example, consider the paired examples below: the one on the right ("Old Man with a Beard") exhibits a more linear or teleological structure, while the one on the left ("Old Person of Dean")[9] is circular in that it ends with a return to the first line, thereby resembling the refrains found in ballads and villanelles:

There was an Old Man with a beard,
Who said, 'It is just as I feared!
Two Owls and a Hen,
Four Larks and a Wren,
Have all built their nests in my beard!'

There was an Old Person of Dean,
Who dined on one pea and one bean;
For he said, "More than that
would make me too fat,"
That cautious Old Person of Dean.

Thus the narrative aspects of limericks warrant further study, including their narrative structure, punchlines and jokes (which can range from the subtle to the vulgar), twists in the story, and more. A related feature of limericks is their semantic integrity: despite the limerick form's association with nonsense verse because of Edward Lear's *A Book of Nonsense* and their oftentimes silly content, good limericks still make sense, cohere, and have aesthetic qualities that can be appreciated. For example, can a machine discern that the limerick immediately below[10] is more successful than the one below it[11] because of the latter's non-sequitur conclusion? Moreover, can it readily detect the non-sequitur?

There was an Old Man in a tree,
Who was horribly bored by a Bee;
When they said, 'Does it buzz?'
He replied, 'Yes, it does!'
'It's a very regular brute of a Bee!'

[8] All three poems were written by one of the authors of this paper.

[9] by Edward Lear, 1920

[10] "There was an Old Man in a tree", by Edward Lear, in *The Book of Nonsense* (1887)

[11] Derived from "There was an Old Man with a beard", by Edward Lear, in *The Book of Nonsense* (1887), by changing the last sentence.

	Filter Statistics	
Original data set	Rhyming	Rhythm
98454	69446 (0.70)	93681 (0.95)
Original data set	Rhyme & Rhythm	
98454	65971 (0.67)	

Table 2: Filter statistics. This is a summary of our results. We analyze our data set using various filters to satisfy two of the conventional criteria of a limerick. In other words, (1) it has to follow the AABBA rhyming scheme, and (2) it has to follow the 3-3-2-2-3 accentual pattern.

There was an Old Man with a beard,
Who said, "It is just as I feared!
Two Owls and a Hen,
four Larks and a Wren,
and mutton is best boiled, not seared.

A third potential area of investigation is wordplay, some of which depends on poetic devices such as assonance, alliteration, and puns and innuendo. The problem of machine recognition and subsequent classification of such literary devices pose interesting challenges for a next generation of machine limerick readers.

The long range goals we mention above – indeed the entire setting of this work – places these kinds of investigations and challenges within the context of machine learning and language and thus, broadly in the space of natural language processing (NLP). In that setting, there is a strong thread of work focused on probing the linguistic knowledge of the increasingly complex language models (e.g., Transformer-based deep learning architectures). Of interest are the "minimal pair" challenges in which the architecture is "asked" – after suitable training – to assign a likelihood of correctness (in the sense of a model's "preference") between an original and presumably correct instance of some phenomenon and a minimally corrupted (relative to a given grammatical rule) version as evidence of some ability to distinguish a particular linguistic characteristic. In (Warstadt et al., 2020) 12 kinds of phenomena are investigated and each phenomenon is further deconstructed into "paradigms" and paradigm is the source of 1000 instances of minimal pairs.[12] This minimal pairs approach is being extended to poetic devices – specifically, in the investigation of language models to encode rhyming information (Abdibayev et al., 2021). One extension of this work would be the comparison of a "correct" limerick and a variation minimally corrupted in terms of meter or rhyme scheme to test the poetic knowledge in language models and whose results will produce benchmarks (and a fixed test set) for the deep learning community. It is our general sense that poetic knowledge is a challenging domain that productively probes the linguistic capabilities of advanced language models. Moreover, we could well imagine an even broader set of minimal pair benchmarks to interrogate the "writerly" or "stylistic" knowledge of language models.

It is also possible to envision applications for language models that possess poetic knowledge. As Roman Jakobson showed, political slogans (like "I Like Ike") can have rich aural, orthographic, and rhythmic patterning which augment their catchiness (Jakobson et al., 1987). Such poetic knowledge could extend to the large scale analysis of popular music, advertising and marketing copy, and perhaps even political speeches, propaganda, and disinformation – all with an eye toward examining what makes certain non-poetic instances of language which are nevertheless suffused with poetic features so effective or memorable to large audiences.

At its most speculative, this kind of work trains an odd light on the seemingly impenetrable process of how we learn to write even the simplest forms of poetry like the limerick. A young child learns to rhyme, decide syllable breaks, and can develop a sense of poetic meter very quickly – say, in a single grade school class (if the plethora of teachers' worksheets available on the internet is any indication). That a language model with billions of parameters and thousands of examples isn't yet perfect says a lot about both the models we develop and the human process of learning as well.

References

Accessed July 1, 2021. For Better for Verse. https://prosody.lib.virginia.edu/.

[12]For example one minimal pair that tests subject-verb agreement (see Table 1 of (Warstadt et al., 2020)) is *These casseroles disgust Kayla.* v. These casseroles disgusts Kayla.

Almas Abdibayev, Allen Riddell, and Daniel N. Rockmore. 2021. BPoMP: The benchmark of poetic minimal pairs – limericks, rhyme, and narrative coherence. In *Proceedings of Recent Advances in Natural Language Processing*, pages 1–9. Association for Computational Linguistics.

M. H. Abrams. 1999. *A Glossary of Literary Terms*, 7th ed edition. Harcourt Brace College Publishers.

V. Joshua Adams, Joel Calahan, and Michael Hansen, editors. 2016. *Special Issue: Historical Poetics*, volume 77 of *Modern Language Quarterly*.

Manex Agirrezabal, Iñaki Alegria, and Mans Hulden. 2017a. A comparison of feature-based and neural scansion of poetry. In *Proceedings of the International Conference Recent Advances in Natural Language Processing, RANLP 2017*, pages 18–23, Varna, Bulgaria. INCOMA Ltd.

Manex Agirrezabal, Iñaki Alegria, and Mans Hulden. 2017b. A comparison of feature-based and neural scansion of poetry. *arXiv preprint arXiv:1711.00938*.

Khalid Alnajjar and Mika Hämäläinen. 2018. A master-apprentice approach to automatic creation of culturally satirical movie titles. In *Proceedings of the 11th International Conference on Natural Language Generation*, pages 274–283, Tilburg University, The Netherlands. Association for Computational Linguistics.

Arto Anttila and Ryan Heuser. 2016. Phonological and metrical variation across genres. *Proceedings of the Annual Meetings on Phonology*, 3(0).

Derek Attridge. 1982. *The Rhythms of English Poetry*. English language series. Longman, London; New York.

Dzmitry Bahdanau, Kyunghyun Cho, and Yoshua Bengio. 2014. Neural machine translation by jointly learning to align and translate. *arXiv preprint arXiv:1409.0473*.

William S. Baring-Gould. 1988. *The Lure of the Limerick: An Uninhibited History*. Clarkson Potter.

Timo Baumann, Hussein Hussein, and Burkhard Meyer-Sickendiek. 2018. Style detection for free verse poetry from text and speech. In *Proceedings of the 27th International Conference on Computational Linguistics*, pages 1929–1940, Santa Fe, New Mexico, USA. Association for Computational Linguistics.

George Belknap. 1981. History of the limerick. *The Papers of the Bibliographical Society of America*, 75(1).

Cyril Bibby. 1978. *The Art of the Limerick*. The Research Publishing Co., London.

Jonathan D Culler and Ben Glaser, editors. 2019. *Critical Rhythm: The Poetics of a Literary Life Form*. Fordham University Press. OCLC: 1076879939.

Javier de la Rosa, Alvaro Perez, Laura Hernandez, Salvador Ros, and Elena Gonzalez-Blanco. 2020. Rantanplan, fast and accurate syllabification and scansion of Spanish poetry. *Procesamiento del Lenguaje Natural*, 65:83–90.

Alex Estes and Christopher Hench. 2016. Supervised machine learning for hybrid meter. In *Proceedings of the Fifth Workshop on Computational Linguistics for Literature*, pages 1–8, San Diego, California, USA. Association for Computational Linguistics.

Poetry Foundation. 2021. There was an Old Man with a Beard by Edward Lear.

Marjan Ghazvininejad, Xing Shi, Jay Priyadarshi, and Kevin Knight. 2017. Hafez: an interactive poetry generation system. In *Proceedings of the 55th Annual Meeting of the Association for Computational Linguistics-System Demonstrations*, pages 43–48.

Erica Greene, Tugba Bodrumlu, and Kevin Knight. 2010. Automatic analysis of rhythmic poetry with applications to generation and translation. In *Proceedings of the 2010 Conference on Empirical Methods in Natural Language Processing*, pages 524–533, Cambridge, MA. Association for Computational Linguistics.

Thomas Haider. 2021. Metrical tagging in the wild: Building and annotating poetry corpora with rhythmic features. In *Proceedings of the 16th Conference of the European Chapter of the Association for Computational Linguistics: Main Volume*, pages 3715–3725, Online. Association for Computational Linguistics.

Michael Hammond. 2013. Calculating syllable count automatically from fixed-meter poetry in English and Welsh*. *Literary and Linguistic Computing*, 29(2):218–233.

S. Blair Hedges. 2002. The origin and evolution of model organisms. *Nature Reviews Genetics*, 3(11):838–849.

Sepp Hochreiter and Jürgen Schmidhuber. 1997. Long short-term memory. *Neural Computation*, 9(8):1735–1780.

Roman Jakobson, Krystyna Pomorska, and Stephen Rudy. 1987. *Language in Literature*. Belknap Press, Cambridge, Mass.

John D. Lafferty, Andrew McCallum, and Fernando C. N. Pereira. 2001. Conditional random fields: Probabilistic models for segmenting and labeling sequence data. In *Proceedings of the Eighteenth International Conference on Machine Learning*, ICML '01, page 282–289, San Francisco, CA, USA. Morgan Kaufmann Publishers Inc.

Sidney Lanier. 1979. *The Science of English Verse*. Folcroft Library Editions, Folcroft, Pa.

Jey Han Lau, Trevor Cohn, Timothy Baldwin, Julian Brooke, and Adam Hammond. 2018. Deep-speare: A joint neural model of poetic language, meter and rhyme. In *Proceedings of the 56th Annual Meeting of the Association for Computational Linguistics (Volume 1: Long Papers)*, pages 1948–1958, Melbourne, Australia. Association for Computational Linguistics.

G. Legman. 1969. *The Limerick. 1700 Examples, With Notes, Variants and Index*. Bell Publishing Co., New York.

G. Legman. 1980. *More Limericks. 2750 Unpublished Examples, American and British*. Bell Publishing Co., New York.

Marjorie Levinson. 2007. What is new formalism? *PMLA*, 122(2):558–569.

Yinhan Liu, Myle Ott, Naman Goyal, Jingfei Du, Mandar Joshi, Danqi Chen, Omer Levy, Mike Lewis, Luke Zettlemoyer, and Veselin Stoyanov. 2019. Roberta: A robustly optimized BERT pretraining approach.

Hoyt Long and Richard Jean So. 2016. Literary pattern recognition: Modernism between close reading and machine learning. *Critical inquiry*, 42(2):235–267.

Guillermo Marco, Javier de la Rosa, Julio Gonzalo, Salvador Ros, and Elena González-Blanco. 2021. Automated metric analysis of spanish poetry: Two complementary approaches. *IEEE Access*, 9:51734–51746.

Nina McCurdy, Vivek Srikumar, and Miriah Meyer. 2015. RhymeDesign: A tool for analyzing sonic devices in poetry. In *Proceedings of the Fourth Workshop on Computational Linguistics for Literature*, pages 12–22, Denver, Colorado, USA. Association for Computational Linguistics.

Kevin P. Murphy. 2012. *Machine Learning: A Probabilistic Perspective*. The MIT Press, Cambridge, MA.

Naoaki Okazaki. 2007. CRFsuite: A fast implementation of conditional random fields (CRFs).

Mary Poovey. 2001. The model system of contemporary literary criticism. *Critical Inquiry*, 27(3):408–438.

Alex Preminger, Terry V.F. Brogan, and Frank J. Warnke, editors. 1993. *New Princeton Encyclopedia of Poetry and Poetics*. Princeton University Press.

Ashish Vaswani, Samy Bengio, Eugene Brevdo, Francois Chollet, Aidan N. Gomez, Stephan Gouws, Llion Jones, Łukasz Kaiser, Nal Kalchbrenner, Niki Parmar, Ryan Sepassi, Noam Shazeer, and Jakob Uszkoreit. 2018. Tensor2tensor for neural machine translation. *CoRR*, abs/1803.07416.

Ashish Vaswani, Noam Shazeer, Niki Parmar, Jakob Uszkoreit, Llion Jones, Aidan N Gomez, Łukasz Kaiser, and Illia Polosukhin. 2017. Attention is all you need. In *Advances in Neural Information Processing Systems*, pages 5998–6008.

Jianyou Wang, Xiaoxuan Zhang, Yuren Zhou, Christopher Suh, and Cynthia Rudin. 2021. There once was a really bad poet, it was automated but you didn't know it. *CoRR*, abs/2103.03775.

Alex Warstadt, Alicia Parrish, Haokun Liu, Anhad Mohananey, Wei Peng, Sheng-Fu Wang, and Samuel R. Bowman. 2020. BLiMP: The benchmark of linguistic minimal pairs for English. *Transactions of the Association for Computational Linguistics*, 8:377–392.

8 Appendix: A Random Selection of "Failed" Limericks

Here is a random sample of an additional five limericks that did not pass our rhyme test. Author names listed along with OEDILF number.

- Beriberi's a scary disease;
  It appears when one vitamin B's
  Too deficient. You need
  To remember to feed
  On more egg rolls and liver and peas.
  `Author: Chris Doyle, #21528`

- Lulu Glaser, a lucky chorine,
  Shone on Broadway at just 17.
  Did she dream, as a child,
  That the stalls would go wild,
  Shouting, "Lulu! The great actorine!"?
  `Author: Janet McConnaughey, #100961`

- God a code virus bloggig by doze,
  Ad by 'puter's god dutz. I subboze
  Dat a virus idfected
  Ids code. I'b dejected.
  Wud virus is bad. Doo just blows.
  `Author: Janet McConnaughey, #99468`

- A caper who's all caper-witted
  Is not a corsair who's well fitted
  For fightin' and luffin'.
  He'll cut capers on nuffin'
  When brainier pirates have flitted.
  `Author: Janet McConnaughey, #63637`

- In Osoyoos, BC (this is rare),
  All four tires went flat! We'd no spare.

What did CAA say?
“You are kidding us, eh?
Like this desert, you’re full of hot air.”
Author: MikeAq, #110550

Unsupervised Adverbial Identification in Modern Chinese Literature

Wenxiu Xie[1], **John S. Y. Lee**[2], **Fangqiong Zhan**[3], **Xiao Han**[2], **Chi-Yin Chow**[1]
[1]Department of Computer Science, City University of Hong Kong
[2]Department of Linguistics and Translation, City University of Hong Kong
[3]Department of Linguistics and Modern Languages, The Chinese University of Hong Kong
vasiliky@outlook.com, jsylee@cityu.edu.hk, zhjade2000@gmail.com
xhan42-c@my.cityu.edu.hk, tedchow@gmail.com

Abstract

In many languages, adverbials can be derived from words of various parts-of-speech. In Chinese, the derivation may be marked either with the standard adverbial marker DI, or the non-standard marker DE. Since DE also serves double duty as the attributive marker, accurate identification of adverbials requires disambiguation of its syntactic role. As parsers are trained predominantly on texts using the standard adverbial marker DI, they often fail to recognize adverbials suffixed with the non-standard DE. This paper addresses this problem with an unsupervised, rule-based approach for adverbial identification that utilizes dependency tree patterns. Experiment results show that this approach outperforms a masked language model baseline. We apply this approach to analyze standard and non-standard adverbial marker usage in modern Chinese literature.

1 Introduction

In many languages, adverbials can be derived from words of other parts-of-speech (POS). The adverbials are often morphologically marked in the derivation process. In English, the most common marker is the suffix "-ly", for example in the derivation of "happily" from the adjective "happy". In Chinese, the focus of our study, the standard adverbial marker is DI (地)[1], which can be suffixed to a wide variety of adverbs, adjectives and verbs to form adverbials. However, a non-standard adverbial marker, the suffix DE (的), is also used frequently, in some contexts on par with the standard marker (Zhang, 2012a).

Chinese parsers tend to be trained on standard texts that mostly employ the standard adverbial marker. Indeed, many Chinese treebank guidelines (Yu et al., 2001; Xia, 2000) mention only DI as the adverbial marker. As a result, even state-of-the-art parsers might not accurately detect adverbials formed with the non-standard marker. This affects not only parser accuracy but also downstream NLP tasks, as well as linguistic research on the DE vs. DI choice.

This paper investigates the task of adverbial identification, including adverbials marked both in the standard and non-standard manner. Due to the lack of annotated data for non-standard adverbials, our research focus is on unsupervised methods. We propose a simple yet effective approach for adverbial identification based on POS tag and dependency tree patterns. In an evaluation on texts drawn from modern Chinese literature, our approach achieved over 87% accuracy, outperforming a state-of-the-art masked language model.[2] To our knowledge, this is the first reported study on identifying DE- and DI-adverbials in Chinese text.

The rest of the paper is organized as follows. The next section provides the necessary linguistic background for adverbials in Chinese. Section 3 summarizes previous work. Section 4 describes our approach and the baselines. Section 5 presents our evaluation dataset. Section 6 discusses experimental results. Section 7 applies our research to the analysis of adverbial marker choice of a prominent Chinese author. Finally, Section 8 concludes.

2 Adverbials in Chinese

Every suffixed adverbial in Chinese can be rendered in one of two forms. The adjective *gaoxing* 高兴 'happy', for example, can be transformed into an adverbial either with the standard DI suffix (*gaoxing-DI* 高兴地 'happily') or the non-standard DE suffix (*gaoxing-DE* 高兴的 'happily'). We will

[1]Although the suffix is pronounced "de", we use the shorthand DI based on the character's pronunciation "di" in other contexts, in order to differentiate it from the non-standard marker, which has the same pronunciation "de".

[2]All evaluation data is publicly released at https://github.com/wxx2021/Modern-Chinese-Literature-Adverbial-Marker-Datatset-LaTeCH-CLfL-2021.

Proceedings of LaTeCH-CLfL 2021, pages 91–95
Punta Cana, Dominican Republic (Online), November 11, 2021.

henceforth refer to the former as "DI-adverbials" and the latter as "DE-adverbials".

Detecting the DE-adverbials can be challenging because of the dual role of the DE suffix: it serves both as the non-standard adverbial marker and as the (standard) attributive marker. A DE-suffixed word can therefore potentially be either an adverbial or an adjectival phrase. For example, *gaoxing-DE* is an adverbial in the expression *gaoxing-DE chang zhe ge* 'happily sing a song', but it is an adjectival phrase in the expression *gaoxing-DE rizi* 'happy day' (Table 1). The former is often parsed incorrectly as an adjective since training data tend to favor the standard marker.

In the rest of this paper, we will use the term *base word* to refer to the word from which the adverbial is derived, and *head word* to refer to the word modified by the adverbial. In Figure 1a, the adverbial *gaoxing-DE* 'happily' has *gaoxing* 'happy' as its base word and *chang* 'sing' as its head word.

3 Background

During the Vernacular Language Movement (Weng, 2020), Chinese intellectuals proposed to use DE as the standard attributive marker and DI as the standard adverbial marker (Table 1). Many Chinese treebank guidelines, such as those from Peking University (Yu et al., 2001) and the Chinese Treebank (Xia, 2000), also focus on the DI suffix in their treatment of adverbials. However, the division of labor between DE and DI has never been strictly observed, and the non-standard DE-adverbials have persisted.

Neglection of the DE-adverbials hampers both parsing accuracy and linguistics research. When parsers fail to recognize DE-adverbials and other adverbials that modify adjectives, adverbs or a sentence (Yang, 1999), accuracy in adverbial identification would be affected (Xing et al., 2020). Research on linguistic variation in Chinese often addressed DE as possessive and attributive marker, but not as adverbial marker (Zhang, 2012b). Because of the ambiguity with the DE suffix, most quantitative analyses on DI- vs. DE-adverbial usage required manual annotation or was restricted to relatively small sample sizes (Tan, 2004; Zhang, 2012a; Ho, 2015).

Previous research has utilized both rule-based and machine learning approaches to study Chinese numeral classifiers that form quantity noun phrases (Guo and Zhong, 2005; Peinelt et al., 2017).

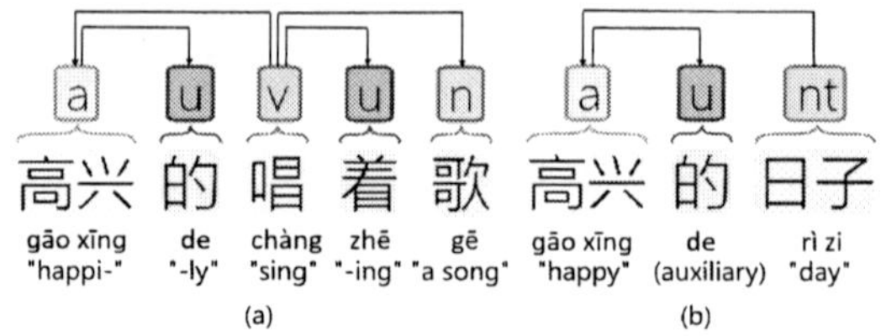

Figure 1: Use of the DE suffix as adverbial marker and attributive marker and its disambiguation through dependency relations: (a) DE marks the base word *gaoxing* 'happy' to form the adverbial *gaoxing-DE*, with *chang* 'sing' as its head word; (b) DE marks the base word *gaoxing*'happy' to form the adjectival phrase *gaoxing-DE*, with *rizi* 'day' as its head word

Similar to our study, it was found effective to leverage syntactic criteria and linguistic rules to analyze relations between numeral classifiers, nominal head words and nouns.

4 Approach

While the DI suffix is a reliable identifier for DI-adverbials, a naive search for the DE suffix would yield low precision in retrieving DE-adverbials since DE may also mark attributives. It is essential to determine the POS of the head word: DE marks an adverbial if the head word is an adjective or verb, but it marks an attributive if the head word is a noun.

4.1 Proposed method

We investigate a parser-based approach in the following three settings, using the HanLP Chinese parser (He, 2020) for word segmentation, POS tagging and dependency parsing.[3]

POS only This baseline predicts "adverbial" if the base word is tagged as "adverb" (`d` in HanLP, e.g., *gaoxing*/`d` DE/`u`). Note that the DE-adverbial in Figure 1a would be falsely rejected. If the word segmentor combines the base word and suffix as one word, the POS tag of the word is also required to be "adverb" (e.g. *gaoxing-DE*/`d`).

POS+base This second baseline aims to improve recall with more relaxed POS constraints. It predicts "adverbial" when the base word is tagged as "adjective" (`a`) or "verb" (`v`), in

[3]Full description of the POS tag set can be accessed at http://www.hankcs.com/nlp/part-of-speech-tagging.html#h2-8.

Suffix	Role	Status	Example
DI	adverbial marker	standard	*gaoxing-DI chang zhe ge* 高兴地唱着歌 'happily sing'
DE	adverbial marker	non-standard	*gaoxing-DE chang zhe ge* 高兴的唱着歌 'happily sing'
DE	attributive marker	standard	*gaoxing-DE rizi* 高兴的日子 'happy day'

Table 1: Examples illustrating the various syntactic roles of the DI suffix and DE suffix

Method	DI			DE			All
	Precision	Recall	F1	Precision	Recall	F1	Accuracy
MLM	1	0.8344	0.9097	**1**	0.6600	0.7951	0.7833
POS only	1	0.7232	0.8393	0.9970	0.7628	0.8643	0.7843
POS+base	0.7666	**0.9462**	0.8470	0.7645	**0.9732**	0.8563	0.8382
POS+base+head	**1**	0.9356	**0.9667**	0.9725	0.7920	**0.8730**	**0.8743**

Table 2: Adverbial identification performance

addition to "adverb" (d) as above. If the word segmentor combines the base word and suffix as one word, the tags for "auxiliary" (u) and idiom (i) are also accepted. This approach would correctly recognize the DE-adverbial in Figure 1a, but also falsely identify Figure 1b as an adverbial.

POS+base+head Our proposed approach aims to balance precision and recall with an additional constraint on the head word, which is automatically identified via dependency relations in the parse tree (Figure 1). It predicts "adverbial" only when the head word is tagged as "verb" (v), "adjective" (a), "idiom" (i), "abbreviation" (j), or "preposition" (p), since Chinese prepositions often function like verbs. The POS requirement on the head word is waived if the head word has a child word in a "subject-predicate" dependency relation, since the relation strongly suggests the head word can be modified by an adverbial. This approach would correctly reject Figure 1b as an adverbial since the head word *rizi* 'day' is tagged as a noun.

4.2 Masked language model baseline

As an additional baseline, we evaluated BERT[4], a state-of-the-art masked language model (Devlin et al., 2018; Wolf et al., 2020). Similar to the parsers, BERT is trained mostly on standard Chinese text (e.g., Chinese Wikipedia) that skews towards the standard adverbial marker. We mask the characters DE and DI in the input text.[5] We predict "adverbial" if BERT ranks DI higher than DE as a candidate word for the masked position.

5 Data

There is no publicly available, large-scale corpus of Chinese text with annotations on adverbial markers. We focused on modern Chinese literary works written during and after the Vernacular Language Movement, when the division of labor between DE and DI was formalized. We created a corpus by extracting all works by four prominent Chinese authors (Guo Moruo, Lao She, Lu Xun, and Mao Duo) posted on the *Baiwan Shuku* website.[6] There are a total of 911 works containing over 6 million characters.

A native speaker of Chinese with formal training in linguistics examined three words in this corpus: *manman* 慢慢 'slow', *keqi* 客气 'courteous', and *gaoxing* 高兴 'happy'. Each of the 1,057 occurrences was labelled as a base word in a DE-adverbial (447 instances); a base word in a DI-adverbial (465 instances); or neither (145 instances).

6 Experimental Results

POS+base+head. As shown in Table 2, our proposed approach achieved 87.43% accuracy in adverbial identification. It outperforms POS+base, which has the second highest accuracy at 83.82%, indicating the effectiveness in examining the head word.[7]

[4]https://huggingface.co/bert-base-chinese

[5]For example, *gaoxing-DE chang zhe ge* (Figure 1a) would be masked as *gaoxing* [MASK] *chang zhe ge*

[6]http://www.millionbook.com/mj/index.html, accessed in July 2019.

[7]The improvement is statistically significant at $p < 0.0158$ by McNemar's Test. The improvement is also significant against MLM at $p < 0.0001$ and POS only at $p < 0.0001$

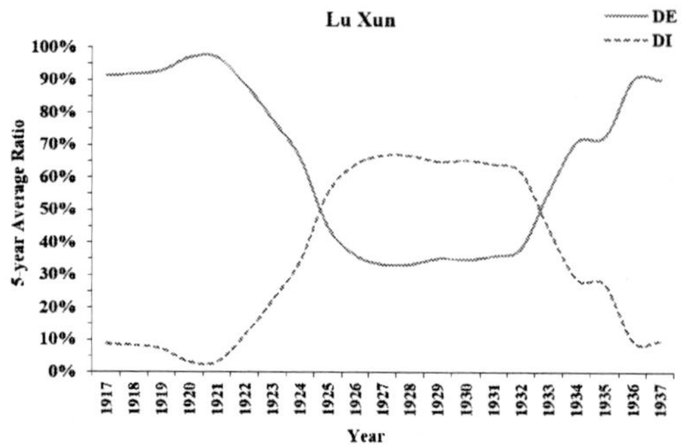

Figure 2: The proportion of DE-adverbials and DI-adverbials in the works of Lu Xun from 1917 to 1937.

The proposed approach also scored the highest F1 in identifying DI and DE adverbials. The relatively low recall resulted from the POS ambiguity for the head word. The parser sometimes erred on interpreting DE as marking attributives rather than adverbials, as many Chinese verbs share the same form as nouns. Recall was also affected by word segmentation errors, and parser errors where the base word is parsed as root.

POS only. The adverbials extracted by this approach were almost always true positives, with high precision for both DE- and DI-adverbials. The recall, however, was affected by noise in POS tagging, especially for DE-adverbials that do not modify verbs.

POS+base. This method outperformed the proposed approach in recall both for DI-adverbials (94.62%) and DE-adverbials (97.32%). However, it suffered from low precision (76.66% for DI-adverbials and 76.45% for DE-adverbials), partly due to false positives with incompatible head word POS.

Masked Language Model (MLM). This model achieved 100% precision but at the expense of low recall, especially for DE-adverbials (66.00%). It had difficulty recognizing a DE-adverbial especially when the verb is located at a long distance, in which case it tends to rank DE higher than DI.

7 Application

As an application of this research, we present a case study on the DE- vs. DI-adverbial usage of Lu Xun, arguably the most influential writer in modern Chinese literature. Literary works are ideal for studying adverbial markers since marker choices are more likely to be consciously rather than randomly made.

We used the POS+base+head method (Section 4.1) to automatically label *all* suffixed adverbials in his writings in our corpus. Over his career Lu Xun chose the DE suffix 56.9% of the time and the DI suffix in the rest. This overall figure, however, masks three distinct periods in which his marker usage varied.

Figure 2 shows a diachronic analysis, where each data point represents the average percentage of DE-adverbials and DI-adverbials within the 5-year window centered on the year on the horizontal axis. The initial period, from 1917 to 1924, was dominated by the non-standard marker DE. As he came under the influence of the Vernacular Movement, Lu Xun entered a second period around 1925. The DE percentage dropped dramatically from 65.7% in 1924 to 44.7% in 1925, reflecting his "innovative work in style" in several significant publications in 1925 (Gunn, 1991). In the 1930s, the call for a "mass language" gathered steam towards the end of the Vernacular Movement, with the goals of eradicating illiteracy and giving ordinary people access to writing. Subsequently the Latinized New Writing movement blurred the distinction between the two markers, leading to the re-emergence of the unified use of DE. An advocate of Latinization, Lu Xun reverted to non-standard markers, with the DE percentage approaching a similar level as the initial period.

8 Conclusions

This paper has presented the first study on identifying both standard and non-standard adverbial markers. We have proposed an unsupervised, rule-based algorithm based on dependency tree patterns. In an evaluation on modern Chinese literary text, our proposed method achieved an accuracy of over 87%, outperforming a state-of-the-art masked language model. Finally, we applied it on a diachronic analysis of adverbial marker choice in the works of a prominent author.

In future work, we aim to further improve performance in adverbial identification by incorporating supervised methods. As the DE vs. DI choice continues to evolve, it would also be interesting to examine contemporary authors and analyze their adverbial marker usage in comparison to those in the last century.

References

Jacob Devlin, Ming-Wei Chang, Kenton Lee, and Kristina Toutanova. 2018. Bert: Pre-training of deep bidirectional transformers for language understanding. *arXiv preprint arXiv:1810.04805*.

Edward Gunn. 1991. *Rewriting Chinese: Style and innovation in twentieth-century Chinese prose*. Stanford university press.

Hui Guo and Huayan Zhong. 2005. Chinese classifier assignment using svms. In *Proceedings of the Fourth SIGHAN Workshop on Chinese Language Processing*.

Han He. 2020. HanLP: Han Language Processing.

James Ho. 2015. From the use of three functional words "的, 地, 得" examining author's unique writing style–and on dream of red chamber author issues. *BIBLID*, 120(1):119–150.

Nicole Peinelt, Maria Liakata, and Shu-Kai Hsieh. 2017. Classifierguesser: A context-based classifier prediction system for Chinese language learners. In *Proceedings of the IJCNLP 2017, System Demonstrations*, pages 41–44.

Yongkang Tan. 2004. 状中结构助词混用的几个影响源 [in Chinese]. *Journal of Chongqing Radio Television University*, 3:42–43.

Jeffrey Weng. 2020. *Vernacular Language Movement*. Oxford University Press.

Thomas Wolf, Lysandre Debut, Victor Sanh, Julien Chaumond, Clement Delangue, Anthony Moi, Pierric Cistac, Tim Rault, Rémi Louf, Morgan Funtowicz, Joe Davison, Sam Shleifer, Patrick von Platen, Clara Ma, Yacine Jernite, Julien Plu, Canwen Xu, Teven Le Scao, Sylvain Gugger, Mariama Drame, Quentin Lhoest, and Alexander M. Rush. 2020. Transformers: State-of-the-art natural language processing. In *Proceedings of the 2020 Conference on Empirical Methods in Natural Language Processing: System Demonstrations*, pages 38–45, Online. Association for Computational Linguistics.

Fei Xia. 2000. The part-of-speech tagging guidelines for the Penn Chinese Treebank (3.0). *IRCS Technical Reports Series*, page 38.

Dan Xing, Endong Xun, Chengwen Wang, Gaoqi Rao, and Luyao Ma. 2020. Construction of adverbial-verb collocation database based on large-scale corpus. In *Workshop on Chinese Lexical Semantics*, pages 585–595. Springer.

Rongxiang Yang. 1999. On early modern Chinese adverbs. *Journal of Peking University (Humanities and social Sciences)*, 3.

Shiwen Yu, Jianming Lu, Xuefeng Zhu, Huiming Duan, Shiyong Kang, Honglin Sun, Hui Wang, Qiang Zhao, and Weidong Zhan. 2001. Processing norms of modern Chinese corpus. Technical report.

Yisheng Zhang. 2012a. On the selection of adverbial markers in contemporary Chinese [j]. *Chinese Linguistics*, 4.

Zheng-Sheng Zhang. 2012b. A corpus study of variation in written Chinese. *Corpus Linguistics and Linguistic Theory*, 8(1):209–240.

Data-Driven Detection of General Chiasmi Using Lexical and Semantic Features

Felix Schneider[1] and **Phillip Brandes**[2] and **Björn Barz**[1] and **Sophie Marshall**[2] and **Joachim Denzler**[1]
[1] Computer Vision Group
[2] Institut für Germanistische Literaturwissenschaft
Friedrich Schiller University Jena
Jena, Germany
firstname.lastname@uni-jena.de

Abstract

Automatic detection of stylistic devices is an important tool for literary studies, e.g., for stylometric analysis or argument mining. A particularly striking device is the rhetorical figure called chiasmus, which involves the inversion of semantically or syntactically related words. Existing works focus on a special case of chiasmi that involve identical words in an A B B A pattern, so-called antimetaboles. In contrast, we propose an approach targeting the more general and challenging case A B B' A', where the words A, A' and B, B' constituting the chiasmus do not need to be identical but just related in meaning. To this end, we generalize the established candidate phrase mining strategy from antimetaboles to general chiasmi and propose novel features based on word embeddings and lemmata for capturing both semantic and syntactic information. These features serve as input for a logistic regression classifier, which learns to distinguish between rhetorical chiasmi and coincidental chiastic word orders without special meaning. We evaluate our approach on two datasets consisting of classical German dramas, four texts with annotated chiasmi and 500 unannotated texts. Compared to previous methods for chiasmus detection, our novel features improve the average precision from 17% to 28% and the precision among the top 100 results from 13% to 35%.

1 Introduction

Knowledge about the use and distribution of stylistic devices, such as the chiasmus, can be used for stylometric purposes such as attribution to a certain author or genre (Pasanek and Sculley, 2008). Current computational methods for stylometry focus on analyzing word distributions and do not take more complex stylistic devices into account (Burrows, 2002; Jannidis, 2014; Dimpel et al., 2016). However, since styles may also differ in their use of stylistic devices, this is an important factor to consider. Different stylistic devices can also be an indicator of the structure of arguments (Mitrović et al., 2017; Lawrence et al., 2017). Automatic detection of stylistic devices is an important prerequisite for enabling such analyses at scale.

The chiasmus is a stylistic device that is found in texts since the antiquity. Chiasmus is defined as an inversion of semantically or syntactically related words, phrases, or sentences in an *A B B' A'* pattern (Fauser, 1994). It can be used, for example, to emphasize contrasts. One example for it is:

> **Eng** ist die **Welt**,
> und das **Gehirn** ist **weit**
> (**Narrow** is the **world**,
> and the **brain** is **wide**)
> *Wallensteins Tod* (Schiller, 1799)

The semantically related words are narrow and wide, as well as world and brain.

Existing works for automatic chiasmus detection focus on a special case called antimetabole, which consists of an inversion of identical lemmata (i.e. *A=A', B=B'*). An example for this is:

> **Un** pour **tous**, **tous** pour **un**
> (**One** for **all**, **all** for **one**)
> *Les Trois Mousquetaires* (Dumas, 1844)

Here, the inverted words are "all" and "one".

In contrast to this, we are interested in finding general chiasmi, where the lemmata can be different. In this work we present the first machine learning based method for finding general chiasmi. Existing methods find candidates by searching for inversions of lemmata. However, such an approach cannot find general chiasmi like the one by Schiller mentioned above, which does not consist of an inversion of lemmata but of semantic concepts.

We propose searching for chiasmus candidates by finding inversions of part-of-speech *(PoS)* tags in an *A B B' A'* pattern instead of inversions of lemmata. This requires more sophisticated filtering of the candidates, which include much more

Proceedings of LaTeCH-CLfL 2021, pages 96–100
Punta Cana, Dominican Republic (Online), November 11, 2021.

false positives without rhetorical intention. To this end, we use a linear classifier and propose a novel set of lexical and semantic features. Our semantic features are based on word embeddings (Mikolov et al., 2013; Bojanowski et al., 2017) to include information about the semantic relationship between the words constituting the chiastic pattern.

Compared with existing methods, our novel features improve the average precision from 17% to 28% in an experiment on four fully annotated dramas by Friedrich Schiller. Further experiments on 493 unannotated texts confirm the usefulness of our automatic general chiasmus detector, which improves the precision among the top 100 rated chiasmus candidates from 13% to 35%.

2 Related Work

Only few works address the detection of chiasmi, and the majority of those focus on antimetaboles and not the general case of chiasmus. While it is easy to capture all occurences of antimetabole in a text by just gathering all cross-wise repeating lemmata, this approach also yields a disproportionately high number of false positives (Gawryjolek, 2009). Thus the main challenge is to remove the false positives from the set of chiasmus candidates.

The approach of Dubremetz and Nivre (2015) introduces a filtering step for the chiasmus candidates. Here, the authors use hand-crafted features based on punctuation and word repetitions together with a maually tuned classifier. They expanded on their work with more features and machine learning (Dubremetz and Nivre, 2017, 2018), and trained a Kernel SVM and a linear classifier to detect antimetaboles, which constitutes the current state of the art. In contrast to their method, we search for candidates not based on lemmata but on PoS tags. We furthermore include novel features incorporating lemma information and semantic information about the conceptual similarity of the words constituting the chiasmus.

A first approach for general chiasmus detection was presented by Java (2015) by searching for inversions in syntax trees. However, this misses many true positives and they do not filter their results, leading to numerous false positives as well. In our work, we use inversions of PoS tags with an additional learning-based filtering step to find more candidates and discard more false positives.

3 Method

Our method consists of two steps; first the detection of suitable chiasmus candidates, second filtering these candidates using machine learning.

Candidate Extraction First we extract candidates from the text. In contrast to Dubremetz and Nivre (2018), we do not search for inversions of lemmata but of PoS tags. Like them, we limit the candidate phrase length to 30 tokens. With this stragety we find candidates for general chiasmi as well as antimetaboles. However, the candidates do not include lemma information a priori, in contrast to lemma-based candidate mining. We also find more false positive candidates, which raises the performance requirements for the subsequent filtering step. Thus, in addition to the Dubremetz features we include two new types of features in our work.

Dubremetz Features The features proposed by Dubremetz and Nivre (2018) comprise a combination of various elements like the number of identical words between the supporting words, the number of hard and soft punctiation marks at different positions, grammatical dependencies of the words, and n-gram-repetitions. For a full list of these features please refer to their work.

Lexical Features Since our generalized search procedure based on PoS tags does not consider lemma information anymore, we need to provide this information explicitly for the filter. Therefore, we include a novel set of *lexical features* to still capture this information. For all six pairs *AB, AB', AA', BB', BA', B'A'* of supporting tokens, we add a binary feature equaling 1 if the lemmata of the two tokens are identical and 0 otherwise.

Embedding Features To distinguish true chiasmi from random PoS tag inversions, the semantic relationship between the supporting tokens needs to be considered. We use word embeddings to integrate this semantic information, since they represent words as vectors in a space, where the distance between two vectors signifies their semantic relation (Bojanowski et al., 2017). For each pair of supporting tokens, we add an *embedding feature* equaling the cosine similarity (Salton et al., 1975) of the word embeddings of the two tokens.

Candidate Ranking We train a logistic regression classifier using the aforementioned features to distinguish true chiasmi from random PoS tag in-

	Schiller dramas			Dubremetz data
	Antimetaboles	Chiasmi	Combined	Antimetaboles
(baseline) D	0.21 ± 0.18	0.15 ± 0.07	0.17 ± 0.04	$\mathbf{0.73 \pm 0.24}$
L	0.07 ± 0.08	0.01 ± 0.00	0.02 ± 0.00	0.06 ± 0.01
E	0.10 ± 0.07	0.06 ± 0.03	0.09 ± 0.07	0.25 ± 0.13
LE	0.11 ± 0.06	0.05 ± 0.02	0.08 ± 0.04	0.25 ± 0.13
DL	$\mathbf{0.49 \pm 0.32}$	0.14 ± 0.09	0.22 ± 0.07	0.72 ± 0.24
DE	0.48 ± 0.30	$\mathbf{0.23 \pm 0.13}$	$\mathbf{0.28 \pm 0.01}$	$\mathbf{0.73 \pm 0.24}$
DLE	0.48 ± 0.30	0.19 ± 0.09	$\mathbf{0.28 \pm 0.08}$	$\mathbf{0.73 \pm 0.24}$

Table 1: Average precision for different feature combinations. D=Dubremetz features, L=lexical features, E=embedding features.

versions. For ranking candidates, we use the score obtained from the classifier's decision function.

4 Experiments

We perform two types of experiments[1]. First we evaluate the average precision (AP) of different feature combinations using 5-fold cross-validation on an annotated dataset to conduct an ablation study regarding the different feature types. AP describes the area under the precision-recall curve and is common in information retrieval. Additionally, we conduct this experiment on antimetabole candidates used by Dubremetz and Nivre (2018) for a comparison with their approach on their task.

In the second experiment, we evaluate how well our model generalizes to texts from different authors not included in the training data. To this end, we extract PoS tag inversions from the GerDraCor corpus (Fischer et al., 2019) and retrieve the top-scoring 100 candidates using our pre-trained classifier. These results are evaluated manually to assess the precision among the top 100 results.

For PoS tagging, dependencies, and word embeddings we use the *de_core_news_lg* model from spaCy (Honnibal et al., 2020). For the English data from Dubremetz and Nivre (2018), we use the spaCy *en_core_web_lg* model. To create syntax trees, we used CoreNLP (Manning et al., 2014).

Feature Combinations Our dataset[2] consists of four annotated texts by Friedrich Schiller, "Die Piccolomini", "Wallensteins Lager", "Wallensteins Tod", and "Wilhelm Tell". We annotated the whole texts, finding 45 general chiasmi and 9 antimetaboles. To obtain negative examples, we randomly chose 4000 PoS tag inversions from the 1,006,487 inversions in these texts.

Table 1 shows the AP of 5-fold cross-validation conducted with both the antimetaboles, chiasmi, and a combination of both as positive examples. It can be seen that all our additional features improve over the Dubremetz features alone, which are designed for finding antimetaboles in lemma inversions. Adding our novel features improves the detection of general chiasmi in PoS tag inversions. The combination of Dubremetz and lexical features improves the detection especially for antimetaboles. This shows that the lexical features include lemma information that is not present a priori with PoS tag inversions, including the information in the classifier, not in the candidate choice. When using only the novel features, the combination of both improves the results.

When we only search for chiasmi and exclude the antimetabole examples from the data, the combination of Dubremetz and embedding features yields the best results. Both the combinations of either embedding or all new features with the Dubremetz features improve over the baseline. However, in contrast to the antimetaboles-only experiment, the embedding features bring a stronger improvement than the rest. The combination with lexical features even slightly decreases the AP. This can also be seen when using only the novel features.

For the experiment with antimetaboles and chiasmi both considered as positive, the combination of the baseline and both novel feature sets or of the baseline and embedding features improves AP the most. The baseline features with the embedding features yield a better performance than the combination with the lexical features, both improving over the baseline. Lexical features are more important for Antimetabole detection, while embedding features help with the general chiasmus detection.

In addition, we tested our approach on English

[1]Code: `https://git.io/DetectChiasmus`
[2]Data: `https://git.io/ChiasmusData`

	Schiller dramas			Rest of the GerDraCor corpus		
	D method	D features	DLE	D method	D features	DLE
antimetaboles	6	2	**8**	7	2	**25**
chiasmi	5	5	**10**	6	9	**10**
combined	11	7	**18**	13	11	**35**

Table 2: Number of correct examples among the top 100 ranked ones in unseen texts for the Dubremetz method baseline, the PoS inversions with Dubremetz features and the Dubremetz+lexical+embedding (DLE) features.

data used by Dubremetz and Nivre (2018). This data consist of annotated candidates based on lemmata instead of PoS tags, so only the antimetabole detection can be tested. Since the novel features do not introduce additional information for candidates based on lemma inversions, the new features do not improve the detection.

We also tested the approach by Java (2015) on the *Combined* candidates, yielding a precision of 0.2% and a recall of 5.6%, compared to 10% and 69% with our *DLE* approach. This shows that in their approach most positive examples are discarded, while due to the missing filtering step many false positives occur.

Chiasmi in Unseen Texts Since we have shown that both the novel lexical and embedding features and their combination can help with the task of antimetabole and general chiasmus detection, we evaluate the generalization performance of our chiasmus classifier trained on the four annotated Schiller dramas to other texts. The first set of texts comprises seven other dramas by Friedrich Schiller, which contain a total of 2,822,313 PoS tag inversions and 80,606 lemma inversions. To see how well our method generalizes to different authors, we tested it on the remaining 493 documents from GerDraCor. For evaluation, we annotated the top-scoring 100 candidates manually.

We compare the baseline Dubremetz method based on lemma inversions with the full combination of the Dubremetz, lexical, and embedding features based on PoS tag inversions. Table 2 shows the results of this experiment. We can see that the precision among the top 100 rated candidates improved from 11% to 18% for the Schiller dramas and from 13% to 35% for the rest of the dataset. Interestingly, even the lemma-based baseline method finds some chiasmi. This is mainly due to some words with a common lemma, for example, *sich* can take the forms of *mich* and *dich* in the sentence and thus carry a chiasmus. We furthermore observe that the Dubremetz features together with the PoS tag inversions yield less positive examples than with lemma inversions. Since the number of PoS tag inversions is vastly higher than the number of lemma inversions, this is a much harder problem when the same feature set is used. The results show that our additional novel features are not only able to bridge this gap but also find substantially more chiasmi than the baseline.

The number of chiasmi compared to the number of PoS tag inversions in a text is extremely small; in our annotated dataset from the previous experiment, only 0.005% of the inversions were chiasmi or antimetaboles. Thus, our approach is suited to find these stylistic devices.

Since our candidate mining approach also allows all four PoS tags to be identical (i.e., A A A A instead of A B B A), we found that many of the false positives among the top 100 displayed another stylistic device: the parallelism.

5 Conclusion

We present a novel machine learning approach for a problem seldom addressed: the detection of general chiasmi. First, we extend the candidate mining scheme used by methods for the special case of antimetabole detection to general chiasmi by searching for inversions in PoS tags instead of lemmata. We then propose two new sets of *lexical* and *embedding* features, which encode information about the lemmata and word semantics.

Our experiments show that our approach outperforms the state of the art. Especially the semantic embedding features proved useful for detecting chiasmi and antimetaboles. Our approach still falls short of human performance, which is expected, as the number of chiasmi in a text is extremely low compared to the number of potential chiasmus candidates.

An interesting next research step is to test the model on different languages without retraining. Also, applying the method to search for parallelisms using an *A B A' B'* pattern seems promising.

References

Piotr Bojanowski, Edouard Grave, Armand Joulin, and Tomas Mikolov. 2017. Enriching word vectors with subword information. *Transactions of the Association for Computational Linguistics*, 5:135–146.

John Burrows. 2002. 'Delta': a Measure of Stylistic Difference and a Guide to Likely Authorship. *Literary and Linguistic Computing*, 17(3):267–287.

Friedrich Michael Dimpel, Victoria Gutsche, and René Wundke. 2016. Problematische Autorschaft. Zu ersten Anwendungsversuchen stilometrischer Methoden im Rahmen der Edition der Deutschen Politischen Schriften Zincgrefs. *Magazin für digitale Editionswissenschaften*, 2:23–32.

Marie Dubremetz and Joakim Nivre. 2015. Rhetorical figure detection: the case of chiasmus. In *Proceedings of the Fourth Workshop on Computational Linguistics for Literature*, pages 23–31, Denver, Colorado, USA. Association for Computational Linguistics.

Marie Dubremetz and Joakim Nivre. 2017. Machine learning for rhetorical figure detection: More chiasmus with less annotation. In *Proceedings of the 21st Nordic Conference on Computational Linguistics*, pages 37–45, Gothenburg, Sweden. Association for Computational Linguistics.

Marie Dubremetz and Joakim Nivre. 2018. Rhetorical figure detection: Chiasmus, epanaphora, epiphora. *Frontiers in Digital Humanities*, 5:10.

Alexandre Dumas. 1844. Les trois mousquetaires. *Le Siècle*.

Markus Fauser. 1994. *[Art.] Chiasmus, in Historisches Wörterbuch der Rhetorik*, volume 2, pages 171–173.

Frank Fischer, Ingo Börner, Mathias Göbel, Angelika Hechtl, Christopher Kittel, Carsten Milling, and Peer Trilcke. 2019. Programmable corpora: Introducing dracor, an infrastructure for the research on european drama.

Jakub Jan Gawryjolek. 2009. Automated annotation and visualization of rhetorical figures.

Matthew Honnibal, Ines Montani, Sofie Van Landeghem, and Adriane Boyd. 2020. spaCy: Industrial-strength Natural Language Processing in Python.

Fotis Jannidis. 2014. *Der Autor ganz nah – Autorstil in Stilistik und Stilometrie, in Theorien und Praktiken der Autorschaft*, pages 169–195. de Gruyter, Berlin.

James Java. 2015. *Characterization of Prose by Rhetorical Structure for Machine Learning Classification*. Ph.D. thesis, Nova Southeastern University.

John Lawrence, Jacky Visser, and Chris Reed. 2017. Harnessing rhetorical figures for argument mining.

Christopher D. Manning, Mihai Surdeanu, John Bauer, Jenny Rose Finkel, Steven Bethard, and David McClosky. 2014. The stanford corenlp natural language processing toolkit. In *ACL (System Demonstrations)*, pages 55–60. The Association for Computer Linguistics.

Tomás Mikolov, Kai Chen, Greg Corrado, and Jeffrey Dean. 2013. Efficient estimation of word representations in vector space. In *1st International Conference on Learning Representations, ICLR 2013, Scottsdale, Arizona, USA, May 2-4, 2013, Workshop Track Proceedings*.

Jelena Mitrović, Cliff O'Reilly, Miljana Mladenović, and Siegfried Handschuh. 2017. Ontological representations of rhetorical figures for argument mining.

Brad Pasanek and D. Sculley. 2008. Mining millions of metaphors. *Literary and Linguistic Computing*, 23(3):345–360.

G. Salton, A. Wong, and C. S. Yang. 1975. A vector space model for automatic indexing. *Commun. ACM*, 18(11):613–620.

Friedrich Schiller. 1799. *Wallensteins Tod*.

Translationese in Russian Literary Texts

Maria Kunilovskaya[1], Ekaterina Lapshinova-Koltunski[2], and Ruslan Mitkov[3]

[1,3]University of Wolverhampton
[2]Saarland University
[1]maria.kunilovskaya@wlv.ac.uk
[2]e.lapshinova@mx.uni-saarland.de
[3]r.mitkov@wlv.ac.uk

Abstract

The paper reports the results of a translationese study of literary texts based on translated and non-translated Russian. We aim to find out if translations deviate from non-translated literary texts, and if the established differences can be attributed to typological relations between source and target languages. We expect that literary translations from typologically distant languages should exhibit more translationese, and the fingerprints of individual source languages (and their families) are traceable in translations. We explore linguistic properties that distinguish non-translated Russian literature from translations into Russian. Our results show that non-translated fiction is different from translations to the degree that these two language varieties can be automatically classified. As expected, language typology is reflected in translations of literary texts. We identified features that point to linguistic specificity of Russian non-translated literature and to shining-through effects. Some of translationese features cut across all language pairs, while others are characteristic of literary translations from languages belonging to specific language families.

1 Introduction

In this paper, we pursue a comparative analysis of literary texts that include texts originally authored in Russian and Russian translations from a variety of source languages (SLs) using machine learning methods.

We seek to establish if and how non-translated literature in Russian differs from literary translations. More specifically, we test if literary translations from typologically distant languages (in relation to the target language [TL]) exhibit more translationese, and hence, are easier to predict in a text classification scenario.

There are only a few computational studies based on literary translations. Intuitively, literary texts should defy generalisation as each author's style and each literary work is expected to manifest unique forms of artistic expression. Besides, literary translation is viewed as an independent creative endeavour, which, under the dominant covert translation strategy, results in highly readable and fluent texts. Logically, translations in this register might be less dependent on their source texts in terms of frequency of linguistic features. To the best of our knowledge, there were no large-scale investigations into Russian translations of literary texts.

With a view to analysing translationese in literary texts, we formulate two research questions.

First, this study seeks to establish if non-translated literary texts differ from literary translations, and if they do, which linguistic properties distinguish non-translated Russian literature from translations into Russian (RQ1).

Second, this study has the objective to find out if the fingerprints of individual SLs and their typological families can be traced in Russian translations (RQ2).

It has been shown that translationese "dialects" generated by typologically similar languages tend to demonstrate more similarities than those coming from typologically distant SLs (see Section 2). To explore the impact of SLs on the target text properties, we use a set of machine learning experiments automatically classifying translated and non-translated fiction in Russian in binary and multiclass scenarios. This study reports the classification performance and identifies discriminative features of translated and non-translated literature. We conjecture that this investigation can yield empirical evidence of various translational strategies pursued in individual language pairs. All linguistic inconsistencies in relations between translations and non-translations for specific language pairs that we identify can be further tackled from the point of view of critical translation studies, which focuses on social and cultural practices in translation.

Proceedings of LaTeCH-CLfL 2021, pages 101–112
Punta Cana, Dominican Republic (Online), November 11, 2021.

2 Related Work

Translationese and literary texts Translationese studies analyse linguistic features shared by translations that make them distinct from comparable non-translated texts (Gellerstam, 1986; Baker, 1993). The deviations of translations from comparable originally-authored texts in the target language (referred to as 'non-translations' in this paper) are revealed through the analysis of translationese indicators, i.e. linguistic features that exhibit a different frequency distribution in translations as compared to non-translations. These features are used to automatically distinguish translations from non-translations (Baroni and Bernardini, 2006; Volansky et al., 2015; Rabinovich and Wintner, 2015; Rubino et al., 2016; Kunilovskaya and Lapshinova-Koltunski, 2020). The choice of candidate translationese indicators is usually motivated by expectations of specific translational behaviours based on cross-linguistic contrastive properties of a given language pair or by (theoretically) known patterns in translations. Over the decades of translationese research, several dozens of features were tested, with some being especially effective in a number of settings. Features used for analysis of translationese are also widely used in register analysis, variational linguistics and stylometry. Several studies have shown that combinations perform better than individual features in machine learning setting for a number of translationese-related tasks (Lynch and Vogel, 2012; Evert and Neumann, 2017; Sominsky and Wintner, 2019). However, it is also a fact that translationese indicators can be specific for language pairs and registers, and literary translation is an Most corpus-based translationese studies of literary texts offer a single-feature analysis and do not employ machine learning (ML), e.g. passive constructions (Kolehmainen and Riionheimo, 2016), *that*-complementiser (Olohan, 2001), phrasal verbs (Cappelle and Loock, 2017), complex non-finite constructions, clause connectives and keywords (Puurtinen, 2003).

Popescu (2011) and Lynch and Vogel (2012) are the only works known to us that use ML approach to the study of translationese in literary texts. The first study compared originally-written English literary texts with translations from French and German using character 5-grams. The second study reports the results of SL detection based on English literary translations from Russian, German and French. Their four-class classifier achieved the accuracy of 80% on a combined set of 50 features, including such surface features as frequencies of most-used part-of-speech (PoS) bigrams, 15 top token unigrams (mostly functional words) and 19 document-level features such as sentence- and word-length and readability scores. The authors analysed some of the top-ranking features trying to link them to the SLs. We propose a similar experiment: we run a multiclass classification on a set of features trying to identify best predictors. However, we rely on very different – more interpretable, language-specific and translationally-motivated – features and experiment on a twice bigger data from a wider range of SLs. The mapping of individual features to known tendencies in translational behaviour was shown to be disputable, with one feature being associated with various tendencies (Zanettin, 2013; Kunilovskaya and Corpas Pastor, 2021), and we refrain from establishing the indicator-tendency link in the top-down manner.

Source language detection Source language detection task utilises the fact that translations tend to retain enough traces of the SLs involved (shining-through effect, Teich, 2003) for the benefits of linguistic typology and practical purposes of establishing translation direction in parallel corpora. For instance, Rabinovich et al. (2017) showed that the signal from the source language is enough to restore the phylogenetic languages trees. The authors experimented on English translations of European parliamentary speeches from languages representing three families and showed that classification errors most frequently occurred between languages from the same family. SLs with isomorphic structures tend to share more features in translations to a third language. That idea was exploited by Bjerva et al. (2019) who explored genetic, geographical and structural distances between languages and found that similarities between embeddings learnt from translations correlated best with the structural distance values obtained from vectorised treebanks of respective SLs meaning that translations carried over structural properties of their sources, while geographic coordinates and genetic distances calculated from phylogenetic trees did not correlate with the properties of translations as well. Dutta Chowdhury et al. (2020) showed that the more isomorphism was detected between translations into English and non-translated English, the closer the source languages were to English. They learned delexicalised multi-view representations – embeddings based on PoS, semantic tags, and synsets – and used isomorphism between embedding spaces. However, all these studies used parliamentary speeches, which belong to a more conventionalised text type than fiction. These texts, as well as their translations, are more homogeneous in style in comparison to literary texts used in the present paper. The translators are also more constrained in their linguistic choices by the requirements of official and documentary nature of texts. All the studies above cover English as the target language, whereas we focus on Russian.

A recent study by Hu and Kübler (2021) showed that translationese features not discriminative for English translations worked for a different language. The authors analysed Chinese translations of journalistic texts from seven SLs in a ML classification approach. This study stands out, because it defined Chinese-specific translationese features, while most research in the field relied on easily-extractable language-independent features. They made observations on typological traces of the SLs manifested in the TL-unusual frequencies of certain feature groups.

SL-TL distance and the strength of the SL signal in translations is also key to solving the task of translation direction detection: Sominsky and Wintner (2019) found that the more distant were the source and the target languages, the higher the results. The authors achieved accuracy of 80-90%, even though they were challenged to perform classification at sentence-level. Their feature set was designed to address the sparsity of data, inevitable if typical document-level features were used. They relied on alignment of phrases identified as 'minimal translation units' and represented with PoS. The relation between predictability of translations and the divergence between the source and the target languages was also analysed by Nikolaev et al. (2020). The authors used entropy measures to check whether morphosyntactic entropies of original-language corpora are significantly different from those of corpora containing translations[1]. The results showed that translations from similar and distant languages were predictable in different ways: structurally-similar SLs favoured the use of a narrower range of syntactic patterns limited to those shared by two languages, which constituted one type of translation specificity. In translations from highly-divergent languages, however, translators tended to produce non-idiomatic translations, that were not recognised by models trained on the target language.

3 Research Design

3.1 Data

In the current work, all data comes from the parallel subcorpus of translations into Russian of the Russian National Corpus (RNC). We followed a rigid data selection procedure to reduce possible confounding factors. Our sampling frame is aimed at reducing the influence of idiolects, while giving us enough data per language pair for machine learning experiments. It includes the following criteria, applied recursively:

- size and number of available documents (at least 30,000 tokens);
- unique combination of author and translator to avoid the influence of the over-represented authors or translators;
- no auto-translations or novels by bilingual authors (e.g. Nabokov, Vasil Bykov);
- translations produced after 1940 till now (sources are more widely spread in time).

The resulting sample consists of 11 translational subcorpora. We chunked this corpus to ensure direct comparability of results between language pairs and to properly balance our data. To this end, we randomly selected six books from each subcorpus, making sure that the average sentence length of the selected books is in the empirically-established optimal range (9, 22) to provide for generic homogeneity of the data (this constraint excluded novels with considerable parts written in verse or as drama).

From each of the selected books, we randomly extracted 15 chunks of about 150 consecutive sentences. We preferred chunking by the number of sentences rather than by word count as many of our features are normalised to the number of sentences. A comprehensive overview of the size of data in each subcorpus after chunking and lemmatisation is given in Figure 1. Translational data used in our experiments roughly totals 2,538,951 tokens (168,683 sentences), with each subcorpus represented by 90 chunks totalling at least 200,000 tokens (with

[1]The authors use a small pre-existing Parallel Universal Dependencies corpus of 1000 sentences from the news domain and Wikipedia translated from English into eight languages

the exception of Belarusian (187,000 tokens and Swedish 189,000 tokens), the number of sentences being roughly 15,000 per source language. The SLs in the resulting corpus come from four language families: Romance (French, Spanish), Germanic (Swedish, English, German), Balto-Slavic (Baltic: Latvian, Slavic: Polish, Belarusian, Ukrainian, Bulgarian) and Uralic (Finnish) based on phylogenetic languages tree in (Serva and Petroni, 2008). Figure 1 also shows a subcorpus of non-translations (marked as Russian). It was built following the sampling and chunking principles described above from the monolingual part of the RNC.

All translational subcorpora are in one-sentence-per-line format. We discarded by-lines and headings, such as "Chapter 5", "Jane Eyre" and "Charlotte Bronte", empty lines and lines without alpha, including cases where the absence of text was marked with "—". The 11 translational subcorpora and non-translations were annotated within Universal Dependencies (UD) framework using UDPipe (v1, Straka and Straková, 2017).[2] The chunks in the resulting conllu format were used as input to our feature extraction module.

3.2 Features

Fist and foremost, this research aims to shed a light on how the Russian language of translated fiction is different from that used in the original Russian prose. This motivates the selection of the research design focused on features. We included a few well-known translationese indicators and a number of Russian-specific features extracted from parsed sentences. Such features as sentence length, content-lemma-based type-to-token ratio, lexical density, frequencies of discourse markers are known to predict translations well in a range of target languages and registers.

The motivation for including primarily structural features is manifold: (i) these features are less vulnerable to sparsity given a chunk size of around 2000 tokens (used e.g. in Volansky et al., 2015; Hu and Kübler, 2021); (ii) it is a common practice in translationese studies to refrain from using lexical features to avoid the impact of domain differences between translations and non-translations; and (iii) various morphosyntactic features (frequency of demonstratives, relative clauses, modal predicates, etc.) were shown to be effective in translationese detection. In a previous study based on Russian, these structural features were shown to work much better than lexical features (such as n-gram ranks and PMI scores, see Kunilovskaya and Corpas Pastor, 2021). Of several dozens of UD relations, we use the subset of seven relations that was shown to perform well for translationese detection in English-to-Russian mass-media texts (Kunilovskaya and Kutuzov, 2018).

We also included features that are susceptible to change in translation, according to textbooks on practical translations. Due to contrastive differences, translations into Russian (from Germanic languages, at least) are expected to feature higher frequencies of:

- pronominal determiners, e.g. этот, тот, весь, каждый, некоторый (this, that, all, every, some);
- possessive pronouns, e.g. мой, твой, его (my, your, his);
- relative and adverbial clauses that might be used for unpacking dense and unusual syntactic constructions in other languages;
- modal predicates – Он может знать ответ (He might know the answer) instead of a more typical Возможно, он знает ответ (Probably he knows the answer).

At the same time, we expect lower frequencies for:

- negative particles or main sentence negation,
- deverbal nouns and
- simple sentences.

Most of our extraction rules rely on the UD output, and we are constrained by the quality of annotation in this respect. Overall, our feature set includes 45 features[3]; their values are normalised frequencies of various UD tags and their combinations. The features include morphological forms (past tense, passive voice form, etc.), syntactic features (e.g. number of clauses per sentence, sentence length), word classes (e.g. types of pronominal function words, adverbial quantifiers), and dependency relations (e.g. adjectival clause, clausal complement). Besides, we include two features reflecting sentence complexity: mean hierarchical

[2] With the Russian model trained on SynTagRus treebank (v2.5, Droganova et al., 2018).

[3] We provide the full list of features in Appendix A.

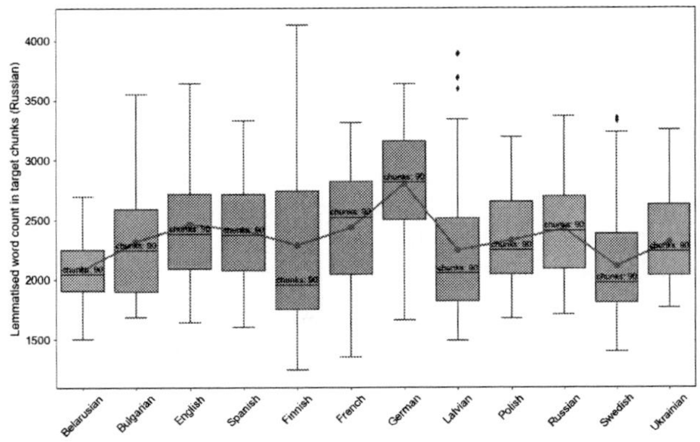

Figure 1: Distribution of chunk sizes (in tokens) in each subcorpus after lemmatisation

distance and mean dependency distance (described in Jing and Liu, 2015) and two features reflecting richness of vocabulary - type-to-token ratio and lexical density.

The normalisation basis varies depending on the type of feature as recommended in (Evert and Neumann, 2017): total tokens for word classes; number of sentences for conjunctions and modal predicates; total verbs for verb forms; total number of dependencies in the sentence for the selected types of dependencies.

3.3 Methods

We run two types of experiments: (i) a set of 11 binary classifications where we compare Russian translations from each of the SLs and fiction originally authored in Russian; and (ii) 12-class classification where we test whether data from any subcorpora stand out as very different from the rest of translated and non-translated Russian. Support Vector Machine (SVM) with Radial Basis Function (rbf) kernel is used as the main algorithm in both settings. Each feature was centred around the mean and scaled to feature standard deviation independently. The models are evaluated using cross-validation.

To avoid overfitting, we used scikit-learn *GroupKFold* algorithm which generated cross-validation folds where training and test sets in each split did not include chunks from the same books. In other words, in each iteration we trained the model on 10 books and tested on the two unseen books, one from each class. If this precaution is not in place, we may end up achieving unrealistically high accuracy for all binary classifications. While we have 6 books for each subcorpus, the maximum number of cross-validation splits that we can afford is six (book-aware 6-fold cross-validation). In the multiclass scenario, we used standard 10-fold cross-validation instead.

The multiclass classifier predicts the source language of translations or Russian for non-translations. In this experiment, we use one-vs-rest decision-making strategy, i.e a binary classifier is fitted on data splits, which cast each class against all the other classes. At test time, an unseen sample is predicted by all classifiers, and the most confident prediction is output.

For all ML experiments below we report accuracy and macro F1-score. Note that our 12 subcorpora are well-balanced with regard to the number of observations: translations from each SL and non-translations are represented by 90 chunks of text. A fair random chance level for binary classifiers is 50%, F1 = 0.5. For 12-class classification, a pseudo-classifier with random predictions on a uniform distribution achieves the accuracy of 9.8%, with F1-score 0.10.

To detect features particularly useful in our translationese classifications, we used two approaches: (i) ANOVA-based feature selection; and (ii) feature weights analysis. The first method utilises significant differences in feature values and helps us to find out an optimal subset of features for better classification results, while getting rid of possible noise in the data. We compare lists of selected features across all 11 classifications to see whether those involving translations from similar languages have a bigger intersection of best translationese indicators.

In the second approach, we followed Teich et al. (2016) and Argamon et al. (2008) to tap into feature weights returned by each classifier. Note, that to get access to feature weights we had to switch to an SVM with a linear kernel[4]. The feature weights indicate which of the features from the list push the classifiers decision towards this or that class. The features assigned to a certain class are interpreted as distinctive for this particular class. The features with the greatest weights, averaged across all folds, are particularly important. Using this methodology, we aim to discover features that are associated with Russian non-translated literature as opposed to any translations in all 11 classification tasks. Similarly, the intersection of the features distinctive for translations in each of the 11 classifications can be seen as universal indicators of translationese in Russian translated literature.

4 Results and Discussion

4.1 Classifier performance

Binary scenario To answer the questions if Russian non-translated literary texts are distinct from literary translations, and if the scale of the differences can be linked to the SL typology, we compare the results from 11 binary classifications, where non-translated Russian is classified against translations from each of the 11 languages in our data (Russian vs. translations from English, vs. translations from Ukrainian, etc.). The results in Table 1 are arranged with regard to proximity to Russian – (1) Germanic, Romance and Uralic, i.e. typologically distant languages (in relation to Russian) including English (en), German (ge), Swedish (sv), Spanish (es), French (fr) and Finnish (fi), and (2) Balto-Slavic, i.e. typologically close languages, i.e. Latvian (lv), Belarusian (be), Ukrainian (uk), Polish (pl), Bulgarian (bg). Our hypothesis was that the more distant a language is with regard to Russian, the better the classification results.

One immediate observation from Table 1 is that all classification results were above the chance level of 50% accuracy. Translations from typologically distant languages returned higher accuracy (over 70% accuracy) than translations from Slavic languages (in the range from 59% to 67%). The two bold exceptions from this generalisation were translations from French and Bulgarian. Texts translated from Bulgarian were easier to distinguish from non-translated Russian literature than texts from other Slavic languages (accuracy 72.22%) This result could be attributed to the peculiar traits of the Bulgarian grammar that is different from other Slavic languages (e.g. absence of noun cases, infinitives, complex conjugation system). Novels translated from French were comparatively difficult to distinguish from non-translated Russian literature (accuracy 60.56%). A very similar low classification accuracy was demonstrated by translations from Ukrainian (59.44%). The greatest differences between translations and non-translations were seen for the German subcorpus, for which the accuracy reached 84.44%. The results for Slavic languages are consistently more than 2% lower than the accuracy for distant languages.

	language	accuracy	F-score
	en	75.56	0.74
	ge	*84.44*	*0.84*
	sv	71.11	0.70
(1)	es	74.44	0.74
	fr	**60.56**	**0.56**
	fi	70.00	0.67
	lv	61.11	0.59
	be	65.56	0.63
(2)	*uk*	*59.44*	*0.56*
	pl	67.22	0.64
	bg	**72.22**	**0.70**

Table 1: Results of 11 binary classifiers

It is noteworthy that relatively low translationese classification results as compared to results reported in other studies on translationese in fiction (Lynch and Vogel, 2012; Popescu, 2011) can be attributed to the rigour of our evaluation setup. If we used standard 10-fold cross-validation ignorant of the book-associated groups in the data, the binary classification results (with the same hyperparameter settings C=10.0, gamma=0.01 for the RGF kernel) would range from 89.44% (Belarusian) to 98.89% (Swedish). This is an indirect evidence that each translated book has its own unique and learnable structural peculiarities.

With regard to the features that might be less useful, we established that reducing the feature set by a third, to 30 features selected by ANOVA by each binary classifier independently, degraded the results by only 1% to 7% (for Finnish and Swedish there was no change in performance). On the reduced feature set the observations about the impact of typological differences on translationese properties were still standing. The description of the selected and discarded features appears in Section 4.2.

[4]The linear kernel accuracy for binary setting differs from the rbf kernel in the range from -10% for German to +5% for Ukrainian

Classification errors in multiclass scenario To further explore the differences in translationese dialects observed in translations from typologically-grouped SLs, we tried to distinguish the 12 classes representing SLs and Russian in our data in a multiclass scenario. In particular, we are interested in classification errors obtained from a confusion matrix that helped us to see if typologically close languages were more frequently confused with each other than more distant languages.

Overall, the 12-class classification achieved the accuracy of 65.4% with a macro F1-score of 0.68 (rbf kernel, 10-fold cross-validation, one-vs-rest strategy, C=0.1, gamma=0.01). The best classification results based on macro F1-score were seen for Russian (F1 = 0.78). Translations from Finnish were second most recognisable (F1 = 0.74). However, the Russian class had much higher recall (as expected, some translations, except those from German and Swedish, were erroneously classified as Russian non-translation). Note that true Russian texts were relatively rare mistaken for translations. The specificity of translations from Finnish was such that it did not attract many misclassifications. To visualise misclassification patterns and to see which SL translations were most often confused with each other, we drew a directed graph based on error statistics, see Figure 2. It has classes as nodes and the number of false positive errors for each language pair on edges. To distil the important error patterns, we retained only the edges with over 5 errors (5% of the size of the expected class).

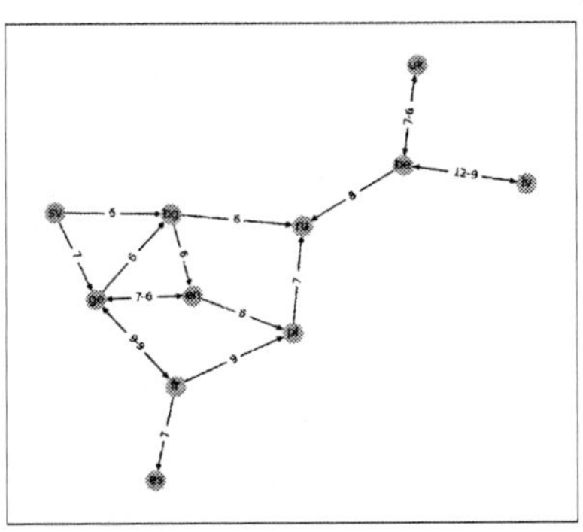

Figure 2: Errors in multi-class classification

Figure 2 confirms our expectations that translations from typologically similar languages are more often confused between themselves. The upper right corner of the graph has East Slavic languages and Latvian, which have the highest number of mutual misclassifications (esp. between Belarusian and Latvian) and are often confused with Russian. The lower part of the graph shows errors between Romance languages, while Germanic languages seem to be grouped together by error statistics on the left. Belarusian, Bulgarian and Polish are the three Slavic languages that are confused with non-translated Russian fiction. At the same time, both Bulgarian and Polish were also confused with either translations from English and other Germanic languages, or French, respectively. The error patterns that emphasised language families got stronger if we reduced the number of features to top 30 (not shown for considerations of space). One curious and unexpected observation from the error network analysis is that Bulgarian and Polish attracted more errors from non-Slavic languages than any other Slavic language.

4.2 Feature Analysis

Feature selection These experiments are aimed at finding the best-performing subset of features for all classifiers, if possible, and for individual SLs.

We assume that the intersection of the best features selected by each of the 11 binary classifiers contains translationese indicators that cut across all language pairs. We found that this intersection included only three features if we capped the number of best features (selected based on analysis of variance [ANOVA] results) at 30: contrastive connectives (`advers`), adverbial clause introduced by a pronominal (`whconj`) and demonstrative pronouns (`demdets`). However, their importance varied across the classifiers. This is confirmed by the difference in their ranks on the ordered lists of selected features and by the volatility of classifiers' performance on this subset of features. The lack of wide feature intersection in the best features for all classifiers indicates that translations from each SL have unique properties that distinguish them from non-translations, and using any universal subset of features can be sub-optimal to achieve the best classification results. To test this assumption, we found the number of features (in the range of 1 to 45) which returned the highest classification accuracy for each of the 11 classifications. Note that the performance of all classifiers in this setting was much higher than reported in Table 1 and ranged between 73.89 (Finnish) and 87.78 (German) for distant languages, and between 73.33 (Belarusian) and 82.78 (Bulgarian) for Slavic languages. It turned out that some translations were recognised best on just a few features, while using more features degraded classification quality. For example, translations from Spanish, French and Polish were best separated from non-translations using just one feature (translations had significantly higher frequencies of relative clauses, demonstrative pronouns and clausal modifiers of nouns, respectively); translations from Swedish seem to have two strong translationese indicators: more demonstrative pronouns and fewer interrogative sentences.

Not surprisingly, close Slavic languages (Belarusian, Ukrainian) require larger feature sets (15 and 21 features, respectively) to achieve best classification results. Their distinctions from non-translations are more subtle and cannot be reliably captured by a few features. Even in this best setting, we were able to achieve 73.33% and 77.22% accuracy for translations from Belarusian and Ukrainian respectively.

At the same time, the largest feature set was called for to achieve the best accuracy for German: the classifier used 38 features to achieve the accuracy of 87.78%, which was higher than for any other SL. The second best result was returned for English: accuracy 86.67% on 14 features. The same feature set was particularly useful for capturing translationese in Russian and German translations from English (Kunilovskaya and Lapshinova-Koltunski, 2020), however on other text types than literature.

Every of the 45 features was selected by at least one of the 11 classifiers as part of the best-performing feature subset. Admittedly, it is best to develop language-pair-specific features for best results in each language pair. Using a universal set of count-based features in a setting similar to ours can introduce noise and degrade the quality of classification. However, a comprehensive feature set can be useful for exploratory purposes in frameworks where the metadata about SLs is not available. The most popular feature was demonstrative pronouns selected by eight classifiers, followed by lexical density, mean hierarchical distance, adverbial clauses and parataxis, found in five best feature sets. The least relevant features, appearing on just one of the best feature lists, included passive voice auxiliaries, lexical type-to-token ratio, copula verbs, temporal-sequential connectives and clausal complements.

With regard to the features selected for typologically similar SLs, English and German rely on 13 shared features (of 14 features selected to identify English translations). The best classification setups to distinguish translations from Belarusian and Ukrainian from Russian non-translations share six features. Interestingly, English-German and Belarusian-Ukrainian intersection had only one feature in common (adverbial clause introduced by a pronominal – `whconj`). This supports the hypothesis that translations from similar SLs have similar translationese properties.

Features of non-translated Russian The analysis of feature weights from the binary classifiers yielded five features associated with the non-translations class in all 11 binary classifications: `simple` (simple sentences), `interrog` (interrogative sentences), `mpred` (modal predicates), `pasttense` (past tense), `ccomp` (clausal complements). This means that these five features were characteristic for Russian literary texts if compared to literary translations into Russian from any language. However, their weights varied across the 11 classification tasks. None of them was shared in the 10 most weighted features, indicating that the classifier found more useful (more weighted) features to take the decision in each given subcorpus.

Past tense was selected among the top translationese predictors in all classifications except the one against translations from Finnish, while interrogative sentences (i.e. ending in '?') were important for Russian in all classifications except those against translations from Ukrainian, Latvian and Finnish.

Interestingly, sentence length was a strong indicator of Russian class and appeared in top 10 features in 9 classifications. It means that using feature weights and ANOVA for identifying distinctive features returned intersecting, but not identical results, which should be taken into consideration in further literary analysis.

A glance at the data table reveals that interrogative sentences were more frequent in Russian non-translated texts than in translations, whereas modal predicates had lower frequency. The low frequency of modal predicates in non-translated literature is in accord with our assumptions about the differences between translated and non-translated Russian (see Section 3.2 above). Interrogatives are typical of narrative texts containing dialogues between characters, but they can also be used as rhetorical means to actively engage the reader as in example (1).

(1) Тут меня охватило раздражение – <кого-кого>? В <каком> округе? Да <что> за китайская грамота такая? (Then I was seized by irritation – who? Which county? What double Dutch is that?)

High frequency of interrogatives may also indicate the authority relations between interactants (Halliday and Matthiessen, 2014).

In our chunks, in most source text collections there were fewer interrogative sentences than in Russian non-translations. Russian translations actually introduced additional question marks, a typical normalisation behaviour. Can it be a sign of the specificity of Russian fiction compared to other national literatures? However, a deep qualitative analysis is needed to find a true explanation of this observation.

Source language translationese Using the same technique as applied for the Russian non-translations, we searched for the overlaps between most-weighted features associated with the translations class in 11 binary classifications. We found five overlapping features, universal for all literary translations in our data: `lexdens` (lexical density), `demdets` (demonstrative determiners), `relativ` (relative clauses), `advers` (adversative discourse markers) and `whconj` (adverbial clauses introduced by a pronominal adverb). However, similarly with the results observed for the non-translations, none of them appears in all lists of top 10 predictors of the translated class. At the same time, `lexdens` has high weights associated with translations from 9 languages (all except German and French), `demdets` – with 8, `relative` – with 7, `advers` and `whconj` – both with 6.

Remarkably, all of them show higher frequencies in translated Russian (with an exception of lexical density). This result is in line with expectations for the four features, based on what is known about translational behaviour from earlier studies: `demdets`, `relativ`, `whconj`, `advers`. For example, the increased use of the adversative markers (наоборот, несмотря на, однако) expressing the relation of contrast and comparison, could indicate explicitation in translation, as there are studies showing that this type of relation is cognitively more complex, and thus is more frequently expressed with explicit signals than other discourse relations (Hoek et al., 2017).

The observation on the low value of lexical density (i.e ratio of PoS disambiguated content words types to the total number of running words) in non-translated Russian if compared to translations into Russian deserves a comment. Since translated texts are predominantly reported to have a lower lexical density than non-translations (see e.g. Laviosa, 1998; Steiner, 2012), our findings are surprising. Steiner (2012) reports lower lexical density for fiction translated from German into English than for the English non-translated texts in the same register. At the same time, this tendency may differ for translations of fiction. According to register studies (see Biber et al., 1999, p. 62), fictional texts are characterised by lower lexical density values (if compared to general language) due to dialogues and complex purposes of fictional writing that combines informational aspects and aesthetic concerns. This means that translations in our data may show a higher degree of colloquial, spoken or source-culture-specific elements than non-translated Russian literature, which relies on a narrower range of vocabulary or has a higher proportion of non-content words.

5 Conclusion

We focused on the phenomenon of translationese in Russian literature to find out that Russian non-translated literary texts are rarely confused with translations, and thus are very distinct. Translated Russian literary texts differ from non-translated ones to the degree that they can be automatically detected and the source language signal is strong enough to be traced in translations. As assumed, typologically close languages are more frequently confused with each other than more distant languages, which points to language typology being reflected also in translations of literary texts. The analysed features that distinguish translations and non-translations help to uncover specificity of Russian non-translated literature. We were also able to detect some universal features of translationese in fiction, as well as language-specific and language-typology-specific translation features. We plan to use these results as guidance in a more qualitative analysis of the features that behave differently in translated language, and of language pairs (esp. Bulgarian and French) which were found diverting from the observed trend, in the framework of critical translation studies.

References

Shlomo Argamon, Jeff Dodick, and Paul Chase. 2008. Language use reflects scientific methodology: A corpus-based study of peer-reviewed journal articles. *Scientometrics*, 75(2):203–238.

Mona Baker. 1993. Corpus linguistics and translation studies: Implications and applications. In G. Francis Baker M. and E. Tognini-Bonelli, editors, *Text and Technology: in Honour of John Sinclair*, pages 233–250. Benjamins, Amsterdam.

Marco Baroni and Silvia Bernardini. 2006. A new approach to the study of translationese: Machine-learning the difference between original and translated text. *Literary and Linguistic Computing*, 21(3):259–274.

Douglas Biber, Susan Conrad, Edward Finegan, Stig Johansson, Geoffrey Leech, Susan Conrad, Edward Finegan, and Randolph Quirk. 1999. *Longman grammar of spoken and written English*, volume 2. MIT Press.

Johannes Bjerva, Robert Östling, Maria Han Veiga, Jörg Tiedemann, and Isabelle Augenstein. 2019. What do language representations really represent? *Computational Linguistics*, 45(2):381–389.

Bert Cappelle and Rudy Loock. 2017. Typological differences shining through : The case of phrasal verbs in translated English. In Gert De Sutter, Marie-Aude Lefer, and Isabelle Delaere, editors, *Empirical Translation Studies. New Theoretical and Methodological Traditions*, pages 235–264. Mouton de Gruyter.

Kira Droganova, Olga Lyashevskaya, and Daniel Zeman. 2018. Data conversion and consistency of monolingual corpora: Russian ud treebanks. In *Proceedings of the 17th international workshop on treebanks and linguistic theories (tlt 2018)*, volume 155, pages 53–66.

Koel Dutta Chowdhury, Cristina España i Bonet, and Josef van Genabith. 2020. Understanding Translationese in Multi-view Embedding Spaces. In *Proceedings of the 28th International Conference on Computational Linguistics*, pages 6056–6062, Barcelona, Spain. Online.

Stefan Evert and Stella Neumann. 2017. The impact of translation direction on characteristics of translated texts : A multivariate analysis for English and German. *Empirical Translation Studies: New Methodological and Theoretical Traditions*, 300:47.

Bruce Fraser. 2006. Towards a Theory of Discourse Markers. *Approaches to discourse particles*, 1:189–204.

Martin Gellerstam. 1986. Translationese in Swedish novels translated from English. In L. Wollin and H. Lindquist, editors, *Translation Studies in Scandinavia*, pages 88–95. CWK Gleerup, Lund.

MAK Halliday and Ruqaiya Hasan. 1976. *Cohesion in English*. Equinox.

Michael A.K. Halliday and Christian M.I.M Matthiessen. 2014. *Halliday's introduction to Functional Grammar. Revised by Christian M.I.M. Matthiessen*. Routledge, London.

J. Hoek, S. Zufferey, J. Evers-Vermeul, and T.J.M. Sanders. 2017. Cognitive complexity and the linguistic marking of coherence relations: A parallel corpus study. *Journal of Pragmatics*, 121:113–131.

Hai Hu and Sandra Kübler. 2021. Investigating translated chinese and its variants using machine learning. *Natural Language Engineering*, 27(3):339–372.

Yingqi Jing and Haitao Liu. 2015. Mean Hierarchical Distance Augmenting Mean Dependency Distance. In *Proceedings of the Third International Conference on Dependency Linguistics (Depling 2015)*, pages 161–170.

Leena Kolehmainen and Helka Riionheimo. 2016. Literary Translation as Language Contact: A Pilot Study on the Finnish Passive. *International Journal of Literary Linguistics*, 5(3):1–32.

Maria Kunilovskaya and Gloria Corpas Pastor. 2021. Translationese and register variation in English-to-Russian professional translation. In *New Perspectives on Corpus Translation Studies*. Springer.

Maria Kunilovskaya and Andrey Kutuzov. 2018. Universal Dependencies-based syntactic features in detecting human translation varieties. *Proceedings ofthe 16th International Workshop on Treebanks and Linguistic Theories (TLT16)*, pages 27–36.

Maria Kunilovskaya and Ekaterina Lapshinova-Koltunski. 2020. Lexicogrammatic Translationese across Two Targets and Competence Levels. In *Proceedings of the 12th Conference on Language Resources and Evaluation (LREC 2020)*, Marseille, France. The European Language Resources Association (ELRA).

Sara Laviosa. 1998. Core patterns of lexical use in a comparable corpus of English narrative prose. *Meta*, 43:557–570.

Gerard Lynch and Carl Vogel. 2012. Towards the automatic detection of the source language of a literary translation. In *Proceedings of COLING 2012*, pages 775–784, Mumbai. Association for Computational Linguistics.

Dmitry Nikolaev, Taelin Karidi, Neta Kenneth, Veronika Mitnik, Lilja Saeboe, and Omri Abend. 2020. Morphosyntactic Predictability of Translationese. *Linguistics Vanguard*, 6(1).

Maeve Olohan. 2001. Spelling out the optionals in translation: a corpus study. *UCREL Technical Papers*, 13:423–432.

Marius Popescu. 2011. Studying translationese at the character level. In *Proceedings of the International Conference Recent Advances in Natural Language Processing (RANLP 2011)*, September, pages 634–639. Association for Computational Linguistics.

Tiina Puurtinen. 2003. Genre-specific Features of Translationese? Linguistic Differences between Translated and Non-translated Finnish Children's Literature. *Literary and Linguistic Computing*, 18(4):389–406.

Ella Rabinovich, Noam Ordan, and Shuly Wintner. 2017. Found in Translation: Reconstructing Phylogenetic Language Trees from Translations. In *Proceedings of the 55th Annual Meeting of the Association for Computational Linguistics*, pages 530–540, Vancouver, Canada. Association for Computational Linguistics.

Ella Rabinovich and Shuly Wintner. 2015. Unsupervised identification of translationese. *Transactions of the Association for Computational Linguistics*, 3:419–432.

Raphael Rubino, Ekaterina Lapshinova-Koltunski, and Josef van Genabith. 2016. Information density and quality estimation features as translationese indicators for human translation classification. In *Proceedings of NAACL HT 2006*, pages 960–970, San Diego, California.

Maurizio Serva and Filippo Petroni. 2008. Indo-European languages tree by Levenshtein distance. *EPL (Europhysics Letters)*, 81(3).

Ilia Sominsky and Shuly Wintner. 2019. Automatic Detection of Translation Direction. In *Proceedings of the International Conference on Recent Advances in Natural Language Processing (RANLP 2019)*, pages 1131–1140, Varna, Bulgaria. INCOMA Ltd.

Erich Steiner. 2012. A characterization of the resource based on shallow statistics. In Silvia Hansen-Schirra, Stella Neumann, and Erich Steiner, editors, *Cross-Linguistic Corpora for the Study of Translations: Insights from the Language Pair English-German*, volume 11 of *Text, Translation, Computational Processing [TTCP]*. Walter de Gruyter GmbH, Berlin/Boston.

Milan Straka and Jana Straková. 2017. Tokenizing, POS Tagging, Lemmatizing and Parsing UD 2.0 with UDPipe. In *Proceedings of the CoNLL 2017 Shared Task: Multilingual Parsing from Raw Text to Universal Dependencies*, pages 88–99.

Elke Teich. 2003. *Cross-Linguistic Variation in System and Text. A Methodology for the Investigation of Translations and Comparable Texts.* Mouton de Gruyter, Berlin.

Elke Teich, Stefania Degaetano-Ortlieb, Peter Fankhauser, Hannah Kermes, and Ekaterina Lapshinova-Koltunski. 2016. The Linguistic Construal of Disciplinarity: A Data Mining Approach Using Register Features. *Journal of the Association for Information Science and Technology (JASIST)*, 67(7):1668–1678.

Vered Volansky, Noam Ordan, and Shuly Wintner. 2015. On the features of translationese. *Digital Scholarship in the Humanities*, 30(1):98–118.

Federico Zanettin. 2013. Corpus Methods for Descriptive Translation Studies. *Procedia - Social and Behavioral Sciences*, 95:20–32.

A Appendix: Features

- 8 morphological forms: degrees of comparison (comp, sup), passive voice (shortpassive, bypassive), non-finite forms of verb (infs, pverbals), nominalisations (deverbals) and finite verbs (finites);
- 7 word classes: pronominal function words (ppron, demdets, possdet, indef), adverbial quantifiers (mquantif), coordinate and subordinate conjunctions (cconj, sconj);
- 7 UD relations following (Kunilovskaya and Kutuzov, 2018): adjectival clause, auxiliary, passive voice auxiliary, clausal complement, subject of a passive transformation, asyndeton, a predicative or clausal complement without its own subject (acl, aux, aux:pass, ccomp, nsubj:pass, parataxis, xcomp);
- 4 syntactic functions: various PoS in attributive function (attrib), modal predicates (mpred), copula verbs (copula), nouns or proper names used in the functions of core verbal arguments(nnargs);
- 7 syntactic features for sentence type and structure: simple sentences (simple), number of clauses per sentence (numcls), negative sentences (neg), types of clauses – relative (relativ) and pied-piped subtype (pied), correlative constructions (correl), adverbial clause introduced by a pronominal ADV(whconj);
- 2 graph-based features: mean hierarchical distance and mean dependency distance (mhd, mdd) (Jing and Liu, 2015);
- 5 list-based features for semantic types of discourse markers (addit, advers, caus, tempseq, epist) and *but* (not followed by 'also' and not in the absolute sentence end). (but). The semantic classification roughly follows (Halliday and Hasan, 1976; Biber et al., 1999; Fraser, 2006);
- 2 text measures: lexical variety, i.e. ratio of PoS-disambiguated content word types to their tokens (lexTTR) and lexical density, i.e. ratio of PoS-disambiguated content words types to all tokens (lexdens). PoS-disambiguation is based on 'lempos' annotation ((look_VERB vs look_NOUN)); content PoS include ADJ, ADV, VERB, NOUN.

BAHP: Benchmark of Assessing Word Embeddings in Historical Portuguese

Zuoyu Tian[†] **Dylan Jarrett**[†] **Juan Manuel Escalona Torres**[‡] **Patrícia Amaral**[†]
[†]Indiana University Bloomington [‡]Cornell University
{zuoytian,dsjarret,pamaral}@iu.edu; jme252@cornell.edu

Abstract

High quality distributional models can capture lexical and semantic relations between words. Hence, researchers design various intrinsic tasks to test whether such relations are captured. However, most of the intrinsic tasks are designed for modern languages, and there is a lack of evaluation methods for distributional models of historical corpora. In this paper, we conducted BAHP: a benchmark of assessing word embeddings in Historical Portuguese, which contains four types of tests: analogy, similarity, outlier detection, and coherence. We examined word2vec models generated from two historical Portuguese corpora in these four test sets. The results demonstrate that our test sets are capable of measuring the quality of vector space models and can provide a holistic view of the model's ability to capture syntactic and semantic information. Furthermore, the methodology for the creation of our test sets can be easily extended to other historical languages.

1 Introduction

Distributional semantics assumes that words with similar contexts have similar meanings (Lenci, 2018), hence, words similar in meaning should be similar in vector representation since word embeddings are learned from context. The success of word embeddings in different tasks in natural language processing verifies such assumptions to some extent. However, it has also been noticed that the quality of word embeddings is critical to different applications since the embeddings are learned in an unsupervised way. Thus, for evaluating embedding models, different tasks appear, but most of these test sets are designed for English, and the multilingual versions are usually created by translation.

As more historical texts have been digitized, we notice the surge of using computational methods to study historical language. Compared to the large amount of digital resources in modern language, researchers normally use very limited resources to generate historical embedding models. However, the quality of embedding models generated from small corpora is not always satisfying (Sahlgren and Lenci, 2016). Thus, assessing embedding models are critical to distributional semantics studies in historical languages. For a number of reasons, there is a lack of evaluation datasets for historical word embeddings. First, it is difficult to directly translate English evaluation benchmarks to historical languages because of the lack of translation tools and mismatch of concepts. Second, creating intrinsic or extrinsic evaluation tasks specific to older stages of a language demands large amounts of manual annotation and requires related expert knowledge. Meanwhile, we notice that prior studies in evaluation benchmark creation typically focus on a single type of test set, and few studies discuss the distinction between different test sets, especially for historical languages and embedding models generated from small datasets.

In this paper, we aim to create intrinsic tasks for evaluating historical Portuguese embedding models in an efficient way. Major methods for assessing word embeddings such as analogy tests and similarity tests are questioned for issues of the appropriateness and informativeness and lower inter-annotator agreement. Building a benchmark containing more types of evaluating methods can avoid the bias from a single method. Efficiency, measured in terms of human effort and amount of resources needed, is another concern for creating the benchmark. We try to minimize the cost of building test sets of historical languages and make the benchmark reliable at the same time. Four types of evaluation sets are adopted. They target different types of relations within word embeddings: syntactic, semantic, and morphological. We then use our benchmark to evaluate word2vec models generated from two historical Portuguese corpora. We find that our

Proceedings of LaTeCH-CLfL 2021, pages 113–119
Punta Cana, Dominican Republic (Online), November 11, 2021.

evaluation datasets can effectively demonstrate the quality of the distributional model.

This paper is structured as follows: we review predominant word embedding assessment methods and existing Portuguese word embedding evaluation resources in the next section. In section 3, we introduce how we created four types of word embedding assessment datasets. Then, the evaluation experiments of word2vec models generated from Medieval and Classical Portuguese corpora are discussed in section 4. We summarize our findings in the last section.

2 Related Work

Analogy tests were first introduced by Mikolov et al. (2013) to evaluate the word2vec models. This analogy test also known as Google Analogy Test (GAT) which contains 9 types of syntactic relations and 5 types of semantic categories has been widely applied in embeddings assessment. But many researchers also pointed out the disadvantages of analogy test, for example, irrelevant neighborhood structure being captured (Linzen, 2016) and drawbacks in appropriateness and informativeness (Schluter, 2018).

Compared to finding the analogy relation within the vector space, word similarity test uses the corelation score between human annotated word pairs and similarity scores from the distributional model to assess the embeddings. Based on the different definition of similarity, such test sets could be divided into word similarity like Sim999 (Hill et al., 2015), word relatedness like MEN (Bruni et al., 2014), and the mix of these two concepts like Sim353 (Finkelstein et al., 2001). The major concern toward word similarity is low human inter-annotator agreement across many datasets (Batchkarov et al., 2016).

Besides the two instrinsic tasks above, other evaluation methods include concept categorization (Baroni et al., 2010), outlier detection tests (Camacho-Collados and Navigli, 2016), and coherence tests (Zhao et al., 2018). These tests can make up for the drawbacks of analogy tests and word similarity to some degree.

Regarding evaluating Portuguese distributional models, we see different types of intrinsic tasks in Modern Portuguese. Querido et al. (2017) translated a set of English intrinsic datasets including an analogy test, word similarity, and concept categorization into Portuguese. Wilkens et al. (2016) used Portuguese BabelNet to create a TOEFL-like test set called BSG targeting semantic relations. Gamallo (2018) created an English 12-8-8 outlier detection set and then translated it into Portuguese. Analogy test set TALES created by Oliveira et al. (2020) is compiled by using existing lexical resources and examines the lexical-semantic relations in Portuguese.

Unlike the resourceful test sets in modern languages, only a few studies developed assessing tasks for historical languages. Schlechtweg et al. (2018) designed a task to measure language change in German by annotating semantic relatedness between diachronic usage of words. This method has been adopted by the following studies and expanded language change detection tasks to English, Latin and Swedish (Schlechtweg et al., 2020). Hu et al. (2021) designed analogy tests for Medieval Spanish. Their analogy test includes seven categories of morphological and semantic relations, with more tests focusing on the former. But, these studies focus only on one type of instrinsic tasks (relatedness or analogy).

3 Test Set Creation

3.1 Historical Portuguese Corpora

In order to have a holistic view of historical Portuguese and present the performance of our test sets, we use two corpora as reference to create intrinsic tasks and generate embedding models. These two corpora include texts from Medieval Portuguese and Classical to Modern Portuguese, respectively.

The *Corpus Informatizado do Português Medieval* (CIPM) is an online corpus of Medieval Portuguese (with texts from the 12th to 16th centuries), with about 2,5 million tokens.[1] Compared to modern corpora used to generate embedding models, the size of the corpus is notably small. Moreover, this corpus lacks systematic punctuation and contains a considerable amount of orthographic and morphological variation, as well as editorial annotations. Even though we normalized some variants and deleted all editorial annotations during pre-processing, [2] we suspect that the quality of the word embedding model generated from this corpus will be clearly affected, since previous work show

[1]We scraped the whole corpus from https://cipm.fcsh.unl.pt/ after getting permission from the corpus creators.

[2]For a full list of normalized variants, please see Amaral et al. (Accepted)

that embedding models generated from small corpora are less reliable (Sahlgren and Lenci, 2016; Antoniak and Mimno, 2018).

The Corpus of Historical Portuguese (COLONIA) (Zampieri and Becker, 2013) is a tagged diachronic corpus containing historical texts representing Classical Portuguese and Modern Portuguese. It contains both European and Brazilian texts from the 16th to the 20th century with about 5,1 million tokens.[3] Compared to CIPM, COLONIA is well pre-processed and contains less orthographic variation, since the degree of variation in Portuguese orthography is moderate after the 16th century (Castro, 1991). Therefore, we directly use the raw corpus in our paper.

3.2 Word Analogy Test

Word analogy tests aim to check whether the vector model successfully captures certain relations between words. The relationship could be semantic, syntactic or morphological. For example, if we have two words: *dog* and *dogs*, they are in a singular-plural relation a morphological and a semantic relation. Given a third word *cat*, we aim to find the word in the same relationship to *cat*, which should be *cats* in this case. In an analogy test, we first calculate the distance between *dog* and *dogs* in vector space and then add it to the vector of the given word *cat*. If it is an optimal vector model, *cats* should be the nearest neighbour of this new vector. For the distance calculation, the cosine similarity is used here. To evaluate the quality of distributional model, we report the accuracy in sets of analogy questions.

Since the other three assessment tests in this paper all target the capacity of semantic representation, we created an analogy test set examining the syntactic and morphological relations in historical Portuguese. Two types of grammatical relations for nouns and four types of relations for verbs are included in our dataset. We first designed some seed word pairs with analogy relations in each type consulting the CIPM corpus. Then, we combined every two word pairs in each relation type to create a standard analogy test dataset. This procedure gives us 2,994 analogy questions in total. For the model evaluation, we use the built-in function in Python package Gensim.[4] In this paper, due to time constraints, we only built an analogy test set using the vocabulary from CIPM, since this corpus is more challenging given its size and variability. We plan on developing a version of this test for COLONIA in future work.

3.3 Word Similarity Test

Considering the small size of the reference corpus we used in the paper, we do not distinguish the two concepts of relatedness and similarity in this dataset. We adopted the semantic relation annotation scheme proposed by Jurgens et al. (2014) (see Table 4), which also corresponds to the construction of SemEval 2017 word similarity test (Camacho-Collados et al., 2017).

To conduct the word similarity test, 100 pairs of common nouns in CIPM were created, resulting in a total of 200 words. During word pair creation, we take frequency factor into consideration. Fifty words were selected from the top 20 percent of vocabulary in CIPM and fifty more were selected from the bottom 20 percent. This ensured that the anchor words in each pairing consisted of some of the most frequent nouns in the corpus and some of the most infrequent. Following this, the anchor words were paired with other common nouns in the corpus. All pairings were created by hand by one of the annotators, an expert in historical Portuguese, using both intuition and the consultation of historical dictionaries of Portuguese. In order to ensure a variety of similarity ratings, approximately one third of the anchor words were paired with words that were synonymous or nearly-synonymous. Another third were paired with nouns related in some way to the anchor words (e.g. cases of meronymy, members of the same semantic category) and the final third was paired with words which bore no perceivable relationship with the anchor words, as shown in Table 1.

The annotation of word pairs were done by two experts in historical Portuguese following the annotation scheme shown in Table 4. The Pearson correlation between two annotators is 0.8928. The inter-annotator agreement measured by Cohen's Kappa is 0.5651. Only 3 pairs have a larger than 2 degree annotation difference or unclear relation perceived by our experts, and were thus discarded. In our final test set, we had 97 word pairs. We report both Pearson and Spearman correlation scores in the final evaluation. As said before, currently, we use the same word similarity test for both CIPM and COLONIA as reported in section 4.

[3] http://corporavm.uni-koeln.de/colonia/

[4] https://radimrehurek.com/gensim/index.html

	Word 1	Word 2
Synonymous	povo 'people'	gente 'people'
Related (not synonymous)	cabeça 'head'	olhos 'eyes'
Not related	morte 'death'	conselho 'advice'

Table 1: Examples of word pairings

3.4 Outlier Detection

This evaluation method was first proposed by Camacho-Collados and Navigli (2016). This task examines whether the vector space models can successfully cluster semantically homogeneous words. In this task, we start with a group of words, for example, *tuna*, *flounder*, *trout*, and *bread*, with the goal of identifying the word that does not belong to this group. We can easily find that *bread* is the outlier in this case since it is not the name of a fish. In the original paper, the authors created a 8-8-8 dataset. This means that eight categories of concepts are included in the dataset, each category is composed of eight words in that category and eight outliers not related to that category. Then, there would be $8 \times 8 \times 8$ tests, or 512 total in one test set. Following their format, we created two outlier detection datasets for Medieval Portuguese and Classical-Modern Portuguese, respectively, based on this 8-8-8 format. To assure the quality of the dataset, we asked an expert in historical Portuguese to come up with the categorization and outlier clusters. Table 3 shows the categorization in each dataset. For the evaluation portion, accuracy and outlier position percentage (OPP) is used. This task yields better results for COLONIA than for CIPM (see Table 2). For this reason, we performed an error analysis for CIPM. For example, in the body parts category the model wrongly predicted *mao* 'hand' to be the outlier. However, this form is also one spelling variant for the adjective 'bad' (current spelling: *mau*). The example shows that the model is capturing distinctions between words and that abundant variations in the corpus can give us a more challenging task to generate word embedding models, which also corresponds to our assumption that the quality of models from CIPM should be lower than that of COLONIA.

3.5 Coherence Assessment

Zhao et al. (2018) proposed a new evaluation method for assessing the quality of biomedical domain-specific word embedding models. They assume that the neighbors of a given word embedding should have the same characteristics of that word.

Analogy Test

	CIPM Accuracy	COLONIA Accuracy
N-Gender	0.0579	0.1215
N-Singular-Plural	0.0232	0.0801
V-1SG.Pres-3SG.Pres	0.0067	0.3911
V-3SG.Pret-3PL.Pret	0.0035	0.6338
V-Infinitive-3SG.Pres	0.0122	0.2226
V-Infinitive-Gerund	0.0252	0.3522

Word Similarity

	Pearson	Spearman
CIPM	0.2759	0.3141
COLONIA	0.5326	0.5482

Outlier Detection

	Accuracy	OPP
CIPM	0.6398	0.9093
COLONIA	0.8742	0.9809

Coherence Assessment

	Top 5 (Acc.)	Top 10 (Acc.)
CIPM	0.8333	0.7542
COLONIA	0.9280	0.8800

Table 2: Results of BAHP in embeddings models generated from two corpora.

	Categorization
CIPM	body parts; Christianity; color; food; geography; parts of buildings; titles/professions; war
COLONIA	furnature; Christianity; color; food; geography; face; titles/professions; kitchen

Table 3: Categorizations in two outlier detection datasets

For example, in their paper, they focus on drug names. The assumption is, then, that the neighbors of drug names should also be drug names if the embedding model is of good quality.

Inspired by their method, we designed a similar test dataset. Given that proper nouns, especially names of people and places, are frequent in our corpora, we decided to assess the model by reporting the percentage of neighbors generated for a proper noun which were of the same category (i.e., proper nouns). In CIPM, many texts are narrations of either historical or fictional events and hence include names of kings, knights, saints, and places. This is true of other diachronic corpora given the nature of the texts produced and the copies of the manuscripts that survived to this day. We chose the 25 most frequent proper nouns in both CIPM and COLONIA to make two coherence assessment sets. For the evaluation, we reported the percentage of proper nouns in the top 5 and 10 neighbors, following Zhao et al. (2018). To give an example from each corpus, in CIPM 7 out of 10 neighbors of the proper name "Galaaz" (the name of a knight) were proper names (names of other knights of the Arthurian legend), while 3 were common nouns, hence the percentage was 0.7. In COLONIA all 10 neighbors of the proper name "Maria" were proper names (other names of women), hence the percentage result was 1.

4 Model Evaluation

To have a better understanding of how our test sets fit into the model evaluation, we examined the quality of two distributional models trained on two corpora in this section

4.1 Word Embedding Training

We employed Skip-gram with negative sampling (SGNS) architecture of word2vec to generate the word embedding models. Considering the randomness of SGNS models, we generated 20 models for each corpus. The results presented below are the average output of these 20 models. We used the following hyper-parameters to generate all the models: minimal word frequency threshold = 20, window size = 7, vector dimension = 300.

Table 3 presents the categorizations used in two outlier detection datasets.

4.2 Results

Table 2 show the evaluation results of the word embedding models on both corpora. It is clear that word embeddings generated from COLONIA are of higher quality across all four test sets than those from CIPM. This observation is not surprising, since texts in COLONIA are well-processed, punctuated, and have less orthographic variation. It means that the benchmark we created can successfully reflect the different properties of the text we used.

Regarding the analogy test, word embeddings generated from COLONIA perform much better than CIPM. We can see that certain grammar relations, especially those concerning verbs, are correctly identified. However, it seems that the SGNS model in COLONIA is not good at capturing the gender change and singular-plural change in nouns. Meanwhile, for the distributional models in CIPM, the accuracy is notably low. It indicates that the analogy test is rather difficult for distributional models generated from small and uncleaned data.

When we look into the other three datasets targeting semantic representation, the quality of word embeddings in COLONIA is better as well in all evaluation indexes. But, unlike the poor performance in the analogy test, we see that distributional models in CIPM also achieve comparable performance in intrinsic tasks examining semantic knowledge.

5 Conclusion

In this paper, we presented a new benchmark for assessing word embeddings in historical Portuguese that includes four intrinsic tasks.[5] The results of our tests reported here show that the cleaner corpus, COLONIA, led to better results, which confirms the findings of Hu et al. (2021) regarding two Spanish corpora. In that study, the medieval corpus (a smaller corpus, with high spelling and morphological variation) was likewise more challenging than the much larger and pre-processed corpus of contemporary Spanish. Moreover, learning from the creation process of existing intrinsic tasks, we find a more economic way to develop test datasets for assessing embedding models generated from historical languages. By bringing together a few experts in the history of Portuguese and a computational linguist, we have provided a feasible method to create multiple reliable intrinsic tasks using raw corpora. Unlike previous work that has relied just on one type of task, our benchmark has the advantage of targeting different lexical relations, thus providing a more thorough assessment. In the future, we plan on doing a more thorough comparison of different embedding methods and we hope that this benchmark can be used to test models for historical corpora of other languages.

References

Patrícia Amaral, Zuoyu Tian, Dylan Jarrett, and Juan Escalona Torres. Accepted. Tracing semantic change in Portuguese: A distributional approach to adversative connectives. *Journal of Historical Linguistics*.

Maria Antoniak and David Mimno. 2018. Evaluating the stability of embedding-based word similarities. *Transactions of the Association for Computational Linguistics*, 6:107–119.

[5]The entire benchmark is available at https://github.com/zytian9/BAHP.

Marco Baroni, Brian Murphy, Eduard Barbu, and Massimo Poesio. 2010. Strudel: A corpus-based semantic model based on properties and types. *Cognitive science*, 34(2):222–254.

Miroslav Batchkarov, Thomas Kober, Jeremy Reffin, Julie Weeds, and David Weir. 2016. A critique of word similarity as a method for evaluating distributional semantic models. In *Proceedings of the 1st Workshop on Evaluating Vector-Space Representations for NLP*, pages 7–12.

Elia Bruni, Nam-Khanh Tran, and Marco Baroni. 2014. Multimodal distributional semantics. *Journal of artificial intelligence research*, 49:1–47.

José Camacho-Collados and Roberto Navigli. 2016. Find the word that does not belong: A framework for an intrinsic evaluation of word vector representations. In *Proceedings of the 1st Workshop on Evaluating Vector-Space Representations for NLP*, pages 43–50.

Jose Camacho-Collados, Mohammad Taher Pilehvar, Nigel Collier, and Roberto Navigli. 2017. Semeval-2017 task 2: Multilingual and cross-lingual semantic word similarity. In *Proceedings of the 11th International Workshop on Semantic Evaluation (SemEval-2017)*, pages 15–26.

Ivo Castro. 1991. *Curso de história da língua portuguesa.* Universidade Aberta.

Lev Finkelstein, Evgeniy Gabrilovich, Yossi Matias, Ehud Rivlin, Zach Solan, Gadi Wolfman, and Eytan Ruppin. 2001. Placing search in context: The concept revisited. In *Proceedings of the 10th international conference on World Wide Web*, pages 406–414.

Pablo Gamallo. 2018. Evaluation of distributional models with the outlier detection task. In *7th Symposium on Languages, Applications and Technologies (SLATE 2018)*. Schloss Dagstuhl-Leibniz-Zentrum fuer Informatik.

Felix Hill, Roi Reichart, and Anna Korhonen. 2015. Simlex-999: Evaluating semantic models with (genuine) similarity estimation. *Computational Linguistics*, 41(4):665–695.

Hai Hu, Patrícia Amaral, and Sandra Kübler. 2021. Word embeddings and semantic shifts in historical spanish: Methodological considerations. *Digital Scholarship in the Humanities.*

David Jurgens, Mohammad Taher Pilehvar, and Roberto Navigli. 2014. Semeval-2014 task 3: Cross-level semantic similarity. In *SemEval@ COLING*, pages 17–26.

Alessandro Lenci. 2018. Distributional models of word meaning. *Annual Review of Linguistics*, 4:151–171.

Tal Linzen. 2016. Issues in evaluating semantic spaces using word analogies. In *Proceedings of the 1st Workshop on Evaluating Vector-Space Representations for NLP*, pages 13–18.

Tomas Mikolov, Kai Chen, G. Corrado, and J. Dean. 2013. Efficient estimation of word representations in vector space. In *Proceedings of the workshop of ICLR.*

Hugo Gonçalo Oliveira, Tiago Sousa, and Ana Alves. 2020. Tales: Test set of portuguese lexicalsemantic relations for assessing word embeddings. In *Proceedings of the ECAI 2020 Workshop on Hybrid Intelligence for Natural Language Processing Tasks.*

Andreia Querido, Rita Carvalho, João Rodrigues, Marcos Garcia, João Silva, Catarina Correia, Nuno Rendeiro, Rita Pereira, Marisa Campos, and António Branco. 2017. Lx-lr4distsemeval: A collection of language resources for the evaluation of distributional semantic models of portuguese. *Revista da Associação Portuguesa de Linguística*, 3:265–283.

Magnus Sahlgren and Alessandro Lenci. 2016. The effects of data size and frequency range on distributional semantic models. In *Empirical Methods in Natural Language Processing (EMNLP 2016)*, pages 975–980. USA.

Dominik Schlechtweg, Sabine Schulte im Walde, and Stefanie Eckmann. 2018. Diachronic usage relatedness (durel): A framework for the annotation of lexical semantic change. In *Proceedings of the 2018 Conference of the North American Chapter of the Association for Computational Linguistics: Human Language Technologies*, pages 169–174.

Dominik Schlechtweg, Barbara McGillivray, Simon Hengchen, Haim Dubossarsky, and Nina Tahmasebi. 2020. Semeval-2020 task 1: Unsupervised lexical semantic change detection. In *Proceedings of the Fourteenth Workshop on Semantic Evaluation*, pages 1–23.

Natalie Schluter. 2018. The word analogy testing caveat. In *Proceedings of the 2018 Conference of the North American Chapter of the Association for Computational Linguistics: Human Language Technologies*, pages 242–246.

Rodrigo Wilkens, Leonardo Zilio, Eduardo Ferreira, and Aline Villavicencio. 2016. B2sg: a toefl-like task for portuguese. In *Proceedings of the Tenth International Conference on Language Resources and Evaluation (LREC'16)*, pages 3659–3662.

Marcos Zampieri and Martin Becker. 2013. Colonia: Corpus of historical portuguese. *ZSM Studien, Special Volume on Non-Standard Data Sources in Corpus-Based Research*, 5:69–76.

Mengnan Zhao, Aaron J Masino, and Christopher C Yang. 2018. A framework for developing and evaluating word embeddings of drug-named entity. In *Proceedings of the BioNLP 2018 workshop*, pages 156–160.

Rate	Relation	Explanation
4	Very similar	The two words are synonyms (e.g., midday-noon or motherboard-mainboard).
3	Similar	The two words share many of the important ideas of their meaning but include slightly different details. They refer to similar but not identical concepts (e.g., lion-zebra or firefighter-policeman).
2	Slightly similar	The two words do not have a very similar meaning, but share a common topic/domain/function and ideas or concepts that are related (e.g., house-window or airplane-pilot).
1	Dissimilar	The two words describe clearly dissimilar concepts, but may share some small details, a far relationship or a domain in common and might be likely to be found together in a longer document on the same topic (e.g., software-keyboard or driver-suspension).
0	Totally dissimilar and unrelated	The two words do not mean the same thing and are not on the same topic (e.g., pencil-frog or PlayStationmonarchy).

Table 4: The five-point Likert scale used to rate the similarity of item pairs from Camacho-Collados et al. (2017)

A Word Similarity Annotation Scheme

Table 4 presents the annotation scheme used for the similarity test. The scheme comes from Camacho-Collados et al. (2017)'s paper and is designed by Jurgens et al. (2014).

The diffusion of scientific terms – tracing individuals' influence in the history of science for English

Yuri Bizzoni and **Stefania Degaetano-Ortlieb** and **Katrin Menzel** and **Elke Teich**
Department of Language Science and Technology, Saarland University
yuri.bizzoni, s.degaetano, k.menzel, e.teich@mx.uni-saarland.de

Abstract

Tracing the influence of individuals or groups in social networks is an increasingly popular task in sociolinguistic studies. While methods to determine someone's influence in short-term contexts (e.g., social media, on-line political debates) are widespread, influence in long-term contexts is less investigated and may be harder to capture. We study the diffusion of scientific terms in an English diachronic scientific corpus, applying Hawkes Processes to capture the role of individual scientists as "influencers" or "influencees" in the diffusion of new concepts. Our findings on two major scientific discoveries in chemistry and astronomy of the 18th century reveal that modelling both the introduction and diffusion of scientific terms in a historical corpus as Hawkes Processes allows detecting patterns of influence between authors on a long-term scale.

1 Introduction

The detection and definition of influence in social contexts is becoming increasingly popular in computational sociolinguistics and related disciplines (Eisenstein et al., 2014; Nguyen et al., 2016; Cork et al., 2020), mainly due to the availability of data from large-scale social media that allow us to study an unprecedented amount of exchanges, but recently also in diachronic settings as shown by Soni et al. (2021) on lexical semantic change. As the diffusion of new concepts and ideas is inherent to scientific writing, one can assume many cases of terminological influence between authors. Also, since scientific communities act as social and collaborative networks (Newman, 2001), the diffusion of new concepts in the history of science might behave similarly to that of recently formed communities such as social media networks. Scientific findings that either introduce new concepts or redefine the understanding of known phenomena are bound to either encourage the acquisition of new words and expressions or to promote existing terminology that gets endowed with novel importance.

We present a pilot application of Hawkes Processes, usually used to trace short-term influences between cascades of events, modeling long-term influences between authors of the Philosophical Transactions and Proceedings of the Royal Society of London, two of the longest-running scientific journals in English. From today's perspective, the 18th century Royal Society network represented a rather narrow circle of professional and private relations (Røstvik and Fyfe, 2018). In the publications of this "scientific club", we assume a reflection of social and thematic networks. Central members may have had a particular influence by crossing disciplinary boundaries that were not yet well established. Relying on previous findings on innovative uses of words in the Late Modern Period of the RSC (Degaetano-Ortlieb and Teich, 2019), we select in a data-driven fashion using Kullback-Leibler Divergence sets of words distinctively used around that period and involved in terminology formation. These sets of words are used to select texts to be fed into the modelling of Hawkes Processes. We present the results of influences between individuals for two specific "revolutionary" periods in the history of science: (1) the discovery of oxygen, leading to the Chemical Revolution in the mid-18th century, and (2) the rapid expansion of knowledge on the composition of structures in the universe (the planetary nebula) through more powerful telescopes around the end of the 18th century.

2 Related Work

Large diachronic scientific corpora are rare and valuable, since they allow us to study the development of a rather big but specialized community throughout historical time spans. One of the largest curated corpora of this kind to date is the Royal Society Corpus (RSC; see Kermes et al. (2016); Fischer et al. (2020) for corpus creation and Menzel

Proceedings of LaTeCH-CLfL 2021, pages 120–127
Punta Cana, Dominican Republic (Online), November 11, 2021.

et al. (2021) for metadata curation). The material of the Royal Society has been used in various diachronic studies to explore the development of English scientific writing and aspects such as the evolution of peer review and community-based editorial processes of scholarly journals (e.g., Halliday (1988); Degaetano-Ortlieb and Teich (2019); Fyfe et al. (2020); Bizzoni et al. (2020)).

Considering work on tracing influences, Hawkes Processes (HP) (Hawkes, 1971), originally designed to model waves of earthquakes' aftershocks (Hawkes, 1973), have gained popularity in sociolinguistics. They have been recently used as powerful means to study influence relationships between authors on a text-based level (He et al., 2015) as well as words' spreading and turn taking in conversations (Li et al., 2014; Guo et al., 2015; Daw et al., 2020) and social media (Goel et al., 2016; Zhang et al., 2018; Soni et al., 2019; Dutta et al., 2020).

The main advantage of using HPs has been found in their ability to model a wide range of different relationships between events through a transfer function (Bonnet et al., 2021). Also, their flexibility in accommodating auxiliary features (Chiang et al., 2021) has made them increasingly popular in fields like criminology (Mohler et al., 2018), economy (Rambaldi et al., 2015; Hawkes, 2018), and epidemiology (Escobar, 2020). Their flexibility has also made HPs particularly apt to finance and market modelling (Bacry et al., 2015; Hawkes, 2018). Naturally, with the growth of social media a number of studies have found HPs suitable to model the spread of information through communication networks (Lukasik et al., 2016; Rizoiu et al., 2017; Li and Bhowmick, 2020). All in all, HPs are a relatively simple and robust method to detect influence from incomplete and noisy data (Da Fonseca and Zaatour, 2014; Yang et al., 2018). We adapt HPs to model long-term influences between scientific authors focusing on the use of newly established terminology.

3 Data and Methods

3.1 The Royal Society Corpus

The Royal Society Corpus (RSC; Kermes et al. (2016); Fischer et al. (2020); Menzel et al. (2021)) is composed of the full set of publications from the period between 1665 and 1996 of the Royal Society of London. As multidisciplinary journals covering the natural sciences, the Philosophical Transactions and Proceedings of the Royal Society originally used to cover all branches of science of the time and became increasingly specialized due to increased competition from commercial journals and publications from specialized scientific societies. Few journals are so deeply embedded in a community of scholars as these (Røstvik and Fyfe, 2018).[1] We use the open access RSC 4.0 version[2] (1665-1869, 9.779 texts, 31.952.725 tokens) as it covers the period where we previously detected major scientific discoveries reported in the RSC such as the Chemical Revolution (Degaetano-Ortlieb and Teich, 2019). The RSC encodes metadata (such as text type (article, abstract), author, title, date of publication, and time periods (decades, fifty years)) and linguistic annotation at the levels of tokens (with normalized and original forms), lemmas, and parts of speech using TreeTagger (Schmid, 1995), achieving 95.1% accuracy on normalized word forms (normalization is based on VARD; see Baron and Rayson (2008)). As the material has been OCRed, pre-processing steps have been adopted to mitigate OCR errors as good as possible (see Kermes et al. (2016) and recently Menzel et al. (2021) for a more detailed description).

3.2 Modeling Event Cascades by Hawkes Processes

A Hawkes Process (Hawkes, 1971) (HP) is a self-exciting point process, where the probability of seeing new events increases based on previous events. This is a way of modeling event cascades, where some events seem to cause or "excite" a number of successive events (consider e.g. an earthquake and its after-shocks). In simpler terms, they are sequences of events happening with some form of domino effect. For example, the first shock of an earthquake happens randomly, while the succession of after-shocks comes only as a consequence of the first one. Since the first shock initiates a cascade of events, the events that immediately follow it will not show an arbitrary distribution. In linguistic exchanges, such as conversations or letters, HPs can be applied to model influence among interactants and be also applied to capture the diffusion of new

[1]The Royal Society of the 17th-19th century was a rather closed circle. Its journals became fundamentally linked to the Society's scientific meetings. Manuscripts could only be submitted by fellows of the RS, a professional and social network dedicated to discussing science and investigating facts via scientific experiments. Fellows could also "communicate" manuscripts for nonmembers.

[2]RSC 4.0 at https://hdl.handle.net/21.11119/0000-0001-7E8B-6 and further releases.

words or linguistic uses, e.g. in a debate or social network (Linderman and Adams, 2014; Soni et al., 2019).

We consider words as events over the time line. If author X introduces a new word, and Y and Z use it in a pattern that resembles that of an event cascade rather than a random occurrence, we may assume an influence from X to Y and Z.[3] Since its aim is to understand who influences whom in a network, HP has an event intensity function (cf. Rizoiu et al. (2017)):

$$\lambda_j(t) = \lambda_{j,0} + \sum_{t'<t} \alpha_{s_e \to j} \kappa(t - t') \quad (1)$$

where α is a scalar excitement parameter, s_e indicates the source of event e (here: a word), $\alpha_{s_e \to j}$ quantifies how much the source event s_e tends to excite target j, and κ is a kernel decay function monotonically decreasing through time, constrained to integrate to 1 over positive arguments – the further away in time, the weaker the influence is expected to be. The model's overall goal is to measure the intensity of the influence of s_e over j for a specific time interval Δt and is modeled as a sum over B simple basis models (here B is equal to the number of authors considered):

$$\kappa_{s_e \to j}(\Delta t) = \sum_{b=1}^{B} g_b^{(s_e \to j)} \phi_b(\Delta t). \quad (2)$$

where $\phi_b(\Delta t)$ is the basis model (an impulse function that sums to 1) and g_b are the dyad-specific weights over the basis models.

As input for the Hawkes Process model[4], we use sentences (as plain text) from the RSC corpus which contain sets of words attributed to major discoveries. The selection procedure of these sets of words is described in the following section. To obtain an overall impression of influencer and influencees, we use a heatmap visualization based on Equation 2 showing the intensity of influence across groups.

[3]Note that the concept of influence is to be held as likely, and not absolutely ascertained. We are de facto observing correlation, not causation. For example, it may be that all parties are being influenced by the same hidden source with a delay, i.e. early adopters would not be influencing late adopters. Saying that X influences Y means that their behavior is consistent with that of an event cascade initiated by X and continued by Y.

[4]https://github.com/degaetano-ortlieb/influencer_RSC_HawkesProcess.

3.3 Selection Procedure

For selection of words as possible events which might trigger cascades from an influencing author to influencees, rather than intuitively choosing words, we use Kullback-Leibler Divergence (KLD) (Kullback and Leibler, 1951) as a more data-driven approach, modeling at a given time period differences between past and future language use following Degaetano-Ortlieb and Teich (2018). Formally, we compare the probability of a word w in a period of 20-years following a given year, $p(w|F)$, to the word's probability in a period of 20-years preceding a given year, $p(w|P)$. Given these probabilities, we model divergence between future language use F given past language use P:

$$D(F||P) = \sum_i p(w_i|F) log_2 \frac{p(w_i|F)}{p(w_i|P)} \quad (3)$$

The words with the highest contribution to the overall KLD at a particular point in time denote words used distinctively in the future compared to the past, i.e. new words or existing words used in novel ways. From this ranking, we observe words related to two major discoveries reported in the RSC corpus. First, we consider the *discovery of oxygen* in 1774 by Joseph Priestley, which substituted the phlogiston theory of combustion. This transition was characterized by the coinage and spreading of words related to the new element. Second, we consider the *discovery of new nebulae* (mainly the planetary nebulae) at the end of the 18th century by William and Caroline Herschel. This expansion of scientific knowledge was characterized by the increased success of existing terminology (like the word *nebula* itself). We select the most distinctive words for each discovery from the KLD rankings.[5] We use these word sets to extract sentences from the RSC corpus, the respective authors and the publication year. This data serves as input for the Hawkes Process model.

For both discoveries (oxygen and nebula), in this pilot study, we limit our analysis to single-author papers of authors who published more than seven papers containing at least one of the words of our selection.[6]

[5]oxygen set: *oxyg(en|enous|ene), phlogiston, dephlogisticated, acid, water, gas, hydrogen(e), substance, solution, oxide, compound, muriatic*; nebula set: *nebul(a|ae|e|osity|ous|ar|osa|as), Saturn, luminous, bright(ness), illuminate, position, cluster, object, lustre, spectrum, eye, star, ray, light, catalogue, formation, rotation*

[6]Note that in the RSC, there are some non-unified au-

4 Influencers and Influencees in the RSC

4.1 The Discovery of Oxygen

Figure 1 shows an influencer heatmap of the most prolific authors during the diffusion of the theory of oxygen. The y-axis denotes the influencers and

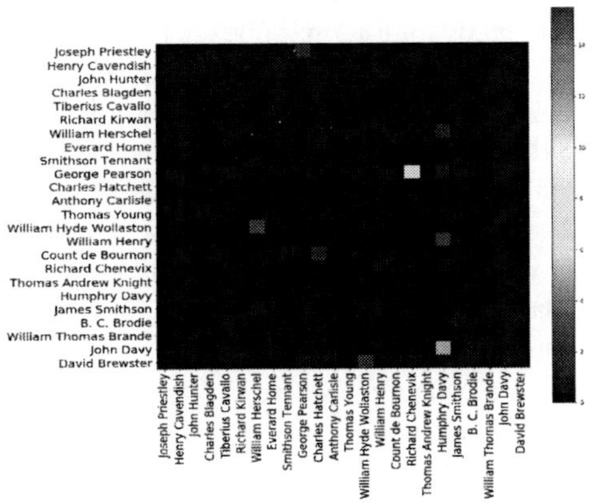

Figure 1: Influencer heatmap (oxygen)

the x-axis the influencees. Stronger influences shift towards the red. The single strongest influence is by Joseph Priestley on George Pearson: after Priestley's first use of words such as *oxygenous* (see Figure 2), Pearson follows with a series of mentions of morphologically related words which our model detects as a highly probable cascade reaction to Priestley.[7] In fact, Pearson was the first English chemist to adopt Priestley's oxygen theory (Coley, 2003), and while Priestley displays the strongest influence of the group, Pearson's work has the most widespread effect, showing direct influence on eleven other scientists we consider, including Chenevix, Davy, and Henry (see Appendix Table 2). Additionally, some authors are influenced by several others, e.g., Humphry Davy (the first to describe the properties of nitrous oxide, a gas still extensively used in anesthesia) by Herschel, Pearson, Henry, Chenevix, and John Davy.

Overall, it seems that oxygen's diffusion happens through three main roles which can be partly related to the Diffusion of Innovation theory (Rogers, 2010): the first user, Priestley, with a strong but focalized influence acts as an *innovator*; Pearson, an influencee-influencer acts as an *early adopter*, reacting strongly to Priestley and in turn influencing a large number of peers; and strong influencees like Davy, reacting to an already widespread use from several authors with a large number of mentions possibly acting as *early majority* adopters.[8]

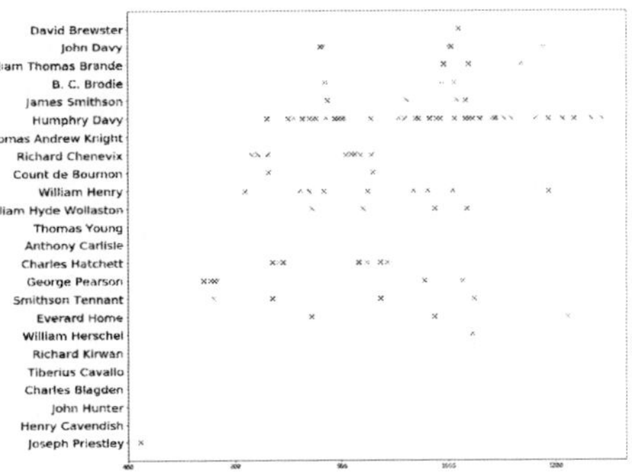

Figure 2: Chronologically ordered mentions of the word *oxygen*

4.2 The Discovery of the Planetary Nebula

Figure 3 shows the most prolific authors using the set of words we selected for the astronomical field in the period between 1761 and 1828. William Herschel is visibly influenced by many other authors. His "big influencee" role seems to reflect his research endeavor of collecting/discussing facts in the community (e.g., Francis Wollaston's catalogue or the relationship to his friend Pigott (Hoskin, 1979)). Note that his strongest influencer was his sister Caroline Herschel (see red square in Appendix Figure 4).[9] The discovery of new instances of pre-existing "objects" like nebulae ultimately lead him to discover the planetary nebula as a different phenomenon from star clusters. William Herschel did not influence this sub-field with new terminology, but did "resonate" to concepts already in the field and mentioned by others.

Beyond the Herschels, this group of astronomers and physicists reveals other valid influences. For example, Henry Kater, famous for his studies on

thor names, i.e. while most authors are covered by dominant spellings, some have several spelling variants, which are however rare. For practical reasons, in this pilot work, we consider only the most frequent spelling variants of the respective author names. Currently, to overcome this issue, unique Fellow IDs for authors that were fellows of the RS are being added to the corpus metadata, allowing us in future work to further increase coverage of spelling variants.

[7] Priestley himself did not use the word oxygen(e) yet, which was coined in France by Lavoisier, who learned the process of making oxygen from Priestley.

[8] The role of Davy as a prolific inventor and President of the RS from 1820 could also be a factor in his behaviour.

[9] Caroline was not a prolific author and does not appear in Figure 3. However, based on her well-known contribution to her brother's work, we added her texts for inspection revealing her strong influence on her brother.

telescopes, has a relevant influence over the pioneer optician and inventor David Brewster (see red square in Figure 3 and Table 3) or Edward Sabine, actively calling for building magnetic observatories, influences Samuel Hunter Christie pursing the same interest (MacDonald, 2015, 416) (orange square in Figure 3 and Table 3).

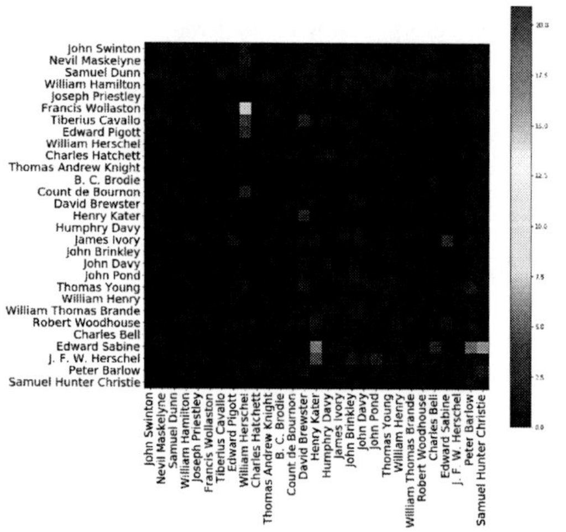

Figure 3: Influencer heatmap (nebula)

Overall, rather than the early adopter role acting as strong influencer as seen for the diffusion of oxygen, here there are writers who start using existing terminology with increased insistence as the influencee William Herschel, wide-spreading influencer as Caroline Herschel and others (see Table 4), and strong individual influencers as Kater on Brewster.

5 Discussion and Future work

This pilot study aimed to trace influences on the diffusion of terms in the history of science. We model long-term influences with Hawkes Processes, usually applied to short-time studies, on the diachronic Royal Society Corpus. We focus on two cases in the Late Modern Period: (a) the diffusion of oxygen terminology, when the competing concept of phlogiston was losing momentum, and (b) the diffusion of specific astronomical terms centered around the discovery of new nebulae. For both, the model detects realistic influences between authors which correspond to qualitative observations of the scientific fields involved. The relationships between influencers and influencees can be quite diverse and contribute differently to the diffusion of innovative knowledge. For example, for the oxygen theory, while Priestley is the innovator, Pearson, the early adopter, is the one influencing a large number of peers. For the planetary nebulae discovery, instead, Caroline Herschel acts as a wide-spreading influencer among other influencers, while her brother William is a strong adopter with no major influencer role. Being supported by empirical observations, these results also validate HPs as a possible tool to study long-term influence between authors.

In future works, a deeper qualitative analysis will allow us to detect more reliably possible benefits and drawbacks of the approach. For example, informing our data-driven approach with knowledge of historians of science, as we have simplistically shown for Caroline Herschel, would be beneficial, and investigating more deeply connections detected by our model will show whether we are able to find latent patterns of influence or detect false positives. To further evaluate the appropriateness of the approach, we might attempt to reproduce the phenomena we model in synthetic data that mimic types of lexical diffusion over longer periods. Thus, we would have an even clearer idea of what types of scientific influence HPs can capture best.

While we here consider the lexical level, we are especially interested in tracing the diffusion of syntactic and/or stylistic patterns shaping the scientific register. The language of science has been shown to increasingly use conventionalized ways of expression to level out the high degree of informativity rendered (Biber and Gray, 2016; Degaetano-Ortlieb and Teich, 2019; Teich et al., 2021). However, influencers originating from minority groups, such as Caroline Herschel, might have had to oblige not only to conventions related to the language of science but also to socio-cultural conventions possibly reflected in their use of language. According to Winterburn (2015, 3,7,8), e.g., Caroline's language is modest, self-effacing and polite highlighting her awareness of the proper codes of conduct for women, but also succinct and rigorous on the accounts of her observations, conclusions and defence of their credibility adhering to the expectations of the scientific community. Also, her use of language does not claim priority as her bother's, but focuses on sharing information. Thus, detecting influencer belonging to particular socio-cultural groups and analyzing their use of language across linguistic levels might help us to better understand the complexity of the diffusion of knowledge and the different possible stages and relationships of influencers and influencees considering social roles.

References

Emmanuel Bacry, Iacopo Mastromatteo, and Jean-François Muzy. 2015. Hawkes processes in finance. *Market Microstructure and Liquidity*, 1(01):1550005.

Alistair Baron and Paul Rayson. 2008. VARD 2: A tool for dealing with spelling variation in historical corpora. In *Proceedings of the Postgraduate Conference in Corpus Linguistics*, Birmingham, UK.

Douglas Biber and Bethany Gray. 2016. *Grammatical complexity in academic English: Linguistic change in writing*. Studies in English Language. Cambridge University Press, Cambridge, UK.

Yuri Bizzoni, Stefania Degaetano-Ortlieb, Peter Fankhauser, and Elke Teich. 2020. Linguistic variation and change in 250 years of English scientific writing: A data-driven approach. *Frontiers in Artificial Intelligence*, 3:73.

Anna Bonnet, Miguel Herrera, and Maxime Sangnier. 2021. Maximum likelihood estimation for Hawkes processes with self-excitation or inhibition. *arXiv preprint arXiv:2103.05299*.

Wen-Hao Chiang, Xueying Liu, and George Mohler. 2021. Hawkes process modeling of covid-19 with mobility leading indicators and spatial covariates. *International Journal of Forecasting*, online print.

Noel G. Coley. 2003. George Pearson MD, FRS (1751-1828): The greatest chemist in England? *Notes and Records of the Royal Society of London*, 57(2):161–175.

Alicia Cork, Richard Everson, Mark Levine, and Miriam Koschate. 2020. Using computational techniques to study social influence online. *Group Processes & Intergroup Relations*, 23(6):808–826.

José Da Fonseca and Riadh Zaatour. 2014. Hawkes process: Fast calibration, application to trade clustering, and diffusive limit. *Journal of Futures Markets*, 34(6):548–579.

Andrew Daw, Antonio Castellanos, Galit B Yom-Tov, Jamol Pender, and Leor Gruendlinger. 2020. The co-production of service: Modeling service times in contact centers using Hawkes processes. *arXiv preprint arXiv:2004.07861*.

Stefania Degaetano-Ortlieb and Elke Teich. 2018. Using relative entropy for detection and analysis of periods of diachronic linguistic change. In *Proceedings of the Second Joint SIGHUM Workshop on Computational Linguistics for Cultural Heritage, Social Sciences, Humanities and Literature*, pages 22–33, Santa Fe, New Mexico. Association for Computational Linguistics.

Stefania Degaetano-Ortlieb and Elke Teich. 2019. Toward an optimal code for communication: The case of scientific English. *Corpus Linguistics and Linguistic Theory*, 0(0):1–33. Online print.

Hridoy Sankar Dutta, Vishal Raj Dutta, Aditya Adhikary, and Tanmoy Chakraborty. 2020. HawkesEye: Detecting fake retweeters using Hawkes process and topic modeling. *IEEE Transactions on Information Forensics and Security*, 15:2667–2678.

Jacob Eisenstein, Brendan O'Connor, Noah A. Smith, and Eric P. Xing. 2014. Diffusion of lexical change in social media. *PLOS ONE*, 9(11):1–13.

Juan V. Escobar. 2020. A Hawkes process model for the propagation of COVID-19: Simple analytical results. *Europhysics Letters (EPL)*, 131(6):68005.

Stefan Fischer, Jörg Knappen, Katrin Menzel, and Elke Teich. 2020. The Royal Society Corpus 6.0. Providing 300+ years of scientific writing for humanistic study. In *Proceedings of the the 12th Language Resources and Evaluation Conference (LREC)*, Marseille, France.

Aileen Fyfe, Flaminio Squazzoni, Didier Torny, and Pierpaolo Dondio. 2020. Managing the growth of peer review at the Royal Society journals, 1865-1965. *Science, Technology, and Human Values*, 45(3):405–429.

Rahul Goel, Sandeep Soni, Naman Goyal, John Paparrizos, Hanna Wallach, Fernando Diaz, and Jacob Eisenstein. 2016. The social dynamics of language change in online networks. In *International Conference on Social Informatics*, pages 41–57. Springer.

Fangjian Guo, Charles Blundell, Hanna Wallach, and Katherine Heller. 2015. The Bayesian Echo Chamber: Modeling social influence via linguistic accommodation. In *Proceedings of the Eighteenth International Conference on Artificial Intelligence and Statistics*, volume 38 of *Proceedings of Machine Learning Research*, pages 315–323, San Diego, California, USA. PMLR.

M.A.K. Halliday. 1988. On the language of physical science. In Mohsen Ghadessy, editor, *Registers of Written English: Situational Factors and Linguistic Features*, pages 162–177. Pinter, London.

Alan G Hawkes. 1971. Point spectra of some mutually exciting point processes. *Journal of the Royal Statistical Society: Series B (Methodological)*, 33(3):438–443.

Alan G. Hawkes. 1973. Cluster models for earthquakes-regional comparisons. *Bull. Int. Stat. Inst.*, 45(3):454–461.

Alan G Hawkes. 2018. Hawkes processes and their applications to finance: a review. *Quantitative Finance*, 18(2):193–198.

Xinran He, Theodoros Rekatsinas, James Foulds, Lise Getoor, and Yan Liu. 2015. Hawkestopic: A joint model for network inference and topic modeling from text-based cascades. In *Proceedings of the 32nd International Conference on Machine Learning*, volume 37 of *Proceedings of Machine Learning Research*, pages 871–880, Lille, France. PMLR.

Michael Hoskin. 1979. Goodricke, Pigott and the quest for variable stars. *Journal for the History of Astronomy*, 10:23–24.

Hannah Kermes, Stefania Degaetano-Ortlieb, Ashraf Khamis, Jörg Knappen, and Elke Teich. 2016. The Royal Society Corpus: From uncharted data to corpus. In *Proceedings of the 10th LREC*, Portorož, Slovenia.

Solomon Kullback and Richard A. Leibler. 1951. On information and sufficiency. *The Annals of Mathematical Statistics*, 22(1):79–86.

Hui Li and Sourav S Bhowmick. 2020. Brunch: branching structure inference of hybrid multivariate Hawkes processes with application to social media. In *Pacific-Asia Conference on Knowledge Discovery and Data Mining*, pages 553–566. Springer.

Liangda Li, Hongbo Deng, Anlei Dong, Yi Chang, and Hongyuan Zha. 2014. Identifying and labeling search tasks via query-based Hawkes processes. In *Proceedings of the 20th ACM SIGKDD International Conference on Knowledge Discovery and Data Mining*, KDD '14, page 731–740, New York, NY, USA. Association for Computing Machinery.

Scott Linderman and Ryan Adams. 2014. Discovering latent network structure in point process data. In *Proceedings of the 31st International Conference on Machine Learning*, pages 1413–1421. PLMR.

Michal Lukasik, PK Srijith, Duy Vu, Kalina Bontcheva, Arkaitz Zubiaga, and Trevor Cohn. 2016. Hawkes processes for continuous time sequence classification: an application to rumour stance classification in twitter. In *Proceedings of the 54th Annual Meeting of the Association for Computational Linguistics (Volume 2: Short Papers)*, pages 393–398.

Lee T. MacDonald. 2015. Making kew observatory: the Royal Society, the British Association and the politics of early Victorian science. *The British Journal for the History of Science*, 48(3):409–433.

Katrin Menzel, Jörg Knappen, and Elke Teich. 2021. Generating linguistically relevant metadata for the Royal Society Corpus. *Challenges in Combining Structured and Unstructured Data in Corpus Development - Special Issue of Research in Corpus Linguistics, Asociación Española de Lingüística de Corpus (AELINCO)*, 9(1):1–18.

George Mohler, Jeremy Carter, and Rajeev Raje. 2018. Improving social harm indices with a modulated Hawkes process. *International Journal of Forecasting*, 34(3):431–439.

Mark E.J. Newman. 2001. Scientific collaboration networks. I. Network construction and fundamental results. *Physical Review E*, 64(016131).

Dong Nguyen, A. Seza Doğruöz, Carolyn P. Rosé, and Franciska De Jong. 2016. Computational sociolinguistics: A survey. *Computational Linguistics*, 42(3):537–593.

Marcello Rambaldi, Paris Pennesi, and Fabrizio Lillo. 2015. Modeling foreign exchange market activity around macroeconomic news: Hawkes-process approach. *Physical Review E*, 91(1):012819.

Marian-Andrei Rizoiu, Young Lee, Swapnil Mishra, and Lexing Xie. 2017. *Hawkes processes for events in social media*, page 191–218. Association for Computing Machinery and Morgan & Claypool.

Everette M. Rogers. 2010. *Diffusion of Innovation*. The Free Press, New York.

Camilla Mørk Røstvik and Aileen Fyfe. 2018. Ladies, gentlemen, and scientific publication at the Royal Society, 1945–1990. *Open Library of Humanities*, 4(1):1–40.

Sandeep Soni, Lauren F. Klein, and Jacob Eisenstein. 2021. Abolitionist networks: Modeling language change in nineteenth-century activist newspapers. *Journal of Cultural Analytics*, 6(1).

Sandeep Soni, Shawn Ling Ramirez, and Jacob Eisenstein. 2019. Detecting social influence in event cascades by comparing discriminative rankers. In *The 2019 ACM SIGKDD Workshop on Causal Discovery*, pages 78–99. PMLR.

Elke Teich, Peter Fankhauser, Stefania Degaetano-Ortlieb, and Yuri Bizzoni. 2021. Less is more/more diverse: On the communicative utility of linguistic conventionalization. *Frontiers in Communication*, 5:142.

Emily Winterburn. 2015. Learned modesty and the first lady's comet: A commentary on Caroline Herschel (1787) 'An account of a new comet'. *Philosophical Transactions of the Royal Society A*, 373(2039):20140210.

Steve Y Yang, Anqi Liu, Jing Chen, and Alan Hawkes. 2018. Applications of a multivariate Hawkes process to joint modeling of sentiment and market return events. *Quantitative Finance*, 18(2):295–310.

Wei Zhang, Fan Bu, Derek Owens-Oas, Katherine Heller, and Xiaojin Zhu. 2018. Learning root source with marked multivariate Hawkes processes. *arXiv preprint arXiv:1809.03648*.

A Appendix

Table 1: Strongest individual influences related to oxygen.

Influence Score	Authors
15.5	Joseph Priestley on George Pearson
6.98	George Pearson on Richard Chenevix
4.80	John Davy on Humphry Davy
3.51	William Hyde Wollaston on Humphry Davy
2.31	David Brewster on William Hyde Wollaston
2.15	William Henry on Humphry Davy

Table 2: Most wide-reaching influencers related to oxygen.

No. of Influenced Authors	Author
11	George Pearson
8	Richard Chenevix
6	William Herschel
4	John Davy
3	William Hyde Wollaston
3	Count de Bournon

Table 3: Strongest individual influences in the astronomical field.

Influence Score	Authors
169.42	Caroline Herschel on William Herschel
22.54	John Hunter on William Herschel
20.89	Henry Kater on David Brewster
16.28	Edward Sabine on Samuel Hunter Christie
7.14	John Ellis on Nevil Maskelyne
5.88	John Brinkley on Peter Barlow

Table 4: Most wide-reaching influencers in the astronomical field.

No. of Influenced Authors	Author
19	Caroline Herschel
17	Samuel Dunn
14	Robert Woodhouse
12	John Swinton
12	Count de Bournon
11	Thomas Young

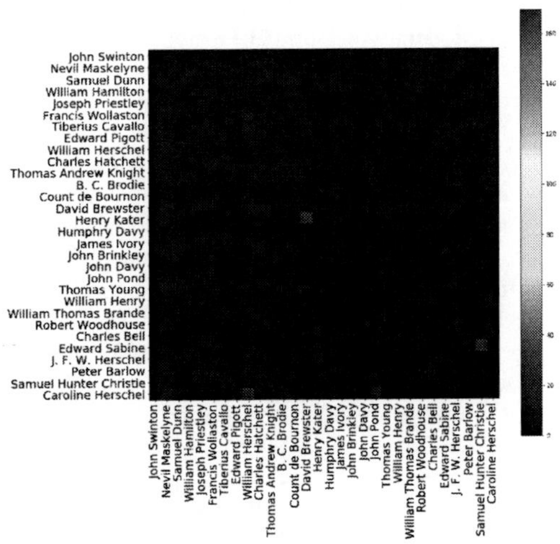

Figure 4: Influencer heatmap (nebula) plus Caroline Herschel.

A Pilot Study for BERT Language Modelling and Morphological Analysis for Ancient and Medieval Greek

Pranaydeep Singh, Gorik Rutten and Els Lefever
LT3, Language and Translation Technology Team
Department of Translation, Interpreting and Communication – Ghent University
Groot-Brittanniëlaan 45, 9000 Ghent, Belgium
firstname.lastname@ugent.be

Abstract

This paper presents a pilot study to automatic linguistic preprocessing of Ancient and Byzantine Greek, and morphological analysis more specifically. To this end, a novel subword-based BERT language model was trained on the basis of a varied corpus of Modern, Ancient and Post-classical Greek texts. Consequently, the obtained BERT embeddings were incorporated to train a fine-grained Part-of-Speech tagger for Ancient and Byzantine Greek. In addition, a corpus of Greek Epigrams was manually annotated and the resulting gold standard was used to evaluate the performance of the morphological analyser on Byzantine Greek. The experimental results show very good perplexity scores (4.9) for the BERT language model and state-of-the-art performance for the fine-grained Part-of-Speech tagger for in-domain data (treebanks containing a mixture of Classical and Medieval Greek), as well as for the newly created Byzantine Greek gold standard data set. The language models and associated code are made available for use at https://github.com/pranaydeeps/Ancient-Greek-BERT

1 Introduction

During the last decades, large collections of digital texts have become available for Ancient Greek and Latin. As a result, classicists are becoming more and more interested to apply Natural Language Processing (NLP) techniques to extract information from these texts in an automatic and structured way. Although there has been a boost in NLP research for Greek and Latin thanks to the introduction of the Classical Language Tool Kit[1] and the development of Dependency Treebanks, such as the The Ancient Greek and Latin Dependency Treebank (AGLDT)[2], there is still a lack of NLP tools that perform well on different historical varieties, such as for instance Byzantine Greek[3].

The presented research is to be situated in the overarching DBBE project[4], where Byzantine epigrams are studied as nodes between textual transmission and cultural and linguistic developments (Bernard and Demoen, 2019). This multidisciplinary project aims to reveal the connections between linguistic patterns and text-historical developments in a corpus of metrical paratexts in Byzantine Greek manuscripts and will develop new digital tools designed to perform linguistic analysis and to detect patterns and variations in this fragmented corpus of Byzantine text.

The linguistic analysis of Ancient (and Medieval) Greek has some challenges. The free word order is expected to create difficulties for automatic linguistic preprocessing, but both Dik and Whaling (2008) and Keersmaekers (2019) conclude that the word order does not cause specific problems for the task of Part-of-Speech (PoS) tagging. Considering we are interested in Byzantine Greek in particular, it is also important to mention there are major differences between Classical Greek and Byzantine Greek, which can be observed on the phonetic, phonological, morphological, syntactical and lexical level. In some cases, Byzantine Greek is reminiscent of Modern Greek, rather than Ancient Greek. As a consequence, many of the systems that are widely used for the analysis of Ancient Greek are expected to struggle with Byzantine Greek. The very popular morphological analysis tool Morpheus (cf. infra) in particular, is expected to not operate well for Medieval Greek.

The remainder of this paper is organized as follows. In Section 2, we briefly discuss some of the relevant research related to linguistic preprocessing of Ancient Greek. In Section 3, we describe the

[1] http://cltk.org/
[2] https://perseusdl.github.io/treebank_data/
[3] In this paper, *Classical* and *Medieval* Greek are used interchangeably with *Ancient* and *Byzantine* Greek respectively.
[4] https://www.dbbe.ugent.be/

Proceedings of LaTeCH-CLfL 2021, pages 128–137
Punta Cana, Dominican Republic (Online), November 11, 2021.

data set used to train and evaluate the morphological analyser and provide details on the creation of a novel Byzantine gold standard data set. Section 4 gives an overview of the BERT language model creation for Ancient and medieval Greek, whereas Section 5 describes the fine-tuning of the resulting model on the task of morphological analysis. In Section 6, we end with concluding remarks as well as indications for future research.

2 Related Research

Previous research has resulted in various tools and resources for the linguistic analysis of Ancient Greek.

The first systems to perform NLP tasks on Ancient Greek relied on morphological analysis tools. In the early 1970s, Packard (1973) already wrote a program to analyze Greek words with a 95% accuracy. Great strides forward were achieved in the 1990s, when the morphological Analysis tool Morpheus was developed in the framework of the PERSEUS project (Kent, 1991). From this point onward, Morpheus has been the standard tool for Ancient Greek morphological analysis. In his paper on Generating and Parsing Classical Greek, Crane (1991) describes how Morpheus operates by combining information from three databases: one database containing stems, a second one containing possible inflections and a third one containing irregular forms. Although this system is accurate in optimal circumstances, it has two distinct weaknesses: (1) all possible morphological analyses are provided, but Morpheus does not decide which analysis is correct in casu, and (2) the rule-based nature does not deal well with unknown words or non-classical Greek forms. The system can deal with some historical and dialectal variation to a certain extent, but Byzantine Greek is not within the scope of Morpheus. A possible remedy consists in manually adding words to Morpheus' vocabulary as shown by Keersmaekers (2019). This approach, however, does not scale very well nor would it remedy the issue of the conjugation and declension of existing words changing. Nevertheless, we can observe that in many of the approaches presented for Ancient Greek, the morphological information provided by Morpheus is fundamental in the analysis.

2.1 Part-of-Speech Tagging

Part-of-Speech tagging is the NLP task of automatically assigning a morphological label to each token in a text, and traditionally refers to assigning a coarse-grained grammatical category, viz. a *part of speech* (such as noun, adjective, verb) to every token. For the analysis of Ancient Greek, however, Part-of-Speech tagging usually refers to a more fine-grained, full morphological analysis, i.e., the part of speech and morphological features such as gender, person, number, mood or tense. Therefore, we will also use the term *Part-of-Speech tagging* and (full) *morphological analysis* interchangeably in this paper.

Treetagger (Schmid, 1994), a probabilistic tagging method employing decision trees, was one of the first Part-of-Speech taggers used to analyse Ancient Greek. Dik and Whaling (2008) enhanced the tool with a lexicon from Morpheus. The efficacy of Treetagger is proven by its continued use: even recently the tagger has been used to achieve state-of-the-art results on the Diorisis Ancient Greek Corpus (Mcgillivray and Vatri, 2018).

Celano, Crane and Majidi (2016) compared five different PoS-taggers for Ancient Greek: Mate[5], Hunpos[6], RFTagger[7], OpenNLP[8] and NLTK unigram tagger[9]. They perform their comparison using a 10-fold cross-validation test on the Ancient Greek Dependency Treebank (AGDT). In this comparison, Morpheus was applied to provide all possible morphological analyses for each word, from which the correct one was manually chosen in order to construct the training (and test) data. Mate achieved the best results (88% accuracy), followed by the other taggers. This relatively low accuracy can be attributed to the very fine-grained nature of the analyses. It is important to keep the standard, classical nature of the texts in mind here when observing the tagging results.

Keersmaekers (2019) offers a second look at the different available part-of-speech taggers. He compares RFTagger, MarMoT[10] and Mate. The results obtained from this study differ from the aforementioned study by Celano et al. (2016). Mate was outperformed by both RFTagger and MarMoT on

[5]https://www.ims.uni-stuttgart.de/en/research/resources/tools/matetools/

[6]https://code.google.com/archive/p/hunpos/

[7]https://www.cis.uni-muenchen.de/ schmid/tools/RFTagger/

[8]https://opennlp.apache.org/

[9]https://www.nltk.org/book/ch05.html

[10]http://cistern.cis.lmu.de/marmot/

a papyrus test corpus. With a reported accuracy of 94.7%, RFTagger and MarMoT both exceed expectations. It is worth mentioning that the addition of a lexicon from Morpheus increased the accuracy of RFTagger by 2.4%. Keersmaekers attributes these divergent results to the difference between tag sets. The relatively worse performance of Mate was attributed to the following factors: (1) the tagging model being unsuitable for Greek, (2) the smaller amount of training data, and (3) the joint parsing model of Mate could be detrimental due to low parsing accuracy. Just like the Byzantine data that we want to analyze for this project, the test data used for this comparison also diverges from classical Ancient Greek, albeit in a different way. At the one hand, the Greek found in the papyrus corpus is closer to Ancient Greek on the morphological level. On the other hand, different constructions can be expected to be encountered on the syntactical level. All in all, the Greek found in the papyrus data can more accurately be analyzed by Morpheus, which will constitute a fundamental difference in possible viable approaches.

The problem caused by the incompatibility of Morpheus with Byzantine is a major concern for our research. Since the final goal is to develop a preprocessing pipeline that will work for the very varied Byzantine DBBE corpus, which contains a lot of out-of-vocabulary words, the use of Morpheus is preferably avoided. As mentioned already, it would be possible to manually add words to partially alleviate this issue, but this is not a viable solution due to the size of the DBBE.

More recently, researchers have started creating Part-of-Speech taggers not incorporating information from Morpheus. Helmut Schmid's most recent creation, the RNNTagger, was of particular interest due to an increased tagging accuracy on the AGDT (Schmid, 2019). The reported results, viz. accuracy scores of 91%, are very impressive considering this system is no longer dependent on separate output from Morpheus. Additionally, if RNNTagger would be trained on sufficient Byzantine Greek data, it is likely to perform similarly, and would be the first system to perform Part-of-Speech tagging on Byzantine Greek with such high accuracy. Unfortunately, no such data is publicly available as of yet.

Finally, some other recent developments can also be mentioned here. Stanford university's Stanza package (Qi et al. 2020) contains two different PoS-taggers, each one trained on a different database, viz. the AGLDT and PROIEL treebanks. A shallow evaluation we performed for these taggers showed that RNNTagger outperformed both of them.

2.2 Language Models for Ancient Greek

Recent state-of-the-art PoS-taggers (see for instance Heinzerling and Strube (2019)) often integrate information from a BERT language model. BERT (Bidirectional Encoder Representations from Transformers) (Devlin et al., 2019) is based on Transformers, a deep learning model where every output node is linked to every input node, whereas the weights between them are dynamically computed during training. As opposed to directional models, which read the input sentence from left-to-right (or right-to-left), the Transformer model is "bidirectional", i.e. it reads the entire sentence at once. As a result, the model learns the representation of a word based on both its left and right context.

Usually, such a BERT neural language model is pre-trained on a huge data set for a particular target language, and then subsequently, the neural network is used as the basis to fine-tune for a specific NLP taks, such as PoS-tagging.

To the best of our knowledge, only Brennan Nicholson has trained a BERT model for Ancient Greek[11], which makes use of character-based embeddings. This model can, however, not easily be fine-tuned to perform tasks other than masked word prediction, since it's a character-based model unlike the standard sub-word model that we strive to train. Therefore, we present in this research a new subword-based BERT model that can be fine-tuned to perform various tasks like morphological analysis for Ancient and Medieval Greek. More details on the creation of this language model can be found in Section 4.

3 Training and Evaluation Data Sets for Morphological Analysis

To train (and evaluate) our novel morphological analyser, we extracted the relevant information from three different treebanks (Section 3.1). To evaluate the resulting model on Byzantine Greek, a novel gold standard data set was created (Section 3.2).

[11]https://github.com/brennannicholson/ancient-greek-char-bert

3.1 Training Data Morphological Analyser

In order to train and validate a morphological analyser for Ancient and Medieval Greek, we used three existing treebanks, viz. the PROIEL treebank[12], the Ancient Greek Dependency treebank[13] and the treebank created by Vanessa Gorman[14].

The **PROIEL treebank** (Haug and Jøhndal, 2008) consists of three different texts: (1) The Greek New Testament, (2) Herodotus' Histories, and (3) Sphrantzes' chronicles. As such, part of the treebank is Byzantine Greek, while the other part stems from the classical period.

The **Ancient Greek Dependency Treebank** (Bamman and Crane, 2011) includes exclusively Classical Greek data. It currently contains 557,922 tokens of various different authors, genres and dialects, ranging from Homer's Epics to various of Sophocles' tragedies, different dialects and periods. The most recent text present in this database is Athenaeus' Deipnosophists.

Gorman's Treebank (Gorman, 2020) aims to collect representative texts from Ancient Greek prose authors. This monumental work annotated by the author contains over 550,000 tokens of Classical Greek Prose, and no Byzantine data.

In conclusion, the main part of the data used to train the morphological analyser is written in Classical Greek, but the presence of a reasonable amount of Byzantine Greek should not be understated. This Byzantine fraction will be likely to help the model in analyses of Byzantine Greek.

To create the training data set for the development of the fine-grained PoS-model, we extracted all tokens and corresponding Part-of-Speech tags from all three treebanks, that had already been converted to a uniform format by Keersmaekers (2020). It is important to mention, though, that the Part-of-Speech tags present in the treebanks have been further refined by Keersmaekers (2020), who for instance makes a distinction between coordinate and subordinate conjunctions, which is not present in the original treebank annotations.

As mentioned before, the Part-of-Speech tags used in this research contain a full morphological analysis as well. The predicted labels consist of nine parts: coarse-grained part-of-speech category, person, number, tense, mood, voice, gender, case, and degree. Elements that are not relevant for a given token are represented by '-'. The label *v2spme—*, for instance, stands for a verb - in the second person - singular - present tense - imperative - mediopassive. This fine-grained morphological information leads to a high number of possible labels, resulting in 558 different class labels for the Gorman Treebank, 483 for the PROIEL Treebank and 599 for AGDT. Needless to say that predicting these fine-grained morphological labels makes the present machine learning task far more challenging than the more traditional coarse-grained Part-of-Speech tagging task.

3.2 Gold Standard Creation for Byzantine Greek

In order to create a gold standard for evaluating the morphological analyser for medieval Greek, we manually annotated part of the existing Database of Byzantine Book Epigrams (henceforth DBBE). This database, made and maintained by Ghent University, consists of Greek book epigrams (poems in and on books) up to the fifteenth century. Two kinds of textual material are distinguished and defined as follows by the DBBE team:

Occurrences: "Book epigrams exactly as they occur in one specific manuscript. The data collected here is largely the result of careful manuscript consultation, either in situ or based on (digital) reproductions. The remainder is compiled from descriptive catalogues and other relevant publications. Individual verses found in multiple occurrences are linked together by means of dedicated Verse variants pages."

Types: "Book epigrams independently of how exactly they occur in the manuscripts, often, yet not always, regrouping several occurrences that have an identical or at least very similar text. If available, the text of a type is drawn from a critical edition. If not, it is a normalised version of a single representative occurrence." For the presented pilot study, we focused on the "Types" data. In future research, we will also annotate part of the more irregular "Occurrences" data.

To create the gold standard, we selected about 9000 tokens (which amounts to 6,5% of the complete "Types" database). To speed up the manual validation process, we bootstrapped the PoS information from the output of the RNN-tagger (Schmid, 2019), that performed reasonably well on this data.

[12]https://proiel.github.io/

[13]https://perseusdl.github.io/treebank$_{data}$/

[14]https://github.com/perseids-publications/gorman-trees

Ancient Greek BERT trained on text from treebanks with random initialisation	18.0
+ Initialization from bert-greek-uncased instead of random **Mixed Greek BERT**	9.8
+ Data from Perseus Digital Library and First1K Greek Database **Expanded Ancient Greek BERT**	4.9

Table 1: Content and perplexity scores of the three flavours of BERT language models trained for Ancient Greek.

Four peculiarities of RNNTagger, however, came to light during the manual correction of the output:

1. Incomplete pronoun PoS-tags: in many cases (62/96 in a manually analysed gold standard sample), RNNTagger did not correctly tag pronouns with the correct person. This is particularly strange as it managed to predict the lemma as the first person singular pronoun in all of these cases, but did not indicate the first person in the provided Part-of-Speech tag.

2. Consistency problems: the same word is analysed in different ways in different loci, even if only one analysis is possible for that specific word.

3. Lemmatization and Part-of-Speech tagging are not corresponding: even when words are analysed as a singular nominative, meaning that the analysed word would in all cases correspond with the lemma, the predicted lemma surprisingly suggests a different word for about one in five tokens.

4. Generally poor predicted lemmata: continuing on the previous remark, it can be noted that the predicted lemmata are generally imprecise (roughly obtaining a 50% accuracy). Especially substantives, adjectives and verbs suffer from this problem, whereas pronouns seem less problematic. As this study focuses on Part-of-Speech tagging only, this is not a major concern, but it might be relevant for further research.

After the output from RNNTagger was manually corrected, an analysis from our own Part-of-Speech tagger output (as discussed in chapter 5) allowed us to correct remaining errors in the gold standard labeling.

In future research, we plan to further annotate the complete DBBE data set, which will make the resulting gold standard also suited to fine-tune a system for PoS-tagging using this Byzantine corpus.

4 Language Modeling with BERT

A shallow linguistic analysis showed that the actual nature of the "Types" diverges from the expected Byzantine Greek. Many of the byzantine irregularities have been normalized, and the text of the Types contains a lot of classical structures. Consequently, this will cause many of the existing systems for Ancient Greek to work remarkably well. Therefore, we decided to train our final BERT language model on a combination of Ancient Greek and Modern Greek data, as the Types are definitely more similar to Ancient Greek than to Modern Greek.

4.1 Ancient Greek Data Used to Train the Model

BERT models are very data greedy. Consequently, we did not only rely on the treebank databases to train the language model, but also used the (much larger) full text databases available for Ancient Greek. The text databases used were the following: (1) The (Ancient Greek part of the) Perseus Digital Library and (2) The First1KGreek Project Database.

The Perseus Digital Library currently contains 13,407,448 words of Classical Greek texts. The First1KGreek collects one edition of every Greek work composed between Homer (9th century BC) and 250 AD, that does not occur in the Perseus Digital Library. The combination of these two databases results in a relatively complete representation of Classical Greek.

4.2 BERT Model for Ancient Greek

In this research, we opted to first train a generic BERT language model for Ancient and Byzantine Greek, and then in a second step fine-tune the model for the task of morphological analysis.

A first version of the BERT language model was trained primarily on Ancient and Byzantine Greek data, considering the affinity of the "Types" and Ancient Greek data. All available Greek texts present in the three treebanks were used to train the model. The model was trained with following conditions: 15% of the words are replaced with [MASK] tokens, the maximum sequence length per sentence was limited to 512 sub-words and we experimented with two random initialisations. The model optimizes for the Masked Language Modelling objective which is formulated as:

$$-\sum_{w=1}^{V} y_{o,w} log(p_{o,w}) \tag{1}$$

where V is the size of the vocabulary, $y_{o,w}$ is a binary indicator, 0 or 1, for the word w being the correct replacement for [MASK], while $p_{o,w}$ is the probability predicted by the Transformer of the word w being a good replacement.

In order to evaluate the various iterations of our language model, we use perplexity as a metric, showing how uncertain any given system is. More formally, Perplexity is the inverse probability of the test set, normalized by the number of words as shown in the formula below:

$$PP(W) = \sqrt[N]{\frac{1}{P(w_1, w_2 ...., w_n)}} \tag{2}$$

The perplexity for this first iteration of our BERT model trained on the available Ancient Greek corpora was 18.0, whereas perplexity of a good language model is expected to be around 10. However, the texts in question did not have a massive vocabulary comparable to, for example, English. Therefore, theoretically the perplexity should be well under 10.

In order to improve (i.e. decrease) the perplexity of our model, we tried to leverage the existing resources for Modern Greek. We started from the publicly available BERT-Greek-uncased (Koutsikakis et al., 2020) pre-trained model. This BERT model for Modern Greek was trained on various modern Greek resources like the Greek Wikipedia. Even though this model initially did not perform well on Ancient Greek (perplexity >20), the pre-training can serve as a better starting point than random initialisation, helping it understand the Greek characters and some common parts of the vocabulary. After training this model on the Ancient Greek corpus using MLM, performance was significantly increased and the perplexity dropped to 9.8 on the held-out test set. From now on, we will refer to this model as the **Mixed Greek BERT model**.

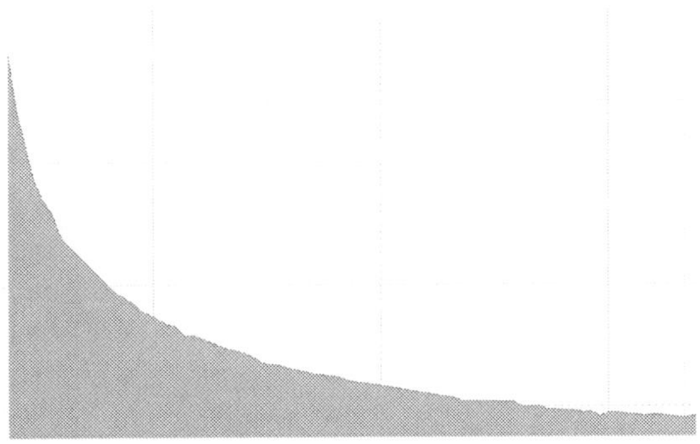

Figure 1: The convergence of loss for the Expanded Ancient Greek BERT model on the held out test set.

However, since we hypothesize that the theoretical perplexity could be much lower than that of a standard BERT model, we wanted to further explore the upper bound of an Ancient Greek BERT. We built a third and final model starting from the pre-trained Modern Greek model, but also including the two large text collections described in Section 4.1, the Greek part of the Perseus Digital library and the First1KGreek database, in addition to the treebank data, overall increasing the original training data by around 300 percent. We also used special lower-casing for Greek, and de-accentuated the text as a pre-processing step. This new model considerably outperforms all the previous iterations and results in a perplexity of 4.9 on a held-out test set. The validation loss convergence as a function of time can be seen in Figure 1. This model is henceforth referred to as the **Expanded Ancient Greek BERT** model. This pre-trained language model has been made publicly available, together with some sample code showing how to use it[15]. Table 1 summarizes the content and perplexity scores of the three flavours of BERT language models we trained for Ancient and Byzantine Greek.

5 Fine-tuning of the BERT model for Morphological Analysis

In a last step, we incorporated the novel BERT language model for Ancient and Byzantine Greek into our morphological analysis system.

[15]https://github.com/pranaydeeps/Ancient-Greek-BERT

5.1 Training of the Morphological Analyser

As explained in Section 3.1, we extracted all tokens and corresponding fine-grained PoS-tags from the three treebanks. We use the contextual token embeddings from the Expanded Ancient Greek BERT model described in Section 4.2, and stack them with randomly initialized Character Embeddings (Lample et al., 2016), which are then processed by a standard Bi-directional Long Short Term Memory (LSTM) encoder and a Conditional Random Field (CRF) decoder, commonly used in sequential tagging tasks. The Expanded Ancient Greek BERT embeddings are the only frozen part of the model, while all the other fragments are trained. We use the FLAIR framework (Akbik et al., 2019) for this set of experiments. While the Bi-LSTM CRF architecture is a staple of many successful sequential taggers, we elect to stack our BERT embeddings with character embeddings that have found extensive use in models for languages with high morphological diversity (Vylomova et al., 2017). We use a hidden size of 256 for our LSTM, and initialize with a starting learning rate of 0.1, which is linearly decreased.

5.2 Evaluation of the Morphological Analyser

For the evaluation of the tagger it is important to keep in mind that we are analyzing Byzantine Greek with models trained mainly on Ancient Greek. The tagger's accuracy will therefore inevitably be lower. Second, inter-annotator agreement on Greek PoS-tagging is most likely a lot lower than for other languages. In various cases, different analyses can be considered correct by experts. Participles, for example, form a middle ground between verbs on the one hand and substantives and adjectives on the other hand. In some cases, a participle that was repeatedly used in a certain form is accepted as a noun or adjective by linguists. This status, however, depends on convention. As such, it is very difficult for a system to detect whether a participle is considered a noun, adjective of verb in many occasions. Even for humans, this issue can be hard to resolve, arguments can sometimes be made for different analyses. For this pilot study, we only constructed a modest gold standard of 9000 tokens. In future research, we intend to construct detailed annotation guidelines and perform inter-annotator experiments to further expand the current gold standard, based on the insights gained during this pilot study.

5.2.1 Validation on the in-domain data

The performance of our trained model obtains state-of-the-art results on the very fine-grained PoS scheme incorporating a full morphological analysis as applied in the treebanks. Table 2 shows the accuracy scores for the different treebank validation sets. These validation sets have been randomly selected from the treebanks data, and have not been used for training the morphological analysis model. The scores presented are the result of a four-fold cross-validation evaluation.

Treebank	Accuracy
AGDT	88.64%
PROIEL	92.87%
GORMAN	91.85%

Table 2: Accuracy of our morphological analysis tagger on in-domain data, viz. validation sets of the three treebanks used for training.

When we compare this to reported scores for the various treebanks, the newly trained PoS-tagger obtains very competitive results. The study of Celano et al. (2016) comparing five taggers for Ancient Greek reports the best score for Mate on the AGDT, incorporating information from Morpheus, with an accuracy of 88%. It is important to note, however, that the scores are not directly comparable, as they are not obtained on exactly the same data partitions.

When we only consider the coarse-grained PoS-tags, viz. the syntactic categories (e.g. *noun, verb*), the results are comparable to state-of-the-art PoS-taggers for other languages. Table 3 gives an overview of the accuracy scores when only taking into account the coarse-grained PoS-tags.

Treebank	Accuracy
AGDT	90.28%
PROIEL	97.40%
GORMAN	95.71%

Table 3: Accuracy for the coarse-grained PoS-tags on in-domain data.

5.2.2 Evaluation on the held-out test data

The gold standard that was created allows to evaluate the performance of existing PoS-taggers on Byzantine Greek data. For this pilot study, we compare RNNTagger with our newly created PoS-tagger. As is illustrated by Table 4, our PoS-tagger incorporating the new BERT language model obtains very promising results, with an accuracy of 86.88% for the full morphological analysis. When we only consider the coarse-grained PoS-tags, the accuracy increases to 92.97%.

Fine-grained PoS Tagger	Accuracy
RNNTagger	76.97%
BERT model	86.88%

Table 4: Accuracy of the two fine-grained PoS-taggers on the Byzantine gold standard data set.

We also performed a qualitative analyse of both taggers' output. The tags predicted by RNNTagger structurally subtly differ from the tags in our gold standard. This leads to reduced accuracy. Our training data, for instance, distinguishes between coordinating and subordinating conjunctions whereas RNNTagger does not make this distinction. On the other hand, in cases where several interpretations were possible, RNNTagger's interpretation is more likely to be adopted as manual correction started from RNNTagger's output.

To offer some insights into the frequency of the detected errors, a small test sample containing 523 fine-grained PoS-tags of RNNTagger and our own morphological analyser (discussed in section 5) was examined and compared in detail. RNNTagger mainly struggles with the following categories:

- Providing full tags for personal pronouns: the person is often omitted (in 8/8 cases in our small test sample).
- Consistently analysing words with only one possible correct analysis (2 occurrences of this phenomenon in the small test sample).
- Recognizing Byzantine names and vocatives in general (8 errors due to incorrectly analysed Byzantine names).
- Detecting '·' as a punctuation mark (the Greek ':', not to be confused with '.'). This is incorrectly analysed as a part of the previous word in about 95% of cases.

On our gold standard, RNNTagger was 76.97% accurate. Considering the nature of the Byzantine text and the slight mismatch between the annotations of the gold standard and RNNTagger, this accuracy is in line with the expectations. Pronouns not being recognized as such, and the wrongly tagged proper names, caused a significant decrease for the accuracy of the tagger.

Finally, our own model achieved an accuracy of 86.88%. The tagger's most notable errors observed were the following:

- Iota subscriptum (a iota in subscript) was often not recognized by the model, leading to incorrect analyses.
- Parentheses and other symbols indicating uncertainty in the text caused the model to not make sensible predictions for the word in question. Even an apostrophe would cause wrong PoS-analyses.
- The perfect tense was sometimes not recognized.
- Proper names that are indeclinable are analysed as a noun without gender, case and number. The gold standard does, however, include this more detailed information, causing all indeclinable names to be evaluated as incorrect.
- As was the case with RNNTagger, '·' is never analysed as a punctuation mark, but as part of the previous word instead.

It is important to remark that comparing RNNTagger with our newly developed morphological analyser is a difficult exercise. The output of both taggers diverges in a different way from the gold standard. In 26 cases in our small test sample of 523 words, an error resulted from an analysis that was in line with how the respective tagger was trained, but was evaluated as incorrect because the predicted label was not corresponding with our gold standard labeling.

To conclude, our new morphological analysis model resolves most of the issues RNNTagger struggled with: Byzantine names and vocatives were almost always correctly analysed, full pronoun tags were provided, and results were consistent. Punctuation, however, appears to be challenging for the new model as well.

6 Conclusions

In this pilot study, we first present a new BERT-based language model for Ancient and Byzantine Greek, the so-called Expanded Ancient Greek BERT model, obtaining very good perplexity results. The model starts from a pre-trained Modern Greek language model, to which Ancient and

Byzantine Greek data (Perseus Digital library, First1KGreek database and AGDT, Proiel and Gorman treebank data) is added. The performance of the language model was further improved by using special lowercasing and de-accentuation for Greek.

Second, we fine-tuned a novel morphological analysis model for Ancient and Byzantine Greek, that does not rely on separate morphological input from Morpheus, as is the case for many existing taggers. As a result, this model is more flexible to analyse irregular forms in Ancient Greek and will perform better at analysing Greek that does not originate from the classical period. The model achieves state-of-the-art performance on a validation set extracted from the PROIEL, AGDT and Gorman treebank data sets. The model also obtains very promising results on a newly created gold standard consisting of Byzantine Greek epigrams.

In future research, we will build on the insights from this pilot study to improve the performance of the fine-grained Part-of-Speech tagger for Byzantine Greek. A first line of research will consist of establishing detailed annotation guidelines and conducting inter-annotator experiments to further improve and expand the gold standard data set. Once a considerable amount of the DBBE will be annotated, this data can be used to further fine-tune the morphological analyser for Byzantine Greek data.

Another venue for future research will consist of adding more diverse Greek data, e.g. Byzatine data from the DBBE, to update the language model, and evaluate whether this impacts the performance of the tagger on Byzantine Greek data.

Finally, we will also experiment with a cascaded approach predicting the various parts of the morphological analysis consecutively, starting with the coarse-grained part-of-speech category (e.g., *noun, verb*). This allows to separate the "classical" part-of-speech from the fine-grained morphological analysis, providing more evidence for each part of the analysis. This approach might, however, introduce error percolation from the various consecutive steps.

To conclude, we are confident that the newly developed BERT-based language model will be a valuable contribution to NLP for Ancient and Medieval Greek, as it can be fine-tuned for a variety of downstream tasks, such as linguistic analysis.

Acknowledgements

Special thanks go out to Dr. Alek Keersmaekers, who provided us with uniform versions of the three treebanks. We also thank Dr. Ilse De Vos, Marthe Nemegeer and Noor Vanhoe from the DBBE team for their help with the creation of the gold standard evaluation set.

References

Alan Akbik, Tanja Bergmann, Duncan Blythe, Kashif Rasul, Stefan Schweter, and Roland Vollgraf. 2019. Flair: An easy-to-use framework for state-of-the-art nlp. In *NAACL 2019, 2019 Annual Conference of the North American Chapter of the Association for Computational Linguistics (Demonstrations)*, pages 54–59.

D. Bamman and G. Crane. 2011. The ancient greek and latin dependency treebanks. pages 79–98. Springer.

F. Bernard and K. Demoen. 2019. Book epigrams. a companion to byzantine poetry. volume 4, pages 404–429. Brill.

G. Celano, G. Crane, and S. Majidi. 2016. Part of speech tagging for ancient greek. *Open Linguistics*, 2:393–399.

G. Crane. 1991. Generating and parsing classical greek. literary and linguistic computing. *Literary and Linguistic Computing*, 6:243–245.

Jacob Devlin, Ming-Wei Chang, Kenton Lee, and Kristina Toutanova. 2019. BERT: Pre-training of deep bidirectional transformers for language understanding. In *Proceedings of the 2019 Conference of the North American Chapter of the Association for Computational Linguistics: Human Language Technologies, Volume 1 (Long and Short Papers)*, pages 4171–4186, Minneapolis, Minnesota. Association for Computational Linguistics.

H. Dik and R. Whaling. 2008. Bootstrapping classical greek morphology. In *Proceedings of Digital Humanities 2008*, pages 105–106, Oulu.

V.B. Gorman. 2020. Dependency treebanks of ancient greek prose. *Journal of Open Humanities Data*, 6.

D. T. Haug and M. Jøhndal. 2008. Creating a parallel treebank of the old indo-european bible translations. In *Proceedings of the Second Workshop on Language Technology for Cultural Heritage Data (LaTeCH 2008)*, pages 27–34.

Benjamin Heinzerling and Michael Strube. 2019. Sequence tagging with contextual and non-contextual subword representations: A multilingual evaluation. In *Proceedings of the 57th Annual Meeting of the Association for Computational Linguistics*, pages 273–291, Florence, Italy. Association for Computational Linguistics.

A. Keersmaekers. 2019. Creating a richly annotated corpus of papyrological greek: The possibilities of natural language processing approaches to a highly inflected historical language. *Digital Scholarship in the Humanities*, 35:67–82.

A. Keersmaekers. 2020. A computational approach to the greek papyri: Developing a corpus to study variation and change in the post-classical greek complementation system.

A. Kent. 1991. *Encyclopedia of Library and Information Science: Volume 48 - Supplement 11: Automated Archival Systems to University-Based Technology Transfer and 2000: Explanation: Example, and Expectations*. CRC Press.

John Koutsikakis, Ilias Chalkidis, Prodromos Malakasiotis, and Ion Androutsopoulos. 2020. GREEK-BERT: the greeks visiting sesame street. In *SETN 2020: 11th Hellenic Conference on Artificial Intelligence, Athens, Greece, September 2-4, 2020*, pages 110–117. ACM.

Guillaume Lample, Miguel Ballesteros, Sandeep Subramanian, Kazuya Kawakami, and Chris Dyer. 2016. Neural architectures for named entity recognition. In *Proceedings of the 2016 Conference of the North American Chapter of the Association for Computational Linguistics: Human Language Technologies*, pages 260–270, San Diego, California. Association for Computational Linguistics.

B. Mcgillivray and A. Vatri. 2018. The diorisis ancient greek corpus. *Research Data Journal for the Humanities and Social Sciences*, 3:55–65.

D.W. Packard. 1973. Computer-assisted morphological analysis of ancient greek. In *COLING 1973 Volume 2: Computational And Mathematical Linguistics: Proceedings of the International Conference on Computational Linguistics*.

H. Schmid. 1994. Probabilistic part-of-speech tagging using decision trees. In *Proceedings of International Conference on New Methods in Language Processing*, Manchester, UK.

H. Schmid. 2019. Deep learning-based morphological taggers and lemmatizers for annotating historical texts. In *DATeCH2019: Proceedings of the 3rd International Conference on Digital Access to Textual Cultural Heritage*, pages 133–137.

Ekaterina Vylomova, Trevor Cohn, Xuanli He, and Gholamreza Haffari. 2017. Word representation models for morphologically rich languages in neural machine translation. In *Proceedings of the First Workshop on Subword and Character Level Models in NLP*, pages 103–108, Copenhagen, Denmark. Association for Computational Linguistics.

Zero-Shot Information Extraction to Enhance a Knowledge Graph Describing Silk Textiles

Thomas Schleider and **Raphael Troncy**
EURECOM, France
thomas.schleider@eurecom.fr | raphael.troncy@eurecom.fr

Abstract

The knowledge of the European silk textile production is a typical case for which the information collected is heterogeneous, spread across many museums and sparse since rarely complete. Knowledge Graphs for this cultural heritage domain, when being developed with appropriate ontologies and vocabularies, enable to integrate and reconcile this diverse information. However, many of these original museum records still have some metadata gaps. In this paper, we present a zero-shot learning approach that leverages the ConceptNet common sense knowledge graph to predict categorical metadata informing about the silk objects production. We compared the performance of our approach with traditional supervised deep learning-based methods that do require training data. We demonstrate promising and competitive performance for similar datasets and circumstances and the ability to predict sometimes more fine-grained information. Our results can be reproduced using the code and datasets published at https://github.com/silknow/ZSL-KG-silk.

1 Introduction

The mentioning of European silk textiles often evokes images of clothes and furniture of the old aristocracies and the lavish lifestyles of kings and queens. Nowadays, the knowledge about the occidental way of producing these expensive items is, however, more and more endangered. Many museums and collections around the globe fortunately still have silk objects, or at least public records with metadata and images illustrating them. Such specific museum data, from many different sources about Cultural Heritage objects that are partly centuries old, have naturally some gaps: sometimes, the production year or place is unknown, but the material and technique used is described; sometimes, a rich textual description is provided with many little details about the object production and what it depicts, but categorical values informing about the exact material or technique used is not provided (Figure 1).

The recent progress in natural language processing and more specifically in information extraction can help to address these problems. In particular, it is common to train text classification models from metadata records in order to predict missing categorical values in other records. However, such models do require a significant amount of annotated data for training, which is expensive to get when the domain is very specific. In this paper, we first briefly introduce the development of a multilingual knowledge graph (KG) about silk textiles production. This knowledge graph, developed with the help of historians and museum experts, uses the CIDOC-CRM ontology and a domain expert designed thesaurus defining the silk textile concepts. Next, we propose a Zero-Shot Learning (ZSL) approach based on the ConceptNet common-sense knowledge graph (Speer et al., 2017), to predict the missing categorical metadata while avoiding to rely on training data. We compare our approach with supervised approaches and we show competitive results and demonstrate the ability to predict more fine-grained concepts despite the specificity of this domain.

The remainder of this paper is structured as follows. We present some relevant related work in Section 2. We summarise the development of the Knowledge Graph and we describe the dataset being used in our experiments in Section 3. We detail our Zero Shot Learning approach as well as two supervised learning baselines in Section 4. We analyze the classification results in Section 5. Finally, we provide conclusions and outline some future work in Section 6.

2 Related Work

Integrating Cultural Heritage data into a knowledge graph can be difficult and time consuming, as data

Proceedings of LaTeCH-CLfL 2021, pages 138–146
Punta Cana, Dominican Republic (Online), November 11, 2021.

Figure 1: Examples from three different museums with missing categorical properties: a) no subject depiction for the record 37.80.1 from the Metropolitan Museum of Art; b) no material for the record Cl. XXIV n. 1748 from the Musei di Venezia; c) no technique for the record GMMP-733-002 from the French Mobilier National

has to be usually collected from many different sources that generally do not use standard formats. For museum data, there are models and ontologies that make such a process less challenging. We consider the CIDOC Conceptual Reference Model (CRM) to be one of them. CIDOC-CRM is an event-centric ontology through which everything can be represented as an event. A man-made object has, for example, been produced at some point in time. Certain materials might have been used during this production that has taken place at a specific location in a specific century. CIDOC-CRM offers not only classes and properties for such an event-based representation, but is also easily expandable with classes from other ontologies. Hence, CIDOC-CRM comes also with useful extensions such as CRMSci (Scientific Observation Model) and CRMdig (model for provenance metadata). CIDOC-CRM is an official ISO standard since 2006 and this status has been renewed in 2014.

There are more and more successful examples of KG development in the Cultural Heritage realm. For example, ARCO (Carriero et al., 2019) is a knowledge graph about the Italian Cultural Heritage that at least indirectly reuses some CIDOC-CRM classes and properties. The Dutch Rijksmuseum collection is available as linked open data (Dijkshoorn et al., 2018) while DOREMUS is the largest knowledge graph available about about classical musical works and interpretations (Achichi et al., 2018).

Information extraction from texts generally rely on supervised machine learning and deep learning classification techniques that require labelled training data. While general purpose transformer-based language models are often used, fine-tuning them often require numerous examples (Dodge et al., 2020). One possible solution to address this lack of labelled data is to use active learning (Yuan et al., 2020) in conjunction with pre-trained models such as BERT (Devlin et al., 2019) that comes with possible bias problems (Papakyriakopoulos et al., 2020). In Cultural Heritage domains, several works are trying to compensate for the lack of labelled data. One method is to leverage human annotations through crowdsourcing together with extracted visual and textual features and automatic annotation through transfer learning (Shabani et al., 2020). In general Convolutional Neural Networks (CNN) are often used for image, audio and video data (Clermont et al., 2020), whereas Recurrent Neural Networks (RNN) is also used for textual Cultural Heritage data (Kambau et al., 2018). Regular neural network (Belhi et al., 2018) for textual data are also used together with word embeddings.

More recently, zero-shot learning approaches have attracted a lot of attention for their ability to offer text classification without relying on training data. It is a form of automatic classification for which textual documents unseen by the model can be analyzed and classified. Several frameworks have been proposed over the years, based on BERT (Zhang et al., 2019), (Ye et al., 2020) or other large pre-trained models (Weller et al., 2020). Our approach relies on ZeSTE[1] (Zero Shot Topic Extraction) (Harrando and Troncy, 2021) that provides a framework for extracting topics from textual documents using the ConceptNet commonsense knowledge graph. In addition, the framework provides explainability of its classification results using the ConceptNet KG neighborhood.

[1] `https://github.com/D2KLab/ZeSTE`

3 A Knowledge Graph of Silk Cultural Heritage

3.1 Knowledge Graph Development

The development of the knowledge graph has followed an established extraction, transform and load (ETL) pipeline. First, domain experts have made a relevant selection of museum websites. We have developed a crawling software that directly scrapes the public records and images from their websites or relies on open APIs when available, and saved the metadata information into a common intermediate JSON format. Next, domain experts have provided mapping rules by interpreting the original metadata to a unified target ontology model based on CIDOC-CRM. This enables to address a first heterogeneity problem as how similar information are differently expressed across museums. For example, the production place of a silk textile is represented in a field named "Culture" in the case of the MET museum and in a field named "Object Place" in the case of the Museum of Fine Arts of Boston. Museums come from all over the world and the field names are also multilingual. For example, the production place would be informed in a field named "Lugar de Producción/Ceca" in the case of the Red Digital de Colecciones de Museosde España.

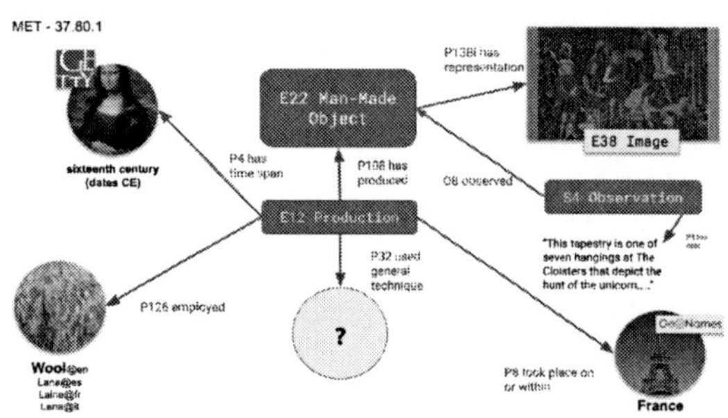

Figure 2: The MET record provided in Figure 1a represented in the knowledge graph using the CIDOC-CRM ontology and controlled vocabularies

The conversion process also addresses a second heterogeneity problem by disambiguating the original metadata field values to common concepts defined in a multilingual thesaurus about the silk production. Hence, specific weaving techniques or materials used that are mentioned in the metadata get linked to these unique concepts (Figure 2). This disambiguation is performed by string matching and simple heuristics. Other controlled vocabularies for normalizing place names (Geonames[2]) and time periods (Getty AAT) are also used. The resulting knowledge graph can be accessed via SPARQL queries or a dedicated RESTful API.

3.2 Dataset and Preprocessing

The multilingual Knowledge Graph of silk textile productions consists of descriptions of 36210 unique objects illustrated by 74527 images in four languages: English, Spanish, French and Italian. While the information integration process has been effective, one general problem of the KG is that many properties have missing values. In this paper, we focus on three important properties describing the silk production namely: the material used, the weaving technique employed and a the subject depicted. Consequently, we extract from the knowledge graph three subsets corresponding to the set of objects having values for those properties.

The silk thesaurus which is being used to normalize the values of those properties contains a very exhaustive inventory of possible materials and techniques, organized in a hierarchy. While some of those materials or techniques are widely used in the data, others are niche and the knowledge graph includes only a very limited number of objects with some of them. One solution is to walk up the thesaurus hierarchy and only consider more general concepts. Ultimately, we need to find a trade off between using fine-grained concepts with the risk of having too sparse data, or too broad concepts with the risk of being non informative. This is a manual process informed by both the thesaurus hierarchy and the available data. Table 1 provides the list of the thesaurus concepts that we finally aim to predict for the three properties (material, technique, depiction) as well as the number of unique objects.

As a general preprocessing step, we also removed all records that have multi-valued properties. Some records have, for example, both "Gold Thread" and "Vegetable Fiber" set as material properties. Including such a record would make the training of a model capable of distinguishing these two concepts harder. We also create language specific subsets. We observe significant differences between the English and Spanish subsets, which highlight the heterogeneous nature of our sources. In particular, subject depiction sticks out as we only have objects from Spanish records having this property informed. The language specific subsets

[2] https://www.geonames.org/

will be used by our Zero Shot Learning approach (Section 4.2) while supervised learning methods will make use of the complete multilingual dataset in the 4 languages (Section 4.1).

Property	Concept	Nb of Objects	
		ES	EN
Material	Vegetal Fibre	225	-
Material	Gold Thread	34	125
Material	Silver Thread	10	176
Material	**SUBTOTAL**	**269**	**301**
Technique	Damask	512	25
Technique	Brocaded	-	190
Technique	Tabby	-	37
Technique	⊢ Muslin	2	37
Technique	⊢Louisine	11	-
Technique	Satin	228	93
Technique	Embroidery	66	343
Technique	Velvet	111	236
Technique	⊢ Voided Velvet	-	1
Technique	⊢ Façonne cut velvet	102	-
Technique	⊢ Giselé velvet	26	-
Technique	⊢ Plain cut velvet	23	-
Technique	⊢ Cut velvet	8	-
Technique	**SUBTOTAL**	**1089**	**955**
Depiction	Floral Motif	965	-
Depiction	⊢ Bunch	39	-
Depiction	⊢ Rose	2	-
Depiction	⊢ Fleur de lis	8	-
Depiction	Vegetal Motif	205	-
Depiction	⊢ Leaf	36	-
Depiction	⊢ Thistle	35	-
Depiction	⊢ Vine	4	-
Depiction	Geometrical Motif	125	-
Depiction	⊢ Rhombus	6	-
Depiction	**SUBTOTAL**	**1425**	**-**
All	**TOTAL**	**3425**	

Table 1: Number of objects exported for each property (material, technique, depiction)

4 Approach

4.1 Supervised Approaches

In order to be able to evaluate our approach, we propose to compare it with two supervised classification methods that we use as baselines. For both of them, we will use the three sub-sets described in the Table 1 and perform a 80%-20% split in order to have training data. We will perform a five-fold cross validation for testing the models.

Classification based on textual descriptions. The goal of this approach is to predict missing categorical values of museum records based on lengthy textual descriptions such as the note of the `S4_Observation` in Figure 2. This approach consists of a Convolutional Neural Network (CNN) built over cross-lingual pre-trained word embeddings which are the aligned fastText vectors trained on Wikipedia (Joulin et al., 2018). More precisely, a series of convolutional blocks with varying kernel sizes (2,3,4), each consisting of 100 filters, are applied to a sequence of such word-embeddings that got mapped from input description texts from the Knowledge Graph. These filters create an output for which a Gaussian Error Unit (GELU) nonlinearity is used and a max-pooling operation is applied for each block. The idea is to, hopefully, select the best features of each block. Afterwards, they get concatenated into one single vector, regularised by a dropout layer and finally sent to a softmax classification layer to come up with the final predictions per input.

Classification based on images and metadata. The goal of this approach is also to predict missing categorical values but this time, using the images illustrating the objects with the other metadata values. The underlying assumption is, that it is to some degree visible on images what materials have been used or which technique was employed to produce a silk textile. For this model, a CNN was also used. More precisely, a pre-trained ResNet backbone network served as a generic feature extraction network. The output is then processed by several fully connected network layers that deliver a joint representation of the images and a final classification layer offers afterwards a probabilistic class score per variable and concept. The model is trained based on multi-task learning to perform predictions for the three properties simultaneously: material, technique and depiction. The training is based on stochastic minibatch gradient descent and using focal loss. For ResNet only, the last convolutional layers are fine-tuned.

4.2 Zero-Shot Prediction

The benefit of our approach is to perform a similar prediction without relying on any training data. The underlying assumption is that a textual document about a topic such as "Embroidery" will probably mention other words that are similar to this concept such as "fabric" or "stitch".[3] Our approach relies on the ConceptNet common sense knowledge graph. More precisely, we need to feed our approach with mappings between the targeted values we wish to predict and the ConceptNet network. These mappings have been manually established (Table 3).

[3]See for example the object described at `https://ada.silknow.org/object/c57358a7-c908-3110-b65d-70b09f5f4c4b`

Approach	Language	Class	Precision	Recall	F1-score	Support
ZSL	ES	Vegetal Fiber	2.7%	100%	5.2%	6
ZSL	ES	Gold	70.6%	10.3%	17.9%	234
ZSL	ES	Silver	50.0%	17.2%	25.6%	29
ZSL	EN	Gold	96%	57.1%	71.6%	210
ZSL	EN	Silver	49.9%	95.5%	64.4%	91
CNN - Image	EN/ES/FR/IT	Vegetal Fiber	36.8%	24.1%	29.2%	
CNN - Image	EN/ES/FR/IT	Metal	32.1%	36.4%	34.1%	
CNN - Text	EN/ES/FR/IT	Vegetal Fiber	79.0%	81.0%	80.0%	229
CNN - Text	EN/ES/FR/IT	Metal	76.0%	61.0%	68.0%	125

Table 2: Results for the material property across approaches

Property	KG Concept	ConceptNet
Material	Vegetal Fibre	/c/es/vegetal
Material	Gold Thread	/c/es/oro, /c/en/gold
Material	Silver Thread	/c/es/plata, /c/en/silver
Technique	Damask	/c/es/damasco, /c/en/damask
Technique	Embroidery	/c/es/bordado, /c/en/embroidery
Technique	Velvet	/c/es/terciopelo, /c/en/velvet
Technique	Voided Velvet	/c/en/velvet
Technique	Cut Velvet	/c/es/terciopelo
Technique	Plain Cut Velvet	/c/es/terciopelo
Technique	Façonne Cut Velvet	/c/es/terciopelo
Technique	Ciselé Velvet	/c/es/terciopelo
Technique	Tabby (silk weave)	/c/en/tabby
Technique	Louisine	/c/es/tafetán
Technique	Muslin	/c/es/tafetán
Technique	Satin (Fabric)	/c/es/raso, /c/en/satin
Technique	Brocaded	/c/en/brocaded
Depiction	Vegetal Motif	/c/es/planta
Depiction	Vine	/c/es/planta
Depiction	Thistle	/c/es/planta
Depiction	Leaf	/c/es/planta
Depiction	Floral Motif	/c/es/flor
Depiction	Fleur-de-lis	/c/es/flor
Depiction	Rose	/c/es/flor
Depiction	Bunch	/c/es/flor
Depiction	Geometrical Motif	/c/es/geometría
Depiction	Rhombus	/c/es/geometría

Table 3: Mapping between the concepts used in our knowledge graph and ConceptNet

ConceptNet is then used to produce a list of candidate words related to the concept of interest, which can be called "topic neighbourhood". Each topic neighbourhood is created by querying every node that is N steps away from the label node. In our experiments, we set N=2. A score for each label is computed based on the content of the text document that we give as input. This score is calculated based on cosine similarity via ConceptNet Numberbatch, the graph embeddings of the network. Even if a word has several meanings, only one neighbourhood per spelling is generated. The score is then supposed to represent the relevance of any other term to the main label inside a neighbourhood. Based on these scores, the whole document (museum record) gets also a score and, therefore, a document label too. This is done by quantifying the overlap between the document content as a list of tokens and the label neighbourhood nodes. Finally, as mentioned before, all predicted document labels can be explained by the model through showing the path between nodes or highlighting the words or n-grams that contributed to the final classification.

This approach has a number of limitations: the concepts that should be predicted must exist in ConceptNet. Furthermore, while ConceptNet is multilingual, the embeddings are language specific. Therefore, our zero shot learning approach will make use of the language specific subsets described in Section 3.

5 Evaluation

In this section, we compare the results of our Zero-Shot Learning (ZSL) approach with the supervised methods described in the Section 4.1. We present the results alongside each of the three properties of interest: material, technique and depiction. It is worth to note that the precision, recall, F1 scores are obtained on 20% of the dataset following a 5-fold cross validation while the figures reported for the ZSL method concerns the entire language specific datasets described in Section 3.

Table 2 shows the results for predicting material concepts. The two baselines approaches can only predict whether the material used is “Metal” or “Vegetable Fiber” while our ZSL approach can predict more fine grained concepts than just “Metal”, such as “Gold” or “Silver”. On the English subset, the ZSL method shows promising results with F1-score of 71.6% and 64.4%) respectively. On the Spanish subset, the prediction results are lower for the ZSL method, in comparison to the supervised approach. The topic neighborhood in this language is also less elaborated. The Text CNN method benefits clearly from the multilingual embeddings.

The results for the prediction of technique concepts are presented in Table 4. On the Spanish subset, we again observe lower scores for the ZSL approach. The problem relies on both the quality of the Spanish textual descriptions and on the Spanish concept neighbourhoods in ConceptNet. On the English subset, the ZSL approach performs in par with respect to the Image CNN baseline but less well than the Text CNN one. We observe that “Tabby”, a very domain-specific concept, is particularly difficult to predict and it was discarded by the Text CNN approach since too little usable textual descriptions were available. The ZSL method performs reasonably well with a similar input and better than the Image CNN baseline.

Figure 3 provides the confusion matrix of the predictions made for the technique property with the ZSL method on the English subset. We can see that the true label is usually predicted the most per class, especially in the case of “embroidery” and “velvet”. We observe that “Brocaded” is often confused with “embroidery” or “"velvet” while “Damask” and “tabby” are rarely predicted. In the case of “damask”, this just reflects a low amount of samples, whereas in the case of “tabby”, the predictions almost do not work at all (F1-score of 2.9%).

Figure 4 shows an example where “Embroidery” is correctly predicted, while Figure 5 depicts a counter-example (the correct technique should have been “Embroidery”). The graph highlights the most relevant words used for the predictions. The first example is based on the text: "*Spot samplers feature motifs that are scattered in a seemingly random fashion over the surface of the foundation fabric, usually linen. These samplers are rarely signed or dated, and often include motifs that are only partially worked, leading to the conclusion that this type of sampler was made as a personal stitch reference for its maker, and not for display, as band samplers were signed by student embroiderers. The sampler features flowers, obelisks on pedestals, and an "S" motif, in addition to geometric designs that are of the type that would have been used to decorate small purses, cushions, and other accessories.*", taken from a record from the MET Museum.[4]

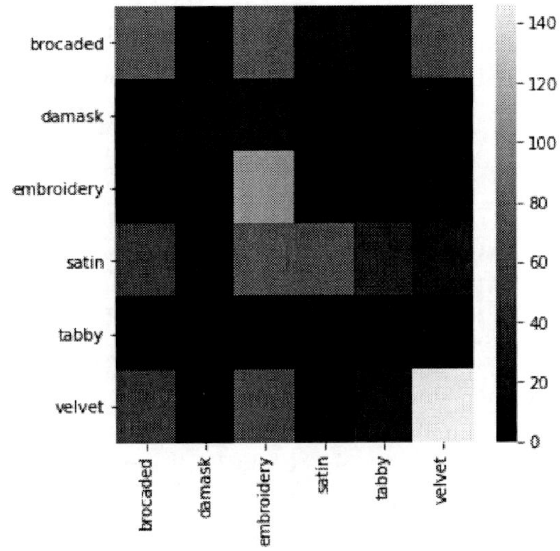

Figure 3: Confusion matrix for the property technique on the English subset for the ZSL method. The Y-axis represents the true labels and the X-axis the predicted ones.

The second text is "*An example of the kind of work [Catherine de Medici] appreciated is the Museum's panel of yellow satin embroidered with silk threads. One of a set of three (the others are in the Musée Historique des Tissus, Lyon), it hung as a valence around the top of a four-poster bed. Various print sources were culled for the airy design of grotesques, while its five vignettes derived from Ovid's Metamorphoses- based on the myths of Europa, Actaeon, Semele, Pyramus, and Salmacis- are adapted from woodcut illustrations published by Bernard Salomon in Lyon in 1557. Its brilliant colors, exquisite design, and sumptuous material would have suited the queen's taste perfectly.*", also

[4] https://ada.silknow.org/object/c57358a7-c908-3110-b65d-70b09f5f4c4b

Approach	Language	Class	Precision	Recall	F1-score	Support
ZSL	ES	Damask	6.8%	63.6%	11.2%	55
ZSL	ES	Embroidery	89.4%	6%	12.3%	987
ZSL	ES	Tabby	0%	0%	0%	6
ZSL	ES	Velvet	10.4%	100%	6.6%	28
ZSL	ES	Satin	3.5%	61.5%	18.8%	13
ZSL	EN	Damask	52.0%	33.3%	40.6%	39
ZSL	EN	Embroidery	32.4%	86.7%	47.1%	128
ZSL	EN	Velvet	61.6%	50.0%	55.2%	292
ZSL	EN	Tabby	1.5%	50.0%	2.9%	2
ZSL	EN	Satin	77.4%	28.5%	41.6%	253
ZSL	EN	Brocaded	40%	31.5%	35.3%	241
CNN - Image	EN/ES/FR/IT	Damask	70.3%	68.9%	68.9%	
CNN - Image	EN.ES/FR/IT	Embroidery	83.9%	83.2%	83.6%	
CNN - Image	EN/ES/FR/IT	Tabby	17.4%	30.8%	22.3%	
CNN - Image	EN/ES/FR/IT	Velvet	70.1%	67.8%	68.9%	
CNN - Text	EN/ES/FR/IT	Damask	98%	90%	94%	135
CNN - Text	EN/ES/FR/IT	Embroidery	96%	98%	97%	230
CNN - Text	EN/ES/FR/IT	Velvet	95%	84%	89%	62

Table 4: Results for the technique property across approaches

Approach	Language	Class	Precision	Recall	F1-score	Support
ZSL	ES	Flower	99.3%	72.1%	83.5%	1397
ZSL	ES	Plant	2.2%	26.1%	4.0%	23
ZSL	ES	Geometry	3.1%	100%	5.9%	4
CNN - Image	ES/FR	Flower	89.9%	88.8%	89.3%	
CNN - Image	ES/FR	Plant	45.1%	38.1%	41.3%	
CNN - Image	ES/FR	Geometry	35.8%	50.0%	41.3%	

Table 5: Results for subject depiction property across approaches

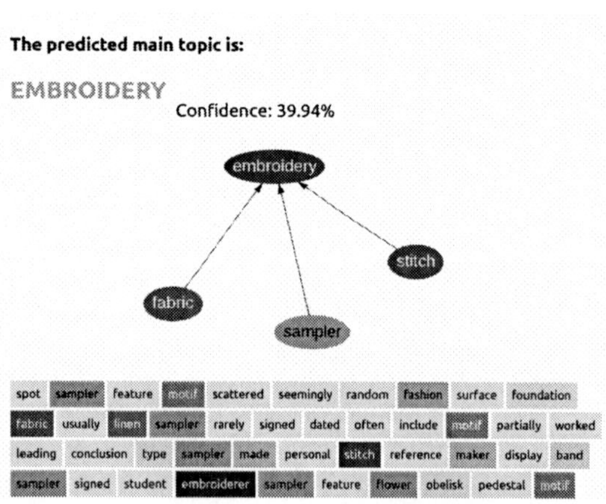

Figure 4: "Embroidery" was correctly predicted by our ZSL approach (English, Technique) in this case. Relevant words in the ConceptNet topic neighborhood are highlighted.

taken from the MET Museum.[5]

The results for the prediction of subject depiction concepts are presented in Table 5. No results are reported for the Text CNN baseline due to the lack of data. We observe that our ZSL approach performs well for predicting the "Flower" concept as does the visual approach. The "Plant" and "Geometry" concepts are however more complicated to predict by the ZSL method. These concepts are general in ConceptNet and the topic neighborhood too broad for the narrower interpretation expected in the silk domain.

6 Conclusion and Future Work

In this paper, we hypothesize that a common sense knowledge graph such as ConceptNet can feed a Zero Shot Learning method for enriching a domain

[5]https://ada.silknow.org/object/e2f34144-9ce4-3bc4-b3e0-c67854cd994f

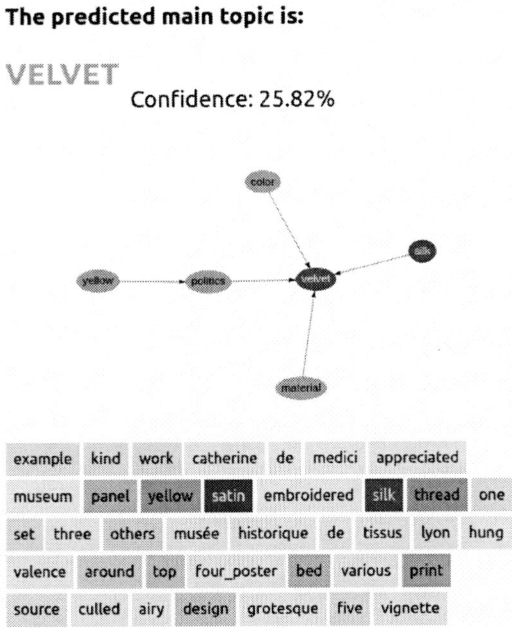

Figure 5: "Velvet" was predicted instead of "Embroidery" by our ZSL approach (English, Technique) in this case. Relevant words in the ConceptNet topic neighborhood are highlighted.

specific knowledge graph such as one describing the silk textile production. Through extensive experiments, we have demonstrated promising results for such an approach in its ability to sometimes reliably predict fine-grained concepts without requiring any training data as supervised classification techniques do. Nevertheless, we observe several limitations: the concepts that should be predicted must exist in ConceptNet with an appropriate topic neighborhood. Our results can be reproduced using the code and datasets published at `https://github.com/silknow/ZSL-KG-silk`.

Even if supervised methods for metadata predictions perform generally better, ZSL remains an interesting method to get accurate predictions even in specific domains that often suffer from data sparsity. We observe that it is also possible to bootstrap the predictions in using first the ZSL method and then applying supervised classification models to further increase performance. We aim to experiment with such hybrid approaches in the future.

Acknowledgment

This work has been partially supported by the European Union's Horizon 2020 research and innovation program within the SILKNOW (grant agreement No. 769504).

References

Manel Achichi, Pasquale Lisena, Konstantin Todorov, Raphael Troncy, and J. Delahousse. 2018. DOREMUS: A Graph of Linked Musical Works. In *International Semantic Web Conference (ISWC)*.

Abdelhak Belhi, Abdelaziz Bouras, and Sebti Foufou. 2018. Leveraging Known Data for Missing Label Prediction in Cultural Heritage Context. *Applied Sciences*, 8(10).

Valentina Anita Carriero, Aldo Gangemi, M. Mancinelli, L. Marinucci, Andrea Giovanni Nuzzolese, V. Presutti, and Chiara Veninata. 2019. ArCo: the Italian Cultural Heritage Knowledge Graph. In *International Semantic Web Conference (ISWC)*.

D. Clermont, M. Dorozynski, D. Wittich, and F. Rottensteiner. 2020. Assessing the Semantic Similarity of Images of Silk Fabrics Using Convolutional Neural Betworks. *ISPRS Annals of the Photogrammetry, Remote Sensing and Spatial Information Sciences*, V-2-2020:641–648.

Jacob Devlin, Ming-Wei Chang, Kenton Lee, and Kristina Toutanova. 2019. BERT: Pre-training of Deep Bidirectional Transformers for Language Understanding. In *Conference of the North American Chapter of the Association for Computational Linguistics: Human Language Technologies*, pages 4171–4186, Minneapolis, Minnesota.

Chris Dijkshoorn, Lizzy Jongma, Lora Aroyo, J. V. Ossenbruggen, G. Schreiber, Wesley ter Weele, and J. Wielemaker. 2018. The Rijksmuseum collection as Linked Data. *Semantic Web*, 9:221–230.

Jesse Dodge, Gabriel Ilharco, Roy Schwartz, A. Farhadi, Hannaneh Hajishirzi, and Noah A. Smith. 2020. Fine-Tuning Pretrained Language Models: Weight Initializations, Data Orders, and Early Stopping.

Ismail Harrando and Raphael Troncy. 2021. Explainable Zero-Shot Topic Extraction Using a Common-Sense Knowledge Graph. In 3rd *Conference on Language, Data and Knowledge (LDK)*, Zaragoza, Spain.

Armand Joulin, Piotr Bojanowski, Tomas Mikolov, Hervé Jégou, and Edouard Grave. 2018. Loss in Translation: Learning Bilingual Word Mapping with a Retrieval Criterion. In *Conference on Empirical Methods in Natural Language Processing (EMNLP)*, pages 2979–2984.

Ridwan Andi Kambau, Zainal Arifin Hasibuan, and M.Octaviano Pratama. 2018. Classification for Multiformat Object of Cultural Heritage using Deep

Learning. In 3rd *International Conference on Informatics and Computing (ICIC)*.

Orestis Papakyriakopoulos, Simon Hegelich, Juan Carlos Medina Serrano, and Fabienne Marco. 2020. Bias in Word Embeddings. In *Conference on Fairness, Accountability, and Transparency (FAT)*, pages 446—457.

Shaban Shabani, Maria Sokhn, and Heiko Schuldt. 2020. Hybrid Human-Machine Classification System for Cultural Heritage Data. In 2nd *Workshop on Structuring and Understanding of Multimedia HeritAge Contents (SUMAC)*, pages 49—-56.

R. Speer, Joshua Chin, and Catherine Havasi. 2017. Conceptnet 5.5: An open multilingual graph of general knowledge. In 31st *AAAI Conference on Artificial Intelligence*, pages 4444—4451.

Orion Weller, Nicholas Lourie, Matt Gardner, and Matthew E. Peters. 2020. Learning from Task Descriptions. In *Conference on Empirical Methods in Naturual Language Processing (EMNLP)*, pages 1361–1375.

Zhiquan Ye, Yuxia Geng, Jiaoyan Chen, Jingmin Chen, Xiaoxiao Xu, Suhang Zheng, F. Wang, J. Zhang, and Huajun Chen. 2020. Zero-shot Text Classification via Reinforced Self-training. In 58th *Annual Meeting of the Association for Computational Linguistics (ACL)*.

Michelle Yuan, Hsuan-Tien Lin, and Jordan L. Boyd-Graber. 2020. Cold-start active learning through self-supervised language modeling. In *Conference on Empirical Methods in Natural Language Processing (EMNLP)*.

Jingqing Zhang, Piyawat Lertvittayakumjorn, and Yike Guo. 2019. Integrating semantic knowledge to tackle zero-shot text classification. In *Conference of the North American Chapter of the Association for Computational Linguistics: Human Language Technologies*, pages 1031–1040, Minneapolis, Minnesota.

'Tecnologica cosa': Modeling Storyteller Personalities in Boccaccio's *Decameron*

A. Feder Cooper* and **Maria Antoniak** and **Christopher De Sa** and **David Mimno**
Bowers College of Computing and Information Science, Cornell University

Marilyn Migiel
Department of Romance Studies, Cornell University

Abstract

We explore Boccaccio's *Decameron* to see how digital humanities tools can be used for tasks that have limited data in a language no longer in contemporary use: medieval Italian. We focus our analysis on the question: Do the different storytellers in the text exhibit distinct personalities? To answer this question, we curate and release a dataset based on the authoritative edition of the text. We use supervised classification methods to predict storytellers based on the stories they tell, confirming the difficulty of the task, and demonstrate that topic modeling can extract thematic storyteller "profiles."

1 Introduction

The *Decameron* is a masterpiece of medieval Italian literature. Completed by 1353, the text is often referred to as "l'umana commedia" (The Human Comedy),[1] a name meant to strike a contrast in subject matter (and a parity in importance) with Dante's well-known "divina commedia" (Divine Comedy) (Branca, 1975). In a structure similar to Geoffrey Chaucer's *The Canterbury Tales*, it is a collection of 100 stories (*novelle*) woven together in the context of a frame tale: an honorable brigade (*brigata*) composed of 7 women and 3 men who have fled the ravages of plague in Florence to the relative seclusion of the Tuscan countryside.[2] The 100 *novelle* are told by the 10 *brigata* members over 10 days, with each day assigned a theme spanning matters of love, wit, and trickery.

While scholarship for *The Canterbury Tales* has engaged with both the stories and the storytellers (Kittredge, 1915; Lawton, 1985; Ginsberg, 2015), storyteller identity has received relatively less attention in the *Decameron*. Instead, literary research has tended to address themes and stories (Migiel, 2004, 2015; Marcus, 1979). Treatment of storyteller identity has thus far been sparse, perhaps due to storyteller personalities seeming generally[3] difficult to distinguish at a high level via close reading.[4]

We therefore ask: **Do the members of the *brigata* exhibit distinct storytelling personalities?** We emphasize that this is not a question of authorship, as the text is attributed to Boccaccio alone, but rather one of thematic and stylistic differences among the fictional characters he depicts. To approach this question, we use computational tools to elicit patterns from the text—patterns that may have thus far remained elusive to scholars and could help constitute unique storyteller identities.

This case study highlights several challenges for digital humanities research. While the *Decameron* is a popular and well-studied text, it is written in medieval Italian, for which there are few language modeling resources; this forces us to rely on language-agnostic methods like classification and topic modeling (Section 4). Moreover, while some digitized resources do exist (Brown University Italian Studies Department; Branca, 2003), the text required multiple rounds of curation to be used for a computational study. To facilitate future digital *Decameron* scholarship, we release our user-friendly digital version (Section 3).[5] In order to build a training corpus for this domain, similar curation

*Corresponding author; afc78@cornell.edu

[1]The first words of the Proem are "Umana cosa," which roughly translate to "It is human" or "human quality" (Boccaccio, 1995); they immediately underscore the secular focus.

[2]The description of the chaos inflicted by plague in Florence has led to renewed international interest in the text (Findlen, 2020; Marcus, 2020; Prime et al., 2020).

[3]"Generally" should be taken very generously; we do not intend to eclipse or elide the small yet rich corpus of scholarship that has either directly (Marafioti, 2001; Grossi, 1991) or indirectly (Richardson, 1978) discussed storytellers.

[4]This is debatable, but perhaps true in comparison to *The Canterbury Tales*. For over 100 years scholars have investigated pilgrim personalities. See Kittredge (1915), at p. 155, "The Pilgrims do not exist for the sake of the stories, but *vice versa*. ... [T]he stories are merely long speeches expressing, directly or indirectly, the characters of the several persons."

[5]https://github.com/pasta41/decameron

Proceedings of LaTeCH-CLfL 2021, pages 147–153
Punta Cana, Dominican Republic (Online), November 11, 2021.

will be necessary for other digitized medieval Italian texts, including additional works by Boccaccio and authors such as Dante and Petrarch.

Taken together, our classification and topic modeling results support existing humanist scholarship concerning storyteller identity and suggest new questions for further inquiry. More broadly, our work here serves as preliminary evidence that such tools can be useful for highly specialized academic digital humanities work—in non-English and non-standard (e.g., bygone language variant) domains.

2 Related Work

As one progresses through the 10 days of the *Decameron*, different members of the *brigata* seem to develop distinct storytelling personalities. Dioneo frequently tells bawdy tales, pushing the bounds of decorum. Emilia seems like she does not quite fit in with the rest of the group, and in fact may be (though we cannot be certain) an actual political outsider—the sole Ghibelline in the group of Guelphs (Richardson, 1978). Lauretta can perhaps be cast as a "bearer of bad news," according to Marafioti (2001). Notwithstanding such standalone examples, scholarship has not addressed whether each of the 10 *brigata* members have clearly identifiable storytelling personalities. As there is no literary consensus, we apply computational tools to extract patterns that might be difficult for human readers to elicit.

Prior work in digital humanities has studied a variety of narrative questions across corpora of multiple texts. For example, research in cultural analytics has compared narrative structure (Chambers and Jurafsky, 2009; Pichotta and Mooney, 2016; Goyal et al., 2010), character arcs and relationships (Bamman et al., 2013; Iyyer et al., 2016), and authorship attribution (Hoover, 2004). Authorship can also be modeled as a latent factor in topic models (Rosen-Zvi et al., 2004). We do not explicitly model authors (or in our case, narrators) but instead rely on a simpler model to extract cross-cutting, interpretative themes. Moreover, unlike studies of focalization (Genette, 1983), we make no attempt to model the perspective or views of a character, but rather simply ask if characters are in any way distinguishable.

In computational studies that similarly focus on sections of a single work, Wang and Iyyer (2019) compare sections of Italo Calvino's *Invisible Cities* and Brooke et al. (2015) investigate distinguishing narrative voices in T.S. Eliot's *The Waste Land*. Wang and Iyyer (2019) circumvent data size limitations by relying on large, pretrained contextual models to cluster the cities and compare thematic patterns; Brooke et al. (2015) rely on preexisting tools that elicit English-language features, including parts of speech and verb tense. Such pretrained models and featurization tools, while available for modern Italian (Polignano et al., 2019), are unavailable for the quite different medieval Italian of the *Decameron* (Salvi and Renzi, 2010; Dardano, 2012). We instead use language-agnostic computational tools for our experiments, which come with the added benefit of interpretability (Section 4).

3 Curating a *Decameron* Dataset

We constructed a `json` dataset of the *Decameron* from an XML version hosted online by the Sapienza University of Rome (Branca, 2003). This digitized version is based on Vittore Branca's authoritative text (Boccaccio, 2014), and was published online in 2003 in the (at the time standard) TEI P4 format (Text Encoding Initiative, 2002). TEI P4 contains a variety of metadata that interrupt contiguous portions of Boccaccio's text, which does not make the format amenable to commonly-used tools. We therefore spent considerable time simplifying this format to be more easily manipulable for modern data analysis. We manually and repeatedly verified that our curation process retained the integrity of the text.[6] Where appropriate, we added metadata to annotate *novelle*, such as the *novella* storyteller, which was absent in the existing online version. Unlike the TEI P4 format, we avoid placing these metadata within the text of individual *novelle*, and provide scripts for those that wish to remove these metadata for their analyses.

We release this dataset publicly. Our hope is that our online version of Branca's text will be more accessible to scholars of medieval Italian interested in engaging with digital tools, as the simplicity of our format should lower the barrier to entry for both computational and humanist scholars interested in the *Decameron*.

4 Case Study: Constructing Storyteller Profiles in Boccaccio's *Decameron*

We use the problem of *Decameron* storyteller identity as a case study for exploring the challenges

[6] We document the process in our repository README.

and opportunities for using digital humanities techniques in specialized literary domains. In particular, **we investigate how such tools can be useful for 1) a small corpus containing a single text 2) modeling language that is no longer in contemporary use.** While the question we ask is specific to our chosen domain—the *Decameron* and medieval Italian—we believe that the lessons we can derive are applicable to other scholarly digital humanities tasks with these same defining elements.

4.1 Problem Formulation

Wang and Iyyer (2019) were able to use pretrained contextual models like BERT (Devlin et al., 2019) for modeling a small, single-text English corpus, analogous tools are not available for studying the *Decameron*. While there is a modern Italian version of BERT (AlBERTO, trained on Twitter data (Polignano et al., 2019)), medieval Italian orthography and morphology are sufficiently different to contraindicate its use (Salvi and Renzi, 2010; Dardano, 2012). Moreover, such pretrained contextual ML models are difficult to interpret, and our goal is to assist humanist scholars in close-reading analysis. Learning about storyteller identity is not just about classification; we already know authoritatively who told which story. Rather, we would like to explain *how* our models distinguish among storytellers. Based on this goal, and the constraints we highlight in Section 4, we choose two language-agnostic, interpretable approaches: logistic regression to try to classify storytellers based on their *novelle* and topic modeling to model storytellers as distributions of lexical themes.

4.2 Modeling Storytellers using Logistic Regression

We first attempt to see if the storytellers can be identified from the *novelle* they tell. We train a logistic regression model for this classification task. For our training data, we divide each *novella* into 100-word chunks (converted to TF-IDF vectors) with the corresponding storyteller as the label. This results in a 10-class logistic regression problem, using an 80/20 train/test split where we ensure that we have equal representation of each storyteller in both sets (i.e., each storyteller tells 10 *novelle*, comprising the 100 *novelle* total; we randomly sample 8 *novelle* for each storyteller in train; the remaining 2 for each in test). We train our model 100 times, with variation coming from randomly sampling the *novelle*. Results are shown in Figure 1a.

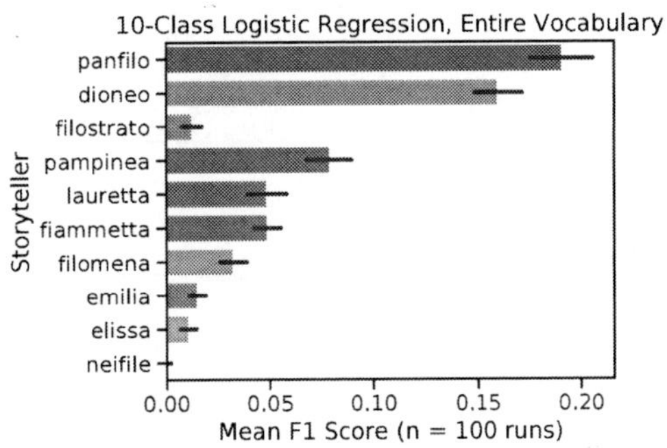

(a)

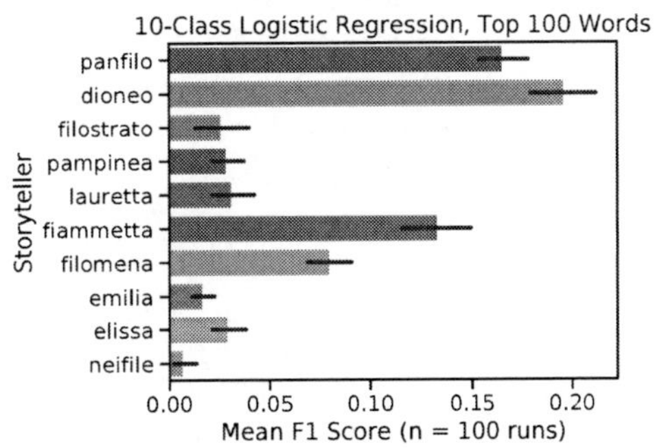

(b)

Figure 1: Mean F1 scores for classifying *novelle* by narrator in 10-class logistic regression. For both experiments, $n = 100$. Using the *Decameron*'s whole vocabulary (1a), the model can identify Panfilo and Dioneo better than random. When we restrict the text to only contain instances of the 100 most frequent words (1b), the model is additionally able to identify Fiammetta.

Since there are 10 storytellers, in order to classify better-than-random, F1 scores would need to be > 0.1. There are only two storytellers, who are both men, that pass this threshold consistently: Panfilo and Dioneo. It is perhaps unsurprising that this is true for Dioneo; he alone among the *brigata* has the special privilege of deviating from the Day's storytelling theme—a privilege he typically exercises to talk about sex. It is however less clear to us why Panfilo stands out in our results, which suggests a potential direction for future research.

We then re-ran this experiment, pre-processing the *Decameron* to only contain the 100 most frequently used words in the vocabulary. In addition to Panfilo and Dioneo, this model is also able to identify Fiammetta, one of the seven women, better than random (Figure 1b). This, too, suggests lines of further investigation, as it is unclear why Fiammetta

	Panfilo	Neifile	Filomena	Dioneo	Fiammetta	Emilia	Filostrato	Lauretta	Elissa	Pampinea
Highest	gentili	veder	amico	famigliare	meco	basciò	fama	gentile	figliuolo	freddo
	compagni	onesta	parenti	conoscere	cuore	vivo	caldo	messere	cavalli	torre
	bocca	gentil	ciascun	primieramente	amava	accidente	cavallo	talvolta	liberamente	fante
	figliuol	credeva	cautamente	signor	nell'animo	maravigliò	oimè	diè	figliuoli	amante
	vicina	vicini	dico	pose	venendo	buone	malvagia	belle	veggendosi	reina
Lowest	freddo	peccato	famigliare	valente	cavallo	vedi	re	incontanente	dormire	veramente
	buone	disidero	sentito	morte	tornare	uom	speranza	animo	allato	ricco
	figliuolo	occhi	porta	corte	signor	famiglia	gentili	medesima	mille	tavola
	aperto	cavaliere	tavola	madre	signore	partito	figliuoli	vedendo	ciascun	bisogno
	pianamente	troppo	corte	cavaliere	figliuoli	cara	amor	fante	giovani	morto

Table 1: The words with highest and lowest PMI for each storyteller (higher scores indicate stronger associations).

is more identifiable than the other women.[7]

We probe our classification results by extracting the words with highest and lowest pointwise mutual information (PMI) for each *brigata* member. This metric uncovers lexical associations with each narrator in comparison to all the narrators. Given a word w and a narrator n, $PMI(w;n) = log\frac{p(w|n)}{p(w)}$. To improve interpretability, we remove words that occur fewer than five times for each narrator, and we manually remove stopwords.[8] Table 1 shows that despite our low classifier performance, lexical differences between the storytellers are interpretable. Neifile, whom our classifier completely misses, scores high for words that signify honorability (e.g., *onesta*), while low for words that connote the opposite (e.g., *peccato*). Filostrato, who reveals his personal heartbreak, scores low for words concerning love and hope (e.g., *amor*, *speranza*).[9]

4.3 Modeling Storytellers using Topic Distributions

Since we were not able to generally distinguish storytellers via classification, as a second experiment we use latent Dirichlet allocation (LDA) (Blei et al., 2003) to model each *novella* as a distribution of topics. We group the results by storyteller to see if the distributions of *novella* topics are distinguishable for each of the 10 members of the *brigata*. In other words, we can view per-storyteller topic distributions as storyteller "profiles"—patterns that may indicate unique thematic features of particular *brigata* members.

[7]We repeated these experiments using one-versus-rest logistic regression to test if each storyteller is distinguishable compared to the other 9. The results were comparable to those presented in Figure 1.

[8][*è, che, la, quale, e, di, fu, le, per, col, aveva, avere, ha, il, lo, gli, i, de, in, ciò, ho*]

[9]Notably, PMI scores do not incorporate semantics. As a result, two words that have the same semantic meaning but different morphology can have very different scores. For example, Panfilo's *novelle* have high PMI for *figliuol* but low PMI for *figliuolo*–words that both mean "son" (in the medieval variant of the modern "figliolo").

To perform this analysis, we used a Python wrapper for MALLET (Antoniak, 2021; McCallum, 2002). We used this framework because its implementation of LDA uses Gibbs sampling (Geman and Geman, 1984), an exact MCMC sampling method that has popularly been observed to have better performance for small datasets than inexact, variational inference-based implementations. We train our model with $k = 20$ topics[10] and allow hyperparameter optimization. Before training, we lowercase the text and process each *novella* to create documents of 200 words each; we remove a custom list of common Italian stop words, and if the resulting document is fewer than 20 words long, we do not use it for training. This creates a training corpus of 1,203 documents.

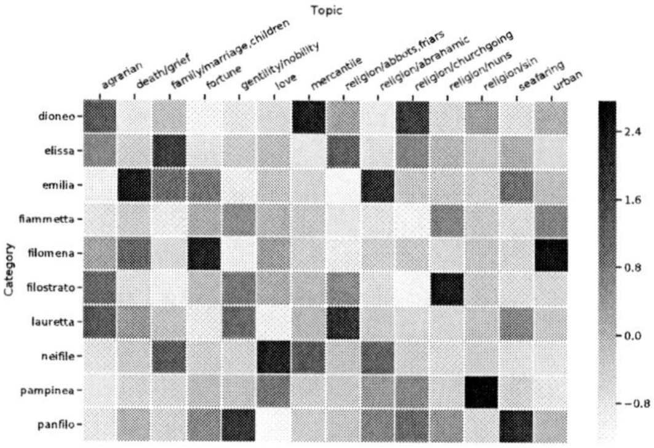

Figure 2: Each storyteller according to their underlying distribution of topics. Columns are normalized to highlight differences across topics.

We manually validated the quality of the resulting topics to see if they were semantically meaningful, and we were able to determine some clear themes. For example, one topic's top words include *nave* (ship), *mare* (sea), *isola* (island), *barca*

[10]We tried different k and found that 20 resulted in the most interpretable, overarching topics for our small dataset.

(boat), and *vento* (wind), to which we assigned overall topic designation `seafaring`. Of the 20 topics, 14 had very clear semantic themes, while the remaining 6 were more illusive. Therefore, to achieve a clearer picture of the variation over storytellers, we removed these 6 topics in our plots.We then validated the remaining topics at the *novella* level, plotting a heat map in which each each row is a *novella* topic distribution. This heat map enabled us to spot-check if particular *novelle* had reasonable topic distributions.[11]

Our storyteller-topic results are summarized in Figure 2, which overall indicates that there are thematic differences between the individual storytellers. If the storytellers were truly indistinguishable, it is unlikely that we would observe variation in the topic signatures. Of particular note are cells in the heatmap that show a uniquely highly-weighted presence for a topic that is relatively absent for each of the other nine narrators. To call attention to three examples, we can see this for `religion/sin` for Pampinea, `mercantile` for Dioneo, and `seafaring` for Panfilo.

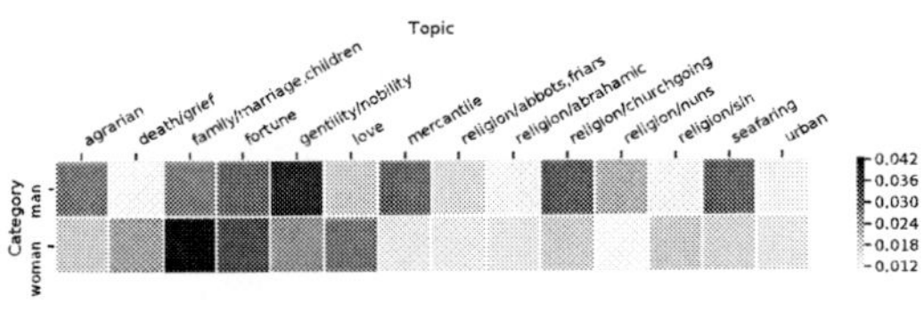

Figure 3: Topic distributions by storyteller gender.

To see another view of these results, we performed a similar analysis, in which we grouped topic distributions more coarsely—by storyteller gender instead of individual storyteller (Figure 3). Two interesting observations for these results are that the men discuss `mercantile` themes considerably more than the women, and the women discuss `love` more than the men. Perhaps the `mercantile` results are unsurprising, given men's unrestricted ability to participate in economic endeavors—a privilege underscored in the Author's Proem (Boccaccio, 2014). However, the result concerning `love` is somewhat surprising. The Author's stated purpose in the Proem is to relieve the suffering of women in love, and the three men are said to be in love with three of the women of the *brigata*, so it may seem unusual for words associated with love to be more strongly collocated with women than with men.

5 Conclusion and Future Work

While our work has focused on a specific question—whether the members of the *Decameron*'s *brigata* exhibit distinct storytelling personalities—we have illustrated broader lessons for small-text, specialized-language digital humanities scholarship. A central tension for work in low-resource domains is whether to focus on building tools and resources to mimic large, English-language resources or to instead work around the lack of resources by relying on methods that do not require much training data. While we have taken the latter path in this paper, we see ample opportunities for both developing models and annotating larger datasets for this domain (Bai et al., 2021). For example, while medieval Italian is syntactically quite different from modern Italian, some linguistic studies on specific texts indicate significant lexical overlap.[12] Based on this observation, future work could modify existing Italian contextual models for high-fidelity use on medieval Italian works.

For scholars of the *Decameron*, our highlighted results indicate areas for further inquiry. For example, a close-reading analysis of the *novelle* could explain when and why the women storytellers talk about more "male" topics (e.g., `mercantile` themes) and would complement our topic modeling results. More broadly, our release of a simplified format of the digitized text will facilitate future digital humanities research related to Boccaccio's *Decameron*.

References

Maria Antoniak. 2021. little-mallet-wrapper.

Fan Bai, Alan Ritter, and Wei Xu. 2021. Pre-train or annotate? domain adaptation with a constrained budget. In *Proceedings of the 2021 Conference on Empirical Methods in Natural Language Processing*. Association for Computational Linguistics.

David Bamman, Brendan O'Connor, and Noah A. Smith. 2013. Learning latent personas of film characters. In *Proceedings of the 51st Annual Meeting of the Association for Computational Linguistics (Volume 1: Long Papers)*, pages 352–361, Sofia, Bulgaria. Association for Computational Linguistics.

[11]This heatmap is available at `https://github.com/pasta41/decameron`.

[12]De Mauro (2001) points out that if we examine the fundamental vocabulary of Italian (i.e., the most common 2000 words) we find that 92% of them are words that Dante used in his *Divina Commedia*.

David M. Blei, Andrew Y. Ng, and Michael I. Jordan. 2003. Latent Dirichlet Allocation. *J. Mach. Learn. Res.*, 3:993–1022.

Giovanni Boccaccio. 1995. *Decameron*, 2 edition. Penguin Books, London, England.

Giovanni Boccaccio. 2014. *Decameron, edited by Vittore Branca*. Einaudi, Torino.

Vittore Branca. 1975. *Boccaccio medievale*, 4 edition. G. C. Sansoni, Firenze.

Vittore Branca. 2003. The Decameron. Digitized by the Sapienza University of Rome, Biblioteca italiana Project.

Julian Brooke, Adam Hammond, and Graeme Hirst. 2015. Distinguishing Voices in The Waste Land using Computational Stylistics. In *Linguistic Issues in Language Technology, Volume 12, 2015 - Literature Lifts up Computational Linguistics*. CSLI Publications.

Brown University Italian Studies Department. Decameron Web.

Nathanael Chambers and Dan Jurafsky. 2009. Unsupervised learning of narrative schemas and their participants. In *Proceedings of the Joint Conference of the 47th Annual Meeting of the ACL and the 4th International Joint Conference on Natural Language Processing of the AFNLP*, pages 602–610, Suntec, Singapore. Association for Computational Linguistics.

Maurizio Dardano, editor. 2012. *Sintassi dell'italiano antico*. Carocci, Roma. Vol. 1, La prosa del Duecento e del Trecento.

Tullio De Mauro. 2001. Dante, il gendarme e l'articolo 3 della Costituzione. In *Dante, il gendarme e la bolletta. La communicazione pubblica in Italia e la nuova bolletta*, pages 3–11. Laterza, Bari.

Jacob Devlin, Ming-Wei Chang, Kenton Lee, and Kristina Toutanova. 2019. BERT: Pre-training of deep bidirectional transformers for language understanding. In *Proceedings of the 2019 Conference of the North American Chapter of the Association for Computational Linguistics: Human Language Technologies, Volume 1 (Long and Short Papers)*, pages 4171–4186, Minneapolis, Minnesota. Association for Computational Linguistics.

Paula Findlen. 2020. What Would Boccaccio Say About COVID-19? *The Boston Review*.

Stuart Geman and Donald Geman. 1984. Stochastic Relaxation, Gibbs Distributions, and the Bayesian Restoration of Images. *IEEE Transactions on Pattern Analysis and Machine Intelligence*, PAMI-6(6):721–741.

Gérard Genette. 1983. *Narrative Discourse: An Essay in Method*. Cornell University Press, Ithaca, New York. Translation (Jane E. Lewin) of Discours du récit, a portion of the 3rd vol. of the author's Figures, essais.

Warren Ginsberg. 2015. *Tellers, tales, and translation in Chaucer's Canterbury Tales*. Oxford University Press, Oxford, United Kingdom; New York, NY.

Amit Goyal, Ellen Riloff, and Hal Daumé III. 2010. Automatically producing plot unit representations for narrative text. In *Proceedings of the 2010 Conference on Empirical Methods in Natural Language Processing*, pages 77–86, Cambridge, MA. Association for Computational Linguistics.

Paolo Grossi. 1991. Per una rivalutazione dei narratori del Decameron: Filomena e la novella di Lisabetta (Decameron IV, 5). *Critica letteraria*, 19:145–57.

David L Hoover. 2004. Testing Burrows's delta. *Literary and Linguistic Computing*, 19(4):453–475.

Mohit Iyyer, Anupam Guha, Snigdha Chaturvedi, Jordan Boyd-Graber, and Hal Daumé III. 2016. Feuding families and former Friends: Unsupervised learning for dynamic fictional relationships. In *Proceedings of the 2016 Conference of the North American Chapter of the Association for Computational Linguistics: Human Language Technologies*, pages 1534–1544, San Diego, California. Association for Computational Linguistics.

George Lyman Kittredge. 1915. *Chaucer and His Poetry*. Harvard University Press, Cambridge, Massachusetts.

David Lawton. 1985. *Chaucer's Narrators*. D.S. Brewer, Suffolk, UK.

Martin Marafioti. 2001. Boccaccio's Lauretta: The Brigata's Bearer of Bad News. *Italian Culture*, 19(2):7–18.

Millicent Marcus. 1979. *An Allegory of Form: Literary Self-consciousness in the Decameron*. Anma Libri.

Millicent Marcus. 2020. Reading the 'Decameron' Through the Lens of COVID-19: The Fallacy of Literary Distancing. *The Yale Review*.

Andrew Kachites McCallum. 2002. MALLET: A Machine Learning for Language Toolkit.

Marilyn Migiel. 2004. *A Rhetoric of the Decameron*. The University of Toronto Press.

Marilyn Migiel. 2015. *The Ethical Dimension of the 'Decameron'*. The University of Toronto Press.

Karl Pichotta and Raymond Mooney. 2016. Learning statistical scripts with lstm recurrent neural networks. *Proceedings of the AAAI Conference on Artificial Intelligence*, 30(1).

Marco Polignano, Pierpaolo Basile, Marco de Gemmis, Giovanni Semeraro, and Valerio Basile. 2019. AlBERTo: Italian BERT Language Understanding Model for NLP Challenging Tasks Based on Tweets. In *Proceedings of the Sixth Italian Conference on Computational Linguistics (CLiC-it 2019)*, volume 2481. CEUR.

Kelly Prime, Mike Benoist, Tommy Orange, and Edgwidge Danticat. 2020. The Sunday Read: 'The Decameron Project'.

Brian Richardson. 1978. The 'Ghibelline' Narrator in the Decameron". *Italian Studies*, 33:20 – 28.

Michal Rosen-Zvi, Thomas Griffiths, Mark Steyvers, and Padhraic Smyth. 2004. The Author-Topic Model for Authors and Documents. In *Proceedings of the 20th Conference on Uncertainty in Artificial Intelligence*, UAI '04, page 487–494, Arlington, Virginia, USA. AUAI Press.

Giampaolo Salvi and Lorenzo Renzi. 2010. *Grammatica dell'italiano antico*. Il Mulino, Bologna.

Text Encoding Initiative. 2002. The XML Version of the TEI Guidelines: <TEI.2>.

Shufan Wang and Mohit Iyyer. 2019. Casting Light on Invisible Cities: Computationally Engaging with Literary Criticism. In *Proceedings of the 2019 Conference of the North American Chapter of the Association for Computational Linguistics: Human Language Technologies, Volume 1 (Long and Short Papers)*, pages 1291–1297, Minneapolis, Minnesota. Association for Computational Linguistics.

WMDecompose: A Framework for Leveraging the Interpretable Properties of Word Mover's Distance in Sociocultural Analysis

Mikael Brunila
McGill University
Department of Geography
mikael.brunila@gmail.com

Jack LaViolette
Columbia University
Department of Sociology
jack.laviolette@columbia.edu

Abstract

Despite the increasing popularity of NLP in the humanities and social sciences, advances in model performance and complexity have been accompanied by concerns about interpretability and explanatory power for sociocultural analysis. One popular model that balances complexity and legibility is Word Mover's Distance (WMD). Ostensibly adapted for its interpretability, WMD has nonetheless been used and further developed in ways which frequently discard its most interpretable aspect: namely, the word-level distances required for translating a set of words into another set of words. To address this apparent gap, we introduce WMDecompose: a model and Python library that 1) decomposes document-level distances into their constituent word-level distances, and 2) subsequently clusters words to induce thematic elements, such that useful lexical information is retained and summarized for analysis. To illustrate its potential in a social scientific context, we apply it to a longitudinal social media corpus to explore the interrelationship between conspiracy theories and conservative American discourses. Finally, because of the full WMD model's high time-complexity, we additionally suggest a method of sampling document pairs from large datasets in a reproducible way, with tight bounds that prevent extrapolation of unreliable results due to poor sampling practices.

1 Introduction: The Paradox of Word Mover's Distance

The present paper introduces WMDecompose, an iteration of the Word Mover's Distance (WMD) (Kusner et al., 2015) model commonly used for determining the semantic distances between pairs of documents. Leveraging word vectors from models such as word2vec (Mikolov et al., 2013), fastText (Bojanowski et al., 2016) and GloVe (Pennington et al., 2014), WMD was presented as a method that was not only hyper-parameter free and thus easy to use, but also highly interpretable (Kusner et al., 2015). Arguably, this still makes the model a viable alternative for document similarity tasks, despite the recent and rapid rise of contextual and rich embeddings from Transformer-type models (Vaswani et al., 2017) such as BERT (Devlin et al., 2019). However, WMD is computationally expensive, with the full model running at cubic time complexity (Kusner et al., 2015). This may explain why, despite its initial pitch as an interpretable alternative, WMD has mainly been further developed and applied in ways that focus on decreasing the model's high runtime, while ignoring or undermining the inherent interpretability of the model (Atasu et al., 2017; Werner and Laber, 2020).

To our knowledge, no current WMD implementation provides an out-of-the-box means of retaining word-level information, despite its utility to many research agendas. To confront this paradoxical situation, we introduce a set of methods and Python code for retaining the individual word distances that make WMD interpretable while simultaneously suggesting a simple trick for efficiently estimating the distance between large sets of documents. Specifically, we propose using implementation of the "relaxed" WMD (Kusner et al., 2015) with linear time complexity (Atasu et al., 2017) to first estimate the distances between a full set of documents, then using optimal pairing with the Gale-Shapley algorithm (Gale and Shapley, 1962) on this estimate to find the pairs between two sets of documents that minimize the average pairwise distance. Next, full WMD is calculated between each pair, while progressively adding the contributions of individual words to the overall distance between document sets. Words are, in turn, grouped using K-means clustering and vector dimensionality reduction to decompose the distances not only by word, but by thematic cluster. Each cluster is defined by its constituent words, and hence highly interpretable.

Proceedings of LaTeCH-CLfL 2021, pages 154–167
Punta Cana, Dominican Republic (Online), November 11, 2021.

Having introduced WMDecompose, we demonstrate its utility in a social scientific context by exploring interrelated trends over time between two social media corpora: `r/conspiracy` and `r/The_Donald`, the primary Reddit communities for self-identified conspiracy theorists and Donald Trump supporters, respectively. While this presents only a cursory and exploratory engagement with these thematically complex data, we hope that it demonstrates the analytic potential of WMDecompose for social science and humanities research.

Finally, we also provide a complementary analysis using a well-known Yelp review dataset, to act as a sanity check on the validity of our method. This analysis can be found in Appendix B.

2 Previous Work

2.1 Word Mover's Distance

Originally proposed by Kusner et al. (2015), WMD has become a popular metric of document semantic distance in computational linguistics and related subfields. An innovation and special instance of Earth Mover's Distance (Rubner et al., 1998; Pele and Werman, 2008, 2009), WMD leverages word embeddings to compute the minimum distance required to "move" the words from one document to another, providing a measure of document-level semantic (dis)similarity as a sum of the distance required to move individual words from one document to another (see Figure 1). Since its introduction, many related algorithms and analytic approaches have been proposed for language engineering tasks (e.g. Atasu et al., 2017; Huang et al., 2016; Ren and Liu, 2018). More recently, WMD and its many variations have also been applied to sociocultural analyses of data ranging from survey response data (Taylor and Stoltz, 2020), to Ancient Greek literature (Pöckelmann et al., 2020), to dyadic conversational dynamics (Nasir et al., 2019).

WMD is typically parameterized in the following manner (Kusner et al., 2015; Huang et al., 2016), using words represented as embeddings produced with algorithms such as word2vec (Mikolov et al., 2013). Let $x_i \in \mathbb{R}^d$ be the ith embedding in d-dimensional space, drawn from a word embedding matrix $X \in \mathbb{R}^{d \times n}$ representing a vocabulary of n words. Let $\mathbf{d}^a$ and $\mathbf{d}^b$ be two n-dimensional, normalized bag-of-words (nBOW) vectors for a pair of documents where d_i^a is the normalized number of times word i occurs in vector d^a. WMD then attempts to find a transportation matrix $\mathbf{T} \in \mathbb{R}^{n \times n}$ that minimizes the total distance required to move all words in the first document to the second document, where $\mathbf{T}_{i,j}$ describes how much of the normalized word vector d_i^a should be transported to the normalized word vector d_j^b. Formally, WMD returns the minimum distance to move from document $\mathbf{d}^a$ to document $\mathbf{d}^b$, given by summing the product of the optimal "flow" $\mathbf{T}_{i,j}$ from all words in the two documents with the "cost" $c(i,j)$ of moving between each word vector in the two documents:

$$\text{WMD}(\mathbf{d}^a, \mathbf{d}^b) = \min_{\mathbf{T} \geq 0} \sum_{i,j=1}^{n} \mathbf{T}_{i,j} c(i,j) \tag{1}$$

Furthermore, the equation is subject to the constraint that the entirety of the "mass" of $\mathbf{d}^a$ should be distributed in the flows to $\mathbf{d}^b$ and vice versa:

$$\begin{aligned} \sum_{j=1}^{n} \mathbf{T}_{i,j} &= d_i^a \ \forall i \in \{1, ..., n\} \\ \sum_{i=1}^{n} \mathbf{T}_{i,j} &= d_j^b \ \forall j \in \{1, ..., n\} \end{aligned} \tag{2}$$

Even though the original implementation of the WMD uses Euclidean distance for the metric $c(i,j)$, the similarity between word embeddings in general and with WMD in particular (Yokoi et al., 2020) is better captured using the cosine distance[1]:

$$c(i,j) = 1 - \frac{\mathbf{x}_i \cdot \mathbf{x}_j}{\|\mathbf{x}_i\| \|\mathbf{x}_j\|} \tag{3}$$

Furthermore, $\mathbf{d}^a$ and $\mathbf{d}^b$ can be normalized using other techniques, such as Term frequency-Inverse document frequency (Tf-Idf), combined with L1-normalization, which allocate more mass to words that are more common in a specific document than the overall vocabulary.

While there is a well-established literature on solving this linear program using the EMD algorithm, doing so is computationally prohibitive. Kusner et al. (2015) note that "the best average time complexity of solving the WMD optimization

[1]The use of the word "distance" here can be slightly confusing, as it is not quite the same as the "distance" in Word Mover's *Distance*. For the latter, the distance between two documents is composed of the cosine distance *and* the "mass" of the nBOW representation of the documents to be moved to one another.

problem scales" $O(V^3 \log V)$, with V denoting the number of unique words in the corpus. Consequently, calculating the distances for large datasets will often prove insurmountable for WMD. Kusner et al. (2015) suggest working around this issue by calculating an approximation of WMD, where the distance from the two pairs are calculated with relaxed constraints, so that $\mathbf{T}_{i,j}$ must contain the mass or flow from the source document, but not the target. This "relaxed" WMD or R-WMD is then instead parameterized with only one constraint:

$$\text{R-WMD}(\mathbf{d}^a, \mathbf{d}^b) = \min_{\mathbf{T} \geq 0} \sum_{i,j=1}^{n} \mathbf{T}_{i,j} c(i,j) \qquad \text{subject to: } \sum_{j=1}^{n} \mathbf{T}_{i,j} = d_i \;\; \forall i \in \{1, ..., n\} \tag{4}$$

Repeating the process, so that R-WMD is instead calculated from $\mathbf{d}^b$ to $\mathbf{d}^a$, gives us an estimate of the bounds within which the full WMD must be located. While R-WMD gives only an estimate of WMD within certain bounds, it has been shown to be a good approximation of the full WMD (Kusner et al., 2015). Notably, instead of the cubic time complexity of WMD, R-WMD can be performed with quadratic time complexity $O(V^2)$. Furthermore, Atasu et al. (2017) have demonstrated how to calculate the R-WMD so that the time complexity is reduced from quadratic to linear with the Linear Complexity Relaxed WMD (LC-RWMD) algorithm. However, this solution does *not* retain the distances contributed by individual words to the R-WMD.

2.2 WMD and interpretability

While these and other suggested tricks and improvements (e.g. Tithi and Petrini, 2021; Werner and Laber, 2020; Yokoi et al., 2020) for efficient WMD make the algorithm a feasible and powerful tool for comparing the semantic distance between large sets of documents, they have been introduced with little regard to the algorithm's initial claims to intuitive and interpretable explanations for document (dis)similarities. Consider, for example, Figure 1, introduced by Kusner et al. (2015) as an example of how the distances between three documents could be decomposed into different parts. Indeed, for sophisticated NLP techniques such as WMD to be maximally useful for sociocultural analysis, the possibility to decompose document-level results

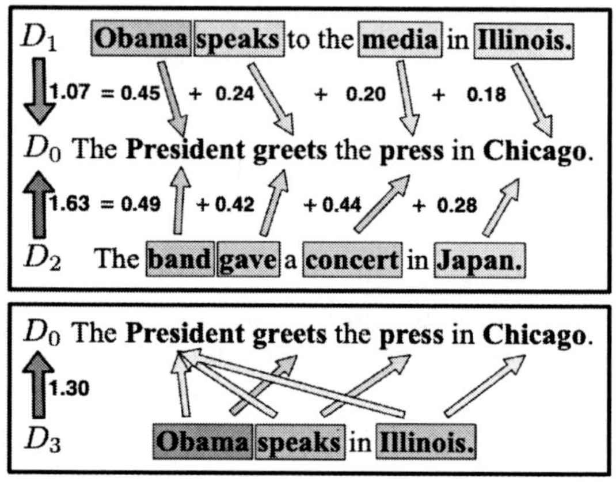

Figure 1: An illustration of WMD in action by Kusner et al. (2015). (Top:) The components of the WMD metric between a query D_0 and two sentences D_1 , D_2 (with equal BOW distance). The arrows represent flow between two words and are labeled with their distance contribution. (Bottom:) The flow between two sentences D_3 and D_0 with different numbers of words. This mismatch causes the WMD to move words to multiple similar words.

into interpretable lexical information is key. For example, if the mean WMD document distances between two longitudinal corpora sampled at some time t_0 and again at some later time t_1 shrink, it might indicate that the corpora have become more similar. However, the change in distance by itself would tell the curious analyst little about the particular lexical phenomena responsible for the semantic changes, and (crucially) how these might relate to extralinguistic social and symbolic processes. In order to tell the full story, fluctuations in distance must be decomposed into interpretable parts.

To invoke Danilevsky et al.'s (2020) classification scheme of explanation in NLP, WMD provides explanations that are *local* (i.e. the distance between any pair of documents can be decomposed to individual words) and *self-explanatory* (i.e., no *post hoc* processing of the model outputs is necessary). However, these explanations have, to the best of our knowledge, not been leveraged in applied research with WMD, most likely due to the prohibitive computational cost of calculating the full WMD and the neglect of interpretability in more efficient elaborations of the model. Moreover, applied WMD research has to date generally begun with an *a priori* interest in the relationship between documents and particular "concept" words (Stoltz and Taylor, 2019, e.g.) or predefined topics

(Wu and Li, 2017, e.g.). Although such analyses are perfectly valid, a fully inductive relationship to words of interest can be useful when the analyst does not have or desire strong assumptions about what lexical changes underlie the phenomena of interest.

To these ends of inductive interpretability, we propose what we believe to be a novel analytic pipeline which combines LC-RWMD decomposed at the word level, optional document pairing based on the Gale-Shapley matching algorithm to ensure robustness, and t-SNE (Maaten and Hinton, 2008) reduced word vectors with K-means clustering (Lloyd, 1982; Elkan, 2003) to enhance interpretability by inducing higher-level thematic groupings. To assist future researchers, we additionally provide a Python package and example code notebooks available on Github.[2]

3 Data

3.1 The corpus: conspiracy theories and American conservatism online

Several researchers have identified conspiratorial thinking as a feature of the (post-)Trump era of American conservative politics (Bracewell, 2021; Hellinger, 2018; Polletta and Callahan, 2019). Many such studies have been theoretical and/or qualitative (e.g. Barkun, 2017; Stecula and Pickup, 2021), survey-based (e.g. Federico et al., 2018; Miller et al., 2016; Uscinski et al., 2020), focused on patterns of "misinformation" dissemination on social media (e.g. Benkler et al., 2017; Marwick and Lewis, 2017), or on the discourse of political elites (e.g., Hornsey et al., 2020; Neville-Shepard, 2019). The present paper chooses a different, though not unprecedented, approach of studying large user-generated text corpora from `reddit.com`. Specifically, we analyze "self posts"[3] from the `r/The_Donald` and `r/conspiracy` communities ("*subreddits*"); the former was the main subreddit for Donald Trump supporters before being banned in June 2020, while the latter remains the largest subreddit for self-identified conspiracy theorists. Others have examined both `r/The_Donald` and its role in alt-right politics (Massachs et al., 2020; Ribeiro et al., 2020; Shepherd, 2020), as well as conspiracy theorists on the platform (Klein et al., 2019; Phadke et al., 2021; Samory and Mitra, 2018). Research has indicated a sizable and statistically significant overlap in users between the two subreddits (Massachs et al., 2020; Nithyanand et al., 2017). However, these observations have been largely based on subreddit co-subscriber networks, and have paid comparatively less attention to large-scale linguistic patterns over time, a gap to which we hope to contribute.

Data was collected using the Pushshift Reddit dataset publicly available on Google BigQuery (Baumgartner et al., 2020). Because we are interested in change over time, we delineate two discontinuous periods of interest: t_0, defined as the twelve months following the creation of `r/The_Donald` (July 11, 2015–July 11, 2016), and t_1, the final twelve months available in the dataset (August 31, 2018–August 31, 2019). These two year-long snapshots, separated by roughly two years, offer a glimpse of the relationship between conspiratorial language and the discourse of self-identified Donald Trump supporters during the Trump presidency.

3.2 Sampling and preprocessing

To reduce computation and run-time, we sample 5,000 posts from each subreddit at t_0 and t_1 for a total of 20,000 posts. Random sampling was restricted to those posts at least 30 words long (to ensure that documents contain adequate lexical information), and having a positive score (2 or greater, as Reddit posts start with a score of 1) to ensure that the lexical content is generally representative of the community. Once sampled, the text is preprocessed using a standard pipeline for NLP applications. The specifics of this pipeline are described in Appendix A. The processed dataset contains 1,509,553 tokens, 596,596 tokens from `r/The_Donald` and 993,957 from `r/conspiracy`.

4 Methods

4.1 Embedding and clustering

After preprocessing, words were converted to vectors using a fine-tuned word2vec model introduced in (Mikolov et al., 2013), originally pre-trained on Google News Vectors containing about 300 billion words. Fine-tuning details and hyperparameters are included in Appendix A. Due to the large number of unique words, and to increase the interpretability

[2] `https://github.com/maybemkl/wmdecompose`

[3] Self posts are forum submissions which contain only text as opposed to links to external sites. We use self posts in lieu of comments, as the latter tend to be shorter and less orderly due to their nested structure. Further, self posts tend to be more regulated by forum moderators, suggesting that they are more likely to reflect the norms of the community.

of the final outputs, words were clustered on the basis of their embedding vectors using t-SNE, an algorithm that is commonly used to reduce the dimensionality of word embeddings while still preserving the original structure of the higher-dimensional form (for uses with WMD, see: Huang et al., 2016; Gülle et al., 2020). In our case, we reduce the dimensionality of the original word vectors from 300 to two and use K-means on the reduced dimensions to generate 100 clusters of words according to their semantic similarity. Clustering words allows us to examine not only the changing usage of individual words across subreddits, but also of these higher-level thematic groupings. The number of clusters was chosen heuristically after inspecting both elbow plots and silhouette scores for clusters in the range of 10 to 200. Our method is robust to using raw embeddings as well as other popular reduction techniques before clustering, such as UMAP (McInnes et al., 2020).

4.2 WMDecompose

We now introduce WMDecompose, the core contribution of this paper, which provides the ability to examine the word-level distances required to move between two sets of documents, such as the self posts in `r/conspiracy` and `r/The_Donald`. The comparison of these documents happens, on the one hand, through retaining the word-level distances of moving between pairs of documents from each set and, on the other hand, by clustering words and aggregating their added distances by cluster.

More generally: Given two sets of documents, S^a and S^b, the matrix $\mathbf{T}_{i,j}$ of flows between all the individual documents in both sets, and clusters for the input word vectors, WMDecompose returns the following information twice, once in terms of movement from the first set to the second and once in terms of movement from the second set to the first:

A The aggregate word-level WMD or WMD_w for each word w in a vocabulary V when moving all documents from one set of documents S^a to another set S^b.

B The aggregate cluster-level or Cluster Mover's Distance (CMD_c) for each cluster c when moving all documents from S^a to S^b, with keywords for each c determined by the words with the highest WMD_w within the cluster.

The WMD_w gives us a good sense of the most important words separating the two sets. The CMD_c allows us to organize this information by cluster, with interpretable cluster keywords that are dynamically ranked, depending on their importance for the particular case at hand.

More formally, WMD_w is calculated in the following manner. Let w^a and w^b be two words contained in S^a and S^b, respectively, and let WMD_{w^a} be the total distance accumulated by word w^a when moving from S^a to S^b. Next, if n is the number of documents in S^a that contain the word w^a, m is the number of words in some document d^b that w^a is distributed over, $\mathbf{t}_{i,j}$ is the vector of flows from w^a in document d^a_i to each word w^b_j in d^b, and $c(w^a, w^b_j)$ is the cost in terms of cosine distance to move from each w^a to each w^b_j, then

$$\text{WMD}_{w^a} = \sum_{i=1}^{n}\sum_{j=1}^{m} \mathbf{t}_{i,j} c(w^a, w^b_j) \quad (5)$$

WMD_{w^b} is counted in the same manner, only this time using the flow and cost from words in S^b to words in S^a.

The CMD_{c^a}, i.e. the CMD_c for movement from S^a to S^b, is then calculated simply by summing over the aggregated distances of all $w^a \in c$, i.e. all words w^a belonging to cluster c. If there are p such words in S^a for some cluster c, then

$$\text{CMD}_{c^a} = \sum_{k=1}^{p} \text{WMD}_{w^a} \quad \forall w^a \in c^a \quad (6)$$

Again, CMD_{c^b} is counted in the same manner. Furthermore, the total WMD_{S^a} when moving all documents from S^a to some pair in S^b can consequently be described as

$$\text{WMD}_{S^a} = \sum \text{WMD}_{w^a} = \sum \text{CMD}_{c^a} \quad (7)$$

In order to further accentuate the differences between the word-level distances WMD_{w^a} and WMD_{w^b}, we subtract the WMD_{w^a} for each word w^a in the vocabulary of S^a from the corresponding WMD_{w^b} (if it exists) in the other set and vice versa. This way results will not be cluttered by words for which the WMD_w is very similar across sets and instead the differences between the two sets will be highlighted. Hence, the final WMD_{w^a} with "difference" or $\text{WMD}^d_{w^a}$ for word w^a is

$$\mathrm{WMD}^d_{w^a} = \mathrm{WMD}_{w^a} - \mathrm{WMD}_{w^b} \quad (8)$$

if there exists such a w^b that $w^b = w^a$. In other cases, the $\mathrm{WMD}^d_{w^a}$ is just equal to the WMD_{w^a}. For the rest of the paper, we will use WMD_{w^a} as a short-hand when writing about $\mathrm{WMD}^d_{w^a}$ as the model with difference yields far better and more interpretable results and is the only one we will consider in our analysis.

Finally, the WMD_w values can be calculated using WMD with or without relaxed constraints. However, while the LC-RWMD cannot be used, we will next suggest a way in which its speed can be leveraged to yield reproducible and conservative estimates of the WMD_w values.

4.3 Gale-Shapley matching for WMD

To run WMD on all 50 million pairwise combinations of documents in our corpus (5000^2 at both t_0 and t_1) would unfortunately be computationally prohibitive in many instances. With larger document sets, even using R-WMD with quadratic time complexity could be too costly in terms of time and computational resources, while using the LC-RWMD with linear time complexity sacrifices word-level decomposability. One solution would be to take a random sample from both sets of documents. However, this is not always ideal, as we will demonstrate next.

We first generate 50,000 random pairs of documents (each pair containing one post from each subreddit) at both t_0 and t_1, yielding a total of 100,000 random pairs. The distribution of distances is displayed in Figure 2. Although a *t*-test confirms high significance ($t = 13.71$), the measured difference in means is very small (0.548 at t_0, versus 0.545 at t_1), and it is difficult to determine to what meaningful extent this reflects increased similarity between user language in `r/The_Donald` and `r/conspiracy` over time. We will return to this point later, in Section 5.2.

Looking at Figure 2, it is clear that merely drawing a small random sample from both sets could produce unreliable results. Researchers working with very long documents and/or lacking computational resources might be limited to drawing small samples if running the full WMD model. If asking whether there is any evidence of document-level semantic alignment—i.e., a reduction in mean document pair distance over time—present in our corpus in the first place, using a random sample to

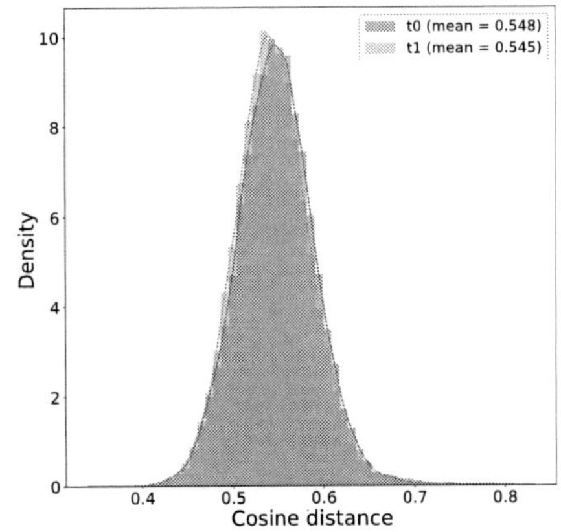

Figure 2: Distribution of WMD distances for random document pairs (one from each subreddit) at t_0 and t_1.

offset computational costs could therefore produce misleading results. We therefore introduce a second contribution of WMDecompose: the option of effective and consistent pairing of documents using the Gale-Shapley (GS) stable matching algorithm (Gale and Shapley, 1962) to reduce the computational burden incurred by analysis.

Originally introduced through the hypothetical problem of pairing colleges with applicants, the GS algorithm iteratively finds the optimal match between two sets of equal size, given the preferences of all members of the two sets. The optimal match is biased towards the party taking initiative, i.e. the "suitor" (Dubins and Freedman, 1981; Iwama and Miyazaki, 2008). To find the "preferences" of documents, we utilize LC-RWMD to first get an approximation of distances between all pairs from two sets of documents. Each document in a set then "prefers" the closest document in the other set. Given these preferences, we can use GS to find the pairs which minimize the distance between the two sets. We posit that GS ensures that our document pairs represent a conservative estimate of the distance between the two sets, making our method reproducible while also ensuring the robustness of results. By reducing computational costs, GS pairing is additionally aligned with mounting calls for NLP and other ML researchers to intentfully pursue algorithms which minimize the growing environmental toll of their technologies (Bender et al., 2021; Strubell et al., 2019).

For our specific case study, we first calculate the LC-RWMD from `r/conspiracy` to `r/The_Donald` and vice versa. This computation on 50M total pairs requires less than an hour on a regular laptop. Next, these relaxed distances from each document i in `r/conspiracy` to all N documents in `r/The_Donald` are used as the preferences of document i vis-a-vis documents $1, ..., N$. We are primarily interested in movement from `r/conspiracy` to `r/The_Donald`, hence the former is given the role of "suitor".

Then, the Gale-Shapley algorithm is executed to find the optimal match, i.e., the set of document pairs that is least costly to move between `r/conspiracy` and `r/The_Donald`. Effectively, this shows one optimal solution to moving the mass of words from former to the latter, if each document in the first set were to be transferred only to the most similar document in the other set. All these steps are repeated for the documents at t_0 and t_1. To summarize, by matching pairs of documents which are more similar in semantic space, WMDecompose produces conservative measures of semantic distance between corpora. Thus, in addition to providing a non-random, reproducible means of reducing computing costs while retaining full WMD calculations, GS ensures the robustness of findings.

4.4 Exploring lexical trends with WMDecompose

Once we have the optimal pairs between `r/conspiracy` and `r/The_Donald`, we can run full WMD for the two sets of pairs, i.e. the set at t_0 and the set at t_1[4]. We do this using `wmdecompose`, a Python package written specifically for this paper with EMD executed using the `PyEMD` library under the hood (Pele and Werman, 2008, 2009).[5]

5 Results

5.1 Overall document distance

After generating document pairs with the Gale-Shapley algorithm, it is worth asking whether mean document distances using GS pairs follow a similar pattern than those generated by random pairs (as in Figure 2). As it turns out, they do; both are normally distributed, with pair distances having a mean of 0.478 at t_0 (versus 0.548 with random pairing), and 0.469 at t_1 (versus 0.545 with random pairing). A t-test again shows significance (t = 8.05), but the absolute difference is small enough as to be difficult to interpret at the document level. We can therefore conclude that, when pairing documents on the basis of semantic proximity with GS and when pairing documents randomly, some modest but statistically significant reduction in distance is taking place from t_0 to t_1. Without further analysis, however, we cannot conclude much else.

5.2 Identifying distinguishing words with WMDecompose

As we have stated throughout, document-level distance measures tell one nothing about the nature and source of that distance. A researcher doing exploratory analysis of a new dataset might look at the relatively small, albeit significant, difference in mean document distance at t_0 and t_1 and conclude, absent any other contextual information, that further analysis is not warranted.

However, distances between documents merely represent the distances between their aggregate words. As such, it is quite possible that relative document-level stability is masking a much greater degree of variation between t_0 and t_1 for specific words, and these words might merit further attention. Figure 3 displays the distribution of changes in word cost (i.e., the total distance contributed at t_1 minus the total distance contributed at t_0) for each unique word in the corpus. As we can see, despite the longitudinal stability of the corpora at the document level, a great deal of lexical and semantic change over time is nevertheless taking place. Though the majority of words show little change in this regard, many words which significantly distinguished the corpora at t_0 no longer do at t_1, and vice versa. Our suggestion is that these words might be qualitatively instructive, motivating a closer inspection of the lexical data produced by WMDecompose. We therefore turn to WMDecompose to examine the sorted list of words and clusters which most distinguish our corpora at each time period, displayed in Table 1.

These top words conform nicely with expectations, with vocabulary directly associated with party and electoral politics characterizing `r/The_Donald`, and words associated with conspiracy theories characterizing their eponymous subreddit. Further, we see the clear effects of temporality and current events: words associated with

[4] Relaxed WMD can also be used to further speed up the calculations. While using R-WMD gives similar results as the full WMD, we focus here on the full WMD results as this is the baseline we are looking to establish.

[5] `https://github.com/laszukdawid/PyEMD`

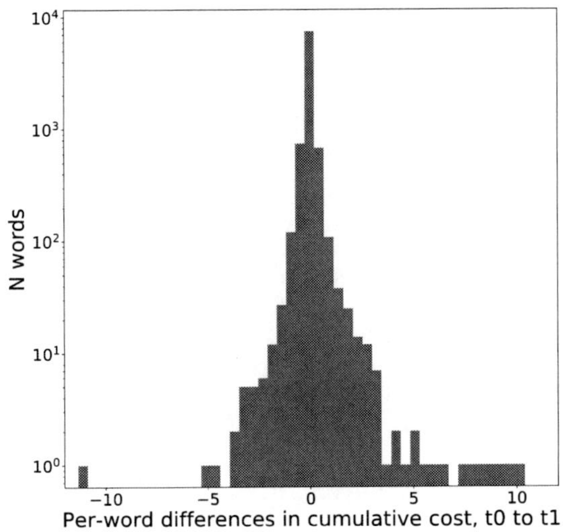

Figure 3: The distribution of word distance changes over time, calculated as the aggregate distance each word contributed to t_1 document pairs minus the aggregate distance it added to t_0 document pairs. Despite the general stability of document-level distances, many individual words show considerable differences in distance contributed from t_0 to t_1.

The_Donald (t_0)		conspiracy (t_0)	
Word	**Cost**	**Word**	**Cost**
trump	45.85	conspiracy	8.79
vote	14.96	government	6.67
bernie	10.79	world	3.90
hillary	10.49	israel	3.72
cruz	10.01	find	3.66
win	9.58	video	3.56
donald	9.58	information	3.08
donald_trump	8.81	documentary	3.00
delegate	7.95	theory	2.97
cuck	7.50	isis	2.97
The_Donald (t_1)		**conspiracy (t_1)**	
Word	**Cost**	**Word**	**Cost**
trump	12.83	conspiracy	11.17
vote	10.70	epstein	8.97
democrat	6.50	video	5.30
president	6.45	control	4.97
dem	5.90	vaccine	4.46
left	5.12	theory	3.94
pedes	4.76	world	3.69
election	4.74	find	3.46
liberal	4.70	government	3.33
win	4.33	cia	2.89

Table 1: Words contributing the most cost between subreddits at t_0 and t_1.

the 2016 election cycle (*bernie, hillary, cruz, delegate*) disappear at t_1, while more general political terms (*democrat, president, liberal*) appear; for `r/conspiracy`, *epstein* and *cia* enter the top ten most distinctive words, while *isis* drops out.

We can also note that, though the top word distances are higher for `r/The_Donald` at each period, the difference greatly shrinks, reflecting both an attenuation of the ritualized, insider language associated with Trump's online following during the 2016 election cycle, as well as an increase in talk related to Trump on `r/conspiracy`. While these results are perhaps unsurprising, they demonstrate the greater richness of WMDecompose for the comparative analysis of corpora by introducing word-level data. Clustering words similarly allows for the discovery of pervasive thematic differences between corpora. Table 2 displays some example clusters, separated by subreddit and time period.

5.3 Inductive discovery of thematic assimilation over time

While WMDecompose can be used to identify distinguishing keywords, it can also be used to uncover fine-grained semantic assimilation. If a word w strongly distinguishes corpus S^a from corpus S^b at t_0, but no longer at t_1, it could represent assimilation (S^b starts using w and related words more frequently), but it could equally represent S^a ceasing to use w (as is often the case with words related to current events).

As such, the change in the distance contribution of a word over time must be considered alongside the change in word frequency. We might thus conceive of each word distance change as occupying a position in three-dimensional space, with axes corresponding to 1) change in aggregate word cost, 2) change in frequency in S^a, and 3) change in frequency in S^b. The same conceptualization can be applied to word clusters as well, wherein a cluster's values are simply the sum of its words' values.

Given our interest in semantic convergence, cases in which word distance contributions go down because usage ceases are of little interest (though they might interest others). Rather, we are interested in words which contribute less distance, while exhibiting comparable or increased use in both subreddits. Examining words meeting these criteria, and excluding low-frequency outliers, we indeed see many conspiratorial words whose cu-

Subcorpus	Cluster Theme	Word 1	Word 2	Word 3	Word 4	Word 5	Word 6	Word 7	Word 8
The_Donald (t_0)	**2016 primary election**	cruz	kasich	campaign	ted_cruz	republican	rubio	party	vp
The_Donald (t_0)	**pro-Trump slang**	trump	donald	donald_trump	maga	high_energy	centipede	america_great	meme
The_Donald (t_1)	**immigration**	wall	illegal	border	immigrant	build_wall	census	illegal_alien	illegal_immigration
The_Donald (t_1)	**Mueller report**	mueller	kavanaugh	trump_supporter	office	hillary	comey	barr	collusion
conspiracy (t_0)	**surveillance**	cia	nsa	secret	operation	agency	agent	intelligence	surveillance
conspiracy (t_0)	**mass shootings**	shooting	police	shoot	shooter	suspect	sandy_hook	kill	paris_attack
conspiracy (t_1)	**Epstein**	epstein	jeffrey_epstein	pedophile	ring	claim	pedophilia	pedo	dr
conspiracy (t_1)	**aliens**	alien	moon	earth	nasa	ufo	space	planet	sun

Table 2: A selection of clusters produced by WMDecompose. Clustering facilitates inductive thematic discovery by grouping semantically similar words.

Word	CC (%)	SWiC
hoax	-99.2	discredit, truth, bogus
fraudulent	-98.5	theft, conspire, scam
brainwash	-95.3	teacher, public_school
threat	-67.0	mitigate, deter
jews	-60.4	jewish, zionist
surveillance	-49.6	nsa, agency, agent
alex_jones	-39.0	infowars, interview
propaganda	-33.8	false_flag, agenda
reality	-23.9	veil, perceive

Table 3: CC (%) = Cost change from t_0 to t_1, represented as a percentage, SWiC = Similar words in cluster (i.e., words from the same cluster whose cost also decreased from t_0 to t_1, while remaining in use in both subreddits).

mulative distance contribution shrank from t_0 to t_1. A selection of such words is presented in Table 3. These include terms such as *hoax, fraudulent, brainwash, threat, jews, surveillance, alex_jones, propaganda,* and *reality*, to name a few. We can then examine other words in these keywords' clusters to get a sense of related words following similar patters of cost reduction and continued usage, as are displayed in the table.

Of course, such observations are of exploratory nature, intended to demonstrate an inductive starting point for a more rigorous analysis, either within or outside the WMDecompose framework. We do not posit this as statistical proof of any process of assimilation. However, this general framework of comparative and longitudinal analysis allows for a much richer engagement with discursive change due to the robust semantic relationships captured by WMDecompose while still providing simple outputs, e.g., for significance testing. Despite its cursory nature, we hope this short vignette has demonstrated the interpretable potential of WMDecompose, and how it might aid social science and humanities researchers with qualitative thematic discovery in large corpora, while also providing a computable metric for quantitative models.

6 Conclusion

We have introduced a novel iteration of WMD, one which departs from the WMD variations which, despite their high performance on a variety of tasks, do away with one of the key contributions of the original model: the inherent and decomposable relationship between document-level semantic distances and the lexical semantics that underlie them. In so doing, we heed a recent, but hopefully long-lived, call for ML and particularly NLP researchers to prioritize models which are interpretable, providing explanatory value at the level of social meaning. We hope that our Python package might aid future researchers similarly interested in interpretable computational approaches. Furthermore, through the Gale-Shapley algorithm, we propose an approach for combining interpretability with environmental sustainability. Down the line, this framework could also be expanded to support dynamic embeddings from models such as BERT, which due to their technical opacity have yet to be widely adapted in sociocultural analysis.

Our vignette presented how one might use WMDecompose in a comparative and exploratory context. That is, we imagine this as somewhat of an inductive starting point—in this case, for an analysis of the relationship between Trumpist and conspiracy theorist online communities—revealing trends related to one's particular research question that can be pursued with more focused and rigorous analysis, be it qualitative, discourse analytic, or statistical. However, because of the rich, word-level quantitative measures WMDecompose provides, future research might attempt to employ it in, for example, causal models seeking to estimate the effect of a treatment condition on particular lexical features, time series analyses, and so on.

References

Kubilay Atasu, Thomas Parnell, Celestine Dünner, Manolis Sifalakis, Haralampos Pozidis, Vasileios Vasileiadis, Michail Vlachos, Cesar Berrospi, and Abdel Labbi. 2017. Linear-complexity relaxed word Mover's distance with GPU acceleration. In *2017 IEEE International Conference on Big Data (Big Data)*, pages 889–896.

Michael Barkun. 2017. President Trump and the "Fringe". *Terrorism and Political Violence*, 29(3):437–443. Publisher: Routledge _eprint: https://doi.org/10.1080/09546553.2017.1313649.

Jason Baumgartner, Savvas Zannettou, Brian Keegan, Megan Squire, and Jeremy Blackburn. 2020. The Pushshift Reddit Dataset. *arXiv:2001.08435 [cs]*. ArXiv: 2001.08435.

Emily M. Bender, Timnit Gebru, Angelina McMillan-Major, and Shmargaret Shmitchell. 2021. On the Dangers of Stochastic Parrots: Can Language Models Be Too Big? In *Proceedings of the 2021 ACM Conference on Fairness, Accountability, and Transparency*, FAccT '21, pages 610–623, New York, NY, USA. Association for Computing Machinery.

Yochai Benkler, Robert Faris, Hal Roberts, and Ethan Zuckerman. 2017. Study: Breitbart-led right-wing media ecosystem altered broader media agenda. *Columbia Journalism Review*, 3(2).

Piotr Bojanowski, Edouard Grave, Armand Joulin, and Tomas Mikolov. 2016. Enriching Word Vectors with Subword Information. *arXiv:1607.04606 [cs]*. ArXiv: 1607.04606.

Lorna Bracewell. 2021. Gender, Populism, and the QAnon Conspiracy Movement. *Frontiers in Sociology*, 5:1–14.

Marina Danilevsky, Kun Qian, Ranit Aharonov, Yannis Katsis, Ban Kawas, and Prithviraj Sen. 2020. A Survey of the State of Explainable AI for Natural Language Processing. In *Proceedings of the 1st Conference of the Asia-Pacific Chapter of the Association for Computational Linguistics and the 10th International Joint Conference on Natural Language Processing*, pages 447–459, Suzhou, China. Association for Computational Linguistics.

Jacob Devlin, Ming-Wei Chang, Kenton Lee, and Kristina Toutanova. 2019. BERT: Pre-training of Deep Bidirectional Transformers for Language Understanding. In *Proceedings of the 2019 Conference of the North American Chapter of the Association for Computational Linguistics: Human Language Technologies, Volume 1 (Long and Short Papers)*, pages 4171–4186, Minneapolis, Minnesota. Association for Computational Linguistics.

L. E. Dubins and D. A. Freedman. 1981. Machiavelli and the Gale-Shapley Algorithm. *The American Mathematical Monthly*, 88(7):485–494. Publisher: Mathematical Association of America.

Charles Elkan. 2003. Using the triangle inequality to accelerate k-means. In *Proceedings of the Twentieth International Conference on International Conference on Machine Learning*, ICML'03, pages 147–153, Washington, DC, USA. AAAI Press.

Christopher M. Federico, Allison L. Williams, and Joseph A. Vitriol. 2018. The role of system identity threat in conspiracy theory endorsement. *European Journal of Social Psychology*, 48(7):927–938.

D. Gale and L. S. Shapley. 1962. College Admissions and the Stability of Marriage. *The American Mathematical Monthly*, 69(1):9–15.

K. J. Gülle, N. Ford, P. Ebel, F. Brokhausen, and A. Vogelsang. 2020. Topic Modeling on User Stories using Word Mover's Distance. In *2020 IEEE Seventh International Workshop on Artificial Intelligence for Requirements Engineering (AIRE)*, pages 52–60.

Daniel C. Hellinger. 2018. *Conspiracies and Conspiracy Theories in the Age of Trump*. Springer. Google-Books-ID: U3hvDwAAQBAJ.

Matthew Honnibal, Ines Montani, Sofie Van Landeghem, and Adriane Boyd. 2020. spaCy: Industrial-strength Natural Language Processing in Python.

Matthew J. Hornsey, Matthew Finlayson, Gabrielle Chatwood, and Christopher T. Begeny. 2020. Donald Trump and vaccination: The effect of political identity, conspiracist ideation and presidential tweets on vaccine hesitancy. *Journal of Experimental Social Psychology*, 88:103947.

Gao Huang, Chuan Guo, Matt J. Kusner, Yu Sun, Fei Sha, and Kilian Q. Weinberger. 2016. Supervised Word Mover's Distance. *Advances in Neural Information Processing Systems*, 29:4862–4870.

Kazuo Iwama and Shuichi Miyazaki. 2008. A Survey of the Stable Marriage Problem and Its Variants. In *International Conference on Informatics Education and Research for Knowledge-Circulating Society (icks 2008)*, pages 131–136.

Colin Klein, Peter Clutton, and Adam G. Dunn. 2019. Pathways to conspiracy: The social and linguistic precursors of involvement in Reddit's conspiracy theory forum. *PLOS ONE*, 14(11):e0225098. Publisher: Public Library of Science.

Matt J Kusner, Yu Sun, Nicholas I Kolkin, and Kilian Q Weinberger. 2015. From Word Embeddings To Document Distances. *Proceedings of the 32nd International Conference on Machine Learning*, 37:957–966.

S. Lloyd. 1982. Least squares quantization in PCM. *IEEE Transactions on Information Theory*, 28(2):129–137. Conference Name: IEEE Transactions on Information Theory.

Laurens van der Maaten and Geoffrey Hinton. 2008. Visualizing Data using t-SNE. *Journal of Machine Learning Research*, 9(86):2579–2605.

Alice Marwick and Rebecca Lewis. 2017. *Media Manipulation and Disinformation Online*. Data & Society Research Institute, New York.

Joan Massachs, Corrado Monti, Gianmarco De Francisci Morales, and Francesco Bonchi. 2020. Roots of Trumpism: Homophily and Social Feedback in Donald Trump Support on Reddit. In *12th ACM Conference on Web Science*, WebSci '20, pages 49–58, New York, NY, USA. Association for Computing Machinery.

Leland McInnes, John Healy, and James Melville. 2020. UMAP: Uniform Manifold Approximation and Projection for Dimension Reduction. *arXiv:1802.03426 [cs, stat]*. ArXiv: 1802.03426.

Tomas Mikolov, Kai Chen, Greg Corrado, and Jeffrey Dean. 2013. Efficient Estimation of Word Representations in Vector Space. *arXiv:1301.3781 [cs]*. ArXiv: 1301.3781.

Joanne M. Miller, Kyle L. Saunders, and Christina E. Farhart. 2016. Conspiracy Endorsement as Motivated Reasoning: The Moderating Roles of Political Knowledge and Trust. *American Journal of Political Science*, 60(4):824–844.

Md Nasir, Sandeep Nallan Chakravarthula, Brian Baucom, David C. Atkins, Panayiotis Georgiou, and Shrikanth Narayanan. 2019. Modeling Interpersonal Linguistic Coordination in Conversations using Word Mover's Distance. *arXiv:1904.06002 [cs]*. ArXiv: 1904.06002.

Ryan Neville-Shepard. 2019. Post-presumption argumentation and the post-truth world: on the conspiracy rhetoric of Donald Trump. *Argumentation and Advocacy*, 55(3):175–193. Publisher: Routledge _eprint: https://doi.org/10.1080/10511431.2019.1603027.

Rishab Nithyanand, Brian Schaffner, and Phillipa Gill. 2017. Online Political Discourse in the Trump Era. *arXiv:1711.05303 [cs]*. ArXiv: 1711.05303.

Ofir Pele and Michael Werman. 2008. A Linear Time Histogram Metric for Improved SIFT Matching. In *Computer Vision – ECCV 2008*, Lecture Notes in Computer Science, pages 495–508, Berlin, Heidelberg. Springer.

Ofir Pele and Michael Werman. 2009. Fast and robust Earth Mover's Distances. In *2009 IEEE 12th International Conference on Computer Vision*, pages 460–467. ISSN: 2380-7504.

Jeffrey Pennington, Richard Socher, and Christopher Manning. 2014. Glove: Global Vectors for Word Representation. In *Proceedings of the 2014 Conference on Empirical Methods in Natural Language Processing (EMNLP)*, pages 1532–1543, Doha, Qatar. Association for Computational Linguistics.

Shruti Phadke, Mattia Samory, and Tanushree Mitra. 2021. What Makes People Join Conspiracy Communities? Role of Social Factors in Conspiracy Engagement. *Proceedings of the ACM on Human-Computer Interaction*, 4(CSCW3):223:1–223:30.

Francesca Polletta and Jessica Callahan. 2019. Deep Stories, Nostalgia Narratives, and Fake News: Storytelling in the Trump Era. In Jason L. Mast and Jeffrey C. Alexander, editors, *Politics of Meaning/Meaning of Politics: Cultural Sociology of the 2016 U.S. Presidential Election*, Cultural Sociology, pages 55–73. Springer International Publishing, Cham.

Marcus Pöckelmann, Janis Dähne, Jörg Ritter, and Paul Molitor. 2020. Fast paraphrase extraction in Ancient Greek literature. *it - Information Technology*, 62(2):75–89. Publisher: De Gruyter Oldenbourg Section: it - Information Technology.

Fuji Ren and Ning Liu. 2018. Emotion computing using Word Mover's Distance features based on Ren_cecps. *PLOS ONE*, 13(4):e0194136. Publisher: Public Library of Science.

Manoel Horta Ribeiro, Shagun Jhaver, Savvas Zannettou, Jeremy Blackburn, Emiliano De Cristofaro, Gianluca Stringhini, and Robert West. 2020. Does Platform Migration Compromise Content Moderation? Evidence from r/The_donald and r/Incels. *arXiv:2010.10397 [cs]*. ArXiv: 2010.10397.

Y. Rubner, C. Tomasi, and L.J. Guibas. 1998. A metric for distributions with applications to image databases. In *Sixth International Conference on Computer Vision (IEEE Cat. No.98CH36271)*, pages 59–66.

Mattia Samory and Tanushree Mitra. 2018. Conspiracies Online: User Discussions in a Conspiracy Community Following Dramatic Events. *Proceedings of the International AAAI Conference on Web and Social Media*, 12(1). Number: 1.

Ryan P. Shepherd. 2020. Gaming Reddit's Algorithm: r/the_donald, Amplification, and the Rhetoric of Sorting. *Computers and Composition*, 56:1–14.

Dominik A. Stecula and Mark Pickup. 2021. How populism and conservative media fuel conspiracy beliefs about COVID-19 and what it means for COVID-19 behaviors. *Research & Politics*, 8(1):2053168021993979. Publisher: SAGE Publications Ltd.

Dustin S. Stoltz and Marshall A. Taylor. 2019. Concept Mover's Distance: measuring concept engagement via word embeddings in texts. *Journal of Computational Social Science*, 2(2):293–313.

Emma Strubell, Ananya Ganesh, and Andrew McCallum. 2019. Energy and Policy Considerations for Deep Learning in NLP. *arXiv:1906.02243 [cs]*. ArXiv: 1906.02243.

Marshall A. Taylor and Dustin S. Stoltz. 2020. Concept Class Analysis: A Method for Identifying Cultural Schemas in Texts. *Sociological Science*, 7:544–569.

Jesmin Jahan Tithi and Fabrizio Petrini. 2021. An Efficient Shared-memory Parallel Sinkhorn-Knopp Algorithm to Compute the Word Mover's Distance. *arXiv:2005.06727 [cs, stat]*. ArXiv: 2005.06727.

Joseph E. Uscinski, Adam M. Enders, Casey Klofstad, Michelle Seelig, John Funchion, Caleb Everett, Stefan Wuchty, Kamal Premaratne, and Manohar Murthi. 2020. Why do people believe COVID-19 conspiracy theories? *Harvard Kennedy School Misinformation Review*, 1(3).

Ashish Vaswani, Noam Shazeer, Niki Parmar, Jakob Uszkoreit, Llion Jones, Aidan N. Gomez, Łukasz Kaiser, and Illia Polosukhin. 2017. Attention is All you Need. *Advances in Neural Information Processing Systems*, 30.

Matheus Werner and Eduardo Laber. 2020. Speeding up Word Mover's Distance and Its Variants via Properties of Distances Between Embeddings. *ECAI 2020*, pages 2204–2211. Publisher: IOS Press.

X. Wu and H. Li. 2017. Topic mover's distance based document classification. In *2017 IEEE 17th International Conference on Communication Technology (ICCT)*, pages 1998–2002. ISSN: 2576-7828.

Sho Yokoi, Ryo Takahashi, Reina Akama, Jun Suzuki, and Kentaro Inui. 2020. Word Rotator's Distance. In *Proceedings of the 2020 Conference on Empirical Methods in Natural Language Processing (EMNLP)*, pages 2944–2960, Online. Association for Computational Linguistics.

A Text preprocessing and word2vec fine-tuning details

The raw text data from the Pushshift dataset was processed as follows, all conducted in Python. Posts were first lowercased, and URLs were removed via regular expressions; stopwords were removed and remaining words were lemmatized, both using spaCy (Honnibal et al., 2020); markdown text and other special characters were removed using custom regex functions; finally, words occurring fewer than 20 times in the corpus (i.e., less than once every 1,000 documents) were removed.

Once processed, the text was embedded with a word2vec model that was fine-tuned on a corpus of 533K self posts from these subreddits as well as other conspiracy and conservative subreddits, with preprocessing following the same steps as above. Fine-tuning was done using the skipgram implementation of word2vec, with negative sampling, a context window of 10 tokens, over four epochs and with a learning rate of 0.01. The model was phrased in a similar manner to the recommendations in Mikolov et al. (2013), such that frequently co-occurring bigrams and trigrams were encoded as single lexical entities (e.g., *president_trump*). Further, each document was represented using Tf-Idf and L1-normalization, in order to prevent frequent words from crowding out information from less common but more salient words.

Positive		Negative	
Word	**Cost**	**Word**	**Cost**
great	41.79	told	19.64
best	33.15	order	19.58
amazing	31.35	rude	18.10
friendly	27.02	never	17.94
delicious	26.18	worst	17.44
highly_recommend	24.93	minute	15.14
staff	19.96	hour	14.97
definitely	19.52	said	14.91
always	18.68	money	13.89
favorite	18.42	terrible	13.57
massage	18.29	called	13.14
portland	16.15	asked	13.05

Table 4: Decomposed word-level WMD_w distances for moving from the full set of positive reviews (left) the the full set of negative reviews and vice versa (right). Only the 12 words w that contributed the most are shown.

B Sanity Check with Yelp Reviews

To further demonstrate the qualities of WMDecompose, we offer an additional case study using a set of reviews from Yelp. This dataset is intuitive and well-known, and should hence complement our main analysis, as it requires less domain-knowledge for illustrating the basic qualities of WMDecompose. To facilitate comparison with earlier work on the WMD, we here rely on Euclidean distances, the metric which was used in the original WMD paper (Kusner et al., 2015), even though cosine distances are arguably preferable when working with semantic similarity tasks and therefore used in the main analysis of the paper. For the analysis in this appendix, we look at trends that are highly predicable, in order to provide a "sanity check" to ensure that our model was behaving as expected. Consequently, we looked at the WMD_w and CMD_c from positive

	Positive to Negative Clusters									
	56	51	92	76	26	30	33	78	47	88
Word (distance)	great (30.91)	made (3.18)	good (7.14)	delicious(21.13)	spot (8.24)	friendly (20.8)	professional (9.19)	year (4.98)	massage (16.45)	quality (2.12)
	best (26.33)	felt (2.85)	really (5.9)	favorite (15.06)	place (6.2)	staff (14.39)	team (6.35)	new (2.89)	relaxing (3.83)	price (1.97)
	amazing (25.21)	soon (2.54)	nice (5.87)	loved (7.27)	town (5.07)	everyone (6.24)	thorough (3.54)	moved (2.77)	facial (3.72)	worth (1.95)
	love (21.88)	quickly (2.07)	well (4.3)	fresh (7.24)	found (3.77)	attentive (5.6)	feel_comfortable (3.48)	weekly (1.58)	spa (3.48)	option (1.94)
	highly_recommend (20.17)	hand (1.87)	kind (4.27)	tasty (4.78)	glad (3.36)	welcoming (4.06)	job (2.84)	st (1.03)	treatment (3.15)	beat (1.74)
	definitely (15.54)	house (1.72)	lot (3.38)	try (4.7)	looking (3.0)	accommodating (3.77)	work (2.74)	year_ago (0.98)	brow (2.81)	every_penny (1.21)
	always (15.27)	next (1.36)	little (3.34)	enjoyed (4.43)	visit (2.95)	pleasant (3.28)	care (2.61)	first (0.86)	gentle (2.47)	size (0.95)
	excellent (12.16)	around (1.22)	also (2.79)	must (4.39)	friend (2.62)	personable (2.76)	efficient (2.27)	monthly (0.73)	calming (2.32)	deal (0.95)
	thank (10.63)	along (1.04)	enough (2.29)	die (2.95)	gem (2.52)	smile (2.38)	felt_comfortable (2.19)	yr (0.71)	hot_stone (2.2)	plus (0.9)
	super (10.52)	totally (1.04)	much (2.0)	special (2.53)	coming (2.21)	met (1.46)	grateful (2.08)	last_week (0.59)	lash (1.57)	penny (0.88)
	Negative to Positive Clusters									
	51	92	44	95	35	52	56	26	78	0
Word (distance)	never (15.84)	like (4.84)	order (15.17)	worst (14.89)	told (16.11)	use (3.06)	ever (2.14)	review (5.09)	went (5.2)	terrible (11.24)
	hour (11.77)	ok (3.46)	minute (12.0)	money (11.35)	said (11.41)	issue (2.41)	treat (1.23)	disappointed (3.2)	closed (4.6)	bad (7.88)
	would (10.22)	hard (3.31)	waiting (7.83)	horrible (9.74)	asked (10.94)	follow (2.17)	unbelievable (0.98)	close (2.49)	month_later (1.89)	awful (7.0)
	u (7.87)	maybe (3.27)	table (7.56)	customer_service (6.39)	manager (9.14)	problem (1.9)	cannot (0.63)	decided (1.6)	changed (1.87)	poor (6.84)
	could (6.59)	however (2.43)	waited (6.24)	waste_time (5.66)	refused (4.05)	frustrating (1.66)	allaround (0.28)	find (1.3)	update (1.85)	star (4.98))
	another (6.41)	used (2.41)	min (5.72)	please (4.4)	ask (2.86)	need (1.51)	every_aspect (0.24)	read_review (1.26)	day (1.8)	slow (4.86)
	even (6.29)	seemed (2.33)	sitting (3.8)	unless (3.82)	asking (2.41)	properly (1.48)	everyday (0.2)	heard (1.24)	month_ago (1.68)	worse (3.8)
	nothing (6.06)	fine (2.31)	waiter (3.71)	somewhere_else (3.63)	mistake (2.26)	multiple (1.27)	commend (0.2)	opened (0.82)	last (1.44)	disappointing (3.16)
	give (5.36)	least (2.03)	hostess (3.59)	avoid (3.56)	stated (2.05)	due (1.17)	speedy (0.16)	somewhere (0.63)	twice (1.43)	sad (2.96)
	left (5.35)	something (1.71)	line (3.32)	suck (2.5)	informed (1.87)	failed (1.12)	always (0.13)	first_impression (0.62)	month (1.23)	unfortunately (2.63)

Table 5: The CMD_c for the top 10 c when moving from the positive review set to the negative (top) and vice versa (bottom). The keywords and their order for each cluster are determined by the WMD_w of each word.

and negative reviews to see whether the distance would, as expected, be composed mainly of different polarized sentiment words, such as *good* and *bad*.

For this analysis, we use the latest version of the Yelp review dataset, accessed in late July 2021[6]. The data was filtered to only include reviews written in the cities of Atlanta and Portland, two geographically and demographically distinct cities, after December 2017. We further filtered the data to only include reviews for establishments that were labeled with the categories *Restaurant* or *Health Medical*. This way we wanted to show that category-specific trends would also emerge among positive and negative keywords, as well as explore whether any trends specific for the two cities would appear in the results. Reviews were then further filtered so that only highly positive (5 stars) or highly negative (1 star) were included. These were labeled positive and negative, respectively. Reviews were sampled from this pool, so that 2000 reviews were selected from both Atlanta and Portland, 500 negative and 500 positive for both restaurants and health services, for a total of 4000 reviews.

B.1 Preprocessing and word vectors

For the purposes of this analysis, we fine-tuned the same pretrained word2vec model that was used for the main analysis, with the same hyperparamters, but using the filtered Yelp dataset. A series of preprocessing steps were also conducted, including removal of URLs and stopwords and phrasing as proposed by Mikolov et al. (2013).

[6]https://www.yelp.com/dataset/

B.2 Clustering and Gale-Shapley

After preprocessing, clusters were detected in the word vectors using K-means. Through inspecting Silhouette scores and elbow plots, the number of clusters was chosen to be 100. Further, instead of performing the analysis on the full set of pairs, we first ran LC-RWMD to find the R-WMD between all pairs and then the Gale-Shapley (GS) algorithm to find the set of optimal pairs.

B.3 Results from WMDecompose

Next, the pairs from the GS matching were analysed using WMDecompose. The words that added the most distance (with difference) when moving from the positive set to the negative and vice versa can be seen in Table 4. As expected, the top set of WMD_w word-level distances for the positive documents is dominated by positive sentiment words, with *great*, *best* and *amazing* on top. However, other trends also appear, such as words specific to restaurants (*delicious*) or health services (*massage*). Interestingly enough, the word *portland* appears as a high expense when moving from the positive to the negative set, indicating that positive reviewers located in that city might be more likely to mention it by name.

On the side of WMD_w word-level distances, the top words include negative sentiment words such as *rude*, *worst* and *terrible* when moving from the negative to the positive reviews, but other patterns are also visible. Words about time, such as *hour*, *minute* and the word *money*, contribute heavily to the semantic distance from negative to positive reviews, as do verbs often associated with verbal commands, such as *told* and *said*. Here, words related to the cities or categories of the reviews do not make the top 12 cut, although category specific words are present when looking at the top 50 (including *insurance*, *manager* and *doctor*).

Switching focus to the CMD_c clusters displayed in Table 5, we see some of the top words from Table 4, now organized by cluster. While there is some overlap in clusters when moving from positive to negative and vice versa (clusters 51, 92, 56, 26, 78), the keywords that define the clusters are different, as they are determined using the top ten WMD_w values of each word in the cluster. In Table 5, we also see how category specific words, such as those in cluster 47 related to spa and massage services, add a significant distance when moving from positive to negative reviews.

Period Classification in Chinese Historical Texts

Zuoyu Tian and **Sandra Kübler**
Indiana University
{zuoytian,skuebler}@indiana.edu

Abstract

In this study, we study language change in Chinese Biji by using a classification task: classifying Ancient Chinese texts by time periods. Specifically, we focus on a unique genre in classical Chinese literature: Biji (literally "notebook" or "brush notes"), i.e., collections of anecdotes, quotations, etc., anything authors consider noteworthy. Biji span hundreds of years across many dynasties and conserve informal language in written form. For these reasons, they are regarded a good resource for investigating language change in Chinese (Fang, 2010). In this paper, we create a new dataset of 108 Biji across four dynasties. Based on the dataset, we first introduce a time period classification task for Chinese. Then we investigate different feature representation methods for classification. The results show that models using contextualized embeddings perform best. An analysis of the top features chosen by the word n-gram model (after bleaching proper nouns) confirms that these features are informative and correspond to observations and assumptions made by historical linguists.

1 Introduction

Traditional studies of language change largely rely on close reading and require researchers to have solid training in understanding historical texts. As a wealth of historical data has been digitized, there has been a surge in recent years in using computational methods to investigate language change (e.g. Popescu and Strapparava, 2015; Hamilton et al., 2016; Rodda et al., 2017). However, most of these studies are limited to a small number of Indo-European languages. Many languages, especially typologically very different ones, are understudied.

One task that often precedes an investigation of language change is automatic text dating, also called period classification or diachronic text evaluation. In this task, a machine learning model's performance in capturing temporal information is evaluated. Such tasks, along with datasets, exist for languages such as Irish (Han and Toner, 2017), Polish (Graliński et al., 2017), Hebrew (Liebeskind and Liebeskind, 2020), and Italian (Menini et al., 2020). To our best knowledge, there is no study focusing on dating historical texts in Chinese.

Therefore, we first built a diachronic Chinese Biji (literally "brush notes") corpus with Biji from four dynasties, spanning about 1300 years. This corpus contains around 33,000 paragraphs from 108 different Biji labeled with dynasty information. Then, we investigate two major questions: 1) Can a classifiers successfully distinguish paragraphs in historical texts from different time periods? 2) Do the features used for classification correspond to what we know from a linguistic perspective, and are the features informative for linguists?

For the first question, we are interested in the classification systems' performance on Chinese, since this is the first approach for this language, and written Chinese is renowned for its lack of change from century to century (Norman, 1988). More specifically, we investigate the performance of different feature representation methods (char/word n-gram, word2vec, contextualized embeddings models) in classifying the time periods of a text. These feature representation methods have been shown effective in previous studies of dating historical texts or lexical semantic change (Zampieri et al., 2016; Schlechtweg et al., 2020; Giulianelli et al., 2020).

Our next question looks closer at the interrelation between text dating and language change. The classification results provide useful information, but they cannot directly tell us which features drive language change. Since language change is an accumulating process and usually happens in neighboring time periods (dynasties), we use a task of distinguishing paragraphs from neighboring dynasties to target lexical change. We can then look at the features that ranked highest in this task and

Proceedings of LaTeCH-CLfL 2021, pages 168–177
Punta Cana, Dominican Republic (Online), November 11, 2021.

investigate whether a high relevance for this task corresponds to linguistic insights. Results show that most of the top features are informative and fit into the observation made by historical linguists.

The paper is structured as follows: We discuss related work in section 2. In section 3, we discuss the process of building a Classical Chinese Biji dataset. We introduce the feature representation methods for classifying historical texts in section 4 and the experimental setup in section 5. We report results of the different feature representation methods and present an error analysis in section 6. In section 7, we analyze the classification for neighboring dynasties, focusing on important features drawn from the training data. We conclude in section 8.

2 Related Work

2.1 Studies in Time Period Classification

Studies using language models to capture temporal information in contemporary diachronic texts date back to the 2000s (de Jong et al., 2005; Dalli and Wilks, 2006), they demonstrate that machine learning systems with textual features can successfully predict the publication time span of documents. The shared-task on Diachronic Text Evaluation in SemEval 2015 (Popescu and Strapparava, 2015) provided resources and publicity for the task of automatic historical text dating. The task was to build automatic systems to identify the time period of English news snippets from 1700 to 2010 in three subtasks. Following Popescu and Strapparava (2015), Menini et al. (2020) hosted a shared-task focusing on the same genre and cross-genre issue in dating Italian historical documents. Like SemEval 2015, they also adopted three similar classification standards: year-based, fine-grained, and coarse. There are also studies simplifying the period classification task with larger time intervals. For example, Liebeskind and Liebeskind (2020) distinguish Hebrew texts spanning around 1000 years into four time periods. We can see that tasks in different languages tend to have different classification standards, and this is closely related to the language in question and the goal of the task.

Regarding feature engineering in dating texts, lexical features including character and word n-grams are most widely used in classifying time periods. For example, Szymanski and Lynch (2015) found that character n-grams are more effective compared to other features such as POS n-grams, word n-grams, and syntactic phrase-structure rules. Zampieri et al. (2016) built an SVM classifier with word and POS n-grams to classify Portuguese texts from 1600 to 1900. Meanwhile, in the related area of lexical semantic change, many studies use word embeddings trained from deep learning models to model the language change and successfully track the semantic shift (e.g. Hamilton et al., 2016; Rodda et al., 2017; Rodman, 2020). Liebeskind and Liebeskind (2020) first implemented deep learning methods in time period classification tasks. They show that CNN and RNN outperform paragraph vectors and conventional machine learning methods. Recently, contextualized embedding models have been introduced to lexical semantic change studies (Hu et al., 2019; Giulianelli et al., 2020; Tseng et al., 2020), with promising results.

2.2 Digital Resources of Historical Chinese

Even though we see an increase of work on Classical Chinese processing, researchers also are aware of the lack of Chinese diachronic resources, which hinders the research process to some extent (Hamilton et al., 2016; Zinin and Xu, 2020). Unlike other understudied languages, many Chinese texts are already digitized, but only a few digitized texts are free to access and process. Most of the datasets are designed for close reading but not for an NLP purposes. There are well-designed POS tagged diachronic corpora and high-quality digitized resources of historical Chinese such as Zhonghua Database of Chinese Classic Books[1] and Scripta Sinica database[2]. However, they are not available for use in NLP due to copyright restrictions.

The Academia Sinica Classical Chinese Corpus[3] is the most representative diachronic Chinese corpus with sub-corpora for Old Chinese, Middle Chinese, and Early Modern Chinese. The corpus has been tagged with POS annotation. But it can only be accessed via an online search function. Recently, Zinin and Xu (2020) created a corpus of Chinese Dynasty Histories for diachronic research. However, the dynasty histories are mainly literary Chinese and normally written by a small number of authors per dynasty within a short period of time. Thus, they cannot represent the language properties through the whole dynasty.

[1] http://www.ancientbooks.cn/

[2] http://hanchi.ihp.sinica.edu.tw/

[3] http://lingcorpus.iis.sinica.edu.tw/ancient/

2.3 Linguistic Periodization of Chinese

For Chinese, different opinions exist wrt. periodization. The most widely accepted framework, proposed by Wang (1958) and Xiang (1993) and accepted by Dong (2019), splits Chinese into four major time periods: Old Chinese (pre-Qin Dynasty), Middle Chinese (Three Kingdoms and Jin Dynasty to Song Dynasty), Early Modern Chinese (Yuan Dynasty to Qing Dynasty), and Modern Chinese (after 1919 May Fourth Movement). Pan (1989) accepts the four major periods but argues that Early Modern Chinese started in Late Tang Dynasty. In contrast, Ōta (1988) proposes a new language period: Early Chinese, which divides Chinese into five periods. In this periodization system, Early Modern Chinese starts in Qing Dynasty. Thus, the major differences concern the question regarding the starting time of Early Modern Chinese. The answers range from Late Tang Dynasty to Qing Dynasty. Unlike other languages, literary (written) Chinese has undergone little change from dynasty to dynasty (Norman, 1988), hence, historical linguists tend to use materials including vernacular language to discover language change and periodize Chinese. One of the major resources for historical linguists to periodize Middle Chinese and Early Modern Chinese are Biji since they thrived during these time periods, include materials from different aspects of everyday life, and consist of vernacular language.

3 Corpus of Classical Chinese Biji

A reliable dataset is the key to dating historical texts. Taking into account the goal of our task, our dataset needs to satisfy the following requirements: 1) It need to be publicly available, so that it can be used for future studies. 3) The time period information needs to be relatively accurate. 3) As only written form is available for historical texts, we need to focus on a genre that has preserved colloquial language as much as possible. Instead of collecting texts from different genres, we concentrate on a single genre: Biji, to minimize the effect of genre differences.

Biji are "fundamentally a set of discontinuous notes of description and reflection written by the Biji author" (Fu, 2007). As suggested by Fu (2007), Biji can be roughly divided into three types based on structural characteristics: 1) Short stories, anecdotes, or biographies; 2) descriptions and reflections on a wide range of affairs; 3) recordings of a single subject such as history or poetry. This abundance of content that Biji cover also leaves us with the issue of definition: Biji and its boundaries with other genres are always controversial in academia. As we are more interested in those Biji containing more informal language, we focus on the first type of Biji, which contains more conversations. The first type of Biji is normally novel-like, also called Biji fiction. To have a professional data selection standard, during dataset creation, we choose Biji according to the book series *Biji Xiaoshuo Daguan* "the collection of Biji fiction" published by Shanghai Classics Publishing House (Shanghai Classics Publishing House, 2000, 2007a,b,c).

Since these Biji fiction collections are published based on dynasties, this also offers us trustworthy dynasty information about Biji with decisions made by professional editors. Given the difficulties involved in dating Biji fiction (Hanan et al., 1973), we use dynasties as our classes, for several reasons: First, since Biji are a set of discontinuous notes written by an author, the writing time could span dozens of years. It is unrealistic to label a specific publication time. Second, most Classical Chinese databases, such as Scripta Sinica and the Chinese Text Project, label texts with their dynasty instead of the exact publication date. This makes our dataset consistent with the widely used corpus format; Third, the most important reason is that labeling books with dynasties is sensible based on studies in historical linguistics (Wang, 1958; Xiang, 1993; Peyraube, 1996), since dynasties are widely used as an anchor point for periodization. Thus, dynasty labels can easily fit into historical linguists' periodization framework. We collect Biji titles from four books in this series: *Biji Fiction in Tang Dynasty and Five Dynasties, Biji Fiction in Song and Yuan Dynasty, Biji Fiction in Ming Dynasty, and Biji Fiction in Qing Dynasty*. All four books have a total of 140 Biji and cover four dynasties sequentially: Tang Dynasty (618-907), Song Dynasty (960-1279), Ming Dynasty (1368-1644), and Qing Dynasty (1644-1911)[4].

We used the wiki section in the Chinese Text Project[5] as the primary source of data. In this section, digitized texts are submitted by the site users, and they are freely available without copyright restrictions. We searched all Biji titles mentioned in

[4]There are a few Biji written in Five Dynasties and Yuan Dynasties in the book series. These Biji are labeled as Tang Dynasty and Song Dynasty respectively.

[5]https://ctext.org

the books and successfully collected 127 of them. However, we deleted some Biji for the following consideration: 1) Biji without punctuation. The original Biji were written without punctuation, and punctuation was generally inserted during modern editing. Thus we take the presence of punctuation as a sign for careful editing and discard the non-edited Biji. 2) Biji with encoding and formatting issues (mainly paragraph segmentation errors) and a significant amount of annotations within the text. 3) Biji which are not collections of short stories or anecdotes. For example, some Biji mainly aim to explain concepts in previous classical work. A majority of the content is sentences citing from the classical work. Such books clearly carry linguistic features from previous dynasties and are not good representations for the dynasty in which they were published.

After applying these filtering rules, 89 Biji were left. We found two problems with this dataset: 1) Due to the issues described above, some Biji from Tang Dynasty have been deleted, which causes an imbalance of the dataset. 2) Since Biji from Ming and Qing are usually lengthy, the *Collection of Biji Fiction* covers only few Biji from these dynasties. To balance the dataset, we used two open-access data sources, *Daizhige*[6] and *Xuge Shang*[7] to collect additional data. For Tang Dynasty, *Collection of Biji Fiction* already covers most of the existing Biji in Tang Dynasty, so we looked in these new data sources for alternative editions of those Biji with format issues. For Ming and Qing Dynasty, we added books from the Biji category and made sure that all these newly added Biji satisfy our filtering rules. Our final dataset includes 108 Biji.

Since Biji are usually a collection of short stories, we essentially treat each story as one instance in the corpus. We also notice that stories can be lengthy in Biji from Ming and Qing Dynasties; for such books, we treat each paragraph as a single instance. To balance the length of each instance, we discard those too long (larger than 1000 characters) or too short instances (shorter than 50 characters). Given our selection process, the quality of our dataset may not be as high as professional Classical Chinese databases since we could not manually examine the correctness of each text.

Table 1 show the statistics of the corpus. The corpus is mainly balanced, but we can see that instances from Tang Dynasty are significantly fewer than the other three dynasties. An example of instance in the corpus is shown in Table 2.

Language Period	Dynasty	Instances	Biji
Middle Chinese	Tang	4541	33
Middle Chinese	Song	10094	46
Early Modern Chinese	Ming	9624	16
Early Modern Chinese	Qing	8898	13

Table 1: Statistics for the Biji Corpus. The periodization of Chinese is based on Wang (1958).

4 Feature Representation Methods

In this section, we present the feature representations that we use for time period classification. These feature representations can be categorized into three major types: n-grams, word embeddings, and contextualized embeddings features.

4.1 n-gram features

n-gram features are widely used in dating historical texts and achieve a high performance (Zampieri et al., 2016). We use n-grams models to capture two types of information: character- and word-level.

Character n-grams Segmentation is always a concern for preprocessing Chinese, especially Classical Chinese. Modern Chinese segmentation tools are not ideal for segmenting Classical Chinese due to major difference in vocabularies. By building character-based models, we can naturally avoid the problem of segmentation. Furthermore, in Classical Chinese, many words are monosyllabic, hence a character n-gram can be an easy yet effective way to characterize Classical Chinese. We use character 1-5 grams and set the frequency threshold to 10.

Word n-grams: For a better understanding of the performance of word and character representations in Classical Chinese, we also construct word n-gram features. We use Jiayan Toolkit[8], a publicly available Classical Chinese segmenter designed for different language periods[9]. It is an unsupervised HMM segmentation tool trained on *Siku Quanshu* 'Complete Library in Four Sections'. We use word 1-5 grams and the same frequency threshold as for

[6]http://www.daizhige.org/

[7]https://www.xuges.com/gdwx/xs/bj/index.htm

[8]https://github.com/jiaeyan/Jiayan

[9]Stanford NLP toolkit Stanza also supports the segmentation in Classical Chinese, but it is trained on an Ancient Chinese corpus. The vocabulary in Ancient Chinese is very different from that in our dataset.

Chinese	陆长源以旧德为宣武军行司马，韩愈为巡官，同在使幕，或讥年辈相悬。 周愿曰：大虫、老鼠，俱为十二相属，何怪之有？
Gloss	Lu Changyuan was promoted to the general of Xuanwu Army due to previous good deed, and Han Yu was the censor of that army. Someone gloated over the generation gap between them. Zhou Yuan said: Both tiger and mouse are zodiac animals, why do you think this is weird.
Book	Wuzazu (Ming Dynasty)

Table 2: Example of a instance in the corpus

the character-based model. To evaluate the segmentation performance, we randomly sampled 50 sentences and checked them manually, the final accuracy is 94.6%.

4.2 Word2vec Features

As discussed in section 2, word2vec models have been shown to be effective in capturing language change across many languages (Schlechtweg et al., 2020). Thus, we conjecture that word embeddings will be good sources for classifying language periods. We are interested in how informative the embeddings vectors are in comparison to other feature types in the task of dating historical texts, which is different from the problem addressed in previous studies.

Assuming that the small size of our dataset would negatively influence the quality of embedding models trained on the dataset, we use pretrained character embeddings instead. We expect that these pretrained features will help us capture subtle semantic relations and infrequent phrases. We use Gensim[10] with 300-dimension skip-grams with negative sampling word embeddings (SGNS) trained on *Siku Quanshu* 'Complete Library in Four Sections' (Li et al., 2018), *Siku Quanshu* is the largest encyclopedia in Ancient China, it contains 3503 books, around 800 million tokens (character). The final feature representation is the average of the individual character vectors in a single instance.

4.3 Contextualized Embeddings Features

Instead of using static embeddings, in contextualized language models such as BERT (Devlin et al., 2019), the same word is represented differently according to its contexts. This is promising for lexical change detection, but it has not been applied to the classification of time periods. Here we use Sentence BERT (SBERT) (Reimers and Gurevych, 2019) to embed the whole instance. Using siamese and triplet network structures, Sentence BERT can efficiently generate the sentence embeddings from pre-trained models of the BERT model family. From the different pretrained models, we chose Guwen-RoBertA[11], a RoBertA model (Liu et al., 2019) trained on a large collection of Classical Chinese, which is ideal for our tasks. The final representation of each instance is the final layer of the Guwen-RoBertA extracted by sentence-transformers[12].

5 Experimental Settings

Since Biji show considerable differences in length, we split them into single paragraphs for classification. However, we need to avoid having instances from the same author distributed over training and testing data since the system may learn to classify authorship instead of time period. Therefore, we perform five-fold cross-validation with a split based on books rather than individual paragraphs. In this way, we use different books for training and testing. We additionally balance the number of paragraphs from each dynasty in each fold as much as possible. For the baseline, we use the majority class, i.e., all instances are labeled as Song Dynasty.

Since our aim is to compare the performance of different feature representation methods, we need to investigate all models using the same machine learning algorithm. We compare three machine learning algorithms widely used in classification tasks: SVM, Logistic Regression, and Naive Bayes. All the classification experiments use the Python package scikit-learn (Pedregosa et al., 2011).

6 Dynasty Classification

In this section, we compare the machine learning algorithms and different feature representation meth-

[10] https://radimrehurek.com/gensim/index.html

[11] https://github.com/Ethan-yt/guwenbert

[12] https://www.sbert.net/

	Acc.	Prec.	Recall	F
SVMs	65.47	65.21	66.21	65.01
Log. Regression	64.63	64.81	65.24	64.47
Naive Bayes	61.38	61.20	63.52	61.02

Table 3: Result for different algorithms (using SBERT).

Representation	Acc.	Prec.	Recall	F
Baseline	30.44	25.00	7.61	11.67
n-gram$_{\text{character}}$	56.37	57.03	55.52	55.48
n-gram$_{\text{word}}$	58.51	59.48	57.30	57.61
Word2vec	46.14	46.31	44.26	44.60
SBERT	65.47	65.21	66.21	65.01

Table 4: Results of different feature representations.

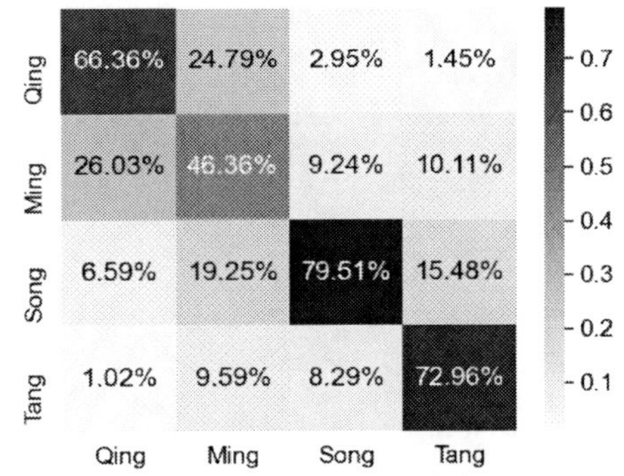

Figure 1: Confusion matrix of system using contextualized embeddings. Row: true label; column: predicted.

ods, and we conduct an error analysis. In order to determine which machine learning algorithms perform well, we first compare different machine learning algorithms using the same contextualized embeddings features[13] and report the results in Table 3. Among the three algorithms, the SVM performs best; it outperforms Logistic Regression by 0.5 percent wrt. the F score. Hence, we assume SVMs to be the best choice for dating historical texts, and all the following results are reported using SVMs.

Table 4 shows the result for different feature representations. We see that SBERT outperforms all the other representations and achieves an F score of 65.01. This shows that contextualized features are more informative in the task of dating historical texts compared to other feature representations. However, if we compare our results to the results in a similar classification task using 4 time periods in Hebrew (Liebeskind and Liebeskind, 2020), the Chinese task is somewhat more challenging for classification systems. In Hebrew, a model using Naive Bayes with 20,000 selected n-gram features achieved an F score of 74.43, i.e., almost 10 points higher than our results. Possible reasons include: 1) Despite our filtering, some instances tell stories from previous dynasties, which is difficult for the classifier to interpret correctly. 2) In some folds, the test set only contains instances from few Biji of certain dynasties, and the skewed authorship makes these dynasties difficult to classify correctly. For example, in some folds, most of the test instances of a certain dynasty are from one Biji. If the classifier performs poorly on this Biji, the final accuracy will be low. A striking case is the Qing Dynasty, for which the F scores of the SBERT model vary from 45% to 85% among the five folds.

The next best feature type is n-gram features. We notice that word n-grams outperform character n-grams by more than 2 points in F score. A possible reason may be the increase of disyllabic words after the Tang Dynasty since disyllabic words increase in frequency from Old Chinese to Middle Chinese and from Middle Chinese to Early Modern Chinese (Norman, 1988). Therefore, word n-grams become more informative than simple character n-grams even when taking segmentation errors into consideration. Surprisingly, using word2vec embeddings as features is not very effective in this task. The F score of word2vec features is 44.6, i.e., about 10 points lower than that of character n-grams. This implies that word2vec embeddings are not very effective in capturing language change outside a neural network architecture.

Figure 1 shows the confusion matrix of the SVMs with contextualized embeddings, averaged over the five folds. It shows that the most challenging time period is Ming Dynasty. Less than 50 percent of its instances are predicted correctly. About 26% instances from Ming Dynasty are wrongly labeled as Qing Dynasty, and we see the same trend for the Qing Dynasty instances as well. Notice that this similarity may be due to the property of language usage and similar content (see section 7). Most instances from Song and Tang are labeled correctly, and we also see that they are seldom labeled as Qing Dynasty. This indicates that Qing and Ming dynasties are similar to each other, but

[13]We also examined the n-gram features and found similar trend of contextualized embeddings. Thus, we only report results from our best model.

Book	Chinese N.	Acc.	Dynasty
Jianhuji	坚瓠集	0.70	Qing
Nanbu Xinshu	南部新书	19.25	Song
Xihu Mengxun	西湖梦寻	21.09	Ming
Yongtong Xiaopin	涌幢小品	27.20	Ming
Jianghuai Yiren Lu	江淮异人录	28.00	Song
Wuzazu	五杂组	28.40	Ming
Duyizhi	独异志	32.00	Tang
Zhinang	智囊	32.10	Ming
Chibeioutan	池北偶谈	36.20	Qing
Qingshi	情史	36.40	Ming

Table 5: 10 Biji with the lowest prediction accuracy.

Song and Tang are each very distinct from any other dynasty.

We have a closer look at the 10 Biji with the lowest accuracy, see Table 5. We can roughly group these 10 books into two categories: 1) The book is written at the end the beginning of dynasty. Examples are *Jianhuji* (Qing), *Nanbu Xinshu* (Song), *Xihu Mengxun* (Ming), *Yongtong Xiaopin* (Ming), *Jianghuai Yiren Lu* (Song),*Wuzazu* (Ming), and *Chibeioutan* (Qing). 2) The book is a collection of short stories from different dynasties such as *Zhinang* (Ming) and *Qingshi* (Ming). Regarding the first category, language change is continuous and happens across dynasties. Thus books written either early in a new dynasty or very late in the previous dynasty will share many language characteristics and are thus difficult to classify. For example, many books from the period of Late Ming and Early Qing are wrongly predicted. According to the periodization assumption made by historical linguist Fang (2010), Ming and Early Qing should belong to the last stage of Early Modern Chinese while Mid Qing to Late Qing constitutes the transition of Early Modern Chinese to Modern Chinese. Content similarity may be another reason for wrong labeling and can explain the low accuracy of Biji in the second category. For example, *Qingshi* collected love stories from pre-Qin to Ming Dynasties, which explains why many instances are wrongly labeled as Tang and Song Dynasty. We can also see the mixture effect of language and content similarities. *Jianhuji* is written in the Early Qing Dynasty but mainly includes anecdotes from Ming Dynasty, and we see that most of the instances are predicted as Ming Dynasty. *Wuzazu* is a similar case. This book is written in the Late Ming Dynasty, and one of the major parts of the book is about the author's thoughts about Song Dynasty's strategy. Therefore, many instances are wrongly labeled as Song and Qing Dynasty. A different case is *Duyizhi*. It was written in Tang Dynasty, but most parts of the original book are missing (Liu and Wang, 2016). The existing edition was published in Ming Dynasty. However, when we look into the classifier's prediction, we find that many instances are wrongly labeled as Ming Dynasty. This implies that the texts may contain language features from the editing during Ming Dynasty, and our classifiers identify such language features.

7 Neighboring Dynasties Classification

We now turn to the second research question, investigating whether the features that our classifier uses correspond to linguistic insights. Instead of classifying the four dynasties, we now look at the classification of neighboring dynasties, which is where the effects of language change should be the most visible. Since contextualized embeddings features are difficult to interpret, we use n-gram features. However, a first trial showed that many of the high ranking features were person names, etc., which are inherently linked to a specific dynasty. Thus, we decided to bleach proper nouns, i.e., we mask words tagged as proper nouns by Jiayan Toolkit. Then, we use chi-square feature selection on the bleached n-gram model, and select the 1,000 highest ranked features for the investigation.

Table 6 shows that contextualized embeddings models perform best for this task as well. We expect bleached models to perform worse than standard word n-grams since many informative features are deleted. This is the case when distinguishing the first two neighboring dynasty pairs but the opposite is the case when distinguishing Ming Dynasty and Qing Dynasty. Across three pairs of neighboring dynasty classification, all models show the same trend that distinguishing instances between Tang and Song Dynasty is easiest for the systems, then Song and Ming Dynasty. The F score of the Ming and Qing pair is the lowest. This supports the view that Ming Dynasty and Qing Dynasty belong to the same language period. Our results provide new evidence in a long standing debate: For the cutting point of Middle Chinese and Early Chinese, there are several assumptions, two consider the late Tang Dynasty (Pan, 1989) and Song Dynasty (Wang, 1958). Our results support the late Tang Dynasty assumption proposed by Pan

Representation	Tang vs Song			Song vs Ming			Ming vs Qing		
	Prec.	Recall	F	Prec.	Recall	F	Prec.	Recall	F
SBERT	86.19	85.26	85.42	80.81	80.11	80.02	69.49	69.13	68.76
n-gram$_{\text{word}}$	81.44	77.92	79.09	77.66	76.72	76.52	59.56	59.13	58.59
n-gram$_{\text{bleach}}$	78.98	74.44	75.83	72.81	72.40	72.37	65.08	64.11	63.69
n-gram$_{\text{bleach}_{1000}}$	77.42	73.24	74.60	70.77	70.15	70.02	62.55	61.55	60.92

Table 6: Results of comparing neighboring dynasties.

Tang vs Song		Song vs Ming		Ming vs Qing	
n-gram	gloss	n-gram	gloss	n-gram	gloss
曰	say	生	born/man	女	woman/unmarried woman
云	say/cloud	而	and	鬼	ghost
则天	person name	矣	final particle	某	certain thing or person
盖	because	俱	all	狐	fox
相国	prime minister	余	first person pronoun	我	first person pronoun
焉	final particle	也	final particle	Proper Noun	proper noun
作	make	女	woman/unmarried woman	一	one
馀	rest	不	no	妇	married women
于	on	云	say/cloud	曰	say
予	first person pronoun	上	top/superior	君	king
用	use	夫人	madam/wife	作	make
正	proper	宋	Song Dynasty/ family name	上	top/superior
知 location	govern place	宰相	prime minister	来	come
亦	also	知 location	govern place	声	sound
令	make	馀	rest	汝	second person pronoun
以	by means of	十余	around ten	忽	suddenly
则	but	情	feeling	笑	smile
刺史	provincial governor	御史	imperial censor	笑曰	smile and say
员外	landlord	天顺	regnal year	主人	master
皆	all	死	die	家	home

Table 7: Top 20 features from the bleached n-gram model when classifying neighboring dynasties.

(1989), since instances are more distinguishable between Tang Dynasty and Song Dynasty.

To look into the features selected by the classifiers, we list the top 20 features extracted from the bleached n-gram models[14], shown in Table 7. These features contain two words that should have been bleached but are listed due to segmentation and tagging error[15]. However, most of these features are very informative and fit historical linguists' observations well: We see the lexical change of the first-person pronoun. Many words are used as first-person singular pronouns in literary Chinese, including 我, 余 and 予. In Modern Chinese, 我 is the only first-person singular pronoun left. From the table, we can see that 我 is listed among the top features only in the comparison between Ming and Qing Dynasty. This shows that it becomes more and more prominent as the time period approaches Modern Chinese (Wang, 2018b). Meanwhile, the results also imply that 予 can distinguish instances from Tang Dynasty and Song Dynasty, and the usage of 余 is different in Song and Ming Dynasty.

Another example concerns the features 皆 and 俱. For both words, the main sense is 'all (adverb)'. Our results show that 皆 is useful in distinguishing instances from Tang to Song Dynasty while 俱 is helpful for classifying Song and Ming Dynasty. These results can be compared to a study by Wang (2018a), who found that the usage of 皆 decreases time, and both 皆 and 俱 are substituted by 都 gradually in modern Chinese. However, the change of 皆 and 俱 is not addressed by Wang (2018a). In contrast, surprisingly, 都 does not appear in our top 20 features. The differences need to be investigated more closely in the future. We also see cultural changes reflected. For example, 相国 is a common title for Prime Minister from Qin to Tang Dynasty, but after Tang Dynasty, 宰相 is used to refer to the Prime Minister. However,

[14]The rank is calculated by averaging the scores of a feature across folds.

[15] 则天 is the given name of a famous female ruler in China, but it is tagged as adverb. 天顺 is the regnal year in Yuan Dynasty but is wrongly segmented.

even after bleaching proper nouns, there remain features containing indirect information about the dynasty. For example, 鬼 and 女 are the names of frequently used main characters in Biji from Qing Dynasty. This makes them informative features, and they rank as the top features in the comparison of instances from Ming and Qing Dynasty.

8 Conclusion & Future Work

In this paper, we have approached the task of dating Chinese historical texts and examined the performance of different feature representations and machine learning algorithms. The first public available diachronic Biji dataset is created for tracking language change[16]. Our main findings are that even though dating historical Chinese texts is a challenging task for different types of feature representation methods, we still find informative features concerning language change, which correspond to historical linguists' observations. However, currently our methods only capture lexical change. In future work, we will investigate models for syntactic change.

References

Angelo Dalli and Yorick Wilks. 2006. Automatic dating of documents and temporal text classification. In *Proceedings of the Workshop on Annotating and Reasoning about Time and Events*, pages 17–22.

Franciska de Jong, Henning Rode, and Djoerd Hiemstra. 2005. Temporal language models for the disclosure of historical text. *Humanities, Computers and Cultural Heritage*, page 161.

Jacob Devlin, Ming-Wei Chang, Kenton Lee, and Kristina Toutanova. 2019. Bert: Pre-training of deep bidirectional transformers for language understanding. In *Proceedings of the 2019 Conference of the North American Chapter of the Association for Computational Linguistics: Human Language Technologies, Volume 1 (Long and Short Papers)*, pages 4171–4186.

Hongyuan Dong. 2019. *A History of the Chinese Language*. Routledge.

Yixin Fang. 2010. *Zhonggu Jindai Hanyu CIHUIXUE (Vocabulary Studies of Middle and Early Modern Chinese)*. The Commercial Press, Beijing.

Daiwie Fu. 2007. The flourishing of Biji or pen-notes texts and its relations to history of knowledge in Song China (960-1279). *Extrême-Orient Extrême-Occident*, pages 103–130.

[16]The dataset is available at https://github.com/zytian9/Chinese-Biji-Corpus.

Mario Giulianelli, Marco Del Tredici, and Raquel Fernández. 2020. Analysing lexical semantic change with contextualised word representations. In *Proceedings of the 58th Annual Meeting of the Association for Computational Linguistics*, pages 3960–3973.

Filip Graliński, Rafał Jaworski, Łukasz Borchmann, and Piotr Wierzchoń. 2017. The RetroC challenge: How to guess the publication year of a text? In *Proceedings of the 2nd International Conference on Digital Access to Textual Cultural Heritage*, pages 29–34.

William L. Hamilton, Jure Leskovec, and Dan Jurafsky. 2016. Diachronic word embeddings reveal statistical laws of semantic change. In *Proceedings of the 54th Annual Meeting of the Association for Computational Linguistics*, pages 1489–1501, Berlin, Germany.

Xiwu Han and Gregory Toner. 2017. Dating texts by multi-class classification with sliding time intervals. In *2017 10th International Congress on Image and Signal Processing, BioMedical Engineering and Informatics (CISP-BMEI)*, pages 1–6. IEEE.

Patrick Hanan et al. 1973. *The Chinese Short Story: Studies in Dating, Authorship, and Composition*, volume 21. Harvard University Asia Center.

Renfen Hu, Shen Li, and Shichen Liang. 2019. Diachronic sense modeling with deep contextualized word embeddings: An ecological view. In *Proceedings of the 57th Annual Meeting of the Association for Computational Linguistics*, pages 3899–3908.

Shen Li, Zhe Zhao, Renfen Hu, Wensi Li, Tao Liu, and Xiaoyong Du. 2018. Analogical reasoning on chinese morphological and semantic relations. In *Proceedings of the 56th Annual Meeting of the Association for Computational Linguistics (Volume 2: Short Papers)*, pages 138–143.

Shmuel Liebeskind and Chaya Liebeskind. 2020. Deep learning for period classification of historical Hebrew texts. *Journal of Data Mining & Digital Humanities*, 2020.

Yinhan Liu, Myle Ott, Naman Goyal, Jingfei Du, Mandar Joshi, Danqi Chen, Omer Levy, M. Lewis, Luke Zettlemoyer, and Veselin Stoyanov. 2019. RoBERTa: A robustly optimized BERT pretraining approach. *ArXiv*, abs/1907.11692.

Zehua Liu and Junde Wang. 2016. The research of writer and edition of duyizhi. *Journal of Qilu Normal University*, 6.

Stefano Menini, Giovanni Moretti, Rachele Sprugnoli, and Sara Tonelli. 2020. DaDoEval@EVALITA 2020: Same-genre and cross-genre dating of historical documents. In *7th Evaluation Campaign of Natural Language Processing and Speech Tools for Italian. EVALITA 2020*, pages 391–397. Accademia University Press.

Jerry Norman. 1988. *Chinese*. Cambridge University Press.

Tatsuo Ōta. 1988. *Chūgokugoshi Tsūkō [Comprehensive Studies of the History of the Chinese Language]*. Tokyo: Hakuteisha.

Yunzhong Pan. 1989. *Hanyu Cihui Shi Gaiyao (Summary of Chinese Vocabulary History)*. Shanghai Classics Publishing House, Shanghai.

Fabian Pedregosa, Gaël Varoquaux, Alexandre Gramfort, Vincent Michel, Bertrand Thirion, Olivier Grisel, Mathieu Blondel, Peter Prettenhofer, Ron Weiss, Vincent Dubourg, et al. 2011. Scikit-learn: Machine learning in Python. *the Journal of Machine Learning Research*, 12:2825–2830.

Alain Peyraube. 1996. Recent issues in Chinese historical syntax. In *New Horizons in Chinese Linguistics*, pages 161–213. Springer.

Octavian Popescu and Carlo Strapparava. 2015. SemEval 2015, task 7: Diachronic text evaluation. In *Proceedings of the 9th International Workshop on Semantic Evaluation (SemEval 2015)*, pages 870–878.

Nils Reimers and Iryna Gurevych. 2019. Sentence-bert: Sentence embeddings using siamese bert-networks. In *Proceedings of the 2019 Conference on Empirical Methods in Natural Language Processing and the 9th International Joint Conference on Natural Language Processing (EMNLP-IJCNLP)*, pages 3982–3992.

Martina A Rodda, Marco SG Senaldi, and Alessandro Lenci. 2017. Panta rei: Tracking semantic change with distributional semantics in Ancient Greek. *IJ-CoL. Italian Journal of Computational Linguistics*, 3(3-1):11–24.

Emma Rodman. 2020. A timely intervention: Tracking the changing meanings of political concepts with word vectors. *Political Analysis*, 28(1):87–111.

Dominik Schlechtweg, Barbara McGillivray, Simon Hengchen, Haim Dubossarsky, and Nina Tahmasebi. 2020. SemEval-2020 task 1: Unsupervised lexical semantic change detection. In *Proceedings of the Fourteenth Workshop on Semantic Evaluation*, pages 1–23.

Shanghai Classics Publishing House. 2000. *Tang Wudai Biji Xiaoshuo Daguan (Brushnotes in Tang Dynasty and Five Dynasties)*. Shanghai Classics Publishing House, Shanghai.

Shanghai Classics Publishing House. 2007a. *Mingdai Biji Xiaoshuo Daguan (Brushnotes in Ming Dynasty)*. Shanghai Classics Publishing House, Shanghai.

Shanghai Classics Publishing House. 2007b. *Qingdai Biji Xiaoshuo Daguan (Brushnotes in Qing Dynasty)*. Shanghai Classics Publishing House, Shanghai.

Shanghai Classics Publishing House. 2007c. *Songyuan Biji Xiaoshuo Daguan (Brushnotes in Song Dynasty and Yuan Dynasties)*. Shanghai Classics Publishing House, Shanghai.

Terrence Szymanski and Gerard Lynch. 2015. UCD: Diachronic text classification with character, word, and syntactic n-grams. In *Proceedings of the 9th International Workshop on Semantic Evaluation (SemEval 2015)*.

Yu-Hsiang Tseng, Shu-Kai Hsieh, Pei-Yi Chen, et al. 2020. Computational modeling of affixoid behavior in chinese morphology. In *Proceedings of the 28th International Conference on Computational Linguistics*, pages 2879–2888.

Li Wang. 1958. *Hanyu Shigao (Manuscript of the History of Chinese Language)*. Science Press, Beijing.

Min Wang. 2018a. Hanyu zongkuo fuci de laiyuan (the source of Chinese blanket range adverbs). *Xiandai Yuwen (Modern Chinese)*, 2018(6):4–11.

Weihui Wang. 2018b. *Hanyu Hexinci de Lishi yu Xianzhuang Yanjiu (The History and Current State of Core Vocabulary in Chinese)*. The Commercial Press, Beijing.

Xi Xiang. 1993. *Jianming Hanyu Shi (A Brief History of Chinese Language)*. Higher Education Press, Beijing.

Marcos Zampieri, Shervin Malmasi, and Mark Dras. 2016. Modeling language change in historical corpora: The case of Portuguese. In *Proceedings of the Tenth International Conference on Language Resources and Evaluation (LREC 2016)*, pages 4098–4104.

Sergey Zinin and Yang Xu. 2020. Corpus of chinese dynastic histories: Gender analysis over two millennia. In *Proceedings of The 12th Language Resources and Evaluation Conference*, pages 785–793.

A Mixed-Methods Analysis of Western and Hong Kong–based Reporting on the 2019–2020 Protests

Arya D. McCarthy and **James A. Scharf** and **Giovanna Maria Dora Dore**
Johns Hopkins University
arya@jhu.edu

Abstract

We apply statistical techniques from natural language processing to Western and Hong Kong–based English language newspaper articles that discuss the 2019–2020 Hong Kong protests of the Anti-Extradition Law Amendment Bill Movement. Topic modeling detects central themes of the reporting and shows the differing agendas toward *one country, two systems*. Embedding-based usage shift (at the word level) and sentiment analysis (at the document level) both support that Hong Kong–based reporting is more negative and more emotionally charged. A two-way test shows that while July 1, 2019 is a turning point for media portrayal, the differences between western- and Hong Kong–based reporting did not magnify when the protests began; rather, they already existed. Taken together, these findings clarify how the portrayal of activism in Hong Kong evolved throughout the Movement.

1 Introduction

On February 12, 2019, the Hong Kong Government revealed its plan to amend the Fugitive Offenders Ordinance and the Mutual Legal Assistance in Criminal Matters Ordinance (Li, 2019). Hong Kong Chief Executive Lam stated that the bill had been inspired by Poon Hiu-wing's murder: a judicial loophole was preventing the Hong Kong courts from trying her killer for murder, and it needed to be closed (Victor and May, 2019). Chief Executive Lam proposed changing the law so that Hong Kong could extradite fugitives, on a case-by-case basis, to jurisdictions it did not have an agreement with, including Mainland China, Macau, and Taiwan.

Opponents of the bill argued that rather than fixing a loophole, Chief Executive Lam's amendment would open the door to extraditions between Hong Kong and Mainland China, something that Beijing sought ever since the 1997 handover. To pass the amendment to the bill before Poon's murderer was released from prison and could (in theory) flee Hong Kong, citizens were only given 20 days to offer their feedback. They saw the bill as threatening their way of life and voiced dissent following the end of the short public consultations. Marches and demonstrations morphed into months of discontent, which were not appeased by Lam's decision to withdraw the bill (Ramzy and Yu, 2019). By then, the protests had evolved into an increasingly violent anti-government, anti-Beijing movement, with demands for greater democracy and police accountability. The Government turned to powers offered by the Emergency Regulations Ordinance (Hong Kong e-Legislation) to end the protests.

Hong Kong–based	Western-based
tensions	
us-china, **tension**, **war**, dispute, **uncertainty**, heightened, prolonged, **worsening**, fallout, **turmoil**	culture, state-owned, protections, tourists, market, base, rise, travel, closer, **argued**

Table 1: 10 nearest neighbors of *tensions*; words indicating negative emotion in LIWC (Pennebaker et al., 2015) are bolded. The Western sources' use of *tensions* is more descriptive and impassive (§5.1).

From a theoretical perspective, this article can be positioned within what Oliver et al. broadly call "the world of news and politics" (2019, 36) and, especially, how "dissonance across media outlets could be socially and politically consequential" (Tsfati and Walter, 2019, 39). The research behind the article is based on a mixed-methods approach that combines the application of a variety of NLP techniques with experts' insights on Hong Kong politics and society. NLP aids in marking inconsistencies in event characterizations as we analyze news articles related to episodes of civil unrest between January 2019 and June 2020, in both western- and

Proceedings of LaTeCH-CLfL 2021, pages 178–188
Punta Cana, Dominican Republic (Online), November 11, 2021.

Hong Kong–based English-language newspapers. Experts' insights help put into perspective how the volatile context of Hong Kong politics, plus newspapers' tendency to report more dramatic events, may result in reporting bias that either emphasises or undermines the legitimacy of either the protests or the regime against which protests are directed (Snyder and Kelly, 1977; Schrodt et al., 2001; Earl et al., 2004). The powerful mixed-methods interplay guides the analyses and enables this work's rich and nuanced discussion of these three research questions about newspaper depiction of the protests:

(§4) *What* do Hong Kong–based and Western-based newspapers discuss about protests in Hong Kong?

(§5) Do Hong Kong–based and Western-based newspapers differ in *how* they portray the protests?

(§6) Does coverage differ before and after the outbreak of protests in June 2019?

2 Related work

In answering our three questions, we benefit from the methods of *content analysis* (Berelson, 1952) by complementing subject matter expertise with the potential for massive scale. In this vein, Lucy et al. (2020) use word embedding similarity, topic models, and dependency parsing to generate clues toward differing portrayals of race and gender in U.S. history textbooks. Field et al. (2018) relate the content of Russian state-run news articles to the nation's economic performance, finding an agenda of distraction. Other content analysis and stylometry considers authorship (Mosteller and Wallace, 1984; Bergsma et al., 2012), native language identification (Koppel et al., 2005; Bergsma et al., 2012), and deceptive product reviews (Ott et al., 2013).

Considering civil unrest generally, Wueest et al. (2013) apply topic models and named entity recognition to protest event analysis. Hürriyetoğlu et al. (2019) show that not all protests are alike, computationally speaking: event extraction models for protests perform much worse on countries outside the training set. Inverting this, we call into question different views on protest in the same location.

Within the specific focus of Hong Kong, the closest work to ours is the contemporaneous Scharf et al. (2021), who perform a longitudinal analysis of Hong Kong news media since Hong Kong's transfer of sovereignty. Our work "zooms in" on the 2019–2020 protests—the largest in Hong Kong's history.

3 Data

We rely on a corpus we have collected of 3398 news articles from six western-based English language newspapers: *The New York Times*, *The Wall Street Journal*, *The Washington Post*, *The Financial Times*, *The Guardian*, and *The Times*; and two Hong Kong–based English language newspapers: *China Daily* and *South China Morning Post*, over a period of 18 months, from January 2019 to June 2020. Although we took steps to include a diverse array of newspapers from within given regions, the newspapers used in this sample were purposefully selected because they were English-language newspapers. This still allows for important insights into differences across cultures and regions. Future research ought to extend news coverage of protest beyond English-only news sources (Earl et al., 2004; Lee, 2014; Du et al., 2018).

The articles were collected through keyword-based searches in ProQuest Newspapers for the western English language newspapers, and Newsbank Access World News Research Collection for the English language Hong Kong newspapers. We searched for the keywords "Hong Kong" + "protests", "Hong Kong" + "rallies", "Hong Kong" + "marches", and "Hong Kong" + "riots". We used the East Coast editions for *The New York Times* and *The Wall Street Journal*; the UK editions for *Financial Times*, *The Guardian*, and *The Times*, and the overseas edition for *China Daily* (which is run and printed in Hong Kong). To be eligible for collection, articles had to be at least 300 words long, and be about the protests.

A one-by-one, manual screening process eliminated irrelevant items such as eventual duplicates within each publication, readers' letters, and articles that included any of the chosen keywords but whose content was not about the protest incidents. Following the manual screening, we retained 3398 articles. The mean length was 783 tokens.

4 *What* do Hong Kong–based and Western-based newspapers discuss about protests in Hong Kong?

The foremost question we answer is about the lay of the land: what is discussed? In this section, we first look at the frequency of articles about protests in Hong Kong: over time, how much are the protests

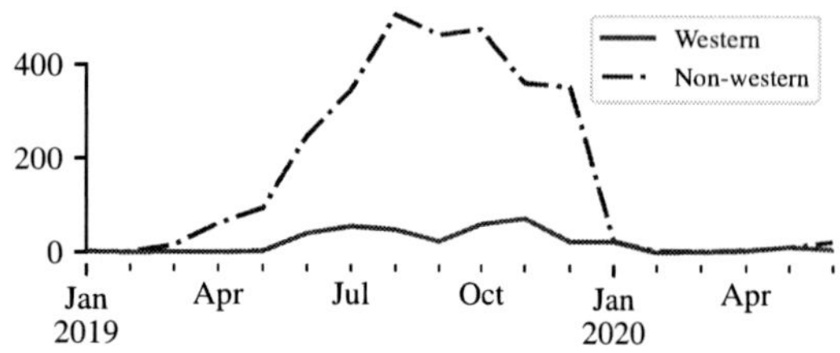

Figure 1: Hong Kong–based sources published far more throughout the protests and tapered off later.

discussed at all? Next, we discover topics that the newspapers tie into the protests, like legislation, air travel, and Mainland China. Bolstered by this, statistical analysis of word counts uncovers a discrepancy between western- and Hong Kong–based sources' use of 15 of 19 protest-related keywords like "protest" and "freedom".

4.1 Publication frequency

Counting articles about a theme is a simple, crude way to gauge its interest or relevance. However, newfound censorship in Hong Kong[1] adds a dimension to these numbers. Here, we report the trends in the number of collected articles over time, and we discuss the causes of the trends.

South China Morning Post and *The New York Times* published the largest number of articles about protests in Hong Kong. *South China Morning Post* published the most articles on Hong Kong protests amongst all newspapers, and *The New York Times* published the most among western-based newspapers. Both Hong Kong– and western-based newspapers published the lion's share of their articles in the second half of 2019 (see Figure 1). Out of a total of 3268 articles published in 2019, 94 % of them were published between June and December 2019.

There are a few reasons for this symmetry. First, *if it bleeds, it leads* (Altheide, 2018). Citizens' disquiet over the proposed amendment to the extradition bill boiled over into direct and violent action during the summer and fall months and, perhaps unsurprisingly, resulted in more articles published in both Hong Kong– and western-based newspapers. Then, the anniversary of the July 1, 1997 handover may have played a role. Historically, Hong Kong–based newspapers have used the handover anniversary as an opportunity to highlight aspects of the *one country, two systems* principle that are proven beneficial for the economic and political wellbeing of both Hong Kong and Mainland China. Western-based newspapers, on the other hand, tend to focus on the slow erosion of the very independence that *one country, two systems* was intended to preserve and guarantee.

Hong Kong has a long tradition of a free and opinionated media, with broad readership in both Cantonese and English. As the main English-language outlet in Hong Kong, *SCMP* shapes the international understanding of events in Hong Kong, whereas the (Hong Kong edition) *China Daily* in its efforts to connect Hong Kong readers to Mainland China finds itself consistently highlighting the *one country* perspective of the *once country, two systems* principles. These differences punctuated these newspapers' coverage of the 2019–2020 protests. *SCMP* published (roughly) ten times more articles than *China Daily* over the course of the 18-month timeline of our research. The articles' style was also markedly different, with the SCMP favoring the use of juxtapositions between positive and negative views towards the government, and the use of polls as indicators of public opinion's sentiment, whereas *China Daily* used academics as apolitical authorities on public affairs, and often adopted rhetorical strategies for the articles to read neutral and objective.

4.2 Topic modeling

Topic modeling characterizes documents by the topics they contain, automatically identifying the topics from corpora. We use latent Dirichlet allocation (LDA; Blei et al., 2003) for our topic models. It is a probabilistic generative model that maintains distributions over the words within each topic and the topics with each article, representing each article in the traditional vector space model (Salton et al., 1975). With LDA, we capture and convey the prevalence of various topics, so that we can contrast these across news sources and over the 18 months of our study.

Method We perform topic modeling with MALLET (McCallum, 2002). To preprocess the articles, we lemmatize all tokens with WordNet's `morphy` feature (Miller, 1995). We also extract common bigrams. The resulting unigrams and bigrams were converted to term–document matrices and provided as inputs to MALLET. We created models, setting the number of topics from $k = 7$ to 60, and evaluated the coherence of the resultant topics according

[1] https://www.nytimes.com/interactive/2020/09/04/world/asia/hong-kong-speech.html

Topic	Top 10 words
Finance	cent, per_cent, hk, market, property, billion, million, price, sale, financial
Social Media	n't, movement, young, have_been, political, do_n't, life, ha_been, hongkongers, social
Legislation	extradition, taiwan, lawmaker, council, election, chan, law, party, mainland, camp
Air Travel	business, mainland, airport, service, staff, august, day, company, tourist, cathay
International	china, chinese, state, world, trade, united, beijing, international, trump, mainland
Force and Order	officer, force, public, court, yesterday, case, arrested, law, post, source
Mainland	beijing, law, china, system, national, country, chinese, central, affair, two_system
Clashes	station, officer, gas, tear, violence, road, sunday, march, rally, tear_gas
Students	student, university, school, group, campus, ho, education, support, event, more_than
Chief Executive	lam, chief, executive, chief_executive, public, carrie, cheng, carrie_lam, extradition, political

Table 2: The 10 topics found in news coverage of Hong Kong's 2019–2020 protests.

to Mimno et al. (2011). We found that using 10 topics produced the highest coherence score. We then identified each of these topics with an identifying label (see Table 2).

Our topic model represents each article as a mixture of topics. More prevalent topics have higher mixture weight, and the weights sum to 1 for each article. (In LDA, these can be interpreted as samples from a k-dimensional Dirichlet distribution.) We can estimate a topic's prevalence in a news source or year by averaging the topic's weight across the articles from that source or year.[2]

Findings Figure 2 shows how the prominence and timing of the ten topics from Table 2 differ. We may expect these differences because of a media organization's desire to appeal to their own readership, preference for big picture issues, and the fact that the local nature of Hong Kong–based media might encourage a focus on the details of domestic issues. The treatment of the topics of MAINLAND, LEGISLATION, and SOCIAL MEDIA help showcase these differences.

MAINLAND Western-based newspapers' coverage of MAINLAND peaks twice. First at the time when the proposal to amend the extradition bill is announced, the short public consultations opened, and citizens become vocal about the amended extradition bill likely to weaken Hong Kong's independent judiciary. The second time, following Beijing's decision on Hong Kong's new security law, whose drafting and approval bypassed Hong Kong's legislature and citizenry. These trends suggest that Western-based newspapers may have used the coverage of the extradition bill to show the failure of the *one country, two systems* concept, and strengthen the perception that the terms of the 1984 Sino-British Declarations were being violated with no recourse for the people of Hong Kong. A toned down coverage of the topic MAINLAND underscores the domestic nature of the issue for the Hong Kong–based newspapers. Coverage, however, picks up at the tail end of 2019, after the amendment proposal was formally withdrawn from LegCo[3] legislative agenda, and even more over the

[2]As a complement to topic models, we also used Linguistic Inquiry and Word Count (LIWC; Pennebaker et al., 2015; Tausczik and Pennebaker, 2010) to analyze the language used in the articles. LIWC characterizes text based on word counts across more than 70 morphosyntactic and psychometric dimensions. There were only discernable trends in two of these categories, so we omit this from further discussion. "Newspaper-ese" has some common stylistic elements across the world, and the subject matter we consider shares one focus: the protests in Hong Kong. We speculate that this leads to the consistency across LIWC categories. The SHEHE and I categories occur with similar frequency because of newspapers' aggregate tendencies to use third- or first-person pronouns with particular frequency. Meanwhile, the INGEST category remains rare due to its irrelevance to the protests. Further, the LIWC categories include finite pre-defined lists of words. We found that the word "fallout", for instance, is not listed in the NEGEMO category, despite its readily apparent negative connotation. Topic modeling adapts to a corpus's extant vocabulary, giving it greater flexibility for our purposes.

[3]The Legislative Council, Hong Kong's legislature, comprises 70 members, 35 of whom are directly elected through five geographical constituencies under a proportional representation. The other 35 are indirectly elected through interest-group-based functional constituencies with limited electorates. Since its establishment in 1843 as an advisory council to the

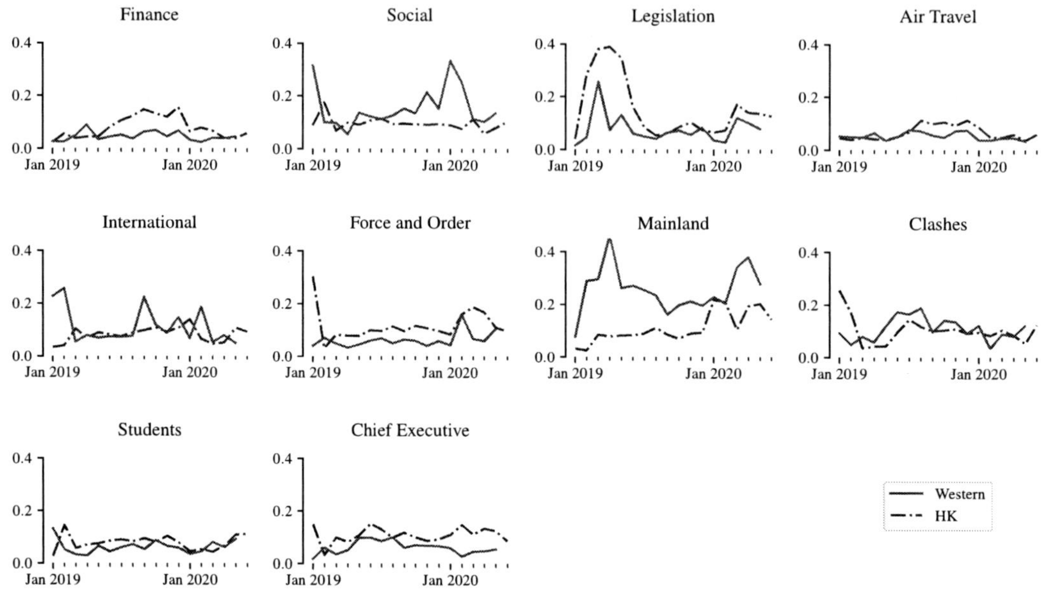

Figure 2: The 10 topics found and used in our topic modeling analysis.

first six months of 2020, (possibly) in an effort to address allegations that Beijing used the amendment to the extradition bill to usher in limitations of Hong Kong's existing civil and political liberties.

LEGISLATION Hong Kong– and western-based newspapers' trends for the coverage of the topic of LEGISLATION mimic each other; however, the volume of coverage is different. Hong Kong–based newspapers published consistently more on LEGISLATION than western-based ones. This is especially the case in the first half of 2019, when the proposal to amend the existing extradition bill was introduced to LegCo, the short public consultations held, and citizens began voicing their criticism; following this, Chief Executive Lam decided to indefinitely postpone the LegCo's vote on the amendment. The local nature of Hong Kong–based media also help explain the larger volume of coverage of an issue that is essentially domestic. In Western-based newspapers coverage is both less voluminous and less consistent. Two, distinct peaks underscore the announcement of the amendment proposal, and Chief Executive Lam's decision to indefinitely postpone the LegCo's vote on the amendment.

SOCIAL MEDIA Social media characterized the protests that engulfed Hong Kong starting in 2019, nurtured a sense of community based on collective, horizontal, and participatory decision-making. As the battleground in Hong Kong's protests, social media emerges as a topic whose coverage in Hong Kong– and western-based media notably diverges. In Western-based media, the discussion of social media peaks and dips as citizens leverage the catalytic features of social media in civic participation to voice their concerns about amending the extradition bill (in the first half of 2019), and civil disobedience, when concerns for the proposed amendment morphed into discontent over the lack of democratic political reforms, starting in the summer of 2019 and continuing through the spring of 2020. Hong Kong–based media's coverage of social media is consistently low, possibly reflecting both the fact that protests' social media use created digital space for activism, and Beijing's unhappiness with such a difficult-to-counter accomplishment.

Governor, its powers and functions have expanded.

Finally, we contrast our findings with those of Scharf et al. (2021). Their longitudinal analysis of unrest in Hong Kong found that the topic of POLICE VIOLENCE became especially prominent in western sources in 2019. Their topic shares many words with our CLASHES and FORCE AND ORDER topics; still, we see no marked discrepancy between these during coverage of the protests.

4.3 Comparing lexical frequency

Having categorized salient themes in the articles, we now turn to the use of specific, protest-relevant keywords chosen by a subject matter expert. Word frequency exposes obvious discrepancies in word choice and word usage. A lack of event-related keywords in contemporaneous articles from different newspapers may signal the omission of events in some of them.

Each source will have some degree of variation in keyword counts. An author's voice accounts for some mismatch in frequency, but not all. It is therefore challenging to determine whether the distribution of keyword counts is due to pure chance or something more meaningful.

We first test for whether there are important differences in the frequencies of 19 protest-related keywords[4]. Our procedure is related to Scharf et al. (2021), though we employ the Holm–Bonferroni correction (Holm, 1979) instead of the overly conservative, low-power Bonferroni correction. We set a significance level of $\alpha = 0.01$.

This statistical analysis cannot, however, reveal the *motive* for a difference in lexical choice. It merely raises the question to subject matter experts. It then befalls those experts to determine whether the difference arises due to intentional omission, niceties of a newspaper's style guide, or some other feature.

Findings The results of the analysis show that 15 of our 19 selected keywords have statistically significant differences in frequency, with *democracy* ($F = 490.5$); *protest* ($F = 354.6$); *protests* ($F = 300.6$); *freedom* ($F = 137.2$); and *occupation* ($F = 119.4$) having the highest F statistics. Our analysis consistently found less discussion of *protests* in Hong Kong-–based sources, with the high values of F statistic for *protest* and *protests* pointing to a statistically significant disparity in the coverage of protests.

Figures 3 and 4 illustrate these differences for *democracy* and *freedom*. In western-based media, the evolution of citizens' dissent over the amendment is cast as citizens' fight for democracy and the freedoms that come with it, resisting the authoritarian tightening in post-handover Hong Kong. This motivates the frequent and recurrent use of

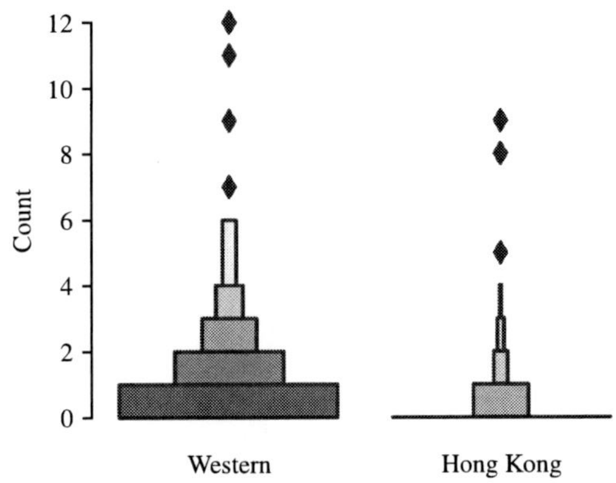

Figure 3: Quantile plot of *democracy* counts per article, by source location

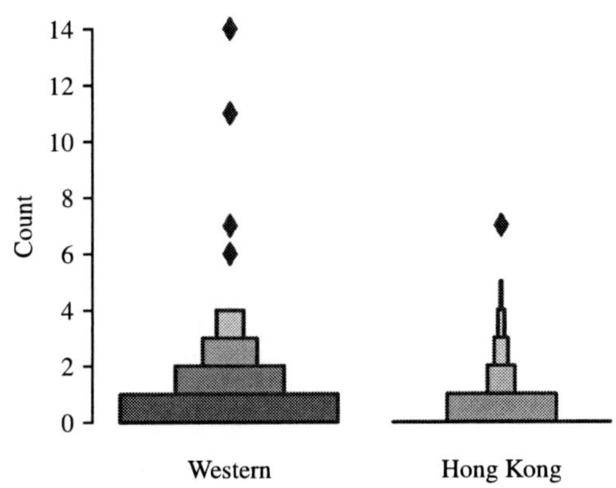

Figure 4: Quantile plot of *freedom* counts per article, by source location

freedom and *democracy*. Hong Kong–based newspapers, on the other hand, use *democracy* and *freedom* sparingly, focusing their discourse narrowly on the actual protest events rather than a broader meaning of them. The following section works to further characterize this contrast.

5 Do Hong Kong–based and Western-based newspapers differ in *how* they portray the protests?

Evidence from word embedding neighborhoods shows that Hong Kong–based sources use more negative, emotionally charged imagery; western-based depictions of concepts like *protest* and *tension* are more impassive and detached.

While the methods from §4 consider *which* words are used, we would like to investigate the evolution of *how* words are used differently between Western- and Hong Kong–based sources. In

[4] *confront, confrontation, crackdown, democracy, freedom, freedom_of_speech, independence, occupation, protest, protests, resistance, rights, riot, rule_of_law, severe, tension, terrorism, terrorist, unrest.*

Hong Kong–based	Western-based
	confront (17th percentile)
retreat, intimidated, abused, reminded, understandable, upset, confronting, provoked, regularly, provoke	work, met, acts, spirit, reasons, decisions, trying, voice, intolerable, tsang
	protest (66th percentile)
rally, sit-ins, demonstration, demonstrators, rallies, campaign, strike, movement, march, demonstrations	demonstrations, umbrella, peaceful, movement, began, streets, activists, mass, 1m, referendum
	tensions (63rd percentile)
us-china, tension, war, dispute, uncertainty, heightened, prolonged, worsening, fallout, turmoil	culture, state-owned, protections, tourists, market, base, rise, travel, closer, argued

Table 3: 10 nearest neighbors of three representative keywords in the Hong Kong–based and western-based articles. For *confront*, HK-based reporting is more emotionally charged. For *protest*, language from both sources is clinical, but HK-based language remains more negative. For *tensions*, the HK-based coverage is emotionally charged, higher-stakes, and more negative.

§5.1, we measure how the contexts that our protest-related keywords differ across sources. Sentiment analysis supports the findings that Hong Kong–based sources' writing is more negative. Analysis of articles' headlines shows that Western sources' headlines are more judgmental.

5.1 Comparing embedding neighborhoods

Diachronic shifts in word usage are often identified with changes in words' neighborhoods in an embedding space (Hamilton et al., 2016; Gonen et al., 2020). For instance, Hamilton et al. (2016) used these to find a shift in the word "broadcast" from agricultural to television contexts between the 1850s and 1900s. The same procedure can identify differences between words' usage when separated by something other than time. A word embedding model seeks to assign similar vectors (measured by dot product) to words in similar contexts, and different vectors to words in different contexts. If the usage of a word changes, then this should be reflected in changes to the word's context and consequent changes in the word's embedding.

We re-implement and extend the difference-in-usage model of Gonen et al. (2020), which measures how the contexts of words differ.

1. Partition the corpus C into C_a and $C_{\overline{a}}$ based on the attribute of interest a.
2. Fit separate word embedding models for each partition: $\mathcal{M}_a$ and $\mathcal{M}_{\overline{a}}$.
3. Select a keyword w of interest.
4. Obtain the set of nearest neighbors $\mathrm{NN}_a(w)$ and $\mathrm{NN}_{\overline{a}}(w)$ of w according to each of $\mathcal{M}_a$ and $\mathcal{M}_{\overline{a}}$.[5]
5. Score the usage-change of w as the size of the intersection, $\left|\mathrm{NN}_a(w) \cap \mathrm{NN}_{\overline{a}}(w)\right|$.

After this process, if w is used differently based on the presence or absence of the attribute, we expect its score to be quite small. Words whose usage does not depend on the attribute will have similar neighborhoods in each split.

To extend the work of Gonen et al. (2020), we contextualize the similarity score of a given word against a reference set. Considering all words that occur at least 100 times, in which percentile does word w's similarity score fall? We find this to be more meaningful than the raw similarity score.

The analysis of lexical usage reveals semantic divergence in certain keywords between Western-based and Hong Kong–based news sources, as shown in Table 3.

A visual inspection of the term's nearest neighbors for the Western-based model suggests the prevalence of neutral or descriptive lexicon (e.g., *work*; *reason*; *rise*). In contrast, the nearest neighbors in the Hong Kong– based model relate to adversarial behavior as in the case of *confront* (e.g.,

[5]Following the recommendation of Wendlandt et al. (2018) and Gonen et al. (2020), we use 1000 nearest neighbors.

retreat; *intimidated*; *provoke*); *protests* (e.g., *rally*; *strike*; *march*); *tension* (e.g., *war*; *dispute*; *uncertainty*; *turmoil*); and *rule of law* (e.g., *safeguard*; *undermined*). These trends are evidence of the dichotomous framing of anti-government demonstrators as well as their actions only having a negative connotation for Hong Kong.

5.2 Sentiment analysis

We corroborate the findings of more negative tone in Hong Kong–based publications with computational sentiment analysis. Sentiment analysis measures the attitude of an author from the tone and connotations of their document. While it is common and interpretable to use hand-crafted sentiment (valency) lexica (Mohammad, 2018), we select a technique that is robust to the specific words that are chosen. We select a BERT-based model to classify a given sentence as positive or negative because of its near state-of-the-art sentiment classification abilities.

We treat sentiment as a binary attribute[6] (+, −) and use a probabilistic classifier trained on the Stanford Sentiment Treebank (SST-2; Socher et al., 2013). The model uses DistilBERT (Sanh et al., 2019) for feature extraction from text; DistilBERT has previously been used for sentiment analysis of product reviews (Büyüköz et al., 2020). We split each article into sentences, then classify each sentence. An article's sentiment is taken as the average sentiment over all of its sentences.

The Hong Kong–based articles' average positivity (31.4 %) is slightly lower than the western-based articles (32.9 %). Across sources, there is wide variation, though; in fact, *The Times* is the most negative overall (28.3 % positive) but writes about the protests rarely. *China Daily* has the most positive tone. Coupled with the word-level negativity we noted in §5.1, this document-level negativity suggests that the Hong Kong press coverage of protests is systemically more negative. While the sentiment score sheds little light on authors' attitudes behind articles and commentaries, it still provides evidence of stylometric differences between news sources. This combined with the analysis of lexical usage and topic modeling helps to construct an informative view into news portrayal of civil unrest in Hong Kong.

[6]There is merit to including a third 'it's complicated' class (Kenyon-Dean et al., 2018).

5.3 Analysis of headlines

Headlines are meant to catch readers' attention while deliberately seeking to influence through the use of narrative mechanisms and sensational or provoking words (Blom and Hansen, 2015). We believe that both the length and the tone of the headline are informative about attempts to influence.

63 % of articles in the corpus have long headlines (i.e., include six or more words), whereas the remaining 37 % have headlines with fewer than six words. The *New York Times* emerges as the newspaper with the highest likelihood to have telegraphic headlines (i.e., 9.7 times more likely), whereas *South China Morning Post* is the least likely to have short headlines (i.e., 11 % less likely).[7]

In terms of sentiment, 52 % of all headlines are neutral, 32 % judgmental, and 15 % are mild, with the Hong Kong–based newspapers being the least likely to have judgmental headlines (i.e., 52 % less likely), and—perhaps unsurprisingly—the *Financial Times* being the most likely to have judgmental headlines (i.e., 2.5 times more likely).[8]

6 Does coverage differ before and after the outbreak of protests in June 2019?

Given that we have found differences between western- and Hong Kong–based reporting on the 2019–2020 protests, we might ask whether there are differences *in these differences* over time. Responding to our observation in §4.3, we use a two-way test and discover no significant interaction between source and the start of the protests on word frequency. We therefore restrict our focus to the aggregate changes in word usage over time, finding that the semantic context of the protest keywords becomes more polarizing and intense.

[7]The full regression model containing all predictors was statistically significant, $\chi^2(8; N = 3398) = 726.788, p < 0.001$. The model correctly classified 74 % of cases, and explained between 14.9 % (Cox and Snell R^2) and 20.5 % (Nagelkerke R^2). The strongest predictor for short headlines is the variable for *The New York Times* with an Exp($\hat{\beta}$) of 9.7, whereas the weakest predictor for short headlines with the *SCMP* with an Exp($\hat{\beta}$) of .89.

[8]The full regression model containing all predictors was statistically significant, $\chi^2(8; N = 3398) = 190.459, p < 0.001$. The model correctly classified 68.7 % of cases, and explained between 4.1 % (Cox and Snell R^2) and 5.8 % (Nagelkerke R^2). The strongest predictor for judgmental headlines is the variable for *Financial Times*, with an Exp($\hat{\beta}$) of 2.5, whereas the weakest predictor for a judgmental headlines is the variable for *SCMP*, with an Exp($\hat{\beta}$) of .48.

6.1 Lexical frequency and interaction terms

A two-way test lets us compare the means of a continuous response variable, modulated by two categorical explanatory variables. This expands on the analysis in §4.3: we can test the significance of not only the two explanatory variables, but also an interaction term between the two. Again, we use the Holm–Bonferroni correction to mitigate false discovery.

In our case, the explanatory variables are the source (western/HK-based) and the date: was the article published before or after July 1, 2019? There were significant differences for five of the nineteen keywords (*unrest*, *democracy*, *rights*, *crackdown*, *protest*). Further, the interaction term is only significant for *occupation* ($p = 2.3 \times 10^{-5}$); for the other 18 keywords, there is no significant interaction between the source and the date. Whatever trends and biases existed were not discernibly altered by the onset of the protests.

6.2 Comparing lexical usage over time

In our analysis, we sought to quantify the degree to which the introduction of the Fugitive Offenders amendment bill acted as a pivotal moment in the style of newspapers' portrayal of the Hong Kong protesters, and found that June 2019 emerges as a turning point, after which the meaning of several keywords shifts for at least the remainder of 2019.

We now split the corpus in "pre-June 30th, 2019" and "post-June 30th, 2019" to investigate whether the way in which Hong Kong– and western-based newspapers portrayed episodes of civic unrest differently following the protests and demonstrations that took place over June 6–12th, 2019.

Neighborhood shift analysis (as in §5.1) revealed significant low scores for *resistance*, *severe*, *riots*, *confront*, *confrontation*, and *terrorism*, which suggests that the context and/or semantic meaning for these words changes from early to late 2019, regardless of whether Hong Kong– or western-based news sources are considered. For instance, In the first half of 2019, neighbors for *riots* include terms like *actions*, *open*, *engage*, and *taken*, which that are not charged, and in the context of either a reporting or an opinion piece descriptively inform readers.

However, in the second half of 2019, the nature of neighboring terms for *riots* changes to include more polarizing terms such as *violent*, *escalated*, *destructive*, *triggered*, *anti-government*, and *sparked*. Similarly, pre-July 2019, neighbors for *terrorism* include, among others, terms like: *covered*, *lawyers*, and *negative*. Post-June 2019, neighboring words become politically charged, and include *criminals*, *destructive*, *extreme*, *lawless*, *punishing*, and *barbaric*. As "Hong Kong Summer of uprising" unfolded (Lee et al., 2019), feelings of social danger prevailed in newspapers' accounts of the events. Citizens' willingness to assert their political and civic agency via marches and demonstartions was described more and more harshly over time. Articles pre-July 2019 focused on general descriptions of protestors' tactics, whereas post-June 2019 the writing focused on detailed description of violent actions that took place during the protests as well as mentions of the negative social impacts that such actions may cause, which are implied to be detrimental to the well being of Hong Kong.

7 Conclusion

The Hong Kong protests captured domestic and international media attention, and their news value increased as their objectives shifted from protesting against a proposed amendment to the existing extradition bill to protecting democracy.

Our research shows that techniques from natural language processing help strengthen our understanding of how the portrayal of activism in Hong Kong profoundly evolved over the 18-month timeline of our study. While Hong Kong– and western-based publishers cover similar topics in their articles on the 2019 protests, the framing of those topics is different, which in turn carries implications for the public's perception, understanding, and support of those events. We also show that, in general, the use of charged words is more prominent in Hong Kong–based sources than western-based ones. This has implications for the extraction of protest-related events from corpora with politically opposed polarities such as ours. Finally, July 1, 2019, emerges as a turning point both for Hong Kong– and western-based news sources: afterwards, lexical choice related to protest descriptions becomes more negative and hostile in articles from both sources.

In exposing these findings, we combined expert domain knowledge and techniques from natural language processing. The interplay allows faster, more efficient analysis with larger sample sizes, which can be contextualized and interpreted to go beyond the descriptive and uncover the "So what?"

References

David L Altheide. 2018. *Creating fear: News and the construction of crisis*. Routledge.

Bernard Berelson. 1952. *Content analysis in communication research.* Free press.

Shane Bergsma, Matt Post, and David Yarowsky. 2012. Stylometric analysis of scientific articles. In *HLT-NAACL*, pages 327–337.

David M. Blei, Andrew Y. Ng, and Michael I. Jordan. 2003. Latent Dirichlet Allocation. *J. Mach. Learn. Res.*, 3(null):993–1022.

Jonas Nygaard Blom and Kenneth Reinecke Hansen. 2015. Click bait: Forward-reference as lure in online news headlines. *Journal of Pragmatics*, 76:87–100.

Berfu Büyüköz, Ali Hürriyetoğlu, and Arzucan Özgür. 2020. Analyzing ELMo and DistilBERT on sociopolitical news classification. In *Proceedings of the Workshop on Automated Extraction of Socio-political Events from News 2020*, pages 9–18, Marseille, France. European Language Resources Association (ELRA).

Y. Du, Lingzi Zhu, and Fan Yang. 2018. A movement of varying faces: How "occupy central" was framed in the news in Hong Kong, Taiwan, mainland China, the UK, and the U.S. *International Journal of Communication*, 12(0).

Jennifer Earl, Andrew Martin, John D. McCarthy, and Sarah A. Soule. 2004. The use of newspaper data in the study of collective action. *Annual Review of Sociology*, 30(1):65–80.

Anjalie Field, Doron Kliger, Shuly Wintner, Jennifer Pan, Dan Jurafsky, and Yulia Tsvetkov. 2018. Framing and agenda-setting in Russian news: a computational analysis of intricate political strategies. In *Proceedings of the 2018 Conference on Empirical Methods in Natural Language Processing*, pages 3570–3580, Brussels, Belgium. Association for Computational Linguistics.

Hila Gonen, Ganesh Jawahar, Djamé Seddah, and Yoav Goldberg. 2020. Simple, interpretable and stable method for detecting words with usage change across corpora. In *Proceedings of the 58th Annual Meeting of the Association for Computational Linguistics*, pages 538–555, Online. Association for Computational Linguistics.

William L. Hamilton, Jure Leskovec, and Dan Jurafsky. 2016. Diachronic word embeddings reveal statistical laws of semantic change. In *Proceedings of the 54th Annual Meeting of the Association for Computational Linguistics (Volume 1: Long Papers)*, pages 1489–1501, Berlin, Germany. Association for Computational Linguistics.

Sture Holm. 1979. A simple sequentially rejective multiple test procedure. *Scandinavian Journal of Statistics*, 6(2):65–70.

Hong Kong e-Legislation. Cap. 241 emergency regulations ordinance.

Ali Hürriyetoğlu, Erdem Yörük, Deniz Yüret, Çağrı Yoltar, Burak Gürel, Fırat Duruşan, Osman Mutlu, and Arda Akdemir. 2019. Overview of CLEF 2019 Lab ProtestNews: Extracting protests from news in a cross-context setting. In *International Conference of the Cross-Language Evaluation Forum for European Languages*, pages 425–432. Springer.

Kian Kenyon-Dean, Eisha Ahmed, Scott Fujimoto, Jeremy Georges-Filteau, Christopher Glasz, Barleen Kaur, Auguste Lalande, Shruti Bhanderi, Robert Belfer, Nirmal Kanagasabai, Roman Sarrazingendron, Rohit Verma, and Derek Ruths. 2018. Sentiment analysis: It's complicated! In *Proceedings of the 2018 Conference of the North American Chapter of the Association for Computational Linguistics: Human Language Technologies, Volume 1 (Long Papers)*, pages 1886–1895, New Orleans, Louisiana. Association for Computational Linguistics.

Moshe Koppel, Jonathan Schler, and Kfir Zigdon. 2005. Determining an author's native language by mining a text for errors. In *Proceedings of the Eleventh ACM SIGKDD International Conference on Knowledge Discovery in Data Mining*, KDD '05, page 624–628, New York, NY, USA. Association for Computing Machinery.

Francis L. F. Lee. 2014. Triggering the protest paradigm: Examining factors affecting news coverage of protests. *International Journal of Communication*, 8(0).

Francis L. F. Lee, Samson Yuen, Gary Tang, and Edmund W. Cheng. 2019. Hong Kong's summer of uprising: From anti-extradition to anti-authoritarian protests. *China Review*, 19(4):1–32.

Jeff Li. 2019. Hong Kong-China extradition plans explained. *BBC News*.

Li Lucy, Dorottya Demszky, Patricia Bromley, and Dan Jurafsky. 2020. Content analysis of textbooks via natural language processing: Findings on gender, race, and ethnicity in Texas U.S. history textbooks. *AERA Open*, 6(3):2332858420940312.

Andrew Kachites McCallum. 2002. Mallet: A machine learning for language toolkit. `http://mallet.cs.umass.edu`.

George A. Miller. 1995. WordNet: A lexical database for English. *Commun. ACM*, 38(11):39–41.

David Mimno, Hanna Wallach, Edmund Talley, Miriam Leenders, and Andrew McCallum. 2011. Optimizing semantic coherence in topic models. In *Proceedings of the 2011 Conference on Empirical Methods in Natural Language Processing*, pages

262–272, Edinburgh, Scotland, UK. Association for Computational Linguistics.

Saif Mohammad. 2018. Obtaining reliable human ratings of valence, arousal, and dominance for 20,000 English words. In *Proceedings of the 56th Annual Meeting of the Association for Computational Linguistics (Volume 1: Long Papers)*, pages 174–184, Melbourne, Australia. Association for Computational Linguistics.

Frederick Mosteller and David L Wallace. 1984. *Applied Bayesian and classical inference: the case of the federalist papers*. Springer.

Mary Beth Oliver, Arthur A Raney, and Jennings Bryant. 2019. *Media effects: Advances in theory and research*. Routledge.

Myle Ott, Claire Cardie, and Jeffrey T. Hancock. 2013. Negative deceptive opinion spam. In *Proceedings of the 2013 Conference of the North American Chapter of the Association for Computational Linguistics: Human Language Technologies*, pages 497–501, Atlanta, Georgia. Association for Computational Linguistics.

James W Pennebaker, Ryan L Boyd, Kayla Jordan, and Kate Blackburn. 2015. The development and psychometric properties of liwc2015. Technical report.

Austin Ramzy and Elaine Yu. 2019. Hong Kong's leader, Carrie Lam, to withdraw extradition bill that ignited protests. *The New York Times*.

G. Salton, A. Wong, and C. S. Yang. 1975. A vector space model for automatic indexing. *Commun. ACM*, 18(11):613–620.

Victor Sanh, Lysandre Debut, Julien Chaumond, and Thomas Wolf. 2019. DistilBERT, a distilled version of BERT: smaller, faster, cheaper and lighter. *CoRR*, abs/1910.01108.

James Scharf, Arya D. McCarthy, and Giovanna Maria Dora Dore. 2021. Characterizing news portrayal of civil unrest in Hong Kong, 1998–2020. In *Challenges and Applications of Automated Extraction of Socio-political Events from Text*, pages 43–52, Online. Association for Computational Linguistics.

Philip A Schrodt, Erin M Simpson, and Deborah J Gerner. 2001. Monitoring conflict using automated coding of newswire reports: a comparison of five geographical regions. In *Conference 'Identifying Wars: Systematic Conflict Research and it's Utility in Conflict Resolution and Prevention', Uppsala*, pages 8–9. Citeseer.

David Snyder and William R. Kelly. 1977. Conflict intensity, media sensitivity and the validity of newspaper data. *American Sociological Review*, 42(1):105–123.

Richard Socher, Alex Perelygin, Jean Wu, Jason Chuang, Christopher D. Manning, Andrew Ng, and Christopher Potts. 2013. Recursive deep models for semantic compositionality over a sentiment treebank. In *Proceedings of the 2013 Conference on Empirical Methods in Natural Language Processing*, pages 1631–1642, Seattle, Washington, USA. Association for Computational Linguistics.

Yla R. Tausczik and James W. Pennebaker. 2010. The psychological meaning of words: Liwc and computerized text analysis methods. *Journal of Language and Social Psychology*, 29(1):24–54.

Yariv Tsfati and Nathan Walter. 2019. The world of news and politics. *Media Effects: Advances in Theory and Research*.

Daniel Victor and Tiffany May. 2019. The murder case that lit the fuse in Hong Kong. *The New York Times*.

Laura Wendlandt, Jonathan K. Kummerfeld, and Rada Mihalcea. 2018. Factors influencing the surprising instability of word embeddings. In *Proceedings of the 2018 Conference of the North American Chapter of the Association for Computational Linguistics: Human Language Technologies, Volume 1 (Long Papers)*, pages 2092–2102, New Orleans, Louisiana. Association for Computational Linguistics.

Bruno Wueest, Klaus Rothenhäusler, and Swen Hutter. 2013. Using computational linguistics to enhance protest event analysis. In *ENCoRe Workshop 'Tools and Techniques for Conflict Event Data Collection'*, Konstanz.

Stylometric Literariness Classification: the Case of Stephen King

Andreas van Cranenburgh
University of Groningen
Department of Information Science
a.w.van.cranenburgh@rug.nl

Erik Ketzan
Trinity College Dublin
Centre for Digital Humanities
ketzane@tcd.ie

Abstract

This paper applies stylometry to quantify the literariness of 73 novels and novellas by American author Stephen King, chosen as an extraordinary case of a writer who has been dubbed both "high" and "low" in literariness in critical reception. We operationalize literariness using a measure of stylistic distance (Cosine Delta) based on the 1000 most frequent words in two bespoke comparison corpora used as proxies for literariness: one of popular genre fiction, another of National Book Award-winning authors. We report that a supervised model is highly effective in distinguishing the two categories, with 94.6% macro average in a binary classification.

We define two subsets of texts by King—"high" and "low" literariness works as suggested by critics and ourselves—and find that a predictive model does identify King's *Dark Tower* series and novels such as *Dolores Claiborne* as among his most "literary" texts, consistent with critical reception, which has also ascribed postmodern qualities to the *Dark Tower* novels. Our results demonstrate the efficacy of Cosine Delta-based stylometry in quantifying the literariness of texts, while also highlighting the methodological challenges of literariness, especially in the case of Stephen King. The code and data to reproduce our results are available at https://github.com/andreasvc/kinglit

1 Introduction

Stephen King, as both a highly successful and critically acclaimed author, has been referred to as "a contradiction in the literary world, a genre novelist who has achieved both popular and critical success," (Anderson, 2020, p. 17). In this paper we investigate the literariness of King's corpus using data-driven stylometric methods.

Stylometry is often operationalized using distances in vector space based on the most frequent words (MFW) in texts. Stylometry was canonically developed for questions of authorship attribution, but it has increasingly been applied to other research questions, including author profiling (e.g. age and gender), and stylochronometry, or the order in which an author wrote their works (Neal et al., 2017). In this paper we propose to further the quantification of literariness as an additional application of stylometry.

The term *literariness* was introduced by the Russian formalist Jakobson (1921, p. 11), although we follow a more general definition: "The sum of special linguistic and formal properties that distinguish literary texts from non-literary texts" (Baldick, 2008). Recent work has approached literariness with data-driven methods. The Riddle of Literary Quality project (2012-2019) focuses on predicting reader judgments of literary quality (Koolen et al., 2020) using textual features. Van Cranenburgh and Koolen (2015) report that machine learning solely using bigrams "can successfully separate novels that are seen as highly literary from less literary ones." Moreover, content and style bigrams achieve comparable accuracy, indicating that literariness is reflected in both thematics and stylistics of texts. Van Cranenburgh and Bod (2017) report that an ensemble of lexical, syntactic, and text complexity features "contribute to explaining judgments of literature," while *individual* syntactic constructions and *individual* bigrams are weak predictors of literariness, as "the top 100 features contribute only 34% of the total [literariness] prediction." Van Cranenburgh et al. (2019) report that even with short fragments of several pages, literariness can be predicted effectively; a keyword analysis reveals that literariness is associated with particular stylistic differences, such as strong and weak pronouns. Piper and Portelance (2016) present another study of contemporary fiction and focus on the distinctions between prize-winning, bestselling, and genre fiction in American novels, employing LIWC fea-

Proceedings of LaTeCH-CLfL 2021, pages 189–197
Punta Cana, Dominican Republic (Online), November 11, 2021.

K03: *The Shining* (Smith, 2002; Hendrix, 2013)
K06: *The Dead Zone* (Smith, 2002; Hendrix, 2013)
K11: *Shawshank* (Romano, 2018)
K16: *Pet Sematary* (Smith, 2002)
K19: *It* (King, 2006; Gates, 1986)
K20, 29, 38, 45-48, 60: *Dark Tower* series (Semenza, 2006, p. 73)
K21: *Misery* (King, 2006; Katzenbach, 1987; Banks, 1987; Smith, 2002)
K32: *Dolores Claiborne* (King, 2006)
K39: *Bag of Bones* (Cruz, 2014; USA Today, GQ: Powells, 1999; Hendrix, 2015a)
K51: *Lisey's Story* (Maslin, 2006)

Table 1: King works categorized as high literary.

K04: *Rage**
K07: *Firestarter**
K09: *Cujo**
K10: *The Running Man**
K15: *Christine* (Allen, 2012; Hendrix, 2013)
K17: *The Eyes of the Dragon**
K18: *Thinner**
K22: *The Tommyknockers**
K37: *The Regulators* (Hendrix, 2015b)
K40: *The Girl Who Loved Tom Gordon* (Allen, 2012)
K43: *Dreamcatcher**
K50: *Cell* (King, 2006; Noonan, 2006)
K52: *Blaze**

Table 2: King works categorized as low literary. Texts with * are suggested by the authors.

tures, multidimensional scaling, and supervised models. Underwood and Sellers (2016) present a study with a similar diachronic aim, demonstrating that a logistic regression based on word frequencies is effective in distinguishing between amateur poetry and critically reviewed poetry.

The studies above demonstrate that literariness is readily reflected in textual features, but these studies worked with sizeable datasets and reliable indicators of literariness. But what if literariness itself is in question in the texts? What if there is only limited data available, as in the case of a single author? Moreover, in the absence of consensus on literariness based on reader surveys or literary award juries, we must contend with a "ground truth" that is potentially more subjective and unreliable. We propose to build upon these studies by exploring stylometric methods for quantifying the literariness of works by a single author, and, again, not just any author, but an author known for occupying an exceptional position across high and low literariness in fiction. Since our data and task are challenging, we opt for a proven stylometric method: Cosine Delta (Smith and Aldridge, 2011; Evert et al., 2017), a variant of Burrow's Delta (Burrows, 2002). While this method has been especially successful for authorship attribution, we expect it to be effective for stylistic aspects in general, of which literariness is an instance.

2 Materials and Methods

King novels and novellas (73 texts). The main corpus contains all fiction solely authored by Stephen King published through 2020. Of these texts, 17 are categorized as high literary (Table 1), 13 as low literary (Table 2), and the rest are not categorized. The motivation for this categorization is presented in the following section.

We contrast the King corpus with two comparison corpora:

Literary fiction (38 novels). Inclusion criteria include: National Book Award winning authors published from 1974–2020, and, to attempt to control for diachronic change, American authors roughly the same age (within 10 years) as Stephen King (born 1947). For each author, we select the novel which won the Award, and an arbitrarily chosen second novel by the same author, to increase the corpus size. No effort was made to control for genre in this corpus, but this could be considered in future work.[1]

Popular fiction (36 novels). Inclusion criteria include: *New York Times* Bestsellers (top 10 only) published from 1974–2020, American authors near the same age (within 10 years) as Stephen King, in genres King himself has written in: thriller and/or horror. We select two novels for each author.[2]

[1]Literary fiction corpus: Thomas Pynchon, *Gravity's Rainbow* (1974). Robert Stone, *Dog Soldiers* (1975). Tim O'Brien, *Going After Cacciato* (1979). John Irving, *The World According to Garp* (1980). Alice Walker, *The Color Purple* (1983). Larry Heinemann, *Paco's Story* (1987). Pete Dexter, *Paris Trout* (1988). John Casey, *Spartina* (1989). Charles R. Johnson, *Middle Passage* (1990). Charles Frazier, *Cold Mountain* (1997). Alice McDermott, *Charming Billy* (1998). Julia Glass, *Three Junes* (2002). Lily Tuck, *The News from Paraguay* (2004). Richard Powers, *The Echo Maker* (2006). Denis Johnson, *Tree of Smoke* (2007). Jaimy Gordon, *Lord of Misrule* (2010). Louise Erdrich, *The Round House* (2012). James McBride, *The Good Lord Bird* (2013). Sigrid Nunez, *The Friend* (2018).

[2]Popular fiction corpus: Allan Folsom, *The Day After Tomorrow* (1994); *Day of Confession* (1998). Anne Rice, *The Witching Hour* (1990); *Taltos* (1994). Catherine Coulter, *Riptide* (2000); *Knock Out* (2009). Charlaine Harris, *Definitely dead* (2006); *Dead Reckoning* (2011). Dean Koontz, *Lightning* (1998); *By the Light of the Moon* (2002). Iris Johansen, *Final Target* (2001); *Countdown* (2005). James Patterson, *Cat and Mouse* (1997); *Cross the Line* (2016). Janet Evanovich, *Hot Six* (2000); *Plum Spooky* (2009). John Grisham, *The Firm* (1991); *The Racketeer* (2012). Michael Connelly, *A Darkness*

The fundamental issue with using this corpus as a proxy for low literariness is whether the identification of "popular" "genre" fiction with "low literariness" is valid, and whether the distinctions between high and low fiction as described by e.g., (Huyssen, 1986) as "the Great Divide" are as great in recent fictional texts. We acknowledge this issue but, in the absence of e.g. large datasets of reader surveys on the literariness of English-language novels, choose this as the best option.

2.1 "High" and "low" literariness King novels

Despite having sold an estimated 350 million books (Heller, 2016), King's texts have been "the object of very little critical study" (Anderson, 2017, p. 5). While this overstates the case, questions of literariness certainly suffuse early King criticism and much academic discourse on King to this day, with early critics providing value judgments on whether King is or is not "literature," whether he is a "mere" horror or "genre" writer or somehow more "literary," most vociferously Harold Bloom, who wrote that "King has replaced reading" (Bloom, 2006, p. 2) and "King's books [...] are not literary at all, in my critical judgment" (Bloom, 2006, p. 207). Despite such criticism, King has gradually attained "high" literary approval, through, *inter alia*, the National Book Foundation's 2003 Medal for Distinguished Contribution to American Letters and publications in such highbrow venues as *The New Yorker* and *The Atlantic*. "King's avowed mission [has been] to dismantle the either/or logic of the binary opposition between popular and serious" fiction, per Birke (2014), through novels which, to this day, fall variously along spectrums of "genre" and "high" subject matter and stylistics.

King himself identified some of his books which may be more or less literary in an interview with *The Paris Review*, suggesting that some of his novels are "entertainments," including *Cell* (a horror thriller in which mobile phones transform people into mindless killers) while others "work on more than one level," including *Misery*, *Dolores Claiborne*, and *It*, the latter of which King assessed as "the most Dickensian of my books" (King, 2006). Scholars are, of course, under no obligation to follow King's classification of his books into "entertainments" and literary novels which "work on more than one level." Although Koolen et al. (2020) have performed literariness experiments benefiting from reader surveys for literariness ratings, no such resource exists for King, which leads us to compare the results of our stylometric experiments with some novels which King and critics have claimed are more or less literary.

Identifying King's high and low literariness texts is certainly a subjective exercise which only foregrounds problematic issues of literariness as a concept. Genre and literariness are related but separate concepts—*Pet Sematary*, for instance, is unambiguously a horror novel, yet has been considered so fine in its execution that it becomes "literary," and media critics who assign value judgments of "good" or "bad" can do so quite separately from issues of literariness; a King novel can be "low literary" but "good"—an unputdownable thriller—or "high literary" but "bad"—ambitious attempts which fail. We have thus begun with two buckets of novels in which critics specifically raise the issue of literariness. While competing critics have sometimes proclaimed the same King novel as high or low literariness (e.g. *11/22/63*), other King works have attained a critical consensus, most notably, the *Dark Tower* series, "what many critics believe to be Stephen King's most literary of works," per (Semenza, 2006, p. 73), with some academic commentators discussing the series in terms of postmodernism, a high literary designation (Anderson, 2020; Buday, 2015). It is easier to find critics proclaiming a King novel to be high in literary qualities than damning a King novel as unliterary trash, however, so we supplement our "low literariness King" bucket with nine more texts based upon our critical judgment, especially examples of relatively straightforward genre exercises which have not been acclaimed by literary-minded critics. This provides us with data points to test stylometric classification of King's literariness.

2.2 Stylometry and Machine Learning

The texts are lowercased and tokenized with a regular expression that includes apostrophes in words (no other punctuation is considered inside words). We apply the Cosine Delta method (Smith and Aldridge, 2011; Evert et al., 2017), a variant of Bur-

More Than Night (2001); *The Wrong Side of Goodbye* (2016). Michael Crichton, *Congo* (1980); *Timeline* (1999). Nelson DeMille, *The Charm School* (1988); *Night Fall* (2004). Patricia Cornwell, *All That Remains* (1992); *The Scarpetta Factor* (2009). Peter Straub, *Ghost Story* (1979); *Koko* (1988). Robert Crais, *Taken* (2012); *Suspect* (2013). Sue Grafton, *H Is for Homicide* (1991); *T is for Trespass* (2007). Thomas Harris, *Red Dragon* (1981); *Hannibal* (1999). Tom Clancy, *The Hunt for Red October* (1984); *Rainbow six* (1998).

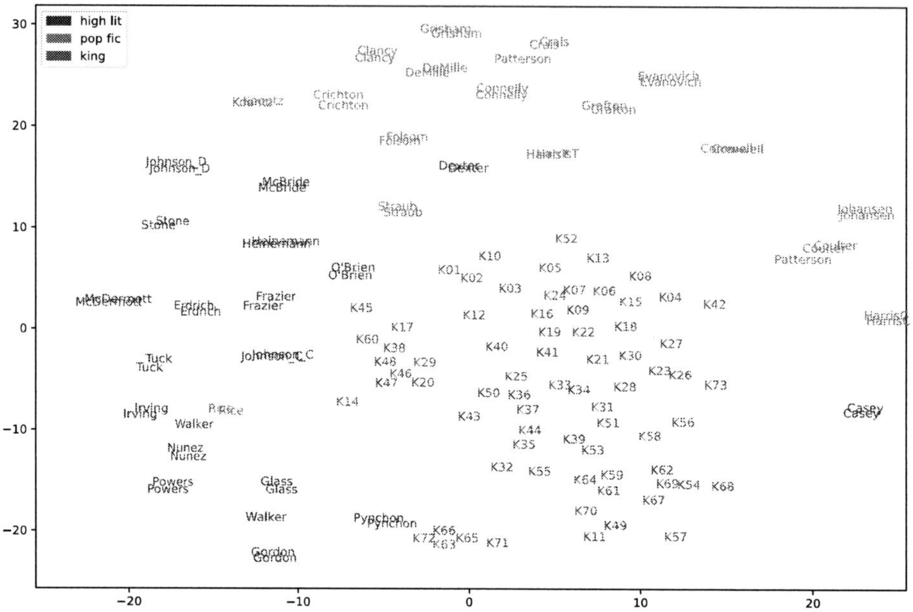

Figure 1: A t-SNE scatter plot of z-scored frequencies of 1000 MFW.

row's Delta (Burrows, 2002), which has proven to be highly effective for authorship attribution. Based on the results in Evert et al. (2017), we work with the 1000 most frequent words; a higher number works as well, but we wished to limit the influence of non-stylistic features such as character names and topical words.

The Cosine Delta method begins by extracting relative frequencies, which are standardized into z-scores. Relative frequencies ensure that document length is ruled out as a factor. Standardization involves subtracting the mean such that each feature has a mean of 0, as well as normalizing to unit variance (standard deviation of 1). This ensures that the differences between document vectors are not dominated by high frequency words, since each feature contributes equally.

We select the 1000 most frequent words and fit the standardized frequencies based on the two comparison corpora (high literary and popular fiction), and apply the same selection and standardization on the King texts. This ensures that the feature selection and standardization is not influenced by the King texts.

The Cosine Delta provides distance measure document vectors which reflect the texts' stylistic similarity, which can be explored in unsupervised fashion with dimensionality reduction and clustering methods. However, as we are particularly interested in estimating the literariness of texts from their word frequencies, we operationalize this by using the popular fiction and high literary novels as proxies for low and high literariness, respectively. Cosine Delta provides a distance between any two texts, and we could classify the literariness of a text by selecting its nearest neighbor, but this assumes that each word frequency is equally important for literariness, and does not tell us where to draw the boundary between popular and literary.

We therefore train a crossvalidated, regularized logistic regression model on predicting whether a text is from the high literary or popular fiction subset (the King texts are not included in this experiment). During crossvalidation, we ensure that both novels by an author are either in the training or in the test fold, not both; this avoids the situation where the model is able to learn a shortcut by exploiting the author signal. Regularization ensures that the model is able to work with a large number of features effectively, even though the number of features is much larger than the number of data points ($1000 > 148$). Logistic regression, despite the name, is a linear classification model, which has an advantage over models such as Support Vector Machines (SVM) in that it produces calibrated probabilities which indicate the confidence of a classification on a scale of 0 to 1. For a given document vector, we use this probability as an indication of how likely it is that the document is a high literary novel, which we then apply to the King texts.

3 Experiments and Analysis

3.1 Unsupervised results

We first present some unsupervised explorations in which we analyze the observed z-scores directly, after which we turn to supervised models that are optimized to predict the literariness labels. By inspecting the mean z-scores in each corpus, we can determine which word frequencies diverge the most (on average) from the comparison corpora (high literary and popular novels) as a whole. The top 15 words with the lowest and highest z-scores are:

Typical for King: ones, kid, thought, one, sounded, least, began, idea, although, mouth, it, sound, mind, gone, almost

Atypical for King: meet, moved, family, figure, attention, we, near, whether, minute, learned, met, worked, within, though, return

Typical for high literature: way, whose, girls, dream, funny, among, fall, each, whole, every, one, sometimes, own, themselves, day

Typical for popular fiction: door, hell, okay, we're, second, opened, check, probably, realized, checked, phone, killed, information, area, minutes

These bags of words resemble the output of topic modeling, an unsupervised method to discover latent semantic structures in texts (Blei, 2012). Even though these lists were not produced by topic modeling, the cautions against naively interpreting bags of words produced by topic modeling are relevant here; Schmidt (2012) suggests that topic models are known for creating "unexpected juxtapositions," while Goldstone and Underwood (2012) argue that "interpreters really need to survey a topic model as a whole, instead of considering single topics in isolation." With these cautions in mind, we observe that the typical words for popular fiction seem action- and procedure oriented, and include markers of informality ('okay,' contractions). These typical words for high literature tend to be conceptual, while these typical words for King display a number of words relating to inner state, such as *thought, idea, mind*, which may relate to claims by e.g. Magistrale (2013, p. 355), who praises "King's ability to place the reader in the consciousness of a character." The keyness of *Kid*, meanwhile, probably relates to the fact that "King regularly makes use of the child protagonist in his novels" (Olson, 2020, p. 2). On the other hand, among the atypical words for King are words related to family and time, which have been reported as distinctive keywords of literary works (Piper and Portelance, 2016; van

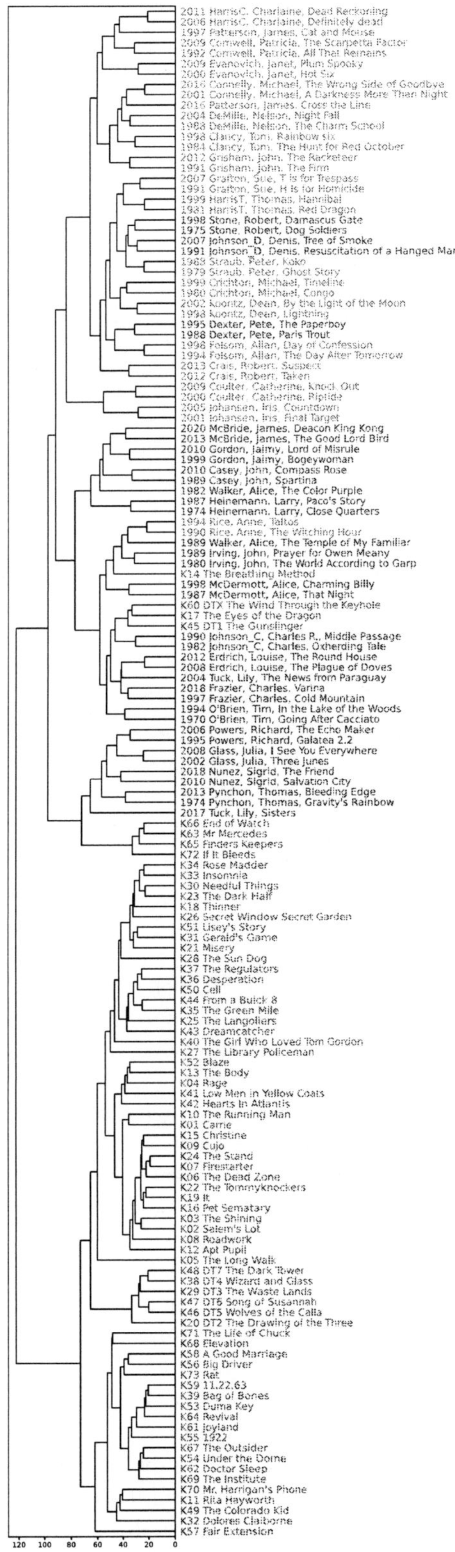

Figure 2: A hierarchical clustering of the whole corpus based on Cosine Delta of 1000 MFW.

	prec.	recall	F1	support
high lit	94.7	94.7	94.7	38
popular	94.4	94.4	94.4	36
macro avg	94.6	94.6	94.6	74

Table 3: Crossvalidated classification scores on predicting high vs popular in the comparison corpora.

	prec.	recall	F1	support
high lit	70.6	70.6	70.6	17
popular	61.5	61.5	61.5	13
macro avg	66.1	67.1	66.1	30

Table 4: Classification scores on the King novels with literariness categorizations, trained on the high lit and popular corpora. The support column shows the number of datapoints in each subset.

	prec.	recall	F1	support
high lit	71.4	58.8	64.5	17
popular	56.2	69.2	62.1	13
macro avg	63.8	64.0	63.3	30

Table 5: Crossvalidated classification scores on the King novels with literariness categorizations, trained on the King corpus.

Cranenburgh and Koolen, 2015). However, it is expected that individual features provide limited information. To get a better understanding of the stylistic differences captured by the z-scores, we should consider all of the 1000 MFW.

Figure 1 shows a dimensionality reduction scatter plot using t-SNE with a perplexity (i.e., number of nearest neighbors) of 15. In this plot, the subcorpora are shown in different colors for visualization purposes. Note that these labels were not given to t-SNE; this scatter plot is therefore still an unsupervised analysis. We can observe that high literary fiction and popular fiction tend to cluster together, with the strongest outlier being vampire fiction author Anne Rice. The texts in the left of King's cluster are those most firmly gravitating toward the high literary cluster, and interestingly, at least eight *Dark Tower* books are placed there by the model, consistent with critical assessments of the *Dark Tower* series as among King's most experimental and even "postmodern." We had suggested *The Eyes of the Dragon* (K17) as a low literariness text, as it is King's only attempt at a Tolkien-esque fantasy (and thus within the purview of the popular fantasy genre), but the model places it firmly within high literary. Another cluster in the bottom left (and thus closest to high literary) features a number of recent King texts which are thematically quite different, but perhaps united in stylistics (K63, 65-66, 71-72). As an aside, one of the King texts suggested as most literary by this model, "The Breathing Method" (K14), is a largely forgotten early novella, but we suggest that the minor power of models such as these to simply highlight texts for literary scholars to revisit (with fresh eyes and a newfound attention to literariness) is a small but worthwhile humanistic contribution.

Another way of exploring the intertextual distances is with a hierarchical clustering, which provides a more ordered way of assessing the stylistic similarities in the corpus (Figure 2). While both the scatter plot and hierarchical clustering highlight which texts are most similar to each other and form clusters, the scatter plot has the limitation of having to summarize the similarities across 1000 dimensions in two dimensions, and since t-SNE is a randomized algorithm with several important parameters that need to be tuned, results can vary and sometimes highlight different aspects in the data. The hierarchical clustering, on the other hand, does not reduce the dimensionality and shows a different kind of structure in the data, in a deterministic fashion. The tree is built bottom up, starting with each text in its own cluster; at each step, the two most similar clusters are then merged based on cosine distance. The horizontal length of the branches are proportional to the similarity of the clusters (Evert et al., 2017). Since Cosine Distance is so adept at detecting authorship, most authors with two novels form a cluster.[3] In other respects, this method confirms clusterings that are also apparent in the scatter plot, which is an indication of the robustness of those results.

3.2 Supervised results

In the unsupervised results, many types of variation in the z-scores may play a role, and we do not obtain a direct measure of how well literariness is reflected in the z-scores. We therefore turn to supervised models in this section.

Table 3 presents classification results for the high literature and popular fiction comparison corpora. The evaluation is done using 3-fold crossvalidation. The classification is highly accurate, indicating that

[3]There are two exceptions: Alice Walker and Lily Tuck.

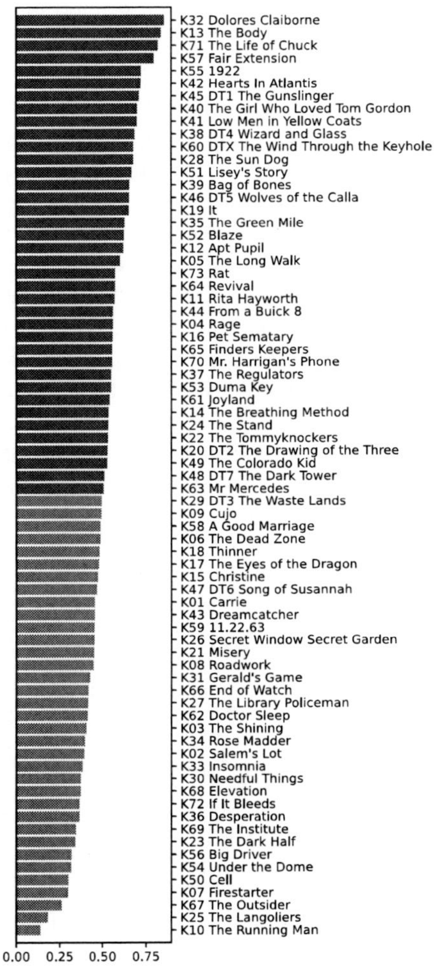

Figure 3: Probability that each King text is high literary according to logistic regression train on popular fiction and high literary novels.

there is a robust difference in word usage across these two corpora, and confirming, as in previous work, that literariness is predictable from textual features. This result also supports the suitability of Cosine Delta for modeling literariness.

Table 4 reports the classification results for the King novels we categorized as high and low literary. In early experiments, the model predicted almost all King novels as literary. There are two possible explanations for this: either all the King novels are indeed literary, or this points to a mismatch of the literariness differences in the King novels compared to the training data which we use as proxy for literariness. Since we know that there are degrees of literariness in the King corpus, we consider the second explanation more likely. In this case we can conclude that the King novels are closer to the literary novels in our reference corpus than to the popular novels. We therefore need to correct for this imbalance in the training data. We achieve this by specifying during training that misclassifications on popular novels are twice as important as misclassifications on literary novels (i.e., a skewed class prior). The result is that about half of King novels are predicted to be literary. With a macro average of 66.1%, the results outperform a random baseline, which produces macro average F1 scores with a mean of 50%.

We can inspect the behavior of the model by looking at predictions for individual novels. Figure 3 shows the probability of being a high literary novel for each text in the King corpus, ranked from most to least literary. Compared to the scatter plot, this provides a more direct way of assessing to what extent literariness is reflected in the textual features, since the predictive model focuses on finding the differences between literary and popular novels while ignoring other variation in the z-scores. A number of the *Dark Tower* novels again score among the highest in the literariness score, while other King novels from the high literary bucket in Table 1 also score high here, including *Lisey's Story* and *It*. The highest scoring novel, *Dolores Claiborne*, is consistent with critical assessment as being high literary for King, with critics such as Senf (1998) praising the realist psychological portraits of its female characters. The literariness of the 2nd, 5th, and 6th top results can somewhat be implied by the fact that these have been adapted as critically acclaimed films, *The Body* as the 1986 film *Stand by Me*, with *1922* and *Hearts in Atlantis* as films of the same titles. Not all of our predicted low literariness texts score particularly low by this measure, but *Cell*, which King singled out as one of his "entertainments," is the fifth lowest-scoring text.

To investigate the possible difference in standards between the categorizations of high literary and popular novels on the one hand, and the labels for low and high literary King novels on the other, we evaluate a different classifier on the same set of King novels, but trained only on the King novels using 5-fold crossvalidation; see the scores in Table 5. For this model we did not use a skewed class prior. The results are slightly worse, but given the much smaller training set, the results are still quite good.

4 Conclusion and Future Work

Our results confirm that popular fiction and high literary novels can be distinguished remarkably effectively, as shown by the classification F-scores. Applying the same model to the King corpus gives promising results, but the classification F-scores are not as impressive. On the one hand, this is entirely expected: the model is evaluated on a different domain than what it was trained on, and some of the patterns it exploits in the training data will not apply. On the other hand, there may be a deeper problem; as many of King's works display aspects of high and low literariness, in both thematics and perhaps style, King may be an exceptionally problematic case in any quantitative measurement of literariness.

Moreover, the lower performance on the set of labeled King texts may indicate that more training data and more sophisticated models are needed, but it may also be a sign that the categorizations of the King novels are not consistent with the textual features or the categorizations of the popular and high literary novels in the comparison corpora. What is taken as a misclassification by the model in our evaluation could also point to a misclassification by critics; moreover, since our labels reflect the perspective of different individuals, they are not necessarily consistent with each other; these critics may have applied different standards. These are methodological challenges that should be addressed in future work.

Robust evidence emerging from the experiments on King's work is the consistent ranking by the models of novels in King's *Dark Tower* series and other texts as being among his more literary works, consistent with critical assessments. This shows promise for Cosine Delta and other stylometric methods in literariness quantification. While the question of King's literariness is not settled, our results confirm the notion that King's work spans the spectrum of low and high literariness.

We also leave for future work the case of literariness and Richard Bachman, a pen name used by King in early novels and two later works. Despite the nom de plume's practical origins (King and his publishers were wary of publishing two novels in one year by the same author), King later described Bachman as a "persona" and "alter ego," stating that the early novels had been written "in a Bachman state of mind: low rage, sexual frustration, crazy good humor, and simmering despair" (King, 1996). We suggest that an exploration of King/Bachman would merit a dedicated, mixed-method study, particularly as there is far from critical consensus on the literariness of the various Bachman books, individually or collectively, let alone whether the Bachman novels (some separated by decades) can convincingly be argued to share distinctive features. *The Running Man*, a Bachman book, was scored by our model as the lowest King novel in literariness, and while a hypothetical critic might dismiss that novel as a low-literary dystopian thriller, the book has many literary aspects, as discussed by Texter (2007). Meanwhile, *The Long Walk*, the second Bachman book, scored relatively highly in literariness in our model, consistent with our own critical assessment of the novel as a fine dystopian allegory of the Vietnam War. Is Bachman a signal, or merely noise?

Acknowledgements

We are grateful to Corina Koolen, Karina van Dalen-Oskam, and three anonymous reviewers for their feedback.

References

Dwight Allen. 2012. My Stephen King problem: A snob's notes. Los Angeles Review of Books.

James Arthur Anderson. 2017. *The Linguistics of Stephen King: Layered Language and Meaning in the Fiction*. McFarland.

James Arthur Anderson. 2020. *Excavating Stephen King: A Darwinist Hermeneutic Study of the Fiction*. Lexington Books.

Chris Baldick. 2008. Literariness. In *The Oxford Dictionary of Literary Terms*. Oxford University Press, USA.

Carolyn Banks. 1987. Summer thrillers from three masters. *The Washington Post*.

Dorothee Birke. 2014. Challenging the divide? Stephen King and the problem of 'popular culture'. *The Journal of Popular Culture*, 47(3):520–536.

David M. Blei. 2012. Probabilistic topic models. *Communications of the ACM*, 55(4):77–84.

Harold Bloom. 2006. *Stephen King*. Infobase Publishing.

Maroš Buday. 2015. Exploring „the dark tower": Stephen King's postmodern epic. *Studia Anglica Resoviensia*, 12:135–145.

John Burrows. 2002. 'Delta': a measure of stylistic difference and a guide to likely authorship. *Literary and linguistic computing*, 17(3):267–287.

Gilbert Cruz. 2014. All 64 Stephen King books, ranked. New York Vulture.

Stefan Evert, Thomas Proisl, Fotis Jannidis, Isabella Reger, Steffen Pielström, Christof Schöch, and Thorsten Vitt. 2017. Understanding and explaining Delta measures for authorship attribution. *Digital Scholarship in the Humanities*, 32(Supplement 2):ii4–ii16.

David Gates. 1986. The creature that refused to die. Newsweek.

Andrew Goldstone and Ted Underwood. 2012. What can topic models of PMLA teach us about the history of literary scholarship? *Journal of Digital Humanities*, 2(1).

Karen Heller. 2016. Meet the writers who still sell millions of books. Actually, hundreds of millions. *The Washington Post*, 20.

Grady Hendrix. 2013. The great Stephen King reread: Christine. Tor.com.

Grady Hendrix. 2015a. The great Stephen King reread: Bag of Bones. Tor.com.

Grady Hendrix. 2015b. The great Stephen King reread: The Regulators. Tor.com.

Andreas Huyssen. 1986. *After the great divide: Modernism, mass culture, postmodernism*, volume 399. Indiana University Press.

Roman Jakobson. 1921. *Novejšaja russkaja poèzija*. Politika, Prague.

John Katzenbach. 1987. Sheldon gets the ax: Misery by Stephen King. *New York Times Book Review*, 31.

Stephen King. 1996. The importance of being Bachman. In *The Bachman Books*, pages v–ix. Plume.

Stephen King. 2006. Stephen King, the art of fiction no. 189. Interviewed by Nathaniel Rich & Christopher Lehmann-Haupt. The Paris Review.

Corina Koolen, Karina van Dalen-Oskam, Andreas van Cranenburgh, and Erica Nagelhout. 2020. Literary quality in the eye of the Dutch reader: The national reader survey. *Poetics*.

Tony Magistrale. 2013. Why Stephen King still matters. In Charles L. Crow, editor, *A Companion to American Gothic*, pages 353–65. John Wiley & Sons.

Janet Maslin. 2006. Her Story of Him, Both Tender and Terrible. *The New York Times*.

Tempestt Neal, Kalaivani Sundararajan, Aneez Fatima, Yiming Yan, Yingfei Xiang, and Damon Woodard. 2017. Surveying stylometry techniques and applications. *ACM Comput. Surv.*, 50(6).

Erica Noonan. 2006. In King's uneven 'Cell,' evil rings up Boston. The Boston Globe.

Debbie Olson. 2020. Introduction: Stephen King's fictional children. In Debbie Olson, editor, *Children and Childhood in the Works of Stephen King*, pages 1–12. Lexington Books.

Andrew Piper and Eva Portelance. 2016. How cultural capital works: Prizewinning novels, bestsellers, and the time of reading. *Post45*, 10.

Powells. 1999. Synopses & reviews of Bag of Bones by Stephen King. Publisher's website.

Aja Romano. 2018. Stephen King has spent half a century scaring us, but his legacy is so much more than horror.

Benjamin M. Schmidt. 2012. Words alone: Dismantling topic models in the humanities. *Journal of Digital Humanities*, 2(1).

Gregory M. Colón Semenza. 2006. Adapting Milton for children: Margaret Hodges's Comus (1996) and the tale of Childe Rowland. In *Milton in Popular Culture*, pages 71–82. Springer.

Carol Senf. 1998. Gerald's Game and Dolores Claiborne: Stephen King and the evolution of an authentic female narrative voice. In Kathleen Margaret Lant and Theresa Thompson, editors, *Imagining the Worst: Stephen King and the Representation of Women*, pages 91–110. Greenwood Press, London.

Greg Smith. 2002. The literary equivalent of a Big Mac and fries?: academics, moralists, and the Stephen King phenomenon. *The Midwest Quarterly*, 43(4):329.

Peter W. H. Smith and W. Aldridge. 2011. Improving authorship attribution: Optimizing Burrows' delta method. *Journal of Quantitative Linguistics*, 18(1):63–88.

Douglas W. Texter. 2007. A funny thing happened on the way to the dystopia: The culture industry's neutralization of Stephen King's The Running Man. *Utopian Studies*, 18(1):43–72.

Ted Underwood and Jordan Sellers. 2016. The longue durée of literary prestige. *Modern Language Quarterly*, 77(3):321–344.

Andreas van Cranenburgh and Rens Bod. 2017. A data-oriented model of literary language. In *Proceedings of EACL*, pages 1228–1238.

Andreas van Cranenburgh and Corina Koolen. 2015. Identifying literary texts with bigrams. In *Proceedings of CLFL*, pages 58–67.

Andreas van Cranenburgh, Karina van Dalen-Oskam, and Joris van Zundert. 2019. Vector space explorations of literary language. *Language Resources and Evaluation*, 53(4):625–650.

Association for Computational Linguistics
209 N. Eighth Street
Stroudsburg, Pennsylvania 18360

ISBN 978-1-7138-9175-8

CURRAN ASSOCIATES INC.
proceedings.com